THE *Economy* OF *Character*

DEIDRE SHAUNA LYNCH

THE

Economy

OF

Character

Novels, Market Culture,

and the Business of

Inner Meaning

THE UNIVERSITY OF CHICAGO PRESS

Chicago & London

Deidre Shauna Lynch is assistant professor of English at the State University of New York, Buffalo.

The University of Chicago Press, Chicago 60637
The University of Chicago Press, Ltd., London

© 1998 by The University of Chicago
All rights reserved. Published 1998

Printed in the United States of America

07 06 05 04 03 02 01 00 99 98   1 2 3 4 5

ISBN: 0-226-49819-0 (cloth)
ISBN: 0-226-49820-4 (paper)

Library of Congress Cataloging-in-Publication Data

Lynch, Deidre.
    The economy of character : novels, market culture, and the business of inner
meaning / Deidre Shauna Lynch.
        p. cm.
    Includes index.
    ISBN 0-226-49819-0 (cloth : alk. paper).—ISBN 0-226-49820-4 (pbk. : alk. paper)
    1. English fiction—18th century—History and criticism.   2. Characters and
characteristics in literature.   3. English fiction—19th century—History and
criticism.   4. Psychological fiction, English—History and criticism.   5. Literature
and society—Great Britain—History.   6. Authors and readers—Great Britain—
History.   7. Books and reading—Great Britain—History.   8. Romanticism—Great
Britain.   I. Title.
PR858.C47L94   1998
823'.509355—dc21   97-40313
                                                                              CIP

For Tom Keirstead

✒ CONTENTS ✒

❧ I L L U S T R A T I O N S ❧

❧ A C K N O W L E D G M E N T S ❧

I am certainly not the first writer to find that acknowledgments join intimate self-disclosure and conventional phrases in curious and discomfiting ways. In chapter 5 of this book I look at the language uses that characterize two of Jane Austen's heroines: Austen, I propose, both shows us how Anne Elliot and Elinor Dashwood re-cite and recycle the polite and hackneyed phrases that everyone uses, *and* she makes their recourse to the pro forma the sign of the depth of their feelings. There are multiple ways in which I would like to *be* Anne or Elinor (I hope that this confession will not detract from the effort this book makes to outline the history of such identifications). I have just revealed one: I would like the people whom I address in these preliminary pages to know that if they encounter sentences here that they have read before, polite formulations so conventional that (to paraphrase Austen) Adam must have met them in the first scholarly book he opened, they should regard the hackneyed style as a sign of how very heartfelt my gratitude to them is.

When I was a beginning graduate student in English at Stanford University, seminars with Bliss Carnochan and Terry Castle taught me to love eighteenth-century literature. As supervisor, with Terry and Bliss, of the dissertation that (after many years) became this book, John Bender made me think harder than I had ever had to before. Other teachers contributed in less apparent ways to my education. Frank Donoghue's conversation sparked my interest in many of the topics pursued in these pages. I am especially grateful to Bill McPheron for encouraging his students to reimagine the means and ends of cultural history.

Since leaving graduate school and entering into the world I have found the academy to be an unexpectedly convivial place; for conversations and epistolary exchanges that help make it so, and for interest and input, I am grateful to Barbara Benedict, Homer Brown, Kelly Hager, J. Paul Hunter, Veronica Kelly, Ann Kibbie, Beth Kowaleski-Wallace, Jayne Lewis, Richard Maxwell, David Miller, Dorothea von Mücke, Tom Otten, Clifford Siskin, and Richard Swartz. Closer to home, my senior colleagues Roy Roussel and Bill Warner devoted much time to searching readings of my dissertation. Bill helped me conceptualize how the project might develop, and Roy helped me understand what I had already tried to say. Robert Devens did superlative work as a research assistant. I hope that if any of the undergraduates who took my courses on Austen encounter this book they will recognize how their enthusiasms and insights helped shape it.

As friends, role models, and intellectual co-conspirators, Nancy Glazener, Stacy Hubbard, Adela Pinch, and Katie Trumpener deserve a paragraph to themselves. The acumen and imagination of their scholarship, their willingness to share insights, and their devotion to this project helped keep me writing. Friends since our graduate school days, Nancy and Katie have asked the right questions for well over a decade now. I haven't always been able to answer the questions that they, along with Adela and Stacy, have posed over the course of many heroic readings of the manuscript, but I know that *The Economy of Character* would have been much impoverished if I hadn't tried. I also would like to thank Katie for introducing me to Doug Allen's cartoons and Doug Allen himself for allowing me to reproduce an episode from Steven's career in my introduction.

Over the last year the editorial staff of The University of Chicago Press have been models of consideration and efficiency. They have belied all the rumors that assistant professors pass on to one another about the humiliations and tribulations of academic publishing. I am grateful to my editor, Alan Thomas, and two anonymous readers for the press for their advice and support. I have been well served by a number of additional institutions. Fellowships from the Stanford Humanities Center, the Mellon Foundation in the Humanities, and the Mrs. Giles Whiting Foundation supported me during the early stages of this project, and, more recently, the Victor S. Johnson and Julian Park funds at the State University of New York at Buffalo assisted with research expenses and the cost of illustrations. Bill Fischer and Ken Dauber, past and present chairs of the department of English, and Kerry Grant, dean of the Faculty of Arts and Letters, ensured that I had the thinking and writing time that my book required. A portion of chapter 1 originally appeared as the essay "Overloaded Portraits: The Excesses of Character and Countenance." It is reprinted from *Body and Text in the Eighteenth Century*, edited by Veronica Kelly and Dorothea E. von Mücke, with permission of the publishers, Stanford University Press. © 1994 by the Board of Trustees of the Leland Stanford Junior University.

Tom Keirstead has lived on intimate terms with this project for many years and reads every sentence of every page without betraying the least impatience. He already knows that this book is, like its author, dedicated to him.

Recognizing Characters

This book engages the changing ways in which British men and women in the long eighteenth century accommodated themselves to their increasingly commercial society. It does this by treating the changing strategies and norms these people implemented in order to value their books and make what they read matter. While it pursues this project, this book also rewrites the history of the literary character. In the late twentieth century, after all, it is (still) the time that we spend with characters that matters most to many readers. At this moment, too, literary character remains the "most problematic and . . . undertheorized of the basic categories of narrative theory." The problems it poses become manifest as soon as, for instance, we try to account for what precisely we're doing when we conceive of characters in the companionable terms I've just invoked, as creatures with whom we spend time and who also have time. Character's "sheer obviousness," one theorist maintains, "disguises the conceptual difficulties it presents."[1] At the outset I should say that it is not the aim of this volume to unmask character's true identity. The questions I pose do not concern what character is "really" like. Instead, trying to displace the approaches to character that have traded in essences and made a variety of disparate practices appear as versions of a singular form, I address character's changing conditions of legibility. I address how definitions of what will count as a character and count as a character reading have operated in culture. From the inception of this project, I have been trying to discover what we can know about character's history if we refrain from using narrative frameworks such as "the rise of individualism" or "the rise of realism." What happens if we do not assume that the history of character and the history of the individual are the same thing? What if we cease to

FIG. 1. Doug Allen, *Steven*

think of the character as our fellow traveler through time and the expressive analogue to ourselves?

Since this book seeks new ways of talking about how characters differ from one another and seeks to illuminate systems of difference that have not been featured in our histories of realism, it seems appropriate to begin with the comic strip *Steven* (fig. 1). Doug Allen's comic reminds readers of what they already knew about how some characters differ from other characters. To be a reader means knowing that some characters are "round" and that others— Allen's Steven being a case in point—are "flat." Documenting the hierarchical distinctions between the two is a routine many Britons and North Americans learn to perform in their elementary and high school classrooms. I like how Allen's cartoon gets us to root for the underdog. The cartoon's wit lies in how Steven gets a rise out of the guy who boasts both "a profile" and "a few different expressions": the cartoon manages to associate the round character, not the flat one, with the banality of an utterly predictable response. Allen's staging of a skirmish in which the flat guy bests the round can be seen as a comment on character's part in the hierarchies that organize cultural production. It is ostensibly the absence of character—of real, round, complex character—from comic strips that dictates that they don't count for much when compared with novels. We see a similar axiomatics at work if we consider literary histories that—focused less on the historicity of their object than on the canonical ordering of works—use concepts such as the rise of realism to separate an inferior eighteenth-century from a fully developed nineteenth-century writing. The rumors in the "comic strip business" that deem it a suspicious circumstance that Steven is always pictured head-on and never "seen from the side" suggest something else about this cultural field: that the unspoken motto of the "character business" has been Buyer Beware. If you position yourself at the wrong angle, you won't know that the flat character has no profile. Duped, you will be unable to tell the difference between the counterfeit and the real thing. In 1832, Thomas Carlyle said something similar as, digressing in his laudatory essay on the novels of Goethe, he described the degraded modernity that he associated with a new mass culture catering to a new mass audience. When Goethe constructs character, Carlyle averred, he "begins at the *heart*": "These Fausts and Philinas have a verisimilitude, and life that separates them from all other fictions of late ages. All others, in comparison, have more or less the nature of hollow vizards, constructed from without inwards, painted *like*, and deceptively put in motion."[2]

While railing against the deceptions of painted characters, the equivalents for him of painted women, Carlyle also acknowledges, indirectly, some commonalities that link the strategies of literary criticism to the strategies that people adopt in order to negotiate the dangerous liaisons, the "opportunities and importunities," of the marketplace.[3] It is by examining such commonalities that I aim to offer an alternative to what literary criticism and literary pedagogy have by and large done with character.

Discussions about whether particular characters are "true" to our individualities—arguments about whether they are round or flat—have, since the last two decades of the eighteenth century, when versions of the latter opposition first become available to readers, worked to validate and naturalize a concept of character *as* representational.[4] Posing our questions in these terms precludes attention to how the truth of character is "a thing of this world." It precludes attention to what Foucault called "the political economy of truth"—"the mechanisms and instances which enable one to distinguish true and false statements[;] . . . the techniques and procedures accorded value in the acquisition of truth; the status of those who are charged with saying what is true."[5] The most familiar ways of narrating the story of the novel and accounting for the transformations that separate eighteenth-century from nineteenth-century writing likewise tend to take character out of history. Ian Watt and a host of successors locate the novel's genesis in the confrontation between internal and external characterization and locate the novel's consolidation in that conflict's resolution, when these rival modes of character-writing enter into complementary rather than contestatory relations. The story they assemble proceeds from Richardson, to Fielding, and finally to Austen, who, the story goes, manages to "complete" the novel's rise because she manages to harmonize the interests in private life and social life that divided her two forefathers. This dialectical movement projects a history in which characterization evolves according to a purely internal logic, protected from material contingency.[6] This is a history that—eighteenth-century scholars' justly celebrated commitment to a sociology of genre notwithstanding—could unfold anytime and anywhere. It is, in Foucault's sense, other-worldly.

There are, however, different ways, less amenable to insertion within schemes of dialectical closure, in which character has over the course of its history differed from itself. In order to illuminate the *local* knowledges that eighteenth-century cultural practices produced, to apprehend these practices in their historicity, I shall be retelling the story of Britons' relations to the imaginary people whom they encountered in books. I shall try to demonstrate that this story does something besides reflect the history of the forms of (non-imaginary) selfhood. Indeed my aim is to make the history of verisimilitude in characterization and the history of individualism and characterization each take a back seat to what I call a *pragmatics* of character. Concentrating on how the opening of new global trade routes, the inauguration of innovative retail practices and spaces, and the rise of new credit arrangements changed the everyday reality of Britons and brought into being a world founded on "the exchange of forms of mobile property and upon modes of consciousness suited to a world of moving objects," this book chronicles the changing ways in which eighteenth-century writers and readers *used* the characters in their books.[7] New commodities, available in new kinds of spaces, put pressure on the norms and the categories that people had formerly invoked to explain the material world and to make its artifacts meaningful. In this context, people used characters, I shall suggest, to renegotiate social relations in their changed, commercialized world, to derive new kinds of pleasure from the changes, to render their property truly private, to cope with the embarrassment of riches. A new "world of moving objects" was one in which new forms for imagining and enforcing social division were requisite. To look closely at the measures eighteenth-century writers and readers adopted to make the character the center of their stories and the source of stories' affective hold is also to understand how the period's discursive transformations went in hand with new protocols for organizing class relations and for dividing a feminine world from a masculine one.

Literary character's history thus converges in particular, unpredictable ways with the history that sees imports of luxury goods into Britain—among them, such quintessentially "English" items as the tea and the chintzes and muslins that were brought from the East Indies—double in quantity between 1715 and 1800.[8] It converges too with a history that sees writing and reading themselves become commercialized, fashionable activities. In this same period, rival syndicates of booksellers went to court over literary property, the first circulating libraries made books available for hire, and books came to be numbered among the possessible keepsakes and knickknacks that people had to learn to use as they learned to personalize the interior spaces of their homes and their selves.

⁂

To take account of these convergences—to take account of the "economy of character"—I begin in my first two chapters in the first half of the eighteenth century. Then, when the starring roles in print culture were assigned to personages who were physiognomists and personages who (as in epistolary fiction) were men and women of letters, character was conceptualized as *reading matter* in the most emphatic way. In their transactions with the preternaturally legible persons of their books, I contend, early-eighteenth-century readers found a coping mechanism. On the one hand, these readers had to negotiate the experience of a marketplace that was chock-full of strange new consumables and that beggared description. On the other hand, they believed themselves, as literate Britons, to be the beneficiaries of a symbolic environment that was founded on principles of perspicuity and accessibility and in which truths could be self-evident. The characters of a Hogarth print or of a Fielding novel provided a coping mechanism in that they assisted English people in reconciling these experiences with these convictions. The uses of character at issue in the first part of the century reveal, in other words, enthusiasms that were adapted to what I will call "typographical culture": an interest in the material grounds of meaning and a fascination with the puns that could link the person "in" a text to the printed letters (alphabetic symbols, or "characters" in another sense) that elaborated that text's surface. In this context, most talk about character was not talk about individualities or inner lives. It was talk about the systems of semiotic and fiduciary exchange—the machinery of interconnectedness—that made a commercial society go.

Part 2 turns to the late Georgian and Regency periods, to novels of manners, and to the development of new romantic guides to making character matter. It is a commonplace that literature took an inward turn at the close of the eighteenth century: that is how it got "romantic." The inner meanings and psychological depths that to many readers have seemed to detach the romantic-period character from mid-century writing's social text and to endow it (as we say) "with a life of its own" are my focus here. My aim is to reconnect these personal meanings to social processes and, in particular, to the market culture of the Regency. In my account, these meanings are the by-product of a transformation in the ground rules that had defined the interrelations of literacy, aesthetic competence, and literariness, a transformation—itself the by-product of an era that saw an increasing demonization of the literacies of the crowd—that involved both a new insistence that reading was an activity pursued by *individuals* and, at the same time, a new determination to produce lines of demarcation between *classes* of readers. Characters acquired inner lives, became associated, that is, with "deep" meanings nowhere stated in print, when character reading itself changed. It did so in two paradoxically linked respects. People's transactions with books came to be connected in new ways, first, to their endeavors to find themselves as "individuals" and to escape from their social context, and, second, to their endeavors to position themselves within an economy of prestige in which cultural capital was distributed asymmetrically and in which not all who read were accredited to "really read" literature.[9] The agoraphobic inflection to the characterization within English novels of manners—which regularly send their heroines into marriage markets where they are misrecognized and objectified and which then go on to reanimate and redeem them from this commodification—is no accident. It is a token of how the character with an inner life has been a useful resource for readers who have to negotiate the irony that sees the circulation en masse of elite culture threaten to turn that culture into its opposite. It suggests too the rich ironies that attend those pursuits of self-fulfillment that unfold in the impersonal space of the market.

As this preview suggests, in reconstructing the uses of character, in emphasizing the many projects writers and readers thought characters were good for, I have not confined myself to representations of the self, and I have been led away from the questions about origins, influence, and development that others have mobilized to tell a story about "the novel." Let me do this précis of my book over again, and in a way that will both foreground those divergences and also (in the standard manner of introductions) name names. The texts that I treat in my first chapter include the much-read books by Defoe, Richardson, and Fielding, as well as the books by Delarivier Manley, Eliza Haywood, and Jane Barker, that feature in the standard and revised editions of that story. But I do not use those books to fill in a line of novelistic succession that would extend from Defoe (or Manley) to Austen. Instead, my project is to ally the characterization we find in these books with the impersonal idioms that contemporaries of these figures described with the term "characteristic writing"—idioms that were mobilized to talk about what English print culture provided and so to talk about reading matter of all sorts, be it "the passions" that were imprinted on the face of the player or the denomination stamped on the face of the coin. In chapter 1, accordingly, those writers whom chroniclers of the novel spotlight have to jostle for center stage with imitators of Theophrastus and La Bruyère, with William Hogarth and the caricaturists whom he decried, and with the actor David Garrick, who had a new way of "looking a character." In my second chapter, when I move forward to the 1750s, 1760s, and 1770s, the familiar figures who have starred in others' discussions of the novel retire even further into the wings. Even Smollett's and Sterne's books are supplanted here by narratives—which temporarily rivaled theirs in popularity—about money that talks: narratives that, like *Adventures of a Bank-Note*, were more intent on imagining society than imagining the self and that only with difficulty can be said to have central characters in the first place.

Together with an increasing number of students of the British book trade, I believe that it is only after the 1770s, in an era that saw the first real growth in the publication of fiction (with a steep increase in the number of new titles published per annum) and that saw critical acclaim granted to the so-called Burney school of novelists, that the cultural construction of the novel, *as* a recognizable mode of writing, is finally accomplished.[10] Only then—in a literary period frequently dismissed as one that was shaped by (ostensibly underqualified) women and as one when novels' numerical increase led to their qualitative decline—do the retrospective acts of definition and canonization that novelized the earlier period's "characteristic writing" finally come to be made. It is therefore the cultural practices of the late eighteenth century that receive the lion's share of attention in this book, and it is to this still-underread period that I turn, starting in my third chapter, in order to show how characterization, understood as the representation of subjectivity, came to define the project of the wide range of writings we now assemble under the retroactive rubric "the novel." Works by Frances Burney and Jane Austen supply me with the end of my story, as they do many accounts of eighteenth-century fiction. Connecting the acclaim given to their drawing of characters to the education in consumer capitalism that they offer their readers, however, I relocate these writers (who, if space had allowed, might easily have been joined by figures such as Charlotte Smith and Maria Edgeworth) within a relatively unfamiliar configuration of objects and practices—one that takes in automatons, circulating libraries, and window-shopping and that also takes in the romantic-period invention of literature.

It is romantic-period characters who first succeed in prompting their readers to conceive of them as beings who take on lives of their own and who thereby escape their social as well as their textual contexts. In discussions of the character as a being who under law has rights on which real persons cannot infringe and has distinguishing attributes that real persons cannot imitate, Bernard Edelman and Jane Gaines have examined at length one telling twentieth-century sign of this success. For entertainment lawyers from the mid-twentieth-century onward, to "protect" characters from those sharp dealers who would seek to "kidnap" them and exploit their profitability has entailed protecting licensed *trademarks*. The provisions of copyright law, provisions that would in fact work to secure the rights of characters' originators—authors—do not apply so far as this branch of entertainment law is concerned. Copyright's irrelevance for the character evokes, Edelman and Gaines comment, a high romantic scenario in which the character abandons its textual origins and disclaims its author: "The author alienates himself within an infernal machine of his own making. The writing takes on a form beyond that of its own origin, a product that moves about freely on a stage, playing out its non-human role."[11] Edeleman and Gaines invoke a *Frankenstein* plot, the very narrative framework about creations' frightening lives of their own that, not incidentally, others have used to tell the story of Richardson and the uncannily popular *Pamela*. It might be argued that this choice of narrative represents the logical extension of the early-nineteenth-century literary histories that identified attention to "original, discriminated, and individual person[s]" as the defining features of a modernized characterization. Romantic literary criticism identified modernity as the belated realist discovery of truths about persons that had been there all along. Walter Scott, reviewing Austen's *Emma*, wrote of how novelists had begun only in his generation to represent what was right under their noses and present characters who, coming from "the ordinary walks of life," could be their readers' friends or neighbors.[12] To continue to narrate the history of literature in this manner, focusing on the intrinsic truths of an individuality that is simply "there" and seems magically to escape the social conditions of its meaning, is to commemorate the values of a handful of romantic critics and canon-makers and dub them Nature.

By contrast, I aim to demonstrate that individuated, psychological meanings did not come naturally to British writers and readers in the long eighteenth century. They do not come naturally to us either. Meanings of all sorts are social productions and, it follows, objects of contest as well as of collaboration. Meanings become intelligible in historically specific, institutionally mediated ways. Tony Bennett has made this point in helpful terms. Meaning, he writes, is "not something that texts have, but is something that can only be produced, and always differently" within the specific "reading formations" that "regulate the encounters between texts and readers." With the grab-bag term "reading formations" Bennett designates the heterogeneous forms of intertextual and institutional relations that regulate (never completely successfully, to be sure) readers' dispositions toward their reading matter—the hierarchies that rank genres, for instance; public discourses about why, where, and with whom one should read; and issues of equal economic and symbolic import such as the price of books.[13] My emphasis on a pragmatics of character calls attention to the social construction of qualities such as interiority or literariness. It serves this purpose by enabling me to underline how it is only within particular series of reading formations that the distinctiveness of literary characters becomes legible and valuable. This is true not only for the distinctiveness that separates the new, improved round characters from their faceless predecessors and from one another, but also for the distinctiveness of mid-eighteenth-century characters, whose legibility comes to matter, however, within systems for categorization and valuation that seem alien to us now.

Whereas we, for instance, sort through characters and characterization using binary terms such as *round* and *flat* or *external* and *internal,* the question that interested countless critics from the middle decades of the eighteenth century was often a surprisingly different one: whether a particular representation might be excessively particularized, or "overcharged." The issues critics most often engaged in treating the protocols of mimesis were issues of discursive economy. They asked the judicious reader to *count,* to think about how many strokes or traits of character it would take for a character's defining difference to be clear, and to take warning from the instances in which a superfluity of strokes pushed representation beyond the bounds of nature and into the domain of the grotesque. It can be difficult, but also bracing, to recognize the sources of our love of literature in the metaphors that critics and authors alike deployed to organize early- and mid-eighteenth-century character reading, metaphors that (as this book's first two chapters show) aligned this enterprise with that of deciphering the signboard of a shop or that of finding out the denomination of a coin.

Obviously, there are moments in the reception history of eighteenth-century literature when it is easier to recognize readers whose incentives for reading are like our own. Still, if the *Pamela* phenomenon—to point to one such moment—offers indisputable evidence of the mid-century reader's determination to enjoy an intense personal involvement with a character,[14] saying as much reveals little about the historicity of "the personal" and little about the ways that, in shifting social circumstances, the relays between the personal, the private, the pleasurable, and the psychological shift in turn. *Identification,* the modern term for what we do with characters, likewise blurs crucial distinctions between a reader's empathy with who a character is and her empathy with what the character feels or does. It obscures the historical specificity, the relative novelty, of our codes of reading. With the beginnings of the late eighteenth century's "affective revolution" and the advent of new linkages between novel reading, moral training, and self-culture, character reading was reinvented as an occasion when readers found themselves and plumbed their own interior resources of sensibility by plumbing characters' hidden depths.

By reconstructing some aspects of the eighteenth century's book culture and of its readers' "working epistemologies," I aim to give novel studies a post-romantic way to consider the mid-eighteenth-century readers who did not complain about the "flatness" of the characters on offer at the booksellers'—who read narratives whose protagonists were talking coins and banknotes (flat by definition) just as avidly as they read *Pamela.*[15] These readers

10

were not dupes who confused the counterfeit character ("painted *like*, and deceptively put in motion") with the real thing. To discard our investment in the history of mimesis is also to discard the notion that earlier readings (or writings) were somehow incomplete—flawed by virtue of missing the whole truth or not realizing all the potential latent in the novel form. The cultural historian's task becomes, rather, that of investigating reading and writing practices as local accomplishments—as social technologies that depend on certain verbal forms, practical exercises, codes of deportment, and capacities for pleasure and that permit their users to engage in particular sets of activities.[16]

Indeed, my own references within this introduction to the history of character should be regarded as a shorthand and nothing more. Character has no autonomous history. Character is not a single object that presents itself in one form at the start of the eighteenth century and another, changed form at the end. Instead, what changes are the plural forces and rules that compose the field in which reading and writing occur. What changes as the eighteenth century unfolds are the pacts that certain ways of writing character establish, at given historical moments, with other, adjacent discourses—discourses on the relations between different sectors of the reading public or discourses that instruct people in how to imagine themselves as participants in a nation or in a marketplace or as leaders or followers of fashion. *Writing* and *reading* are also terms I perforce use loosely. In Britain more than in other national cultures, characters have belonged not only to literary history but also to a transmedia context—the public's experience of the characters in their novels has been experience garnered not only in the seclusion of solitary reading but also at print-shop windows, at waxwork displays, and in shops that sell china figurines. One aspect of the intimate relation between Britain's commercial economy and British characters is that from the early eighteenth century on there have often been so many ways to buy and to collect them. The catalog copy issued by eighteenth-century printsellers categorized humorous prints as "characters." In an era when writers such as Henry Fielding and Tobias Smollett could expect that their descriptions of secondary characters would remind readers of the bits of stage business exploited by David Garrick, the star system of eighteenth-century theater—a system that itself helped to organize what people could do with their theatrical experience—likewise shaped people's reading of fictions. It helped too, as chapter 2 suggests, to create new sorts of relays between character and the norms of sociable commerce and circulation. In the period before readers adapted their uses of characters to altered cultural hierarchies and new ideas of literature, these alternative, extraliterary approaches to making character reading matter counted in ways that they ceased to later on.

One book cannot enumerate the full range of discourses that eighteenth-century writers mobilized when they set out users' guides to character. While I emphasize how characters provided Britons with resources they used to negotiate the pleasures and dangers of the marketplace, I have had to neglect how people's transactions with characters were mediated by, for instance, their experiences with casuistry, newspaper advice columns, and the project of Puritan self-invigilation, as well as by their acquaintance with the techniques of typological reading that enabled such readers to match particular characters with particular roles within the pageant of Old Corruption and Walpole's Robinocracy. It will become evident that there are additional respects in which my account is partial. I have, for instance, drawn on texts from the first part of the century to trace how physiognomy provided one influential account of what an appropriate character reading was—how a "pact" between physiognomic reading and the project of collecting "specimens of English manners" helped render the character a legible, consensual object. But I have not, in part 2, attended to the altered terms under which these two social technologies collaborated by the close of the century, when physiognomy too—in ways that underline how the human face, as much as the literary character, is made and remade over time—became explicitly oriented to depth, rather than, as before, to legibility. When novel readers turned from collecting moral exemplars to pleasing themselves with the example of their own sympathetic capacities, physiognomists—as reading Lavater makes abundantly clear—were likewise becoming men and women "of feeling."

My readings in the economy of character cannot pretend to offer a comprehensive history. Still, because they bypass the tradition in which literary characters *only* represent—in which all that characterization does is memorialize a series of institutionally sanctioned versions of what "the self" is or should be—these readings can, I hope, bring us up against the limits of our unconsciously held assumptions about what makes books matter. To that end I engage throughout this volume with some very familiar ways of thinking about how characters and novels work. In part 1, which delineates how participants in the typographical culture of the mid-eighteenth century debated the overloading of characters, it is possible to identify a draft version of one article of our literary faith, the notion that a fleshed-out representation is the best representation. When these debates about the economy of character are carried on in narratives such as *Roderick Random* or *The Adventures of a Bank-Note* that also examine the claims to general equivalence that are staked by current money and, in a different way, by pretenders to the throne, we can trace the curiously halting way in which the fictionality of fictional characters becomes something that can go without saying. My discussions of Burney and Austen are likewise arranged so that they both rehearse some commonplace ways of thinking about what *real* characters do and are—ways summed up by the oppositions that pit self against society, characters' psychological development against stasis, and unique individuals against types or copycats—and reveal the social claims that Regency readers and writers made while they devised these now-familiar coordinates of our literary experience.

What is tacitly dismissed as the eighteenth-century novel's propensity to overgeneralize and inability to imagine individual variation can, as Carol Kay has observed, be reseen as evidence of writers' determination to produce interconnections between "modes of understanding other people and the social narrative." The eighteenth century's seeming hesitancy about creating individuals looks different, that is, as soon as we acknowledge that not only did self have to be created as a discursive object, so did society.[17] Understanding the history of character writing and reading in conjunction with new techniques for imagining community and new ways of connecting people and objects (and people to objects) reveals unsuspected complexities and depths in the impersonality that we tend to explain away. This impersonality speaks volumes about an era that was gradually developing the new impersonal forms—the mechanisms of credit and currency—that could encompass market relationships. In the more familiar psychological reading formation that is the subject of chapters 3 through 5, character can seem to serve much more to detach one person from another than it does to link them together. Dissociated from extroversion, conspicuousness, and publicity as they are dissociated from the semantic complex that had linked the personal with the typographic and even the numismatic, the truths of character have been redefined as matters of inner meaning; character has become personality. But even this reading formation has its unfamiliar aspects: those, for instance, that become apparent when we consider the links between the practices of window-shopping, picturesque tourism, and that mainstay of literary pedagogy, the character appreciation, a writing practice that first becomes visible in the 1770s.

Putting character into the thick of eighteenth-century book culture can suggest, in fact, that even though characters have been objects of commentary since Aristotle's *Poetics,* there is also a sense in which, until the start of the eighteenth century, characters did not exist. To watch them disappear we might turn to Random Cloud's (Randall McLeod's) discussion of how eighteenth-century editors of Shakespeare, starting with Nicholas Rowe, began to equip Shakespeare's plays with lists of dramatis personae (a device that Samuel Richardson emulated by providing a prefatory inventory of the "Men," "Women," and—notoriously—"Italians" to be found in *Sir Charles Grandison*) and also imposed a new consistency on the speech tags of their texts. (These editors felt themselves obliged to remedy what the earlier nomenclature had said about the solidity—or lack of solidity—of the individual person: in the folio version of *All's Well That Ends Well,* for instance, five speech tags were appended to what the modern aficionado of "characters" would conceive of as a single, unified role, that of the Countess of Rossilion, and each of those tags memorialized a different social relation—"Mother," "Countess," "Old Countess," "Lady," and "Old Lady.") The editors' innovations had the effect of individuating characters and conferring on them existences that preceded, and were detached from, their functions in the plays. Of such stuff "lives of their own" are made.[18] That characters' existence remained tenuous for some time is suggested by the fact that the high-profile conversations about characters in the first two-thirds of the century turned, as I've noted, on issues of discursive economy (how many strokes?), decorum, and readability. These readings of character engaged with whether *characterization,* judged against certain rhetorical norms, was good or bad. Particular characters themselves, good-hearted and malicious alike, seemed to fade from view.

⚜

More than two decades ago, proponents of *nouveaux romans* and of structuralist analyses of narrative also insisted (in terms rather different than those I've just used) that characters did not—do not—exist. Under the rubric "the economy of character," this volume attends to inequalities in and conflicts over the uses of literature. At the same time, with that phrase "economy of character," I am also acknowledging the turn in characters' fortunes that we associate with figures such as Alain Robbe-Grillet, Roland Barthes, Hélène Cixous, and Colin MacCabe and with journals such as *Tel Quel* and *Screen*—

14

that moment when semiotics, drawing on Althusserian Marxism and Lacanian psychoanalysis, called characters' bluff. This was done in the name of an assault on a capitalist order that "classic realism" helped uphold. By creating characters and mobilizing the reader's identificatory fantasies with them, novels, it was argued, made people misrecognize themselves as free subjects. "Classic realism tends to offer as the 'obvious' basis of its intelligibility the assumption that character, unified and coherent, is the source of action"; "the interpellation of the reader in the literary text could be argued to have a role in reinforcing the concepts of the world and of subjectivity which ensure that people 'work by themselves' in the social formation."[19] Intent on demystifying the realist regime of writing and reading, semiotics dissolved the roundest characters into their qualities (semes), into bundles of narrative functions.

There have been, as this volume will demonstrate, many moments in British cultural history that have seen cultural capital redistributed in the name of character. In a roundabout way, the modernist moment of semiotics represents the latest of such moments. Making characters dissolve or disappear represented a new way of shoring up systems of distinctions. It made some sites of reading and writing—in the 1970s, those ostensibly "transgressive" sites farthest from mass culture—and some uses of characters—those programmatically demonstrating the illusoriness of a character's independent existence—more legitimate and more literary than others.

Thinking about character in connection with commerce directs attention to how the critiques intent on exposing the ideological machinery of realist characterization themselves operated within a particular economy of prestige. At the same time, it also underlines how this project of critique defined itself in terms of a particular calculus, pitting one measure of quantity against another. For what this mode of analysis was against, broadly speaking, was "humanist plenitude." It was for "structuralist reduction."[20] Its quarrel with humanism was with the latter's fetishistic assumption that character *exceeded* the formal means of its representation—whereas character was not, in the structuralist schemes, a referent that would preexist its representation but was a signified instead; it was "really" no more than an illusory effect engendered by the words on the page.

In casting character as textual effect, these schemes made it possible to think of "the specificity of character as a function of determinate textual practices."[21] In displacing mimesis, the realism debate paved the way for histories, such as this one, that would attend to the tactics texts use at definable historical moments—for instance, the changing sorts of contracts texts establish with readers to secure their conditions of legibility and the particular formal techniques that produce the relations of mutual reflection between characters and readers. Certainly, Barthes et al. have made it easier for the late-twentieth-century novel reader to appreciate mid-eighteenth-century people's sometimes startling readiness to think of their characters not as persons but as so much writing.

In practice, however, the primary effect of the realism debate was to license a series of readings intent on uncovering, within realism, covert underminings and disruptions of "the subject"—readings that redeemed certain canonical novels from the charges of naive conventionality and ideological complicity. Idealistically conceived, the "subversions" that focused those readings frequently emanated from an unsituated "unconscious" rather than from any alternative sets of conventions—conventions which by their very nature are *agreements*, generated in specific social milieux. In their tendency to glamorize the unconventional, the arguments against realism often rehabilitated the very individualism that they sought to contest.

Let us return for a moment to Doug Allen's cartoon. Steven's reaction when Brock "demystifies" him—"Who cares?"—is a mordant response to the sometimes intensely condescending terms in which the realism debate was conducted. Inverting but also resembling the complaints about the facelessness and flatness of neoclassical characterization, the merely demystificatory critique of the psychologized character dismisses the plenitude it should explain. It does not account for how characters' excesses—the residue left over after the structuralist analysis of narrative roles, the augmented vitality that humanist accounts ascribe to characters who seem to lead lives off the page—have been effective in history. Character reading has no history once it is a matter of ideological misprision. In this respect, the realism debate is hampered by the same ahistoricism and essentialism that are evident in the teleological narratives that couple the rise of the novel with the rise of individualism—the narratives that cast eighteenth-century characterization as inept and nineteenth-century characterization, which expresses a new cultural awareness of the individual, as skillful.[22]

The limitations of the realism debate can be ascribed in part to the debaters' failure to develop organizing concepts any more specific than "capitalism," "the subject," and "the novel." To elide historical particulars in this manner—particulars that manifest what is chancy and volatile about the reproduction, circulation, and intersection of discourses—is, I think, to affirm that there *is* something natural, inevitable even, about the inward turn of narrative and the ensuing psychologizing uses of literary characters. I want to stress this, because although I too am associating literary characters with the emergence of a market culture and am presenting characters as a means by which cultural coherence is produced, I do not impute a monolithic, "bourgeois" design to the British practices of character reading and writing that I trace. Round characters and the practices of emotional keep-fit and self-discovery that they sponsor have inevitably been put to heterogeneous uses. "Identification," after all, has been important in forging new sorts of cultural coherence and alternative publics: feminist communities have been, and still are, created, in Britain and North America, when women in reading groups and classrooms have used their transactions with literary selves both to understand their own gendered selves and to make connections with other people's.[23]

Tacit acceptance of the idea that the structuralist reduction of meaning (the effort to stymie identification and make characters disappear) is the only alternative to "humanist plenitude" has made it difficult for novel studies to make sense of another aspect of the economy of character: the fact that even advocates of "plenitude" have been embarrassed by literary characters' excesses. I have in mind here the nervousness about British literary characters once evinced in Britain's literature classrooms. After a century of edging in that general direction, novels after World War I obtained their entrée into academic precincts on the basis of "the high seriousness of their psychological and social mimesis." For F. R. and Q. D. Leavis, for instance, who took this relative newcomer under their collective wing, this meant that particular responses to novels—and in particular those expressive of a popular cult of characters, which was in some measure a self-congratulatory cult of English eccentricity—had to be ruled out of court. In *The Great Tradition* F. R. Leavis grumbles about the "traditional approach" to " 'the English novel' ": "The business of the novelist, you gather, is 'to create a world,' and the mark of the master is external abundance—he gives you lots of 'life!' . . . Expectations as unexacting as these are not when they encounter significance grateful for it." In *Fiction and the Reading Public* Q. D. Leavis files a similar complaint about a mass audience's desire for a superabundance of characters. She suggests that this desire interferes with recognizing truly valuable fictions: "This readiness to respond to 'characters' will bear some investigation. . . . This kind of interest leads critics to compare the merits of novelists by the size of the

17

portrait gallery each has given to the world."[24] That, for the Leavises, the vitality of lifelike characters is somehow bad for readers has to do, one suspects, with how these lives of their own detach characters from *novels*. The reader of faulty sensibilities who attends too much to the characters indulges in a way of reading that emancipates character from plot. The faulty reader's reading takes characters out of novels' narratives and puts them into a never-never land of eternal life inside "portrait galleries." The relocation dissolves the tensions between plot and character and time and personality that are the mandatory signs of psychological depth; it circumvents the reconciliations of the individual and the social that signal character development and that, for many "serious" readers, are what make novels matter.

That English characters could, in the hands of some readers, overwhelm the project of "psychological and social mimesis" is reflective, as well, of characters' affinities with the world of things. The self-congratulatory references, which become a feature of literary culture at the start of the eighteenth century, to the prodigal, fertile inventiveness that British authors evince in their character drawing go hand in hand with depictions of England as a nation of shopkeepers, a land where domestic goods, bric-a-brac, collectibles, and plain old stuff, abound. Perhaps these references to characters' ebullience—to "the gratuitous doles which rich genius flings into the heap when it has already done enough"—are best studied for their contribution to the process that redefined *luxury*, detached it from its traditional status as sin or moral error, and adapted it to new historical conditions.[25] For the excessiveness that, the Leavises fear, will subvert the economy of the novel and the ecology of a psychological culture has to do with how characters in England—the Leavises would say for a mass audience above all—have propertylike properties. They are objects of merchandising, of commodity tie-ins and spin-offs.

Characters' quality of eerie thing-hood—their quality of being at once "out there" and "other-than-us," the way that, like the commodities in *Capital*, they seem more autonomous, memorable, and real than their makers, our suspicion that their clutter could crowd us out—has been captured best by George Orwell's 1939 remarks on Dickens's pageant of eccentrics. (Orwell's words could apply equally well to the grotesques and remarkable characters to be found in the work of Burney, Smollett, and Sterne and in the chapters that follow.) The "vivid pictures" that Dickensian characters leave in readers' memories, Orwell averred, are pictures of "things. . . . Their first impact is so vivid that nothing that comes afterward effaces it . . . there they all are, fixed for ever like little twinkling miniatures painted on snuff-box lids, . . . solid and . . . memorable."[26] One of the occasions for Orwell's essay was the giveaway scheme launched by John Player and Sons in 1913 that saw a cigarette card with a portrait of a Dickens character included inside every pack of cigarettes. (Through junkshop browsing, I have acquired a Mr. Jingle and a Uriah Heep.) This collaboration between the collectible character and the cigarette—a luxury import that, through its addictiveness, at last becomes a daily necessity—represents nicely the kinds of convergences that the study of the "economy of character" must treat.

I have weighted my book with an insistence on collaborations and convergences such as these in order to offset how "character" has often served to produce differences. Characters have supplied readers with the means with which to implement the work of cultural classification and stratification that Pierre Bourdieu calls distinction. Whether pitted against caricature, as it is for the eighteenth-century readers whose social calculations I reconstruct, or whether it is conceptualized as a kind of private possession that—by being immaterial, a matter of inner meaning—can accommodate both our antimaterialism and our avidity, character has been a resource that some readers have used for purposes like those that Bourdieu describes. Character is some readers' means to distinguish their own deep-feeling reception of texts from other readers' mindless consumption.

For this reason, to trace the reciprocal shaping of eighteenth-century Britain's market culture and its culture of character, to track transformations in the "character business," helps expose the complexity and contingency of the protocols that dictate what our literary experience should be. (As the Leavises' pedagogy suggests, notions of authentically literary characters—characters who "really" do have inner lives—are generally doubled by notions of "true" audiences.) In conditions of near-universal literacy, Terry Eagleton observes, "Literature presents itself as a threat, mystery, challenge and insult to those who, able to read, can nonetheless not 'read.' To be able to decipher the signs and yet remain ignorant: it is in this contradiction that the tyranny of Literature is revealed."[27] My emphasis on the economy of character has, I hope, the effect of historicizing the very category of the literary and of historicizing the disciplinary divisions and divisions of audience and market that sustain it. The cigarettes that have been bought so that people can really own their characters are a salient reminder of how, in market cultures' definitions of the good life, individual acquisitiveness predominates over collective entitlement. But history can also demonstrate something a bit different about our own individuating identification with the characters in our fiction—a consumption practice reshaped by that romantic recasting that made knowledge of characters' truths into personal, private knowledge: that our transactions with characters remain, that change notwithstanding, profoundly social experiences.

The Economies of Characteristic Writing

❧ O N E ❧

Fleshing Out Characters

Not that always where the language is intricate the thought is subtle, or the image always great where the line is bulky; the equality of words to things is very often neglected, and trivial sentiments and vulgar ideas disappoint the attention to which they are recommended by sonorous epithets and swelling figures.
  —Samuel Johnson, preface to *The Works of William Shakespeare* (1765)

Just heaven! how does the *Poco piu* and the *Poco meno* of the Italian artists;—the insensible MORE or LESS, determine the precise line of beauty in the sentence, as well as in the statue! How do the slight touches of the chisel, the pencil, the pen, the fiddle-stick, *et caetera,*—give the true swell, which gives the true pleasure!
  —Laurence Sterne, *The Life and Opinions of Tristram Shandy* (1759–67)

THE INSENSIBLE MORE OR LESS

If Tristram Shandy's talk of true swells and pleasures (nudge, nudge, wink, wink) rudely turns the protocols of neoclassical criticism into a pretext for bawdy, his comment also illuminates the interest that eighteenth-century Britons, preoccupied with ordering the arts, took in an economy of character. It illuminates, that is, what may retrospectively appear a curiosity of British literary history. In the first two-thirds of the eighteenth century, an age known for the rise of the novel, where we would expect to find assessments of a developing verisimilitude in literature, we just as often find wrangling over literary quantity. For neoclassical critics, the process of fleshing out characters raised questions about quantity, about the fine line between the more and the less. Rather than treating matters of quality control, their discussions of what we now call characterization can look instead like attempts to import a project of bookkeeping into the discursive realm. Their discussions of the texts we now call novels were often organized by a scheme in which discursive propriety depended on the difference between enough and too much, the

23

difference between a gestalt in which the component parts added up to the whole and one in which the whole was less than the sum of its parts. In this chapter, I begin reconstructing what eighteenth-century people did with characters by reconstructing a series of debates that was marked by alarm over swelling figures and by a concern with limiting the number of "strokes" of character. To reconstruct the terms in which these debates were conducted will lead us not only to novel readers and writers but also to print shops and theaters. It will suggest how, in the first two-thirds of the eighteenth century, characterization was valued for its usefulness to readers and writers who found themselves dwelling in a new commercial world, one altered by new trade routes and new forms of credit and full of strange commodities that invited the gaze and emptied the pocketbook. At the same time, however, that those debates display the affinities linking concerns over characterization with concerns over commerce, the alarms over the overloading of character also call attention to the proliferation of print commodities in particular. They suggest how printing presses in overdrive—producing ever more fleshed-out characters—destabilized the early-eighteenth-century order of things. As we shall see, that destabilization not only eroded neoclassicism's foundational premises about what made a character legible; it also ushered in new rationales for making persons into reading matter and new decorums for figuring strokes of the pen and the pencil into life.

With Sterne going out of his way to memorialize such instabilities, *Tristram Shandy* has long been notorious for its narrator's problems with (to echo Johnson's remarks on Shakespeare's beauties and blemishes) "the equality of words to things." Tristram fails utterly to get a grip on his self and, his enthusiasm for the finishing touches that produce true swells notwithstanding, fails utterly to get his writing to catch up with his life. (He doesn't get himself born until volume three; his ninth and last volume, which treats Uncle Toby's courtship of the Widow Wadman and hinges on the question of where Uncle Toby got his wound during the Siege of Namur, is concerned with events that unfold, respectively, five and twenty-three years before Tristram's birth.) The disproportion between form and substance, writing and matter, that plagues it suggests how *Tristram Shandy* might be read as a text that never stops at but instead exceeds or falls short of the proper quantity of the finishing touches of character.

Sterne's book recaps a crucial chapter in the history of character in a second respect: Tristram's anxieties about his textual expenditures play themselves out on human bodies. Every reader remembers that references to undersized noses and other preternaturally truncated body parts abound in Tristram's autobiography. Speculations about where Uncle Toby got his wound and about what Tristram means when he states that nothing was well hung in his family may have distracted us from the fact that the Shandys are as troubled by swelling as by detumescence. Voicing a classic lament of the era, Walter Shandy fears, for instance, that the body politic will soon "totter through its own weight," that the nation is unbalanced by the influence of its moneyed interests. "The introduction of trade" has given a "new face to the whole nation," Henry Fielding writes in his 1751 *Inquiry into the Causes of the Late Increase of Robbers,* vexed at having to live in a period marked by accelerated luxury consumption and by the most rapid urbanization in European history. David Hume echoes Fielding's sociophysiognomic metaphor, asserting that "in every kingdom, into which money begins to flow in greater abundance than formerly, every thing takes a new face." In a similar reaction to how the growth of markets and cities seemed to overburden the foundation of native British freedoms, Walter Shandy considers the present state of the commercializing nation and sees a "head [that grows] . . . too big for the body."[1] The rather sensationalist manner in which Walter, Hume, and Fielding exploit the venerable metaphor of the body politic should be noted. The human figure had long provided British men and women with a means of asserting the continuity between their artificial institutions and the natural world: metaphors of the body politic conferred on those institutions a visible definition and stability. The new-fashioned bodies with new visages (or, worse, with distended, overloaded visages) that these comments conjure are, by contrast, cause for alarm. Eighteenth-century writers on political economy seem to wield the image of the disfigured, overloaded body apotropaically, aiming to reinforce ostensibly natural proportions between land and money and between labor and commodities and aiming thereby to regulate the market in which their writings circulated.

Participants in the debates on fleshing out characters, concerned with discursive proportion, easily find their way to a similar figurative practice. My discussion will be guided, accordingly, by the reappearance throughout the debates about overloaded characters of an overloaded countenance, a face overdistinguished by distinguishing features. As a preliminary example of the ways that overloaded faces were used to clinch neoclassical arguments about how and why characters mattered, one might linger a bit longer over *Tristram* and consider the concern with physiognomic surplus that is evident when, digressing, the narrator regales us with a romance by one Slawkenbergius.

In "Slawkenbergius's Tale," an oversized nose, property of a mysterious man who is wandering around Strasbourg, mystifies the scholars of the city. The academic community of Strasbourg despairs of deciding whether gravity will in the end cause this man to fall off from his nose or this nose to fall off from the man (261). The interest of the episode lies in how Sterne uses this overloaded countenance. It gives him a pretext not for commenting on fiscal arrangements but for intervening in the ranking of artistic genres and of their ways of presenting persons. The tale doubles as a sideswipe at the recognition scene, the conventional plot twist in which hidden truths about identity come to light to reunite long-lost friend with friend. At *the* climactic moment in Slawkenbergius's narrative, a visitor to Strasbourg hears through rumor about the big-nosed stranger. The visitor instantaneously falls on his knees, looks up to heaven, and declares, " 'Tis Diego" (268); that accomplished, he rushes off to the requisite reunion. In the eighteenth century, the surplus materiality of the means by which such scenes of anagnorisis were generated became increasingly embarrassing for writers on literature and theater. By the end of the century critics began to sanction only those recognition scenes that arose from action. They were eager to consign recognitions arising from telltale rings, scars, and other distinguishing features to the debased category of popular entertainment. The enlarged nose attached to the now-discovered Diego, or to which the now-discovered Diego is appended, images the inartistic excessiveness that eighteenth-century improvers of the drama discerned in that model of recognition in which personal identity—"character"—might be established through a sighting.[2]

Tristram Shandy is of its time in contesting the old assumptions that recognition scenes made about what was entailed in knowing the truth about a character. Part of what marks "Slawkenbergius's Tale" as a literary throwback, a superannuated museum piece, is the *overstatement* it resorts to when its recognition scene locates what matters about character in a publicly apprehensible, material realm of bodily representation. (Diego's nose is hardly on the same scale as, say, the strawberry mark on his breast that had facilitated Joseph Andrews' reunion with his parents.) Sterne is also using Diego's nose, this oversized token of recognition, to mark the point at which culturally legitimate modes of figuring personhood shade into illegitimate, or popular, modes.

The wrangles over the economy of character that will concern me in what follows produce faces much like Diego's. This overloading of countenances is a sign, as is the decline of dramatic recognitions, of how the pictorialist episteme that associated "characters" with exoteric, visible information such as that conveyed by a birthmark or a ring was losing its credibility and effectualness. It was going downmarket. In the first two-thirds of the eighteenth century *character* was reversing its meaning. Eventually the truths that mattered about the character were dissociated from the effable, public knowledges purveyed by visible bodies. More startlingly, they were also dissociated from the effable, public knowledges purveyed by the graphic characters on the page. Testifying to this shift in an ambivalent way, the texts from the 1740s and 1750s that provide the focus of the third, fourth, and fifth sections of this chapter—the ever more diversified character collections that revamped a Theophrastan tradition of "characters," the artist William Hogarth's polemics on behalf of his "modern moral subjects," and the critical debate on David Garrick's innovative acting style—are marked by hesitations about how one might distinguish between the finishing touch and the added stroke that overcharges representations. These texts persistently fudge the question of whether the added touches that are meant to particularize representations and to assist a more accurate imitation of nature might end up marring rather than mending the character. They fudge the question of whether these added touches might disfigure character into what it is not. The attraction of these texts is that as they wrestle with this question of the "insensible more or less" they show us how the participants in eighteenth-century culture, negotiating their places in a world that had a new face, had been using characters. They reveal this largely because within these texts certain premises about particularization and generalizability and about the relations between individual identity and bodily surfaces and written languages are no longer being taken for granted. The point of historical articulation, when the conventions regulating the economy of characters and countenances had to be emphatically displayed, was also the point of their disarticulation.[3]

The wrangling over economy that occupies the texts of the 1740s and 1750s indexes how the rules for producing and legitimating knowledge were being redefined. That wrangling is also a sign of how, as *character* shifted in meaning and emerged as the primary designation for imaginary personages in works of imaginative fiction, people's ways of knowing and of buying culture were being reorganized. Constructing the cultural history of character also entails telling the story of that reorganization, which would eventually usher in the modern divisions of the disciplines and the principle of market stratification that pits high art against mass culture. The assumptions that were questioned in the first part of the century were those of the typographical culture that endowed characters with their legibility. In the long term, a new order of things would separate literature from this formerly all-encompassing typographical culture—in which communication was a matter of marking, imprinting, and embodying—and so separate the experience of character from the complexly social experiences that eighteenth-century Britons had had when they joined the crowds at the theater and the print shop. This new order of things would also bestow on novel writing a generic identity of its own. Novel writing's claim to a singular distinction among the disciplines would be founded on the promise that it was this type of writing that tendered the deepest, truest knowledge of character.

To say this much is, however, to anticipate the outcome of certain processes (processes of market segmentation, of realigning and hierarchizing modes of communication) that in the mid-century were only beginning. The project of this chapter is to glimpse character and its uses from the vantage point of people who did not yet think of their reading in terms dictated by modern generic conceptions or understandings of literature. The consequence of this chapter's focus on the economy of character is perhaps an eccentric-seeming picture of the first half of the eighteenth century. This period is usually heralded as the era in which "the" novel fully realized its generic identity; it was then, we have learned, that novelists figured out that what their genre did best was mirror subjectivity. In order to offer an alternative account of what changed in the first part of the century, I want to bracket this emphasis on mimesis. I want to set aside as well the notion that the novel is a fixed generic category, a notion that restricts us so that the only texts we can align with novels are either other novels or embryonic or failed exempla of the genre. Rather than isolating the novel's project of characterization, as essentialistic notions of genre—and of literary character—demand we do, I want to understand the so-called novels of the early and mid-eighteenth century as artifacts of the era's typographical culture. Adapted in function to particular relations of reception, those artifacts observe rhetorical protocols and exploit social analyses that were products of a culture-market irrevocably altered by the recent boom in the publishing of printed texts and images.[4]

In the section that follows, thinking in those terms will entail forgetting what we have known for a long time now: how, in the first part of the eighteenth century, Defoe, Richardson, and Fielding founded the tradition of the novel. I want as well to mark my distance from the new "rise of the novel" narrative that has countered this earlier one, a narrative that by altering the canon and recounting "the rise of the woman novelist" has made us resee the novel as a bicultural production that was "mothered" as well as fathered from the start: if the groundbreaking discussions through the 1980s and 1990s of the achievements of female figures such as Delarivier Manley, Eliza Haywood, Jane Barker, and Sarah Fielding have transformed our sense of the gender of early fiction, they have not challenged the investment in genre that motivated the earlier literary historians. I hope to do something different here. When, in the section that follows, I consider the writers celebrated as engineers of the novel's rise, I will present them not so much as novelists but more as participants in a punning argument about the matter of character, an argument that they and their contemporaries elaborated while they thought about what they called "characteristic writing" and while they pondered the relation between the language of characters and the mechanisms of print processes, correspondence, and commerce. And I will go on with my story about the shifting decorums for fleshing out characters by turning from "novels" altogether. Instead, I will consider how Theophrastan character writers decried the overcharging of character at the same time they tried to exploit the market value that fine description had in a post-Lockean age of empiricism; how the arbiters of propriety in the art market responded to a craze for caricatures by trying to distinguish between permissible and excessive attention to physiognomic particulars; and how critics pondered Garrick's new ways of "looking a character" by trying to draw a line between "nature" and "grimace." The terrain to which the second half of this chapter is devoted is unfamiliar to scholars of novels for a reason. To study character within this transmedia context, one in which the innovative caricature seller Mary Darly is as much a contributor to our literary modernity as a Samuel Richardson or an Eliza Haywood, conflicts with a prime disciplinary imperative of eighteenth-century studies—the demand that we look for a genre's origins and cordon off the genuinely novelistic from everything else. Nonetheless, while we follow the debates over added strokes of character, we also see evidence of the shifts that would soon necessitate new, and indeed novel, uses of character. In reconstructing these debates we get an inkling of how it came to be that novels, to be good novels, had to be *about* character.

BODIES OF WRITING, PEOPLE OF LETTERS, AND COPY MACHINES

Before turning to these debates, I begin with the concepts of writing that eighteenth-century people mobilized to regulate the economy of character—

concepts that also, surreptitiously, contributed to characters' overloading. Understanding how character mattered in eighteenth-century Britain entails, first of all, understanding the curiously embodied terms in which literate people conceptualized their reading matter. Reconstructing what Richard Kroll has dubbed the somatic culture of the early eighteenth century will in turn suggest why the matter of character was, first and foremost, a social matter.

The eighteenth century inherited from the seventeenth the conviction that it was best to *image* the linguistic grounds of human knowledge and an eagerness to apprehend the constituents of knowledge through analogies with the human body. According to the understanding of linguistic behavior that prevailed at the opening of the century, discourse was embodied—at ease with its immersion in a print culture in which language necessarily assumes visible, corporeal form. At the same time, the body was discursive, a telltale transcript of the identity it housed. Ideas of the Book of Nature invited people to think of human bodies and the cultural texts humans produced in tandem *and* invited them to think of both humans and their texts as linked to the animal, vegetable, and mineral works of Creation—to natural forms, which themselves were said to possess "signatures" indexing their affinities.[5]

Within this discursive context, a special significative cachet was ascribed to the human face and its representations. Writers of the first part of the eighteenth century seem eager to understand faces less as natural facts and more as signs, prototypical reading matter. The entries under "character" in the *Oxford English Dictionary* suggest one rationale for this special status: among the expected references to notions of personality or of social role (acting "in" or "out of" character), we find that "the face or features [or] . . . personal appearance" defines one sense of "character." With greater insistence, the definitions and etymologies arrayed in the entry also assimilate character to technologies of writing and, particularly, of typography and engraving. In the early eighteenth century's somatic culture the face thus derives its significative centrality from a semantic complex in which the ethical, the physiognomic, the typographic, and even the numismatic merge.

It is not only that faces can be read, exposing persons' inclinations and proclivities, equipping persons with fleshed-out "letters of recommendation" (a phrase that is frequently encountered in eighteenth-century fiction and that points to yet another sense of the term *character*). In eighteenth-century Britain the cognates *countenance* and *character* are both punningly related to terminology denoting the material supports of meaning in a literate culture. From a Greek root denoting either a "brand" or "stamp" or the instrument that produces brands and stamps, *character* was also a term people used to talk about the material and replicable elements from which language, in a culture increasingly dependent on print, was said to be composed. It is in this sense that, to cite just a few instances, Eliza Haywood's amatory fictions pivot, self-reflexively, on the discovery of characters. They are structured not only by scenes in which an incognita is unmasked and her visage, a face that thereafter can be "print[ed]" with kisses, is revealed, but also by scenes in which a wife obtains sure "testimony of [her husband's] infidelity" when an intercepted letter proves to be written in his "character" or in which a lover happily recognizes in the verses of love inscribed on the base of a conveniently situated statue his beloved's "dear, obliging characters."[6]

To identify the technological context for this self-reflexivity about the characters from which characters are composed, we have only to consider the language used by Daniel Defoe, Haywood's sometime rival in the amatory fiction market, when he contributes to this pun-propelled argument about how language mattered for its users. "Characters," he writes, using them himself, are "types impressing their Forms on Paper by Punction or the Work of an Engine."[7] Defoe treats characters in this typographical sense in *An Essay upon Literature: Or, an Enquiry into the Antiquity and Original of Letters* (1726). For Defoe, discussing "literature" (before the sense of the term is narrowed so that it designates good books only) entails sorting through various alphabets, modes of penmanship, inscriptions on money; it directs one to what we, as we reinstate in our own way these puns on *character*, now call typefaces.

Defoe's account of language's embodiment underlines the general implication of his culture's linkages between character and countenance: that each is supposed to be the very epitome of legibility and that this legibility is a function of an incarnation. Such legibility is also a social desideratum. When well drawn, characters and faces will materialize the presuppositions about language's operation that commentators of the first part of the eighteenth century tend to deem vital to commerce and to a well-run society. Richard Kroll explicates the somatic emphases of Restoration-era language theories in these terms: "The plastic qualities of the elements of language ensure that any argument cast in linguistic terms cannot escape from some form of public, institutional accountability or scrutiny." By virtue of being embodied in "characters," "language participates in the phenomenal world and resists mystification from being treated as a purely private or hidden property."[8]

For many early-eighteenth-century writers on the usefulness of letters, a visible language that is embodied in characters obviates disputes. Jane Barker's concern with linguistic consensus informs the account that her preface to *The Lining of the Patch Work Screen* (her 1726 follow-up to the 1723 *A Patch-Work Screen for the Ladies*) gives of how ladies who might once have understood Barker's proverbs no longer do so, now that they have abandoned their country seats for the town and adopted a fashionable "jargon of Babel." This concern with rebuilding common sense in the wake of a process of linguistic breakdown initiated in the era of Oliver Cromwell (when "the Saints and the Ungodly spoke a Dialect so different, that one might almost take it for two Languages") also influences the form in which Barker casts her work.[9] Unlike the French précieuses, whom she emulates in earlier work, Barker does not ask us to imagine her books of the 1720s as originating in conversations, but instead stresses the texts' origins in other, transcribed texts, the "Pieces of Romances, Poems, Love-Letters, and the like" that Galesia discovers in her baggage and that substitute for the clothing this heroine had begun to look for when her hostess first asked her to contribute some patches to her patchwork screen (*Patch-Work Screen*, 74). To conceptualize a book as a patchwork is determinedly to address the eye rather than the ear; it is to stress the materiality of the printed book (a concatenation or patchwork of accumulated graphic signs), as well as to image writing's powers of conciliation. Barker's written language can make contention yield to pattern, can draw a "Set of Ladies together," "Whigs and Tories, High-Church and Low-Church" whose "Sentiments are as differently matched as the patches in their Work" (*Patch-Work Screen*, 52).

Defoe for his part adduces the story of the tower of Babel as evidence that there was no writing during the epoch chronicled by Moses' Book of Genesis. Had the builders been possessed of a "Knowledge of Letters," they would also have had a "settled Rule of Speech": they would never have lapsed into "differing Dialects, and differing Pronunciation of Speech" and, even if geographical distance forbade their frequently conversing together, they would nonetheless have continued to "understand one Another" (61). Within *An Essay upon Literature* such panegyrics to letters, it should be noted, operate to convey a particularly derogatory view of peoples without writing—Catholics who did without the Scriptures, Quakers who trusted in ineffable movement of the Spirit; the Egyptians, the Japanese, and the Chinese, all users of that ostensibly "poor shift" for writing that Defoe dubs "hieroglyphics" (4); and also the ladies of England, who, Defoe assures us, are notoriously bad spellers. These are all people without character, in a doubled sense of the term. The *Essay* clinches its self-congratulatory panegyric to the lettered Englishman by casting God as the original source of characters, for on Mount Sinai he used his finger to trace his laws on Moses' tablets.

This body talk, which calls attention to God's body parts and registers the English preference for alphabetic writing over the ephemeral, disembodied emanations of oral language, reinforces the synonymy between character and countenance. But even eighteenth-century speakers who used the term *character* in its most abstract sense—as a "kind of Mark . . . indicating [a being's] peculiar Nature," a "distinctive feature," "that which distinguishes one object from another," or that by which a thing "separates itself from others of its kind"—would ascribe a special cachet to the face.[10] In this way of explicating character and how it matters, it is the face's singularity—and, by extension, its part in upholding a foundational sort of private property— that are crucial. "Every face must be a certain man's," the earl of Shaftesbury wrote in *Second Characters, or, the Language of Forms,* the treatise on neoclassical aesthetics he was completing at the time of his death in 1713. As if by providential arrangement, whereas "the other Parts and Members of our Bodies are in comparison so little different," as John Evelyn noted in 1697, each face was one of a kind. Within the Book of Nature, the human face seemed to function as a rigid designator, a distinct sign belonging to the same distinct person in all possible worlds. Imagining the situation if the case were otherwise, if the faces of men were as like "as Eggs laid by the same Hen," John Ray exclaimed in 1692, "What a Subversion of all Trade and Commerce? What hazard in all Judicial Proceedings?"[11] At the same time that individual faces functioned as the somatic correlate of a proper name, characterizing persons in the sense that they permitted them to "separate" themselves and their property from others of their kind, faces also, contrariwise, referred to human nature in general. A face indexed character: in one sense of that word, then, it indexed a social norm, a determinate place on the moral map where every person had a proper place and where distinction was contained within limits. Reading a face was the most basic sort of reading in this sense. Recognizing a face, or putting a name to a face, one replayed what eighteenth-century philosophy of mind valued as the most basic cognitive operation: that of discriminating and then weighing samenesses and differences. Such activities epitomized the act of reading the Book of Nature.

In his description of cognition in the *Essay Concerning Human Understanding* (1690), simultaneously the eighteenth century's most important description of the production of personality, John Locke exploits these multiple connotations of *character*. They come in handy as he describes human consciousness as a documentary genre, founded not just on observation, as twentieth-century commonplaces about empiricism maintain, but also on transcription. Locke usually figures in literary studies because of the links Ian Watt adduced between empiricism and the formal realism that defines the novel; but his philosophy is also of interest for what it tells us about how people thought about the relation between their selves and their books. For Locke, cognition is the process whereby experience imprints the mind, inscribing ideas on what was initially "white Paper, void of all Characters, without any Ideas."[12] The imprinting of a surface and the acquisition of characters produce "character," or personality, where before there was a blank. At the center, then, of the *Essay*'s account of the operations of human understanding is an analogy that links the getting of ideas, the techniques of typography, and the process of individuation—the process of developing a self that will be (to return to the definition of *character* laid out in the previous paragraph) separable and distinguishable from other selves. In understanding ideas as characters, Locke is not only able to make a point about the legibility that renders these distinctive selves, in a sense, self-evident. Conceived as characters, ideas come across as so many discrete, distinct building blocks of knowledge, as alphabetic characters are the building blocks of language. Accordingly, Locke is also able to employ in the Essay an analogy with much appeal in his cultural moment (as Barker's method in *A Patch-Work Screen* also suggests): that of ideas as collectibles and wisdom as a matter of idea collecting. His *Essay* incites readers to design their own personal histories. They are invited to personalize the blank spaces of their consciousnesses in the same ways that they might use transcribed quotations to personalize the blank pages of their commonplace books. Their activity is to be understood in tandem with the conscientiously modern practices of the early-eighteenth-century gentlemen and ladies who filled up their libraries and curio cabinets with collections of coins, medals, and paintings or—when compiling "grangerized" *Biographical Histories of England* became the rage—assembled series of engraved portrait "heads." Since these practices in particular depended on buying, selling, exchanging, or stealing, the acquisition of character comes, in Locke's account, to seem congruent with the activity that was defining the modernizing marketplace.[13]

At the same time, however, that its organizing metaphors appealed to readers who might be eager to be modern, the Lockean account of character formation also developed the commonplaces of a much older homiletic discourse that had aligned the traits composing the moral character with the marks identifying the denomination of a coin, as well as with the marks identifying persons and rendering one face distinct from another. Preachers had long seen in the piece of metal a symbol for the person. Much as a coin is transformed into legal tender by virtue of the inscriptions it bears, the preacher's commonplace held that it was lineaments, or "characters," of virtue and vice that made the individual soul individual: corresponding in turn to the lines, birthmarks, and features discovering themselves on the individual face, these lineaments set that soul apart from its originary state of innocence, vacancy, or sheer lumpishness. The individual face, in its turn, could be seen either as the original issue of God's Mint or as a transcript that documented the wear and tear to which currency was liable in the marketplace of experience.[14]

The usage of *character* that engages me in this book is the one that is in question whenever we say something like "Lady Catherine de Bourgh is a character in *Pride and Prejudice*," but the fact is, such usage is merely a postscript to an understanding of character that permitted eighteenth-century people to talk at once about legible faces, minted money, and imprinted texts. First and foremost, "character" was a rubric that licensed discussion of the order of things in a conversible, commercial society. In designating the qualities that separated an object from some things and bound it to others, *character* in its most abstract sense was a tool geared to analysis of the basic elements of the town-dweller's contemporaneity. The understanding that character is one of the elements of fiction, along with plot and setting and theme, emerges tardily, as does the sense of *character* as (to cite the *OED*) "a person regarded as the possessor of specified qualities . . . a personage, a personality."

That makes it important to acknowledge that the context that gave meaning to numismatic, typographic, and physiognomic characters was also the context that gave meaning to many of the eighteenth-century writings we now call novels. Supplying quotations from *Tom Jones*, two of the entries in the *Oxford English Dictionary* identify Henry Fielding as an originator of the modern and novelistic usages of *character*. To pick up on the dictionary's cue, however, and use the term *novel* as a license to isolate Fielding from his context—to set out to identify how his forward-looking "new species of writing" pioneered a novelistic rendering of characters—obscures the ways in which Fielding assiduously complied with arrangements that gave priority to the legible countenances of characters. The metaphor Fielding elaborates in *The Adventures of Joseph Andrews* (1742) as he meditates on "divisions in authors" is noteworthy. When he lauds his own practice of signposting his readers' journey through his book, Fielding not only compares the chapter titles that divide that book to "inscriptions over the Gates of Inns," but he also uses the trope of sign reading to model how readers become informed about characters and how they use them to read the world.[15] The group of personages whom Joseph, the readers' surrogate, encounters on his journey includes a publican, Tim. Tim keeps an inn that is known by the "Lion on the Sign-Post," and the physiognomy by which Tim is recognized matches the inn's signpost. As the narrator says, in a passage that signals Fielding's interest in the connections between persons and the discourse denominating persons, Tim "in Countenance doth . . . greatly resemble that magnanimous Beast" (44). At a subsequent stage in his journey, Joseph encounters a shrewish innhostess: she plies her trade, aptly, under the sign of "the Dragon" (54).

In *The Fortunate Mistress, or, a History of . . . Roxana* (published two years before the *Essay upon Literature*), Daniel Defoe has his heroine give the reader her "own Character" and describe herself as "a standing Mark of the Weakness of Great Men in their Vice" and "a standing Monument of the Madness and Distraction which Pride and Infatuations from Hell runs us into."[16] Roxana conceives of herself as Fielding conceives of Tim and the hostess of the Dragon: in externalized terms, as a sign—a character who, making "an impression" on the consciousness of the reader of her history, will imprint and reform it. At earlier moments in this history of a repentance that never quite takes, Roxana inadvertently "makes a deeper Impression" than she means to when, appealing to his conscience, she talks to her princely lover about the misfortunes that await their love child (81). Noting how Defoe emphasizes his characters' typographic activity does not preclude valuing the complex effects of self-estrangement that distinguish *Roxana*'s self-condemning first-person narrative, a narrative in which the self that is supposed to be condemned never seems to gel, even though such reconciliation and atonement (at-one-ment) were the raison d'être of the spiritual autobiographies that Defoe revamped. When she deceives her Dutch merchant lover about her motives for wishing to leave England, Roxana says of her specious arguments that "all this was but a Copy of my Countenance" (233): she uses terminology ("copy") that came into use when copyhold property became a prime object of litigation and when, as the manorial rolls came to be recopied and counterfeited, title to real estate came to seem a mere matter of falsification.[17] Later, when a chance social encounter obliges her to feign ignorance of her long-lost daughter's identity, Roxana again raises the topic of her countenance but here, contradictorily, in order to acknowledge the limits to the control she has over her self-disclosures: "[W]hat my Face might do towards be-traying me, I know not, because I could not see myself" (284). Roxana's tragedy derives, as many readers have noted, from her failure in those self-disclosures to monopolize the means of representation. The character she gives herself in *Roxana* is shadowed, and challenged, by the characters others give her. Amy, her "right-hand" woman, as "faithful to me, as the Skin to my Back" (25), acts for her in ways that, Roxana insists, misrepresent her. In Amy's victim, our narrator's daughter and namesake, Susan, Roxana again has to cope with indiscreet, telltale "flesh and blood" ("my own Flesh and Blood, born of my Body" [277]), since Susan knows her mother as "a meer Roxana" (182). The Turkish costume that the girl recognizes docu-ments a past when Susan's mother "play'd the Whore" (269), when she was true to the name Roxana (a hyperliterary name that in the early eighteenth century would have smacked of other authors' she-tragedies and secret histo-ries). Such bodily appurtenances, like Roxana's body doubles, reconnect Roxana to a public character inscribed from without.

It is a communicative, prolix world that is conjured up by texts such as *Joseph Andrews* or *Roxana*, with their telltale bodies, signposts, marks, and mon-uments. Fictions by Defoe's and Fielding's noncanonical contemporaries call attention to the protocols of their culture's communications systems in a simi-larly self-reflexive way. The world of the early eighteenth century's secret histories and amatory fictions is saturated with texts. Erotic passion makes people into writers, producers of letters, employers of "pages," and carriers, like Haywood's Melantha, of little "pocket-books" in which to inscribe bits of amorous verse. At the same time, passion makes people's bodies legible, a corpus of amatory signs: " 'a thousand times you have read my rising wishes, sparkling in my eyes' " (*Love*, 119). In this world, furthermore, texts displace people as prime movers of plot. In *The New Atalantis* (1709), Delarivier Manley casts her heroine Charlot as a figure who is in the end to be remembered (much as Roxana is) as a "true landmark to warn all believing virgins from shipwracking their honour upon (that dangerous coast of rocks) the vows and pretended passion of mankind"; at the same time Manley underlines that Charlot's undoing is really texts' doing. Manley might be scoring a satiric point against the Duke of Portland, who is the original for Charlot's guardian, but the duke merely supplies the book (Ovid) that corrupts his ward, and he is himself a creature of letters, actuated by precepts he has culled from the pages of Marcus Aurelius and Machiavelli. Choice quotations—whose ca-pacity for cultural action derives in part from the portability that enables them to be conveyanced from book to commonplace book—become the duke's "oracle."[18] Jane Barker's Galesia inhabits the same new age of communications as Charlot and her guardian. The stories Galesia transcribes for the lady's patchwork are set up so that each verifies a proverb: each delivers the sort of punch line that allows the printer to alter his typeface and display eye-catching words such as *"One good Turn deserves Another"* (63)—a catchphrase that, by definition, we have already read. In his *Roxana* Defoe's achievement was to render the showiness, the volubility, that distinguishes all these characters about characters into the vehicle by which identity is rendered a secret.

Whatever else they are doing in fleshing out their characters, the figures we credit for the rise of the novel are also registering their culture's investment in the eloquence of the material surface—the face of the page, the outside of the body—and their culture's idealization of what was graphically self-evident. Eighteenth-century culture, we should remember, made *person* both a word for someone's physical appearance and a word for someone. It made *trait* signify a minimum unit of the stuff of personality, one of the identifying marks that set persons apart, and it made *trait* cognate with words such as *stroke* or *line*—words for the graphic elements from which both pictorial and written representations are composed and through which they are identified. It is punning like this that dictates that reviewers in the eighteenth century will talk about how characters are "drawn," "coloured," "marked with traits," and made diverting through "strokes of fancy, gaiety, or humour." Indeed, the particular Englishness of the continuing national enthusiasm for character owes much to the fact that the English (even the sometime playwright Fielding) conceptualize the characters they read about not as the French do, as "personnages" (that is, not as so many theatrical masks), but semiologically (as so many marks in a book).[19] *Character,* the term that is privileged in English usage, ascribes discursive centrality to the marketable products of the press and to the voluble (but also depthless and two-dimensional) face of the page.

Another manifestation of the print market's centrality can be discerned if we take seriously eighteenth-century people's tendency to view the print products of their age as a group. Historically, English culture's cult of character has been the joint production of a wealth of signifying practices. To apprehend why, perhaps we might consider how in *Second Characters, or, the Language of Forms* Shaftesbury seems inclined to minimize the difference separating his "first characters" of "designatory art"—the term Shaftesbury uses for the

"marks" that we call writing—from his "second characters" of visual art—
from signs that "plastically, . . . lineally, or graphically by lines and colours"
imitate the "superficies" of real forms (90). In Shaftesbury's aesthetics both
verbal and visual arts employ characters. Both are associated with the activity
of mimicry—for Shaftesbury, the foundation of learning. His scheme downplays the distinctions that separate abstracted from more closely representational imitations. This scheme suggests, in effect, that because the forms of
things themselves come in universally apprehensible shapes, because the
forms too speak a "language," characters of both sorts, first and second, lexi-
cal and graphical, can appear to be directly, iconically, correlated with what
they designate. In this scheme, then, the "character of nature [or] reason of
the thing"—that distinctive trait, the very stuff of eighteenth-century natural
history, that makes something or somebody what it is and nothing else—is
redoubled by the characters in works "epic and historical" and by the characters of painting. And these characters of all sorts announce, in chorus as it
were, "Such a one he is! You see him in his true colours! This is the man"
(101).

The theory of knowledge that informs Shaftesbury's aesthetics postulates
a relationship of transcription between ideas and the external objects of sensation they image: basically, this is Locke's theory, as recollection of Locke's
reference to the characters that experience imprints on the mind should suggest. That the process of knowing was a process of transcribing the embodied
language of forms suggests the relative insignificance of distinctions between
visual imitation and verbal documentation.

It suggests too how in the eighteenth-century context characters drew
together different modes and media. In a 1754 preface, Sarah Fielding
described her own narratives and those authored by her brother—works
we now class as novels—as "characteristic writing." In his *Critical Essay on
Characteristic-Writings* (1725), Henry Gally (a translator of Theophrastus) had
used identical nomenclature to refer not to *narratives* chronicling characters'
development but to the verbal *portraits* of ethical types, as well as to the so-
called character sketches of motley social types (a Critic, a Cutpurse)—both
of them ways of writing character that were popular through the seventeenth
century and for the first part of the eighteenth.[20] In the typographical climate
of the period, *characteristic writing* provided debaters on the arts with a locution
that covered, indiscriminately, the iconic and the narrative, the visual and
the verbal. *Characteristic writing* designated many of the printing press's motley
productions: the character sketches that inventoried character traits; the Fiel-

dings' representations of their heroes and heroines; the contents of the print shop windows of mid-eighteenth-century London—engraved (and, by definition, two-dimensional) pinups of "celebrated Ladies, Generals, Players" and the effigies of "Truly humourous . . . droll characters" (a "Hen-peck'd Husband" or a "Female Botanist").[21]

Perhaps the redundancy of the term *characteristic writing* contributed conceptually to forming this transmedia context. Taken literally, the term means something like "writing writing." Thinking about the production of characters in the terms this literalization suggests—as a recopying of documentation that was already in place, as a transcription that matched stroke with trait in an equal exchange—eighteenth-century consumers could think of the print products of their period as a group. In this sense, likewise, eighteenth-century fiction writers assembling characterological compendia of human nature and their contemporaries, the engravers either memorializing the characteristic lineaments of local celebrities or inventing new characters, could understand themselves to be engaged in a common project. *Character* is a word that works in the same way as *characteristic writing:* in addition to bearing the meanings I outlined earlier, *character* can, opportunely, designate both the person described and the verbal portrait that does the describing. It is a word that, like *landscape* or *history*, trades on similitudes that blur the distinctions between human institutions and nature. Recall how in a similar way the narrator of *Joseph Andrews* emphasizes the affinities that link the verbal designations for persons (the host of the Lion, the landlady of the Dragon) to their bodies and to their moral qualities. This is also the program of the Theophrastan characters of the period, which foreground the homology between the characters that we can read off the body of the person and the characters that compose the discourse that we use to designate him. Thus in Samuel Butler's *Characters* (written between 1667 and 1679 and published for the first time in 1759 in Butler's *Genuine Remains in Verse and Prose*) the reader encounters a world of bodies that live for the page and that strain to make themselves recognizable, self-evident. Butler's Busy Man "frequents all public Places, and like a Pillar in the *old Exchange* is hung with all Men's business both public and private." His Hypocrite takes a printer's composing stick for his model of being and "sets his Words and Actions like a Printer's Letters, [so that] he that will understand him must read him backwards."[22] Both Busy Man and Hypocrite embody the media that exhibit, and transmute them into, reading matter. In this respect, each is a typical product of his typographical culture.

More to the point, such characters represented for their readers devices for thinking about typicality as such, for thinking about how, by expediting the diffusion and uniform legibility of information, printed characters supplied the social order with its impersonal mechanisms of coherence and comprehensibility. Perhaps the repowering of the classical copy theory of knowledge that engaged eighteenth-century philosophers such as Locke and Shaftesbury ought to be viewed as a testimony to how taken these writers were with the experience of living in a print culture. They were taken with the ways in which the print technologies that produced uniformly reproducible and imitable texts (and the similar technologies that produced the legal tender) seemed to make society go: these processes fostered correspondence and commerce in the social body. The printing press, Jerome Christensen suggests in his work on the eighteenth-century man of letters, modeled a social goal of "generalizability"—how "the particular [could] be redirected into the general, the individual into the social whole."[23] Certainly, copy machines of all sorts, including the "polygraph" Thomas Jefferson used to maintain a record of his correspondence and the "pentagraph" English portrait painters used to expedite the taking of profiles or copying of images, attracted much attention. At the eighteenth century's start Isaac Newton preempted Defoe's account of God as the first writing master, adopted a Greek usage, and used the word *Pantocrator* to refer to God; Newton also bestowed the name on a copying machine of his own invention.[24] Newton's equation of the copy machine and the divine principle suggests how central the systems of copying that underwrote the semiotic understanding of character were to the early modern mentality. Consideration of the bureaucratic enterprises that enabled Britain's emergence as an imperial power indicates how, for many literate people, copying was also an aspect of everyday life. Because the permanent naval and military armaments on which the empire depended were financed through energetic tax collection and assessment, "no other European state assembled so much quantitative data about the nation's activities," and this effort depended in turn on the clerical labor of copying and recopying literally tons of documentary records.[25]

Eighteenth-century ways of thinking about the relation of personal identity to the articulate surfaces and the verbal signs that made it public knowledge were not only bound up with the metropolitan culture market of bookselling and printselling. They were also bound up with the institutions that the state developed to increase wealth and expedite commerce by accelerating the circulation and exchange of information and value. As I noted earlier in remarking on the importance that the numismatic sense of *character* would have had for early modern audiences, the transformations that the Royal Mint wrought on pieces of metal were seen as analogous to the divine or experiential marking that rendered characters and faces legible. The activity of the British Post Office, established in 1711, was also important to the ways in which characteristic writing made sense. Christensen, who notes that the invention of the printing press highlighted "three discrete features of text production [, namely,] uniform replication, infinite reproduction, and indefinite dispersion," also notes that the last, the possibility of a distribution that could saturate the market, remained merely *in potentia* until the eighteenth century. Then the development of a regular system of post roads expedited the advertisement and the distribution of the press's products. "[T]he booksellers' commerce rode piggyback on the . . . postman: they sent one sort of communication, advertisements, in order to excite demand for another, books, which were transported along routes expressly designed as lines of communication."[26] Post roads served as lines of communication in a second way, as readers of *A Patch-Work Screen* or *Joseph Andrews* would know: the result of the alliance between early-eighteenth-century "novels" and modern commerce and communications is that coach travel is the novels' paradigmatic occasion for the exchange of stories.

The "letter" with which the alphabetic "character" was readily identified could, of course, also designate a missive conveyed by post. Exchanges of letters through the eighteenth-century mails perhaps shored up the Butlerian and Lockean conceptions of the person that we have already noted—those conceptions in which people figure as bodies of writing. Such exchanges sent feeling along the lines of communication that also carried commercial traffic and that had the effect of integrating snug circles of epistolary intimates into pan-national institutions. They seem also to have made people think about the expectation of "generalizability" I have associated with characteristic writing's typical products of typographical culture. The correspondence in which people articulated their personal particularities was also conceptualized as a system geared to semantic coherence and social homogeneity. This suggests the proximity of, on the one hand, the characterization that transpires in epistolary fiction and, on the other, the punning arguments in which character mattered because it represented the material supports of meaning in a literate culture and because its embodiment ensured the public accountability of language.

This is worth stressing because in numerous appraisals of novels-in-letters,

the definition of correspondence as "intercourse or communications of a secret . . . nature" has priority over the definition that understands it as "con-
gruity, harmony, agreement" and that calls attention to the social and socializing nature of letters. We have inherited a view of the eighteenth-century
epistolary novel as a form precociously capable of delivering psychological
verisimilitude. As an 1804 retrospect on Samuel Richardson maintains, the
novel-in-letters enables readers to "slip invisible, into the domestic privacy
of [its] characters, and hear and see everything that is said and done." As
early as the mid-eighteenth century it was a commonplace that Richardson
was an investigator of the human heart: no less an authority than Samuel
Johnson said so. He said (accounting for characterization with a mechanistic
metaphor that now feels troublingly dehumanized) that, where Fielding could
tell the time, Richardson, looking past surfaces, knew how watches were
made. But if the heart that Richardson investigated was the sanctum of individual inner life, it also, in an era when knowledge and money both could
be figured as the nation's "blood," represented the metaphoric center of the
systems of "circulation"—of converse, of commercial exchange, and of common and prevailing sympathies—that drew feeling individuals into a social
order. Thus what for Johnson counts as inner meaning doesn't for us fit the
bill.[27] Carol Kay counters the proposition that the epistolary form is a medium that gives us the otherwise hidden psychology of characters. She comments that "by its very promise the letter form, however detailed or believ-
able, cannot be a direct view of an entirely individual psychology, since letters
are addressed to another person. . . . The intimate friends and relations addressed are not . . . merely a medium in which private personality crystallizes.
The correspondents are addressed as representative social authorities."[28] We
should note too that, notwithstanding the claims nineteenth-century commentators were wont to make in lauding the access we have to the private
lives of Richardson's characters, we do not "hear and see" anything in epistolary fiction. The nineteenth-century commentator I cited above forgot that,
instead, the audience of a novel-in-letters reads the written records (or the
transcriptions of written records) of what there was to be heard and seen.
The form dramatizes the fortunes of pieces of writing; the action pivots on
the mediation of *characters* in the semiological sense of the term.

The category of "characteristic writings" I have been describing may seem
to accommodate the satirical side of early novels more easily than their sentimental (or Richardsonian) side. The bite satirists inflict on their victims was,
after all, readily equated with the bite of the engraver's acid—with the mate-

rial process that incises a surface and produces a printed character. In other
words, if we return to Johnson's dualistic portrait of early fiction, characteristic writing may seem to accommodate what he called "characters of manners" more easily than it does "characters of nature"—writing attentive to
the outside of the watch rather than its inside. Still, it might be a mistake to
overplay Johnson's opposition between external and internal characterization (reinstated by modern critics whose comments on Richardson's "feminine sensibilities" give it a gendered spin): the contrast may be a more
productive one for modern readers trained to recover the "inner," protopsy-
chological meanings in eighteenth-century investigations of the heart than it
was for Johnson's contemporaries. I would like to point out that *sentiment*
is, in fact, another of those loaded words, like *character*, that calls attention
to that externalizing of meaning that accommodates what is personal to social scrutiny, that describes a private process as if it occurred in public. In
eighteenth-century usage *sentiment* designated both a feeling and the language,
the piece of writing, the "epigrammatical expression . . . often of the nature
of a proverb," that articulated that feeling. Letters of sentiment were involved
in circuits of exchange; one message elicited another and so forth. What
Richardson learned from foremothers such as Manley, Haywood, and Barker
is that an epistolary fiction's project of characterization (by definition limited
to characterization of people who are literate) can be as much a means of
exemplifying the powers of writing as a way of representing individuals.

To stress these aspects of sentiment can mean reseeing *Clarissa* (1747–49),
for instance, in ways that can make sense of its preoccupation with record-
keeping and reproduction, legibility and replicability. Besides boasting a talent for writing in shorthand, Richardson's Lovelace has the power to compose the countenances of his confederates, to stand with them before the
glass, twist and untwist their features, and thus rescript their characters. (At
Mrs. Sinclair's house, the servant girl Dorcas's face is Lovelace's page: "let
me see what a mixture of grief and surprise may be beat up together in thy
pudden-face"; "you have a muscle or two which you have no command of,
between your cheek-bone and your lips, that should carry one corner of your
mouth up towards your crow's-foot, and that down to meet it.")[29] Richardson
aims to counter Lovelace's black arts with a model of the good work that
writing (including Richardson's own writing) does; for this reason he strongly
suggests that the virtue of his heroine consists in the way she tries to approximate the attributes of the very book in which her writing is encountered.
Richardson has Belford, who is taken with the idea that Clarissa is more

angel than woman, write of how he hardly wishes to see her married or a mother yet wishes still that "there were a kind of moral certainty that minds like hers could be propagated" (2:243–44). This celebration of desexed, virtual reproduction—a fantasy of a copying machine—forecasts the activities of transcription and distribution that will engage Belford in the final volumes. All that copying will indeed re-produce Clarissa as *Clarissa.* After she leaves a letter for Lovelace that states her determination to stay at Harlowe Place, Clarissa writes to Anna and anticipates an imminent interview with him in these terms: "I will, for the last time, go to the usual place, in hopes to find that he has got my letter. If he *has,* I will not meet him. If he has *not* I will take it back, and show him what I have written. That will . . . save me much circumlocution and reasoning: and a steadfast adherence to that my written mind is all that will be necessary" (1:470).

In nineteenth-century novels it is precisely the temporality of the letter, its fixity—the quality that Clarissa here seems to view as redemptive—that disqualifies it as a vehicle of authentic self-expression. The proliferation of blackmail plots in the nineteenth century suggests how the letter was faulted for misrepresenting individuals' capacity for change. As Jane Austen's Elizabeth Bennet puts it, " 'Think no more of the letter. . . . The feelings of the person who wrote, and the person who received it, are now so widely different from what they were then, that every unpleasant circumstance attending it, ought to be forgotten.' "[30] Nineteenth-century fiction regrets writing's failure to be true to the self's complexities, laments writing's ineluctable exteriority. Clarissa does not. She molds her character after her writing, as that strange phrase "that my written mind" indicates. Writing provides this heroine's self with "stable and stabilizing commitments."[31]

The male heroes of epistolary fiction have the capacity to augment the powers their literacy grants them by allying their writings with the apparatus of the law courts and the state. To modern eyes looking for the language of the heart, novels-in-letters look most curious when they tout the efficacy of public institutions of communication. Such is the case when, anxious to find out the identity of her anonymous benefactor, the heroine of the duchess of Devonshire's *The Sylph* (1779) places a kind of personal ad seeking out her invisible friend in the *St James's Chronicle* and then takes pains to tell the reader that this is the "fashionable vehicle of intelligence," or when the personal letters in *Sir Charles Grandison* (1753) suddenly give way to the documentation that a hired shorthand writer produces to record the "conference" between Sir Charles and an authorized representative of the rake Sir Hargrave Pollefexen. The mid-eighteenth-century novel-in-letters shows a surprising enthusiasm for documenting business methods, the processes whereby men, in particular, hire scriveners and notaries, become signatories to contracts, draw up articles and settlements: in *Memoirs of Miss Sidney Biddulph* (1761), Orlando Faulkland remakes Sidney's marriage in an episode that involves ghostwriting a letter sent by the husband's mistress and employing a "notary of reputation" to draw up the settlement that will marry off the mistress to his valet.[32]

Indeed, the heroism of figures such as Sir Charles or Orlando cannot be dissociated from the ability they have as men of the gentry to exploit the power of public institutions such as the law. (Eighteenth-century readers would have known that the real-life equivalents of these characters would all be justices of the peace.) It cannot be dissociated, that is, from the ability with which their power to wield and make law endows them: the ability to ensure that writing—indeed *characters* generally in all the senses of that term—realizes the unifying potential that figures such as Daniel Defoe ascribed to it. With this power Sir Charles Grandison, one modern reader has commented, is a "register of unanimity," "a resolver of differences," and "the remaker of broken conversation." His interactions with the other characters of the novel are geared to securing what, in a telling phrase, novels-in-letters in the period like to call the correspondence of sentiments. " 'Where is he, at this moment!' asks Emily during [Sir Charles's] visit to Italy . . . ; everywhere where there is correspondence could be the answer."[33] Famously, Richardson would like this to be true of himself and his work. It is important to note that such powerful ubiquity not only expresses the mid-eighteenth-century writer's idealization of what a good man's writing can do but also suggests how the century's gendered meanings intersected with the meanings of character.

What comparing them with epistolary heroines makes especially evident is how Sir Charles Grandison and his avatar Orlando Faulkland are, in their remaking of marriages, their securing of correspondence, less characters in our modern sense than they are incarnations of a principle of coherence or generalizability. This means that, recalling Defoe's remarks on how literacy would have given Babel's builders a mechanism of conflict resolution, they incarnate the principle of writing itself.

In the line of thinking opened up by the new, print-based understanding of the social activities of knowing and writing and copying, the character is located—optimally—at the interface of what is particular and what is general. In the typographical context I have described in this section, the individual specimen of character is meant to refer to an overarching standard of impersonal uniformity. A seventeenth-century imitator of Theophrastus, Samuel Person, maintains that the character has not only the "*Signatura rerum* but also *Personarum* stamped upon it." He argues, that is, that the meanings saturating a character are at once generic *and* individual. A similar confidence in a typographical culture's capacity to induce the particular into the general and to make the imprint refer to the type informs another seventeenth-century definition of "the character" as "some person" or, equally, "some sort of person."[34] Under the aegis of "characteristic writing" character is freighted with social meanings.

EMPIRICISM, OVERPRODUCTION, AND THE CHARACTER COLLECTION

Despite the ease, however, with which character writers such as Person move from individuals to *types* of individuals, the enhancement of communications technologies in the early modern period does more than draw writers to this harmonizing vision of types and general principles. The boom experienced by Britain's typographical culture also had the effect of generating disturbing visions of excess. The copy theory of knowledge that underpins and unifies characteristic writing postulated a mimetic relation between ideas and the external objects of sensation that ideas imaged. In the classical version of this theory, the communication and acquisition of information had consisted in the production of a resemblance, of that sort of likeness that subsists, in Plato's account of cognition, for instance, between the stamp and the surface that bears its imprint. By the early modern period technological change had re-placed the stamped wax tablets that gave Plato his framework for appre-hending cognition with the printing presses that organized the thinking of a Samuel Richardson (a printer before he was a writer), of a Jane Barker, and of a John Locke alike.

This transition, I want to suggest, laid the ground for a shift in the econ-omy of characteristic writing: in this sense, the debates over overloaded coun-tenances and added strokes of character to which I now turn were incipient in characteristic writing from the start. In the ways of linking up writing and generalizability that I traced in the previous section, eighteenth-century people found prescriptions for public harmony and peace. This link de-pended, however, on a particular equilibrium between two ways of constru-ing what characters did. The printed characters of writing were freighted with assurances about the legibility and, in their uniform replication, about the coherence of the social body. These assurances, which defined the program of characteristic writing, were implicitly in tension with a second use of character, which was based on an understanding of character as (recalling the definition of the term that preoccupied natural history of the period) the peculiar feature that distinguished one thing from others. Character was also that which articulated a difference. For two reasons, the dynamics of the print market may have altered the economy of character, shifting the balance between (to cite once again the Abbé Pernetti's definition of *character*) an emphasis on the sign that indicates a being's "peculiar Nature" and an emphasis on the system that made this sign readable, tipping it in favor of peculiarity. The eighteenth century's accelerated trade in printed words and images had the potential to raise questions about quantity—questions about "how much" and about "how many strokes"—that could disrupt the equilibrium in which these two emphases in the culture of character were maintained. It could compromise the legibility of character.

Once copies are prints, an unprecedented attention to the fine detail is demanded of the viewer who adjudicates between the claim that an original and its imitation are similar and the claim that they differ. The wax tablets that Plato invoked in the *Theaetetus* to speak of the mimetic relations between ideas and their objects might be of various consistencies. They might register impressions differently, with relative blurriness or clarity. By contrast, the print-centered Enlightenment metaphor that reinflects the copy theory of knowledge permits a newly intense emphasis on uniform reproduction. Faithful imitation is conceptualized in narrower terms than before, and in terms not so much of resemblance but of high fidelity, or virtual equivalence. As a result of the enhancement in technologies of copying, the replica is scrutinized with a new thoroughness, because it is now necessary to check out the particulars in which it manages or fails to be strictly faithful to the original.

For a start, then, modern print technology raises the question of the "more or less," of the nuanced difference that in modern, mass-mediated times especially is, recalling Tristram Shandy, "insensible." Precisely because, unlike Plato's tablets of wax, the imprinted page cannot easily be construed as a register of differences, precisely because it is a standard of uniformity, one response to the new technology is a new attention to particularity *as* particularity (and hence a new attention to *character* in one sense of that term). In the eighteenth century, God, we have seen, is a writing master or a copy machine: reacting to the ways that the advent of print, in a dialectical reversal, makes deviation and difference both more significant and more scarce, eighteenth-century character writers also seem to decide that God is in the details. The discernment and the rehabilitation of the particularity that print technology threatens to make indiscernible become a compelling project.[35] In this way, the expansion of eighteenth-century Britain's print market put pressure on the conceptual parameters people invoked in setting the limits beyond which a replica became an imitation and beyond which sameness became similarity. Portrait caricatures, those blatantly unfaithful yet some-how recognizable portraits that are by mid-century best-sellers, can be con-sidered a by-product of this pressure and the attention to particularity that it fosters: the invention of that form of characteristic writing presupposes "the theoretical discovery of the difference between likeness and equivalence" that print cultures facilitate.[36]

A second effect of the boom market in printed words and images was the development of that cultural politics Julie Stone Peters describes as "anti-print romanticism": the project of reinforcing the social hierarchies and the divisions between artistic kinds that had been destabilized by the swollen masses of print products, the first truly mass-produced commodities of com-mercial capitalism.[37] The new ease of copying engendered an anticommer-cial, antimodernist position, thoroughly elaborated by the late eighteenth century, that disdained "mere" copies, holding that meaning is vulgarized by the modern traffic in signs, that truth lies beyond the compass of names and pictures. "Anti-print romanticism" imperiled the organizing power as-cribed to the metalanguage of character, sign, and copy. In *Second Characters*, Shaftesbury speaks of a particular character or dramatic personage, Dryden's Spanish friar, as being "pleasing, although reiterate" (135); Shaftesbury's hes-itation in the face of what is "reiterate" suggests what was unstable about the economy of character. He anticipates the era, subsequent to the late eighteenth century's stratification of the culture market and rethinking of characterizing, when some characters could be dismissed as *mere* types.

To get a preliminary sense of how the relations between sameness and similarity, equivalence and likeness, were revamped with the expansion of the print market, and also to understand how this revamping could be mani-fested as a project of "refinement," I want to return for a moment to Locke's *Essay Concerning Human Understanding*.[38] The *Essay*, I have suggested, expounds at length the implications of casting the processes of copying as metaphors for explaining acts of knowledge and communication. From moment to mo-ment, Locke compares ideas to pictures. Words are for him the "marks" of ideas. Nature "stamps" its workmanship with "characters" or marks of distinction, and experience, as we have seen, imprints the mind as if it were a page. Within the *Essay*'s description of cognition, meaning itself hinges on generalizability and reproduction: it hinges on the correspondences linking the particular to the general and those linking the copy to the original.

Locke presents the *Essay* as piece of public policy, a campaign against antisocial forces that menace the generation of common meanings and common sense. Crucial to such a campaign is the correspondence between the data of sensation or of reflection (that is, "such Combinations of simple *Ideas* as are not looked upon to be characteristical Marks of any real Beings") and the word that "ties [those data] fast together" (*Essay*, 288, 434). The empiricism for which Locke is remembered involves correcting for semantic fraud and negligence by disengaging singularities from projectors' and schoolmen's notions of species and essences. Locke aims to emancipate particularity from the thrall of conceptual categories and systems of names. To that end, throughout the *Essay*, he directs readers' gaze to things heterogeneous and seemingly one of a kind, things occluded by the generalities of others' language. Locke was an original founder of the Bank of England and a member of the British Board of Trade with a special interest in the expanding empire. It is notable that the exotic flora and fauna—cassowaries, parrots, and pineapples, for instance—that were introduced into a commercializing England under the aegis of his sort of enterprise are, throughout his *Essay*, held up as specimens of a diversity that is ill served by the crudity of current modes of utterance (for example, *Essay*, 323, 333). As Chandra Mukerji remarks, "Material novelties . . . were so varied and so new to European travelers and traders that they created a crisis of meaning only solved by new attention to the material world, i.e., by envisioning ways to explain and use it."[39] The cassowary (no ordinary "bird") and the pineapple (no ordinary "apple") provided Locke with examples of how much, if the human mind were sufficiently attentive to the nuance and nonpareil, there would be to talk about. With this emphasis on finding out characters, in the sense of the term that has to do with peculiarity of a thing, he sets his public an example. He finds out new ideas for the inquiring mind to collect.

By striving to connect the abstractness of language to the singularity of these new things, Locke aims to refine language. He means to render it accountable to the complexity of phenomenal experience. This means, however, that redirecting the mind back to general concepts, back to the labor of sorting and assembling a "bundle" of things (*Essay*, 420), is perforce a tricky matter. In these circumstances drawing boundaries between sameness and similarity and likeness and equivalence is problematic. Yet the crux for the *Essay*—a crux, as we shall see, that troubles its confidence in the legibility of characters and countenances—is that this rerouting from the particular back to the general is requisite if common sense is to be preserved and if cognition is to be a social event.

Throughout the *Essay* the problems Locke builds into the empiricist project of transcribing nature—problems in selecting the particular accidents and differenda that will be "pared away" to form general concepts, in regulating the relation of those parts to wholes, in balancing abstraction with particularization—are played out, luridly, on the body's surfaces. The abstraction that Locke subjects to piecemeal particularization is more than once the gestalt of the human face, and the semiotic convention he denaturalizes is the expressive connection that is supposed to obtain between this physiognomic surface and the interior selfhood it images. More than once, that is, Locke undertakes an exercise in disfiguration that disrupts the economy of character by disrupting the relation of the part to the whole and the relation of what is meaningful to what is publicly apprehensible.

Locke's philosophic interests in copying and in the semantics of the *alter idem*—the dissimilarity that can be detached from seeming synonymy—lead him to consider human reproduction as an instance of semiosis. For Locke, birth involves, above all, the perpetuation of a family resemblance and the transmission of the human form. Especially attentive to aberrant products of human reproduction, Locke turns repeatedly to the example of a "changeling." This infant's congenital deformities, which are in some manifestations bodily and in others mental, signal a disturbance in the sequential copying and recopying of the human body and mind. The changeling makes his most spectacular appearance in the *Essay* when Locke reviews arguments about how the knowledge that is registered in humanity's names for things has no relevance to things' "real Frame[s] and secret Constitutions." To put us in a position where we may judge of the fictions of identity that are registered by names, Locke initiates a step-by-step mutilation and inflation of his changeling's face. He fleshes out this character:

> The well-shaped *Changeling* is a Man, has a rational Soul, though it appears not; this is past doubt, say you. Make the Ears a little longer, and more pointed . . . and then you begin to boggle: Make the Face yet narrower, flatter, and longer, and then you are at a stand: Add still more and more of the likeness of a Brute to it, and let the Head be perfectly that of some other Animal, then presently 'tis a *Monster*. . . . it hath no

51

rational Soul, and must be destroy'd. Where now (I ask) shall be the just measure; which the utmost Bounds of that Shape, that carries with it a rational Soul? (572)

Two problems in the knowledge of identity are dramatized through Locke's overloading of the face. First, at each stage in the passage it is increasingly the case that the face, as a sign by which a changeling gets recognized, is dissociated from what it signifies: it is displaced from any substantial ground. Locke demonstrates how, regardless, the fate of the changeling continues to hang, as he puts it elsewhere, on the "sort of Frontispiece" he is joined up to (519). Locke raises, that is, the problem of judging the book by its cover, of appraising character by face value. Second, Locke unfixes the system of differences underwriting our notion of what is proper to humans. The general names "Brute" and "Man" and even "Changeling" or "Monster" (these the terms that mediate between the first two) one by one prove inadequate to the task of labeling the welter of states of being that have come to occupy the interstices among the names. Locke produces objects that beggar description. The proliferation of nameless faces (of various ear-lengths and degrees of flatness) highlights the difficulties that the knowledge-seeking subject of empiricism must take on in adjudicating between identity and difference or, to put it otherwise, in determining the point at which the resemblance of the human image that is blazoned on the well-shaped changeling's body no longer resembles. The questions bringing us to "a stand" as we witness the alteration of the well-shaped changeling's looks are, At what stage in this process is the human no longer the human? Does the body possess one feature or stroke of character that is crucial to the preservation of human image, and, if so, which is it? These correspond to the questions that surreptitiously trouble Locke's program for more attentive vision and more refined utterance: At what stage in the particularization of a thing or the fleshing out of a character does it become something other? When do differences and peculiarities count as part of the thing's intrinsic meaning, and when do they count as mere accessories to its significance? The predicament of each changeling is like that of the bookseller Locke mentions in a parable that, in its focus on business practices, both makes a point about the legibility of personal identity and warns of dire consequences when manufacturers' production outstrips their plans for distribution. This bookseller "had in his Ware-house Volumes, that lay there unbound, and without Titles; which he could therefore make known to others, only by shewing the loose

Sheets" (505). Saddled with *their* frontispieces, the changelings cannot identify themselves with any more success.

Given the cachet the human face possesses in early modern thinking about character and the infrastructure of communications, the stretching of the original changeling's ears and the lengthening of its visage appear acts of semantic vandalism. Locke's fiddling with the changeling's face puts an intolerable pressure on the culture's arrangements for figuring forth meaning. Worse still, his writing adds to rather than subtracts from the lineaments of the well-shaped changeling. Progressively distending and overloading the face, it produces what Renaissance teratology, the science of congenital deformities, classified as a *monstre par excès* and not a *monstre par défaut*. Locke's empiricist way of seeing is *productive*. It disengages differences from seeming similarities and fills the perceptual field with more things that the knowledge-seeking subject may single out. In this sense the *Essay* responds to the requirements of a world altered—in some eyes disfigured—by the introduction of trade: as Chandra Mukerji's work would suggest, its empiricism envisions new ways to explain and use a marketplace being filled up with novelties. However, the *Essay* would seem to register some ambivalence about this diversified, replete world, insofar as the question of "the just measure" that Locke poses at the end of the changeling passage—the problem of the line between the *"Poco piu"* and *"Poco meno"*—haunts it.

As the *Essay* progresses, its imagery comes increasingly to connect propriety of language to bodily size and personal identity. Locke asserts, for instance, that the ideas he communicates in the *Essay* are "fitted to Men of my own size" (8). He wishes that men would back their words with ideas and so realize how "small [a] pittance of Reason . . . is mixed with those huffing Opinions they are swell'd with" (438).

It is for this reason ironic that Locke makes his case for economy—his argument that the production of knowledge would be stepped up if people maintained a strict proportion between their ideas and the names that they give them—in the context of a book that, as he himself avows, "grew insensibly to the bulk that it now appears in." In his "Epistle to the Reader" Locke recalls how, during the composition of the *Essay*, "New Discoveries" led him on and on (8). This covert predilection for an overproduction that results in disproportion also manifests itself in the changeling passage: Locke seems never to finish adding finishing touches to the face, adding more and more strokes. Locke's practice points away from conceptions of embodied words and discursive bodies and points toward notions of the body and the signifier as surplus to significance.

The character writers who were Locke's contemporaries worked according to the same logic of more-is-better that informs the *Essay*'s overloading of the face. Their imitations of Theophrastus were books whose contents grew, in a Lockean manner, ever more motley from edition to revised and expanded edition. In striving to encompass an increasingly quirky assortment of social particulars, the collections of character sketches produced by Samuel Butler and others stymied the cataloging capacity that had been established for their form by Theophrastus' typologies of ethical types. They did the same with the imaginative order that had been set out in Renaissance literature of the estates—catalogs of the characters and defects of each social estate, from the clergy to the peasantry. This sort of setting for character exerted pressure as well on the classifications of the temperaments suggested by humor theory. There *were* four humors, but in Butler's character book, "the humourist" is one character among almost two hundred.[40]

The book of characters makes it apparent that the social and ethical divisions set out in representational schemes developed by earlier generations—divisions regulating the relation of the individual to the totality and asserting the permanence and unity of character beneath contradiction and transitory appearances—have the potential to be subdivided ad infinitum. After a hiatus that began in the 1670s, there was between 1725 and 1760 an effort to revive and update the Theophrastan practice of character collecting. In this interval Butler's character sketches were published for the first time in the *Genuine Remains in Verse and Prose,* and John Earle's *Microcosmography* was reissued and updated frequently; 1750 witnessed the publication of *Characterism, or, the Modern Age Display'd,* the only original character book in the seventeenth-century mode that the eighteenth century produced. This minor revival at mid-century was perhaps motivated by people's determination at this moment to use the device of the character to fabricate a sense of the typical and so a sense of social coherence. One could not just depict, but produce, a nation, if one could get all of its component parts or characteristics down in writing—if, inventory style, in the manner of the political arithmeticians of the era, one could, for instance, supply representatives of all the diverse trades that sustained the marketplace. (The latter is a goal close to being realized in Tobias Smollett's *Roderick Random* [1748], which depicts forty-nine different sorts of tradesmen and tradeswomen.)

But reconciling the pursuit of legibility and coherence, on the one hand, with the pursuit of variety, on the other, is no easy task; and indeed by the mid-eighteenth century character writers operated in an environment in which little authority could be attributed to concepts of a social *type* or concepts of a character portrait that bore a "signatura rerum." The character writers had to proceed, accordingly, by, on one level, begging the question of how many characters it might take to anthologize and to sum up human nature and, on another, begging the question of how many traits, or characteristics, must be set down for a portrait to be complete. Even in the seventeenth century Richard Flecknoe's "character" of the "character" (1658) tried in vain to legislate between "matter" and "superfluity."[41] In the Stationers' Register publication record for Wye Salstonstall's book of characters (1631), the phrase "Picturae Loquaces" appears in the place of "Picturae Loquentes," the phrase that had in fact appeared on the title page of Salstonstall's book. The Register's error speaks volumes about how it was in effect expected that the book of characters would go on too long.

Like the narratives by Smollett and others that we now call novels and with which the mid-century character collections competed as they promised to purvey both variety and legibility, the books of characters had to win a place in a culture market in which distinction, and not typicality, was a selling point. Consumption was fueled by the fiction that the commodity was a nonpareil. Character writers knew that theirs was the age of the novelty item. (Such is the status of the pineapple in Locke's *Essay*.) Drawn in a Lockean manner to refinement, the practitioners of characteristic writing pursued the singularity that could not be contained within existing systems of names and categories; they pursued as well a more comprehensive, "truer" account of a diversifying population and a diversifying human nature. And while they cast their nets more widely and augmented their materials, they called into question the ongoing identity of their project and of the "character" they purported to write up. In what sense was their enterprise the same as that of their predecessors? In what sense did a modern character remain, as the very term *character* pledged, the ne plus ultra of readability? In their updating of Theophrastus, the character writers raised the question that Locke posed while disfiguring the changeling: At what stage in the differentiation of a thing does it becomes something other?

Not surprisingly, by the mid-eighteenth century commentators were prone to call for a zero-growth policy. With one eye on contemporary character books, Joseph Warton in 1753 lamented La Bruyère's propensity for "overcharging" his characters as he fleshed them out: to Warton, La Bruyère's individual portraits seemed overloaded, with "many ridiculous features that cannot exist together in one subject."[42] In the *Critical Essay on Characteristic-Writings* Henry Gally was similarly worried about the discursive economy of the character. He urged authors not to dwell too long on a single idea but rather to pass on to another as soon "as the masterly stroke is given" (39). (He neglected, however, to set out a method for discriminating a master stroke from any other sort.) Gally declared the characters published in seventeenth-century England to be "far-fetched" (89) and asserted, with a dig at La Bruyère, that anything French "convert[ed] Men into Monsters" and "turn[ed] Nature into Grimace" (74). In the meantime, mid-eighteenth-century commentators who cast their eyes on the printsellers' shops and the stage began to suspect that the excesses that arose from Locke's overloading of the changeling's physiognomy and La Bruyère's conversion of man into monster were being repeated.

THE ADDED TOUCH AND THE FINISHING TOUCH: HOGARTH, THE ROYAL ACADEMY, AND THE PHIZ-MONGERS

So far I have presented the eighteenth century's overloading of the character as an aspect of a project of refinement—a project registering the emphasis on the value of the particular that was commended by Lockean empiricism and made compelling by the pressures print technologies brought to bear on people's ways of discriminating sameness from similarity. This commentary on the excessiveness of character writing points to the difficulty of distinguishing between what it means to refine a representation and what it means for it to be frittered away with details. As Gally's reference to what the French do to men suggests, however, such commentaries were not a purely theoretical matter but also a forum for cultural politics or, bluntly, for turf wars. Participants in these debates over added strokes were intervening into the distribution of cultural capital.

Turning to the fortunes of characters and countenances in the print shop and on the stage reveals the utility of these repudiations of the excesses perpetrated by other character writers. Denouncing others' excesses functioned as a way to alibi one's own departures from ideals of discursive economy. It was a measure cultural producers used both to keep up the appearances of discursive probity and at the same time adapt to a contemporary realignment of generic and social hierarchies. The middle decades of the eighteenth century were a watershed era for the development of a "middling" culture, one that was to be founded in part on a renegotiation of the forms proper to an inherited court culture, but even more so on gentlefolks' increasing estrangement from the forms of crowd recreation that constituted the culture of the common people. "Grimace," to return to Gally's terminology, was un-English. More important, at a moment when the differences distinguishing polite from popular culture were being recast in polarized terms, and when belonging comfortably to both spheres had become impossible, grimace was *low*. With this metaphoric effort at physiognomic regulation Gally joins the ranks of those who attempted to refine middling culture by expelling the entertainment afforded by the fairground, the ballad sheet, and the almanac from the category of respectable pleasures. This is the crucial stake of the debates over the overloading of character: what the participants in these debates sought at the same time that they renegotiated the idea of the type was a means to rationalize and to control the passage from proper to popular or illegitimate modes of inscribing character.[43] In this context, the value of the specimen of character came to be a matter of what it was not. In the graphic arts, onstage, and eventually in novels, above all, character came to be something that was constituted through its interrelations, because enjoying a *character* became a way of asserting that one did not belong to the sort of undiscriminating audience that would take pleasure in either caricatures or the "monstrous over-done Grimaces" of the burlesque actor.[44]

In the 1730s some habitués of the London art scene got especially voluble while they decried the way that other habitués were transforming nature into grimace. It was in that decade that the fashion for portrait caricatures was introduced into England by gentlemen returning from the Grand Tour and by enterprising printsellers; then, one especially interesting episode in the construction of an English middling culture and the renegotiation of character was inaugurated. Between 1736 and 1742 Arthur Pond, who had acted as cicerone to the English in Rome, published a series of engraved copies of Italian drawings. His *Tetes de Caractères* reproduced grotesque heads designed by Leonardo da Vinci and Annibale and Agostino Carracci, as well as portraits executed by Pier Leone Ghezzi, who specialized in satiric likenesses of the tourists visiting eighteenth-century Rome. Pond also expedited the printing of the portraits his aristocratic patrons executed of one another after he had tutored them in caricature drawing. Thus, beginning in the 1750s he paved the way for equally enterprising printsellers, Matthew and Mary Darly above all, to print, distribute, and show "due Honour to" the pictorial inventions of "ladies and gentlemen."[45] Initiating England's caricature craze, Pond enabled printsellers to profit from the vanity of well-to-do amateurs.

Eighteenth-century commentaries on this new import divide their attention between two of its features—features that, from our perspective, caricature appears to have shared with the expanded and diversified book of characters. According to this commentary, caricature couples the act of willfully carrying character drawing to excess—of swelling figures and being prodigal in one's handling of the signs of humanity—with the tendering of a truth claim, the claim that the drawing improves on extant modes of imitating nature and conveys truths about the person more truly. One of the ways in which the producers of caricature differ from the writers of Theophrastan characters is in their audacity: caricaturists *flaunted* their excesses. For the caricaturist, or so it was perceived, conveying the identity of the person was a matter of producing a surplus—producing too much.[46] The term *caricature* derives from the Italian *caricare*, to load: as the definition of the practice offered in 1788 by *The Artist's Repository and Drawing Magazine* puts it, a caricature is (in keeping with this etymology) "a likeness of any person; but loaded, exaggerated, heightened, and rendered generally ridiculous." It is, as the French synonym, *portrait chargé*, indicates, a loaded portrait (that is, *rittrati carichi*), a portrait with extras. A 1773 complaint against the caricature-drawing Marquess of Townshend maintains that the loaded portrait aims "With wretched pencil to debase / Heaven's favourite work, the human face, / To magnify and hold to shame / Each little blemish of our frame."[47] Caricaturists concern themselves with the metamorphosis that ensues when the part is released from the whole. The caricaturist's magnification of a blemish reverses priorities. One looks at a caricature and finds oneself gazing not so much at a nose appended to a face but at a supernumerary face that has attached itself to a nose.

This particularization of the individual's physical appearance, neoclassical critics pointed out, was a crime against decorum. Emphasizing how bodies differed rather than what they had in common, caricature diverted beholders from truths of general application. The social satires that were marketed alongside caricature portraits and that brought the chaos and trivia of commercial modernity into representation were liable to be charged with the same transgression—the same sort of indulgence in "low-plane reality" that Norman Bryson identifies when he discusses the still life's ways of allying wealth with excess in the sphere of representation. In the late eighteenth century the artist Henry Fuseli used revealing terms to plead the cause of the type: even if, according to Fuseli, "comic painting"—his general rubric for graphic satire—did not "degenerate into caricature, . . . the history-book of the vulgar," it would still become "unintelligible in time."[48] That is, comic painting annoyed Fuseli because it portended a state of oblivion in which the concrete particulars of images would not be matched with verbal messages set out in captions, a state in which nondescripts would proliferate. Departing from general truths, devoted to low details, comic painting would find itself in the plight that Locke associated with the bookseller who has forgotten about his books' frontispieces; through comic painting's deviations from the typical, the system of differences underpinning intelligibility and identity would be torn asunder.

Critics who delivered these strictures on the relative values accruing to the particular and the general were, however, by and large whistling in the wind. With the aid of West End printsellers such as the Darlys, the eighteenth-century public consumed and produced "droll subjects, comic figures, sundry characters, caricatures, &c" with considerable gusto and so helped to engender a new phase of style wars in the art world. High art set about defining itself in contradistinction to popular and amateur art by identifying itself with an ideal of "pictorial abstemiousness" and identifying others with excess.[49] Thus members of the Royal Academy of Art insisted vehemently in the last four decades of the century that "real" art depended on the artist's getting above (in Joshua Reynolds' words) "singular forms, local customs, [and] particularities."[50] In the academy's map of the cultural field the caricature's allotted place was alongside waxworks and so-called Flemish pictures—with the works of "copyists," who engaged in a mercenary and "mechanical trade" rather than a "liberal art" (4:57), who excelled in "minute finishing of the features" (14:259), and who, "unwilling that any part of [their] industry should be lost upon the spectator, [took] as much pains to discover, as the greater artist does to conceal, the marks of [their] subordinate assiduity" (4:59). To avoid the excesses that disrupted the economy of character, and to secure their claims to high-cultural status, some academicians were seemingly all but ready to forego character (and so difference) altogether. Thus James Barry explained to his pupils that "character" related to beauty as a "distortion" of "the central form of the species" related to that form. In Barry's tripartite division of the field of figural representation, "character" differs from "deformity" only in being constituted by a lesser degree of distortion, in having fewer qualities superadded to it, and, consequently, in not being completely nondescript. For Barry, character's only saving grace is that it doesn't beggar description utterly, but instead intersects with a name.[51]

Even the national physiognomy could seem a risky object of representation to the Royal Academicians. As cast from nature's die, the English face could appear too particularized and marked up to be a proper, readable figure. The countenances that Appelles and Zeuxis had at their disposal provided those ancients with a means to intuit humanity's central form from particular somatic circumstances and to move easily from the particular to the general. By contrast, the face of the modern English model was liable to look busy. It displayed "numerous little hollows, too many and too conspicuous dimples." The English face looked as if it were not "complete" and as if it had not quite "integrated" its surfeit of "parts."[52] There were ways to redeem this excess, even if the untrammeled particularity of the English face seemed to jeopardize any notion that there might be a concord between the particular and the general or the individual and the generic—precisely the harmonizing vision that the body talk of the period was, with the talk of character, expected to provide. Physiognomic unruliness could be construed as evidence of English "liberty" and, like the Magna Carta, like Britons' eccentricity or failure to exhibit the social graces, or like Shakespeare's flouting of the dramatic unities, it could be made into a cause for celebration: it could be numbered among the differences that distinguished Britain from Europe.[53] The microcosm of teeming social detail that was exposed to view in the windows of the typical English print shop captured metonymically what many liked to cast as a peculiarly English world of abundance. (These shop windows stocked with pinups of odd physiognomies were themselves frequently subjects for the comic prints, which characteristically emphasized the social and bodily diversity of the farrago of characters who came to gaze at these imaged characters.) Views of (to quote a typical advertisement) "Mezzotinto's colour'd, plain / Prints of Hogarth's fertile brain" envisaged a world where the common pledge of empiricism and of commercial modernity—that there would always be more than enough—was fulfilled.[54]

Certainly, their surplus marks notwithstanding, modern English faces represented so much money in the bank for English cultural producers—so many shillings per "mark of the painter's . . . assiduity." The Royal Academy's professors cast aesthetic value as a function of painters' transcendence of the particulars that make it possible to recognize an individual person. Nonetheless, commercial realities dictated that portraits of real, individual sitters comprised the largest percentage of works submitted to academy exhibitions,[55] and engraved versions of those portraits of the upper gentry or crowned heads also found their way onto the public market. They were to be found cheek by jowl with cheap portraits of popular preachers, with the Marquess of Townshend's political cartoons, and a farrago of Jack Tars, Cits Turned Macaronis, French Ladies in London, and so forth.

Such conditions of proximity make visible another rationale eighteenth-century people had for associating faces with money, an association based not on the legibility that linked faces and coin-faces but on the fact that both were tokens of pecuniary gain. Faces made money—the overloaded faces of the popular print market and the minutely detailed portraits that Reynolds relegated to the bottom of the artistic barrel especially so. An uneasy response to this commercialization of the face is at the core of William Hogarth's campaign against caricature drawing and for character. The key texts of his campaign, his treatise *The Analysis of Beauty* (1753) and his engravings *Characters and Caricaturas* (1743) and *The Bench* (begun in 1758), are informed, on the one hand, by Hogarth's ambivalent relation to the popular market and the popularity of the overloaded face and, on the other, by his equally ambivalent relation to the abstracted Raphael formulae that were favored by the Royal Academy. Hogarth's appearance above, in my quotation from a print shop's advertising, suggests the complexities these ambivalent relations engender. *The Analysis of Beauty, Characters and Caricaturas* and *The Bench* recycle, that is, the equivocations that characterized Hogarth's actions as, for instance, he settled accounts with the connoisseurs ("picture-jobbers") who dismissed portraiture as the expression of a mere mechanic ability and as he warded off the connoisseurs' charge that he was in the art business for the money, and at the same time took the unprecedented step of advertising his print series in the papers. Such equivocations also characterized the measures to which Hogarth turned in order to reconcile the universal moral applicability ascribed to the idealized forms of history painting with the attractiveness but meaninglessness of the empirical particular. He was perpetually frustrated by the dearth of commissions that might enable him to work in the grand style of history painting but Hogarth was also capable of defying, as well as deferring to, the traditional hierarchies that ranked artistic kinds and members of British society.[56]

The craze for caricature that took hold of the British public in mid-century was bound to exacerbate the complicities and collisions between high and low culture that Hogarth's career exposes to view. The caricature-drawing Marquess of Townshend was, for instance, denounced for catering to the mob in "every ale-house and every gin-shop."[57] Yet, at the same time that they smacked of the low, the caricature drawings that Townshend and the

Darlys championed also represented the sort of aristocratic in-joke that could draw together a coterie audience. In the games of recognition that Townshend's or Pond's personal caricatures invited the spectator to play, it would take an aristocrat to know one. In this second respect, too, caricatures would have vexed a man-on-the-make such as Hogarth—the industrious apprentice who could voice a reverence for the classical ordering of the arts and the social world but who nonetheless found participation in the portrait and print market to be necessary to his own social aspirations.

In his autobiographical writings Hogarth complained that, after the success of his "comic history paintings" (Henry Fielding's term for Hogarthian fictional narratives such as *The Harlot's Progress* [1732] and *The Rake's Progress* [1735]), "the whole nest of Phizmongers were upon my back every one of whome has his friends and all were taught to run em down [and to call] my women . . . harlot and my men charicatures" (*Analysis,* 218). Explaining the genesis of *Characters and Caricaturas,* Hogarth states that the engraving was executed to distinguish the meanings of two words—*character* and *caricature*—that were too often confused, even though (as Hogarth later wrote in the inscription to *The Bench*) "there are hardly any two things more essentially different." The strong claim about difference is so much bravado. In mingling together "droll subjects, comic figures, sundry characters, caricatures, &c.," without bothering to identify what distinguishes one from another, the catalog, quoted earlier, in which Mary and Matthew Darly advertise their wares suggests the degree to which that difference was only in the eye of the beholder; it suggests synonymy more than it does antithesis. Hogarth's polemicizing identifies, or more precisely *invents,* a confusion of categories specifically so as to correct it, and through that fine-tuning alter the position in the cultural hierarchy that might be assigned to Hogarth's own "uncommon way of Painting"—his *"true* comedy" (*Analysis,* 210, 212).

Ronald Paulson puts this in different terms: "[Arthur] Pond's series of caricature portraits . . . opened [Hogarth's] own position to misunderstanding. [Hogarth] was surely aware that 'caricature' was applied to the work of any artist who ventured beyond the Raphael formulae."[58] The problem was, in a sense, that through their deviation from the Royal Academy's system of ideal types, through their engagement with the diversified world of commercial modernity, those who were called caricaturists had taken up a position of opposition that Hogarth would have liked to have had to himself. They got there first. The craze for caricature testified, as much as Hogarth's renditions of Moll Hackabout and Tom Rakewell did, to what was dissatisfying about the existing decorums for particularizing representations.

More generally, the problem was that Hogarth wanted to ensure that the recognition he received from those who admired creations such as Moll and Tom was recognition bestowed for fleshing out *character*. Caricatures provoked identity crises for Hogarth, and this is why he expended energy attempting to adjudicate between departures from the ideal that don't go too far and those that, frittered away by detail, do. For Hogarth, caricatures disarranged the ideological matrix where bodily seemliness, the distinction of art forms, and the distinction of persons intersected. For a start, the adepts of caricature drawing, who consciously aimed to do a bad job of imitation while nonetheless seizing the "air" of their subjects, embodied a threat to the professional identity that an artist such as Hogarth pieced together in his academic training. Furthermore, caricature added to its association with the frankly mercenary print market an association with genteel amateurism (after all, even women were invited by the printsellers to try their hands at caricature) or courtly *sprezzatura:* the genre gives place of privilege to the likeness that proves the artist to be above taking pains over what he or she is doing. Aristocrats could breezily refuse to even try to earn a place in the art world's economy of prestige; caricature sanctioned such refusals. Nonetheless, the grounds of Hogarth's opposition to caricatures are not nearly as clear-cut as they would be if in his mind the genre's only transgressions were its enshrinement of venality and feckless draftsmanship. The problem was that, on the contrary, character resisted Hogarth's attempt to establish it as the antithesis of caricature and so as one pole in a tidy binary opposition. Questions about quantity undermined Hogarth's attempt to assert differences of quality.

Character's unruliness in the face of Hogarth's efforts to make it make sense is significant because, with the new attractiveness of low-plane reality, with the need to negotiate the newly rigid boundaries between high and low culture, practitioners of characteristic writing in all media were trying to get away with new ways of fleshing out characters. When in *Joseph Andrews* Henry Fielding seeks "to secure [for his new species of writing] a place in the classical (and contemporary) hierarchy higher than satire, the grotesque, or the comic," he turns to Hogarth. As Ronald Paulson's overview of the mid-century style wars suggests, Hogarth's polemicizing in his advertising, in his subscription tickets to his progresses, and in his campaigning for copyright reform provided a useful precedent when Fielding and other mid-century practitioners of characteristic writing found that they needed to validate and alibi their own, potentially "low" departures from ideals of discursive economy.[59] Hogarth's example taught them to point the finger at others' excesses. On this occasion, seeking to define and validate his particular project of characteristic writing by showing what it is not, Fielding separates his "comic epic in prose" from the burlesque. To do this he puts character center-stage, and he evokes the preference that people of taste give to Hogarth over the caricaturist who "paint[s] a Man with a Nose, or any other Feature of a preposterous Size" and who exhibits "Monsters, not Men" (5–6). *Characters and Caricaturas* (fig. 2)—in which Hogarth plugs Fielding in his turn and directs public attention to *Joseph Andrews*—aims to polarize the grotesque overstatement and what Fielding called "the exactest copying of Nature." Yet Hogarth's print seems instead to be about the *fine line* differentiating the particularizing vision implemented by the character from that implemented by the caricature. Only a fine line separates the marks that individualize the countenance from the marks that exaggerate it.

The bottom fifth of Hogarth's print is divided vertically into two parts, one dedicated to "Character" and the other to "Caricatura." In the left half, Hogarth has installed copies of profiles from Raphael's Cartoons—images that in 1743 represented the quintessence of history painting. The matching space in the engraving (the lower right side) is occupied by heads that duplicate those of the persons who flaunted their oddity in Arthur Pond's anthology of Italian caricatures. Above this strip of heads one sees a jumble of one hundred heads more. Each profile, Hogarth asserts, making sure that we know that his practice is integrated with his theory, is modeled after that of a minor character appearing in his *Marriage A-la-Mode*. (*Characters and Caricaturas* served originally as the subscription ticket for that 1745 series.) Not one profile, Hogarth boasts, is exaggerated.

The odd effect of Hogarth's engraving derives from these extra hundred heads. They invite the beholder to probe the limits of resemblance and identity. We find ourselves frantically trying to specify the characteristic particulars in which the countenances differ. This is no easy task—it is obvious that Hogarth set out, in delineating these hundred characters, to keep to a minimum the different kinds of strokes he would have to deploy. (The visages differ, but not overmuch; all are male, seen in profile, beardless.) The quantity of physiognomic detail does not flesh out but overwhelms the contrast that ostensibly gives the print its meaning. In fact, this overloaded image

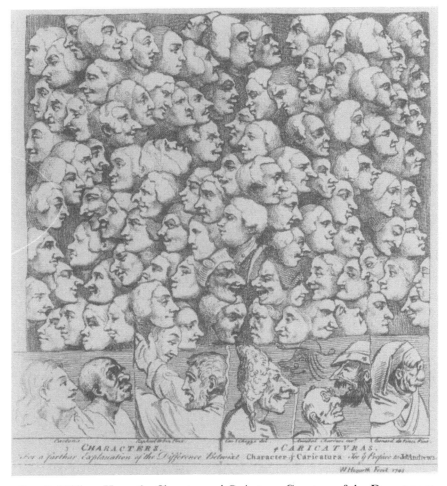

FIG. 2. William Hogarth, *Characters and Caricaturas.* Courtesy of the Department of Special Collections, University of Chicago Library.

suggests the qualities of "minuteness and particularity [that] are," according to Walywn's *Essay on Comedy,* "necessarily assumed of caricature."[60] The proliferation within Hogarth's image of copies that copy copies (copies of Pond's copies of the Italian masters) shows how Britain's printing-press-driven phizmongering allows excess—the overaccumulation of images—to threaten cognition.

Furthermore, the longer one looks at the engraving, the more it seems that Hogarth's subject is *literally* the fine line between character and caricature. Hogarth puts into play the opposition he means to exemplify. The line that divides the heroic Raphael heads from Ghezzi's, Carracci's, and da Vinci's quizzical phizzes is continued, subtly, into the area of the engraving assigned to characters, by a line formed initially by the ornamental braid or epaulette on the shoulder of one character and then extended partway up the print. Hogarth has not drawn a dividing line through the plate from top to bottom, but such a line is suggested. At the lower center of the image, the profiles from the right-hand side meet up nose to nose with the profiles from the left-hand side: playing the games of recognition that caricature responses, we can recognize in this group the face of Hogarth himself, posed eyeball-to-eyeball with the face of Henry Fielding. And when we look closely at the two "characters" who are positioned immediately below Hogarth and Fielding and immediately above the Italianate heads, it appears that these unfortunates have managed to snub their noses against that fine line between character and caricature. The dividing line between good and bad characterizing itself becomes the cause of this physiognomic distortion.

In the catalog published by Sayers and Bennett's print warehouse in 1775, an advertisement for *Characters and Caricaturas* described Hogarth's manifesto as demonstrating "Character to be a small deviation from general Proportions, and [showing that] Caricatura is only that deviation exaggerated." The ad rewrites Hogarth's attempt to polarize the two modes of characterizing and the two kinds of art. It opposes them, precariously, in terms of a quantitative rather than a qualitative difference. This makes the inscription of character liable to the overstatement that, for instance, Henry Gally had earlier aimed to circumvent when he made "Characteristic Justice" (by analogy with poetic justice) hinge on the "strokes of character" being neither "too faint" nor "too strong." Characteristic justice could only be done if the character writer avoided the "paraphrastical manner" and resisted the temptation to repeat the "masterly stroke" and to reiterate the same idea (38–40).

At the same time, the catalog's reinterpretation retailors Hogarth's aesthetics to suit the categories of academic neoclassicism. Sayers and Bennett's refining of Hogarth's definition of character suggests how the Royal Academicians also situated their ideal forms, precariously, on the slippery slope that leads to overloading; how James Barry's "beauty," for instance, was only uncertainly and ambiguously distinguished from "character" as well as from "deformity." Joshua Reynolds proposed in his third Discourse to the Academy that the artist might, without impropriety, conceive of the human "species" as being divided into a certain number of "characters" or "classes," each possessing its own central form, as exemplified for the class of strong men by, for instance, the Farnese Hercules, or for the class of active men by the Borghese Warrior (3:46–48). This scheme maintains the doctrine of the central form while introducing character into painting (a necessary introduction if, as a history painter, the artist is to communicate a story). Its flaw, however, is that it makes no logical provision for limiting how far beauty might be subdivided.[61] The painter's options appear to be confined either to painting the classically beautiful body, which is to say the same body over and over again, or filling the canvas with a riot of characters. To permit even a single division of the central form is to initiate a drift that leads inexorably beyond types and forms and from orderly deviation to deformity.

As if in illustration of this slipperiness, in his second attempt to diagram the nature of character Hogarth found that he could no longer get by with only the two categories "character" and "caricature." In *The Bench* (fig. 3), Hogarth refined *Characters and Caricaturas* by adding a third category, that of the "outré," or the exaggerated: the heads exemplifying the new category are the same heads that in the engraving of 1743 represented caricatures. In this revision, however, *caricature* denotes, in contradistinction to the outré, the sort of minimalist squib that, for example, seizes the look of "a certain Italian Singer" by means of "a Streight perpendicular Stroke with a Dot over it."

Such a definition of caricature was, the *Monthly Review* commented, "by no means to the purpose"; there was no reason why an image of a straight line and a dot should have prompted Hogarth to worry about his characters' getting confused with others' caricatures.[62] Indeed, further on in the inscription appended to *The Bench,* Hogarth betrays himself and all but admits that it is not abbreviation but excess that jeopardizes the identity of character. As an afterthought Hogarth has edited the part of the inscription that explicates the outré—and that cites as examples "a Giant," who may be considered "a common man Outré," and "a Nose or a Leg, made bigger than it ought to be." He has added to the passage, as a finishing touch, the words "a Dwarf" and "lesser," attempting through this emendation to make it clear that the category also comprehends the deviations from the form of character that involve deficiency rather than surplus. The fact that Hogarth evidently forgot that hyperbole extends in two directions—that it means augmenting *or* diminishing to excess—indicates the ambivalence in his attitude toward caricature's techniques of overcharging and its manipulations of physical dimension, an ambivalence he has covered up here by using his odd definition

FIG. 3. William Hogarth, *The Bench*. Courtesy of the Department of Special
Collections, University of Chicago Library.

FIG. 4. Details of plates 1 and 2 of William Hogarth, *The Analysis of Beauty*

of *caricaturas* as a decoy. His mistake reminds us of the attractions of the added touch, even as Hogarth repudiates them. What jeopardizes the decorums of the characteristic face is abundance, a condition of too much rather than too little.

Hogarth did discover a way to sample the dangerous attractions of the added touch. In the two series of figures (fig. 4) that accompany his chapter on "The Face" in *The Analysis of Beauty*, the human visage becomes malleable. In the first series (numbers 97 and 99 to 104 in plate 1 of the *Analysis*), Hogarth sets up a cartoon strip illustrating the degrees of deviation that lead from the masculine visage whose lineaments satisfy the most demanding taste to a figure "totally divested of all lines of elegance, like a barber's block" (*Analysis*, 136). In the second (numbers 110 through 114, 117, and 118 in plate 2), he demonstrates that the variety and number of lines on a female face are augmented as a woman passes from infancy to maturity and as she is progressively marked, in conformity to Locke's documentary paradigm, by experience.

The conditions of the face that are polarized in *The Bench* and *Characters and Caricaturas* are recast by the *Analysis*'s drawings. The face possessing character and the caricatured face are in the *Analysis* rendered points on a continuum. Caricature becomes a contingent stage into which character passes, and vice versa. Caricature, far from being the antithesis of character, may be read as its extension. The conflict between these notions of character and the conflict between these notions of the function of the added stroke point to a significant pattern of disavowal. Here, the finishing touch, the increase in detail that enables the image to realize its claim to truth value, is reconceived as, past a certain limit, something else—something low that disrupts rather than extends. As "comic history painting" adjusts the economy of character, bidding, as one of the arts of middling culture, for its own distinctive place in the eighteenth-century economy of prestige, character breeds a monster—caricature—and then it disavows this constituent part of itself.

Tellingly, when he outlined his *Rules for Drawing Caricaturas* (1788), Francis Grose conjured up a picture of semiotic and physiognomic inflation that very much resembled Hogarth's. (When it was published Grose's manual was bound with the *Analysis of Beauty:* the proximity of Grose's caricatures to his characters must have caused Hogarth to roll in his grave.) Grose writes:

> The sculptors of ancient Greece seem to have diligently observed the forms and proportions constituting the European ideas of beauty; and upon them to have formed their statues. These measures are to be met with in many drawing-books; a slight deviation from them, by the predominancy of any feature, constitutes what is called *Character,* and serves to discriminate the owner thereof, and to fix the idea of identity. This deviation or peculiarity, aggravated, forms *Caricatura.*

Logically, there is no reason for the accumulation of differentiae that Grose plots to halt once the image has prompted the beholder to zero in on an individual's identifying features and to recognize and label that person. Accordingly, Grose advises caricaturists to be wary of "overcharg[ing]" the "peculiarities of their subjects." With too many strokes of the pen, they will produce "the hideous instead of [the] ridiculous and instead of laughter excite horror."[63] Grose's attempt to arrest the snowball effect that ensues from the added stroke—from the introduction of a notion of difference into the canons of representation—is clearly hopeless.

GARRICK'S FACE

Judging by the complaints that David Garrick's critics made, especially when they remarked on his face, the player's acting also exemplified the dangers of extra strokes. What happened on the stage in the first two-thirds of the eighteenth century was not necessarily conceived of as distinct from what transpired on the page. The intimate relation between Britain's print culture and performance culture is suggested by the way both Hogarth and Fielding found it politic, while they promoted their own ways of negotiating the economy of character, simultaneously to promote what Garrick was doing in the same line. (The poet Christopher Smart declared in his *Hilliad* [1752] that "Hogarth [was] the Garrick of his art"; Hogarth had painted Garrick in the character of Richard III in 1745.) Neoclassical theories of acting shared with prevailing conceptions of the graphic and verbal inscription of character the notion that mimesis proceeded through the assembly of discrete strokes.[64] Furthermore, the mid-eighteenth-century stage was not so much a place where characters created by the playwright were fleshed out as it was a place where the passions were put through their paces, delineated by the players in isolated actions and declamations for which the soliloquy and the set speech provided pretexts. We could think of eighteenth-century acting as an exercise in calligraphy in which the players embodied the passions in much the same way that a writing master might produce specimens of the embodied characters of writing. The eloquent motions of the players' bodies—of their faces especially—were the conditions of a knowledge that was effable and publicly apprehensible. While demonstrating that "anger, fear, pity, adoration . . . and almost every other passion ha[d] a look, attitude, and tone of voice, peculiar to itself," the players confirmed that the motions of the human mind were externally manifested, and in uniform, predictable, and so readable ways.[65]

Commentators on the immensely successful career David Garrick launched in 1741 lauded him for delineating in his performances as finely tuned a taxonomy of these human passions as had ever been seen—an achievement he supposedly secured via his introduction of what Joseph Warton praised as his "little touches of nature."[66] Commentators who were less impressed with Garrick's innovations saw in the added touches of his performances not naturalism but a surplus that threatened sense. The debate about whether Garrick was a good or a bad actor did not focus on how he interpreted, say, the characters of Hamlet or Richard III. Instead it focused on quantity. The emblem for the extravagance with which detractors charged him was Garrick's face, which was like the countenance that manifests the extreme stage of the caricaturist's process of overcharging: it exhibited too many lines and too many of the marks that make a character. Samuel Johnson called Charles Burney's attention to the traces of "wear and tear" discernible on their friend's visage; he also said to Hester Thrale that, "David, Madam, looks much older than he is, because his face has had double the business of any other man's."[67] The debate over Garrick's face—was it comely or not?—that Johnson spoke for constituted a forum, like the contro-

versies over the added strokes of caricatures, for renegotiating what people
wanted from character and renegotiating the relation of character's personal
truths to the visible body and to systems of shared meaning.

The player's face was supposed to serve as a screen on which the operations of a natural semantic system might be viewed with special distinctness.
That face was a model simulating nature's production of "marks and impressions on the body [in general]." Through this visual "imitation of the passions," the player provided spectacular evidence of how the passions, working
by means that were consonant with the copy theory of knowledge, "stamped"
the muscles of the face.[68] This mid-eighteenth-century account of the purpose
of playing prescribed, at least in theory, an indifference toward the particularity of the player's looks. The individuating particularities of the players' persons were supposed to be subordinated to the common language of the passions that their delivery made legible. The spectator was supposed to regard
not the players' bodies but the sentiments written across them. With its pictures of the passions articulating to onlookers the ways in which nature operated within their own breasts, the player's body could be viewed as a register
of unanimity—much like the printing press or Galesia's patchwork screen
or the character Sir Charles Grandison.

The celebrated "ductility" of his facial lineaments—the fact that their particularity was their lack of determinate character—made Garrick's fortune.
Even rival thespian Samuel Foote conceded that Garrick's features were ad-
mirably configured for "what is called the looking of a Character."[69] Thus
in one scene Garrick's countenance was observed to evince consecutively, in
five seconds, the distinct signs of wild delight, temperate pleasure, tranquillity,
surprise, blank astonishment, sorrow, "the air of one overwhelmed," fright,
horror, and despair, with spectacular transitions between each passion.[70]
When Garrick became a theater manager he devised new techniques for
illuminating the stage with wing lights and footlights, the better to frame
these moving pictures of the face. For some, these moving pictures imaged
nature more precisely than ever before. For others, Garrick overdid it, and
this was so much "grimace."

Garrick's accumulations of kinesthetic details could be viewed as so much
overloading of the face, and, by extension, repudiated as déclassé transgressions of the boundaries dividing patrician from popular culture. In an era
of refinement, when the disembodied pleasures of the reading man or woman
were beginning to be pitted against the visceral pleasures of crowd entertainments, the physicality of Garrick's performances looked to some like trum-

1 pery meant to "draw in" the "Groundlings" (Foote, *Treatise*, 18). Theophilus
Cibber bemoaned in this spirit Garrick's "over-fondness for extravagant attitudes, frequent affected starts, convulsive twitchings, jerkings of the body,
sprawling of the fingers, slapping the breast and pockets—a set of mechanical
motions in constant use, the caricatures of gesture suggested by pert vivacity;
his pantomimical manner of acting every word in a sentence," and so on,
and so on. The bits of stage business with which Garrick supplemented his
lines exceeded what his detractors, troping the language of commercial eth-
ics, called "the fair business of character."[71]

For those detractors, Garrick's strokes of character were somatic static—
over-visible frivolity that interfered with the information character should
display. Expressing his part "more by the grimaces of his face, than the
proper modulation of his voice," Garrick effaced textual meaning.[72] And with
this gestural overlay, overloading even the nonverbal moments of the play
text, Garrick threatened the legibility of character.

One can detect in criticisms of the business of his person traces of neoclassicism's aesthetic canons, which underscored the baseness of particularized
representations by associating them with a putatively female enthusiasm for
"baby-sizes, toys, miniatures," and trinkets (Shaftesbury, *Second Characters*,
131). According to this axiology Garrick's use of accessories was particularly
vexing. It was low, and it was effeminate. Foote reacted to Garrick's Lear
by complaining about unmanly snivelling and demanding that the player get
a painter to "draw an enraged Monarch, and see whether he will make any
use of the Handkerchief" (*Treatise*, 17–18). The added touch of nature Garrick brought to his Hamlet was still another accessory: for the ghost scene
he put on a specially commissioned wig, the hairs of which he activated by
means of a mechanical device that he hid in his costume. With this physiognomic prosthesis he was able to satisfy to a tee aestheticians', history painters',
and tragedians' strictures on the appropriate expression of fright, which
maintained that this passion causes "the Hair of the Head [to stand] on
end."[73]

What was troubling about these added touches was compounded by
Garrick's association, in his critics' rhetoric and his professional life, with
the pantomimic harlequinades that were the toast of the impolite part of
the town. The harlequinades owed some of their popularity in the mid-
eighteenth century to the immense sums that producers such as John Rich
invested in their special effects. These apparently took in kinetic and nonverbal thrills of the sort described in a *London Chronicle* of 1772, which reports

on a performance in which the contents of a kitchen—pots, pans, chairs—began to dance, while the crockery began to smash itself. In a criticism of the unnatural frenzy he perceived in Garrick's naturalistic style, Horace Walpole commented sourly on the "exhibitions of the animal or inanimate part of creation, which are furnished by the worthy philosophers Rich and Garrick."[74] In support of this coupling of Garrick's and Rich's names, it was rumored that Garrick's acting début was not, in fact, in the role of tragic Richard III but as "Harlequin student."

Harlequin regularly invaded England's high art in just this way: testing the dividing lines that composed the cultural hierarchy, transforming and deforming his body, and so assaulting the categories and figures with which the eighteenth-century culture of character made sense. To escape from Pantaloon, Harlequin would adopt the guise of an ostrich or would arrange for his own and others' decapitation. Harlequin's deliquescent body dealt an insult to culture's basic theorems of identity: in Garrick's own play *Harlequin's Invasion* (1759), Harlequin's arm is lost and then reappears, skipping about the stage to taunt him.

It could be difficult to distinguish between the insults Harlequin tendered when he turned nature into grimace and the improvements David Garrick, with his added touches and new way of looking a character, brought to nature's representation. Garrick's alterations of the lighting at Drury Lane, which darkened the house, and his banishment of spectators from the stage inaugurated a process that eventually brought to an end a turbulent, "socially complex experience of theatre-going, involving a continuous awareness of rank and clique, conversation, argument, flirtation and the risk of rioting."[75] Granting audience members a kind of privacy, enabling them to be alone together, Garrick's innovations helped make playgoers more like readers, their attendance at a play less a matter of unrefined participation in a crowd and more a psychological experience. Nonetheless, Garrick and John Rich could seem accomplices in crimes against character, rather than patrons of, respectively, a naturalistic and newly refined theater for the respectable middle classes and an unredeemed crowd culture.

In his references to Garrick and Rich, therefore, Henry Fielding runs something like the risk that Hogarth does in attempting to prove *character* to be essentially different from *caricaturas*. Not only declaring allegiance to character over caricature in the preface to *Joseph Andrews*, Fielding has a second way to define his species of characteristic writing, to define what it is by showing what it is not. As noted earlier, he is insistent that his comedy be differentiated from the burlesque (4–6), the low theatrical entertainment in which John Rich "turns Men into Monkeys" and strangely "metamorphose[s] the human Shape" (32). Fielding's allusions to Rich allow him to ally himself with a culture of reading and distance himself from the kind of reception he associates with non- and semiliterate spectators of burlesque theater. At the same time, these allusions to illegitimate culture serve to certify that Fielding's engagement with the low-plane reality of character is not an engagement with deformity. Fielding pursues the flip side of this strategy in *Tom Jones,* in which praise for Garrick's new ways of impersonating a character permits Fielding to soak up some of the player's reflected glory. One wonders, however, about the extent to which, for Fielding, the references to Harlequin's burlesque escape artistry at Rich's Lincoln's Inn are meant to take in practices at Garrick's Drury Lane as well. Examining Joshua Reynolds's portrait of a genre-bending Garrick choosing between the allegorical figures of Tragedy and Comedy (1761), Walpole was full of scorn: "Comedy is a beautiful and winning girl—but Garrick's face is distorted and burlesque."[76]

Like the pictorial effects wrought by caricatures, the theatrical effects wrought by Garrick's overloaded, distorted face aroused controversy because they necessitated a reconsideration of character in its relations to notions of the typical and the legible. The overloading of the theater's iconography of character—Garrick's refinements of drama's gestural language—seemed not only to produce richer representations but also to construct a character whose body, monstrously, defied or exceeded writing up. On the one hand, in the declarations of alliance and the declarations of war that were made in the cause of character, in the bewildering series of cultural contests in which the selfsame figure can be accused both of enhancing character's legibility and of overwhelming it altogether, we can trace the refinement of reception and the realignment of generic hierarchies that would secure the hegemony of literature. The adjudication between sufficiency and excess in mid-century debates was a pivot on which a concern with the semantics of character—a concern with the legibility of the mark of self-distinction and self-evidence—could swing into a concern with the boundaries separating polite from plebeian culture. Commentators could point to the overloaded character precisely in order to either adjust or fortify those boundaries. On the other hand, the energy invested in these debates—the lack of consensus about how much particularization was enough—suggests a dissatisfaction with the programmatic ways of valuing character that I've traced. The dissent is a prelude to the emergence of the notion that characters might be valued for their indescribability, their exceptionality, and their polyvalence and of the notion that the truth of a character should be an inside story of secrets, hidden motivations, and unplumbed depths. This dissent suggests, too, how the very notion that character drawing demanded engagement with the question of "the insensible more or less"—that a character was the sum of its traits or strokes—was under pressure.[77]

Fielding might have been as fascinated by Rich as he was admiring of Garrick, for the same reason that Hogarth might have allowed himself to sample the dangerous attractions of the added stroke of character. The symbolic confusion that popular entertainment and popular print culture introduced into eighteenth-century systems of character was attractive to the very texts that denounced it. Securing a text from the charge that it was low, the denunciation could also enable a covert rethinking of character. Certainly, these would-be founders of new kinds of characteristic writing were aware that the differences of quality that they asserted were undermined by the differences of quantity that they allowed.

The narrative fictions Tobias Smollett published in the 1740s and 1750s, which I will engage at length in my next chapter, also illuminate this covert rethinking of character. Smollett reiterates critics' denunciations of the low excesses of Garrick's face. Roderick Random, for example, finds out the inside story of Mr. Marmozet's social success: the player is admitted into genteel company only because of "his talent of mimicking Punch and his wife Joan." Peregrine Pickle must listen as a Frenchman jeers at Garrick's grimaces: " 'his whole art is no other than a succession of frantic vociferation, such as I have heard in . . . Bedlam.' " Hogarth fares no better. In *Peregrine Pickle* Smollett indicates how contemptuously he views Hogarth's claim to be engaged by comic history painting by having Mr. Pallet, a painter who is touring the artistic treasures of the Continent, wax rhapsodic over Flemish art's close-up views of nature's particularity and by having him paint a picture that "in execution . . . equalled, if not excelled, the two ancient painters who vied with each other in the representation of a curtain and a bunch of grapes; for he had exhibited the image of a certain object so like to nature that the bare sight of it set a whole hogsty in an uproar."[78] We might, however, speculate that Garrick's overloaded delivery and Hogarth's overenthusiastic engagement with the empirical particular were useful to the novelist, deflecting attention from the way he himself wavered between different options for construing the interrelations of characters, bodies, and writing. Smollett found in Garrick's and Hogarth's surplus touches of nature an alibi for the problems of readability and closure that he brought upon himself in his efforts to elaborate a social knowledge that would adequately inventory all the characters composing a vastly diversified society.

The problem of the added stroke is, after all, still at issue in that loose baggy monster the novel. Novels' address to private individuals and private families, their promise that literature would offer something more refined than the collective culture of the crowd, is founded, we might note further, on the notion that it is (as Sterne put it) "nonsensical *minutiae*" and the "small sweet courtesies of life" that exhibit the truth of character most truly. Telling its own tale of refinement, the meticulousness of the piece of discriminating characterization signifies in itself, according to the signifying practices of class.[79] This meticulousness is also what makes novels liable to the charge that they go on too long. When John Locke attended to the nuanced and nonpareil and enabled himself to get at least two birds in the hand by discriminating the cassowary from any and every other sort of bird, he was, we might recall, indulging in just that sort of practice that made his book grow "insensibly to the bulk that it now appears in."

What would it mean to understand the history of character in the era when everything is rising—the novel, a distinctively British school of painting, a new style of acting—not as a (teleologically biased) story of the ascendancy of a naturalistic or realistic practice in the arts but as a history of social practices? It would mean, I have tried to suggest, acknowledging the competitions and alliances that divided and united these media prior to the age of literature, a rather different project than engaging with each medium in isolation. And it would mean not attempting to define what a character is (a project that very often turns prescriptive and dictates what a character should be), but instead attending to the desires that have been formulated in the name of character.

One more instantiation of the new desires wrought by the eighteenth-century marketplace that I would like to consider in closing is the marketing blitz that by the 1760s and 1770s surrounded the puzzling, extravagant persons of so-called remarkable characters or real characters. The hot commodities of the mid-century print market were portraits and texts devoted to beings whose vigorous, preternatural particularity—whose excessive ways of being themselves—made them nondescript in the eighteenth-century sense of that term. At the end of the seventeenth century the "real character" had (as in John Wilkins' *Essay Towards a Real Character and a Philosophical Language*

[1668]) been associated with projects for universally legible languages. Usage in the mid-eighteenth century, when the English eccentric, that lover of English liberty, flourished, indicated by contrast that the phrase "real character" had by then taken on the sense we give it now. This is the sense that the *OED*, recording Oliver Goldsmith's usage in *She Stoops to Conquer* (1773), glosses with the definition "odd, extraordinary, or eccentric person." It is the sense we have in mind when we talk not about someone "having" but about someone "being" a character. Real characters are, in the idiom of the period, "strongly marked": their traits (quirks) are writ large.

By mid-century comic prints were frequently marketed under the rubric "A Real character." In 1770 the correspondents' pages of *The Town and Country Magazine* sponsored a London-wide search for "Oddities" to which even the otherwise melancholy Thomas Chatterton contributed. Chatterton marveled over a person encountered at Slaughter's Coffee House, who absent-mindedly took twenty pinches of snuff in as many minutes and who, though "inoffensive and good natured," was convinced that he was in imminent danger of being possessed by the devil. The signature Chatterton puts to this exercise in the genre of the urban picturesque, "A Hunter of Oddities," suggests how characters in this style of social reportage—one endowing real people with the fantastic aspect and entertainment value of the creatures of fiction—are also collectibles. Curios, they cater to the pleasures of possession. The appeal of such oddities—that they can be understood only in themselves—seems inseparable from the appeal of the new commodities that were transforming the metropolitan marketplace. The collector who compiled a scrapbook titled *Remarkable Characters, Exhibitions and Fireworks* included among his mementoes a number of mid-eighteenth-century broadsheet accounts of two eccentrics named Pinchbeck. The Pinchbecks, father and son, paraded their foibles as a means of drawing custom to a shop where they sold things that we would now call novelty items or gizmos: clockwork models, the patent alarm for stopping sedan coaches, "the royal mourning buckle, button, and snuff box." The Pinchbecks' place of pride in the scrapbook speaks volumes about the affinities between the overloading of characters and the diversification of economic production that occurred as Britain made the transition to commercial capitalism.[80]

If we are to understand what it meant in the first two-thirds of the eighteenth century to flesh out a character—in other words, if we are to engage with the history of how *character* has exceeded its meaning—we might well take into account the craze in the print and book markets for the "queer card," the "original" (a character without precedent), and the "rum fellow" (so called because books too arcane to find a readership in Britain were shipped to the West Indies and traded for rum). A particularly interesting label for the odd character came into use in the latter part of the century when a Dublin theater manager, having laid a wager that he could in a single day introduce a word of no meaning into the language, chalked up the mystic letters Q-U-I-Z on all the blank walls in town.[81] The "quiz" who puzzled the dupes of this eighteenth-century Dubliner *is* legible. This quizzical device *is* composed from characters in the alphabetical sense of the term, but only just. A real character who comes packaged as a quiz cannot be figured out. By this period, by the time its "realness" had come to depend on its indecipherability, *character* had begun to designate its own opposite.

☙ T W O ❧

Fictions of Social Circulation, 1742–1782

Who would not be a bank-note to have such a quick succession of adventures
and acquaintances?
       —Thomas Bridges, *The Adventures of a Bank-Note* (1770–71)

GRAND TOURING

A detail George Kahrl supplies about the reception in 1748 of *The Adventures
of Roderick Random* sheds light on how, at a time when new ways of making
character matter were beginning to be articulated, the actor David Garrick's
face was good to think with. Apparently, the first readers of *The Adventures*
were cued to think of Garrick's trademark performance of Scrub (the apothecary's assistant in Farquhar's *The Beaux' Stratagem*) each time they read a description of Strap, loyal attendant to Smollett's eponymous hero: it was Garrick's physiognomy that they imaged when Roderick described the "visible
effect" that "bad luck" had "on the muscles of Strap's face, which lengthened
apace" and when Roderick pictured his manservant immobilized in a "ludicrous attitude, with his mouth open, and his eyes thrust forward considerably
beyond their station."[1] Smollett is willing to trade on his audience's familiarity with Garrick's new, pumped-up ways of looking a character, but as he
delineates an anarchic physiognomy in which the parts do not know "their
station" he also wields the charge of lowness in a way that allows him to
disown as well as indulge Garrick's physicality. Scrub and Strap have their
base station in life in common. The extravagant terms in which Strap is
envisaged are an effect of the division of labor that orders Smollett's narrative
and many other mid-century fictions. This arrangement dictates that the
manservant should have a face on behalf of his master—that he should, in
a sense, materialize the gentleman.

80

In this chapter I engage with a dominant mid-century model of characterization by engaging with the numerous mid-century fictions that treat the education of a gentleman who eventually becomes worthy of the station assigned him. Characterization is conceived of as the medium of this education. Worth accrues to the gentleman-in-the-making in proportion as, launched on a Grand Tour of some sort, he samples the world's variety and familiarizes himself with a range of social conditions and degrees. The reader's surrogate, he is to collect the characters of experience as he scrutinizes the characters of others. His touring is the device by which the author generates examples—the discrete cognitive images, the "pictures" of the passions, and so forth, that were the very stuff of knowledge in a culture that modeled the process of knowing atomistically. Henry Fielding declares in *The History of Tom Jones* (on this point concurring with Smollett) that the real gentleman is acquainted with "every kind of character from the minister at his levee, to the bailiff in his spunging house; from the dutchess at her drum, to the landlady behind her bar." The resolve that propels the hero of *The Adventures of David Simple* (1742) through the world is, similarly, "to go into all publick assemblies, and to be intimate in as many private Families as possible": David travels between the spheres of low life and high life, with the aim of entering into "the Characters of Men." Sarah Fielding makes London's Royal Exchange her hero's first port of call. Fittingly, his exercise in characterizing is inaugurated by his exposure to the polyglot space of the stock market, where, as Mr. Spectator had remarked, "a [rich] Assembly of Country-men and Foreigners [consult] together upon the private business of Mankind," where, Fielding's narrator observes in a less tolerant mood, "Men of all Ages and all Nations [are] assembled, with no other View than to barter for Interest."[2]

To begin in this manner underlines the motive informing authors' and protagonists' program for collecting characters: their program is implemented when the narrow, interested "views" of the merchants at the Exchange are trumped by the extensive views that define the gentleman. In eighteenth-century political and moral philosophy, to qualify for the title of gentleman is to possess what passes for a disinterested viewpoint, a way of knowing uncompromised by attachments to a particular locale or a determinate vocation. As Joshua Reynolds asserts in his third Discourse to the Royal Academy, it is only this "mental eye," which overlooks the accidental deficiencies that allow people to recognize each other as individuals, that can apprehend "general figures"—the "central form" of the human.[3]

The man of enlarged views acquires this cognitive privilege by partaking in a universal conversation. The sociable exchanges that carry him across the divisions of eighteenth-century society, making him familiar with specimens of humanity found in high life and low, are the means by which—to use the language of Locke's *Essay*—the gentleman turns collector and lays in a good "stock" of ideas. (The shoppy resonances of this Lockean metaphor for experience register the fact that, fully at ease in a commercial society, even the gentleman pursues a program of acquisition, the prevailing insistence on distinguishing between his acquisitions and the tradesman's notwithstanding.) The program of characterizing that writers such as Smollett and the Fieldings implement served additional, more explicitly formulated purposes. The protagonist of their narratives ends up undertaking a survey of the condition of England while he acquires his genteel credentials. His observations literally put a face on the crowd: the physiognomic digest the would-be gentleman assembles over the course of his journey makes the nation make sense. In an era requiring new evidences of social cohesion, these tours were reparative. The protagonists' reading of the nation, by translating it into text and rendering its various parts commensurable, provided a means of restoring balance to a social order turned topsy-turvy by the explosive growth of the marketplace. The knowledge stockpiled within the physiognomic digest was meant to serve as a kind of symbolic capital, which, introduced into the economy, would correct the disequilibrium. The social world that writers such as the Fieldings and Smollett conjure up is divided, accordingly, between those qualified to observe and those who are objects of others' observation.[4]

The bodily sign for the universal conversation that makes the protagonist a gentleman (nobody particular, that is, but at the same time an acceptable representative for everybody) is his bland handsomeness. The gentleman boasts the classically regular features that belong, as Reynolds proposed of the beautiful because generalized form, to nobody and everybody. He is, to quote Smollett's introduction of Peregrine Pickle, "cast in the same mould with the Apollo of Belvedere." Those he encounters are, by contrast, emphatically embodied. Their persons assail Vitruvian ideals of human proportion or assign them to fixed places in the physiognomist's tables: the uncouth, one-eyed, one-legged body of Peregrine Pickle's uncle Trunnion seems, for instance, to have metamorphosed into a mute and immobilized effigy of itself, so that it is a real question "whether that was the commodore himself, or the wooden lion that used to stand at his gate."[5] In an age still marked by neoclassical hauteur toward the circumstantial detail, this arrangement gives us Strap's grimaces and manic expressions of sorrow (his face, Roderick says, was "particularly adapted by nature for such impressions" [374]). In *Tom Jones* it gives us the voluble body of Strap's fellow barber Partridge, which has a knack of falling into "so violent a Trembling, that his Knees knocked against each other" (657).[6]

One of the many so-called characteristic anecdotes that traded on David Garrick's glamor also says something about the fluid identity that distinguishes, or, more precisely, fails to distinguish, Strap's and Partridge's genteel employers. Garrick and his friend Préville one day found themselves killing time in a carriage that was marked for Versailles: "but [the] driver refused to move until a total of six passengers entered the vehicle. Garrick had gotten out four times, addressed the driver each time in a different voice and with an altered gait, and had finally succeeded in convincing the man that he had six fares—at which point the entire 'group' had headed off for Versailles."[7] If viewed from one vantage point, Garrick appears an extravagantly visaged oddfellow, if he appears a real character in the self-consciously modern sense in which people had begun to use that term, viewed from another, Garrick appears a Proteus and so in this sense characterless. From the second perspective, Garrick's gift is his capacity to play with equal ease *both* Shakespeare and Harlequin, tragedy and comedy: Garrick here fleshes out the figure that mid-eighteenth-century characteristic writing was devising so as to conceptualize a project of comprehensive knowledge. The anecdote about the coachman's deception also hints, however, at how this ideal of the man of universal conversation could provoke almost as many anxieties about the legibility of the social world as it resolved. Garrick, the story shows, could apply his versatility as a confidence-man.[8] This is the figure who puts a disreputable edge on the neoclassicized indeterminacy of the man of the world.

It might be useful to consider how a couple of eighteenth-century readers—one a spy, the other a hack writer—alluded to the narratives of the versatile gentleman: their allusions can illuminate the sorts of low-life panache to which, paradoxically enough, impersonality could be linked. In the 1750s, a decade that saw the last gasps of both Jacobite and anti-Jacobite conspiracies, the names Peregrine Pickle and Roderick Random were adopted as aliases by a Scottish spy for the English government who pretended to pledge himself to the cause of the young Pretender. In the 1740s, the self-crowned King of the Beggars Bampfylde-Moore Carew also crossed the Pretender's path, first in Edinburgh, where Carew declared himself a Jacobite supporter and joined the rebel army, then in Carlisle, where, discovering that this army had begun its retreat, Carew hastily began to cheer for King George. The adaptability he manifested in this instance merely extended his usual practice as a beggar of applying to "all Sorts and Degrees of Persons, and that in all Shapes and Characters" (to quote from the first of the two accounts of Carew issued in the decade). Addressing the charitable as, by turns, a Welsh Bedlamite, an unfortunate seaman, and a grazier whose cattle had drowned in a flood, Carew pursued a way of life that, one of his biographers asserts, however far from "reputable or commendable, [is yet] full of agreeable Amusement and Instruction." It "gives a young Man opportunities of seeing the World." No doubt it is the patent similarity between this pretext for narrating the career of a con man and the rationales that Henry Fielding and Smollett supplied for their narratives that inspired the unidentified hack writer who is Carew's second biographer to write Carew's life over again. Up-to-speed in the conventions of characteristic writing, he not only aligns the King of the Beggars with the would-be king Charles Stuart; he also repeatedly compares his subject to Roderick Random and Tom Jones.[9]

Coupling the anecdote demonstrating Garrick's characterlessness with Smollett's take on the player's performances of Scrub reveals how the example of Garrick enabled conflicting emphases in the discourse of character to be floated in relation to each other. For mid-eighteenth-century characteristic writing, as I began to suggest in the previous chapter, talk about Garrick was useful because his example absorbed diverging constructions of what it meant to be or have "a character." Navigating between the "high" and the "low," the genteel and the beggarly, Garrick looked to be both over- and underidentified. He looked to be both excessively individuated and excessively detached from a determinate identity. This willingness to have things two ways is equally in evidence in the narratives of social circulation. Their flexibility lies in how they balance between undercharacterizing and overcharacterizing the gentleman. Eventually we will have to consider how this balancing, evidence of the breakup of a consensus on the place of the circumstantial in characterization, registers the emergence of a new discursive order in which the history of the character will become unthinkable apart from the history of fiction and the fictive.

Let us start, however, with the under- and overcharacterizing of the hero. On the one hand, being cast in the same characterless mold as Apollo Belvedere is the license that authorizes the protagonist to expose other characters' pretensions, read each into his or her proper place, and classify the diversity that might confuse class relations. It renders the gentleman the very principle of characterization. Yet these same narratives also seek to annex the contemporary enthusiasm for the implacably individuated oddity, the real character, whose excesses put categories and labels to the proof. And so, on the other hand, many mid-century practitioners of characteristic writing look as if they wish to rewrite the characterless gentleman. Smollett in particular seems to be on the verge of making his protagonist into a jaunty eccentric. What might motivate this rewriting?

As I've suggested, much mid-century fiction implements Locke's model of the self-made consciousness, which aligns the acquisition of knowledge with the acquisition of property. (That legal convention made women's ownership of property tenuous, that there were no Grand Tours for young gentlewomen collectors, suggests how this model suited some consciousnesses better than others.) Locke reimagined the interior space of the mind along the lines suggested by simultaneously public and private spaces such as the portrait galleries and botanical gardens of the great country houses, or, less grandly if more exactly, along the lines suggested by that simultaneously collaborative and customized artifact, the grangerized book of printed portraits. Cast as a collector, the Lockean individual is the cumulative product of his private stockpile of sensations and reflections. This model tracing the formation of the subject does not, from a modern vantage point, seem to offer satisfactory answers to the questions it begs about the relations between wholes and parts and between the self and its properties. When is the mental museum's collection complete? At what point in its sequence of collecting is the self itself?

With its weakness for the added touch, the *Essay*, needless to say, does not dictate how many "characters of experience" are enough. Works such as *Roderick Random*, along with sentimental narratives such as Sterne's *A Sentimental Journey Through France and Italy* or Mackenzie's *The Man of Feeling*, join Locke's model to the traditions of the picaresque narrative: hence their allegiance to a logic of parataxis that puts the narrative part before the whole and that seems to emphasize the particular character portrait and play down the specimen's relation to the impersonal patterns of human nature. Accumulating incident, a picaresque narrative can begin again and again. Roderick and Strap become acquainted with this fact of narrative theory more than once, repeatedly falling victim to cardsharks' deceits and losing the capital they have acquired so far. Inverting Roderick and Strap's situation, Harley, Mackenzie's Man of Feeling, and Parson Yorick, Sterne's sentimental traveler, seem to be forever in funds, and the result is that their narratives delineate one act of charity, one demonstration of the protagonist's sensibility, after another. Twentieth-century critics comment on how the farrago of events in a picaresque narrative are anarchically "reversible" and "infinitely rearrangeable." Irredeemably episodic, the picaresque is characterized by "a proliferation of signifiers and a relative poverty of signification, of meaning."[10] In much the same way, the quest for experience Locke recommended, as he wrote innate ideas out of existence, and made the self the cumulative product of a career of acquisitive cognition, has no predetermined limit.

From the 1740s through the 1770s, the fiction of social circulation offered a framework for exploring what this limitlessness, which underwrites the gentleman's extensive views and the gentleman's gentility, might mean for the ascriptive ties that bind characters to their properties. This fiction offered a framework, in effect, for exploring what made personal effects, or characteristics, personal. To suggest how the narratives performed this service, I will in the next two sections of this chapter trace the connections that link the gentleman's characterlessness to his fictionality and to the practice of sympathy—the social passion that readers' engagement with their books, increasingly their engagement with fiction in particular, was supposed to inspire. Turning from these meditations on the usefulness of the impersonality of the mid-eighteenth-century character, my final two sections engage with what was eventually even more useful about an emphasis on an (overcharacterized) character's private properties.[11]

PRETENDERS AND NOBODIES

In his dedication to *Ferdinand Count Fathom* (1753), Smollett is forthright about what he considers to be at stake in the enterprise of reading a character:

> A Novel is a large diffused picture, comprehending the characters of life, disposed in different groupes, and exhibited in various attitudes, for the purposes of an uniform plan, and general occurrence, to which every individual figure is subservient. But this plan cannot be executed with propriety, probability or success, without a principal personage to attract the attention, unite the incidents, unwind the clue of the labyrinth, and at last close the scene by virtue of his own importance.[12]

Smollett's minimum conditions for a novel are not ours. This talk about "the characters of life" is not precisely about fleshed-out representations of people. Drawing on notions of the book of life, Smollett is using *character* here in its quasi-semaphoric sense, the sense that gives us Theophrastan characters of virtues and vices—characters, that is, to be valued primarily as visual aids. Smollett's "principal personage" is conceptualized analogously, as the instrument that integrates the plot. A Peregrine Pickle or Count Fathom, by this accounting, is the vehicle for the narrative's representations. Complaints that he is insufficiently characterized—that he lacks individuality—miss the point. To a degree, this character is supposed to be a means for producing a sense of social context (rather than the social context counting as a means for producing our sense of a character): this character is the prosthetic device that enables readers to apprehend the comprehensive, impersonal systems that bind them together.

Under the conditions the dedication to *Ferdinand Count Fathom* delineates, such social knowledge is produced when an eye encounters an array of objects. Smollett's *Roderick Random* and Fielding's *Tom Jones* each regale us with the comic recognition scenes and reversals that can occur whenever the break of day discloses to a company of travelers the persons and identities of those with whom they have been journeying through the night. Thus the light of day makes it possible to match a body with the voice of the ferocious "man of war" who has terrorized Roderick and Strap over the course of their stage-coach journey. Once materialized the army captain is, as it happens, scarcely material at all—"about five foot and three inches high, sixteen of which went to his face and long scraggy neck; his thighs were about six inches in length, his legs resembling spindles or drum-sticks, two feet and an half, and his body, which put me in mind of extension without substance, engrossed the remainder;—so that on the whole, he . . . was almost a *vox & preterea nihil*" (50). Underpinning this example of what it takes for Roderick to produce a true portrait of another is the assumption that the concept of "enlightenment" can be taken literally. This device for disclosing the true nature of the person requires, that is, little in the way of interpretation from the observer. Assuming meaning's transparency once the light is right, this device requires only that a body be exposed to a gaze. Indeed, as the definition of the novel from *Ferdinand Count Fathom* indicates, Smollett finds it possible to think of his minor characters as anticipating his gentleman protagonist's work of surveillance and representation. They "exhibit" themselves, "dispose" themselves into "groupes," and in effect render the gentleman's labor redundant.[13]

To identify the degree zero of this mode of characterization, one could turn to Delarivier Manley's *Memoirs of Europe* (1710), where the raconteur-narrator, the count de St. Gironne, guides the reader around a mansion in Constantinople/London: the "crystal door" with which each apartment in the mansion is equipped ensures that the stories of pleasure that are enacted within are for us "all yielding to the Sight." Or one could turn to Alain René Le Sage's *Le Diable boîteux* (1726), known in Britain as *The Devil on Two Sticks*. (Smollett translated Le Sage's *Gil Blas* in the same year that he published *Roderick Random*.) Asmodeus, Le Sage's limping devil, uses his supernatural powers to advance the education of his protegé, the hero of the fiction, whose introduction into the story occurs when he happens on Asmodeus at the precise moment when the latter is attempting to escape the bottle in which a rival demon had corked him. Taking Léandro Perez to the top of a church spire and removing the roofs from the buildings below, the devil gives the gentleman visual access to the goings-on that unfold behind Madrid's closed doors. There are a thousand stories in the now-naked city, or almost. Epistemological mastery is secured in Le Sage's fantasy through the device of miniaturization: from the vantage point Asmodeus and our hero occupy, the townhouses, the prison, and the armory appear as little dollhouses. Claude Lévi-Strauss has remarked that what happens when we consider miniatures, "in contrast to what happens when we try to understand a . . . living creature of real dimensions, [is that] knowledge of the whole precedes knowledge of the parts": his contrast suggests that what is at stake in this mode of characterization, particularly after Le Sage transfers it from the court to the environing city, is not only the assembly of a satiric anatomy but, perhaps more important, the materializing of a new sort of space—that of the social "whole," that new medium that the eighteenth century invented to conceptualize persons' interconnectedness. At the same time, the perceptual field that Asmodeus miniaturizes is made more manageable by being split into so many microscreens. At the devil's prompting, Léandro Perez, as well as the reader for whom Perez acts as surrogate, shifts his gaze from one exposed interior to another and from one character to another.[14]

In the preface to *Roderick Random* Smollett takes a dim view of such "bare Catalogue[s]" of characters," because, he maintains, unless they divert through their "variety of invention," they will tire readers (xxxiii). He sorts out his priorities differently than he later does in the dedication to *Count Fathom*. When he defines the novel in the dedication, Smollett seems to imply that the position of the protagonist must be filled simply because *somebody* has to survey the "large diffused picture"; in the preface to *Random*, by contrast, the protagonist comes first in the account of what it is Smollett wants novels to do. Smollett casts his eponymous hero as the irreplaceable primum mobile on which the text pivots, the means of forestalling any strain on the reader's powers of attention: "The reader gratifies his curiosity in pursuing the adventures of a person in whose favour he is prepossessed; he espouses his cause, he sympathizes with him in distress . . . the humane passions are inflamed" (xxxiii). Insisting in this manner that the reader should feel for the character, Smollett speaks to a concern that will in his lifetime put increasing pressure on discussions of what novels do. With ever more explicitness, concern with the character will be a concern with a being that, through its capacity to prepossess, can train the reader in sympathizing and so in participating in a social world that was being reconceived as a transactional space, as a space that held together through the circulation of fellow feeling. I will move to this new way of making character matter shortly. For now, though, we might note that if, on the testimony of the preface to *Roderick Random* Smollett aims for his hero to be the prepossessing cynosure of all eyes, for their part the heroes in the Smollett novels seem to aspire to blankness. Curious passages in *Peregrine Pickle*, for instance, relate how, in the wake of fights, the pugilistic hero avoids appearing in public with "scandalous marks upon his visage" (206). Peregrine refuses to be seen with characters, in one sense of the term, on his countenance. Beginning ab ovo, Peregrine's story starts as an account of the frenzied measures his aunt Trunnion takes to ensure that her pregnant sister-in-law will give birth to a child who is without those "disagreeable mark[s]" (the so-called longing marks) that would memorialize the mother's baulked passions and would disturb the transmission of a family likeness (21).

Together with Peregrine, Mrs. Trunnion believes heroes to be by definition lacking in the birthmarks and scars that modern passports list under the euphemistic rubric of "distinguishing features." As a group, the narratives of the mid-eighteenth century tend to credit this belief. Yorick, who in *A Sentimental Journey* recounts the story of "H— [Home] the poet" and "H— [Hume] the historian" being confused with one another (30), also has an adventure in which he himself is taken for Shakespeare's Yorick. The aptly equivocal moral appended to both episodes is voiced by the churchman who, protesting against the publication of the sermons written by a Danish jester, then reminded that there are in fact *two* Yoricks, says, " 'Twas all one" (86).[15] Mid-century narratives make it easy, that is, for their protagonists to change places with or to be mistaken for others. As I have noted, they tend to emphasize the generalizability or typicality that endows the protagonist with his ability to describe the social world's connectedness. By virtue of this emphasis, the narratives sometimes read as if their authors had chosen to tone down the diacritical code that dictates that (recalling Shaftesbury) "each face must be a certain man's" and that no face can be nobody's. Characteristic writing sometimes acts on its commitment to a notion of a primal unity and plays down the differentiations—the "characteristic" markings—that convert that unity into variety. In Henry Fielding's narratives, the depiction of heterosexual love is one occasion when this commitment to nature is expressed. Like Joseph Andrews and Fanny before them, lovers who as infants shared the bond of having been exchanged for one another in the cradle, Tom Jones and Sophia Western often seem cast as mirror images of each other, the difference of the sexes notwithstanding. The blushes of one are answered by the blushes of the other; the circulation of the blood in one's body is mirrored by the circulation of the blood in the other's. When he arranges it so that when Tom's eyes meet Sophia's "the Blood rushed into his Cheeks" and when he has his narrator tell us that "Sophia was at no loss to discover the Cause, for indeed she recognized it in her own Breast" (179), Fielding's point is that both have hearts; that nature has repeated one essential model in both.[16]

The mid-eighteenth-century writers' interest in what is impersonal and indefinite about their fictional personages is perhaps most evident if we consider the regularity with which the confusions over their protagonists' identities are exacerbated through the narratives' references to the Young Pretender—Charles Stuart, whose landing in Scotland in 1745 inaugurated the Stuarts' third and final attempt to reclaim the British throne from the Hanoverians. Eighteenth-century fictions frequently align their characters with the historical figure of an imposter prince whose own claim to a determinate identity was shaky, not least because of the shakiness of his family history. (Defenders of the Glorious Revolution of 1688 maintained, against King James II, that the latter's heir was not born from the body of James's queen but that the infant had instead been smuggled into the royals' bedchamber in a covered warming pan. It was this secret history that rendered the Old Pretender, or would-be James III, a "suppositious Child," to use the language of the anti-Jacobite pamphleteers—someone who was kin to neither his father nor his mother, but instead the product of a "New English Way of getting and bearing Children.")[17] In several respects, pretenders, old and young, represent the paradigmatic subject of the narratives of social circulation. I have already considered how in claiming a universal conversibility that allowed him to put himself in every man's place, the gentleman overseer also took on attributes of the confidence man. Like the pretenders, then, this gentleman protagonist is a potential impersonator. Peregrine Pickle distinguishes himself through his talents for mimicry (for example, 155); he distinguishes himself, that is, as Garrick's face distinguishes him, through not being strikingly or even recognizably distinctive. The versatility of Ferdinand Count Fathom, the rogue who takes up the place that Smollett's narratives formerly reserved for their designated hero, is manifested when he visits a fashionable Parisian dining place, distinguishes among the babble of tongues the sounds of high and low Dutch, French, Italian, and English, and has the address to "accost a native of each different country, in his own mother tongue" and to "adapt himself to the humour of each individual" (138, 139). (This linguistic virtuosity turns out, predictably, to be a means of bilking the entire company.) The deceptions and quick-change artistry practiced by the protean Bampfylde-Moore Carew are relevant here, as is the epithet given to Carew: in yoking the top of the eighteenth-century social hierarchy with the bottom, his title, "King of the Beggars," not only suggests the movement across social divisions that advances the gentleman's project of characterization but also indicates a feature linking Carew to the pretender—the latter is likewise king over nothing, an imagined king only.

For the mid-century fictions of social circulation to press the pretenders into service or those who pretend to support them into service is in perfect keeping with the logic that dictates their undercharacterizing of their central character. Manifesting this logic, Smollett provides an episode that sees Fathom arrested at Canterbury on suspicion of being himself the Young Pretender—that sees one impersonator arrested for another: "If he was not really the person they suspected him to be, the thing would speak for itself; for, if he was not the young pretender, who then was he?" (188). During a spell of fortune-hunting that takes him to the assemblies and gaming tables of the town, Roderick Random is accused of being the Pretender's agent (284). In her flight from her father's house Henry Fielding's Sophia Western is taken for Jenny Cameron, the Pretender's mistress.

Oddly, these episodes of misrecognition are played out against the backdrop of a royalism that insisted on the impossibility of Charles Stuart's being anyone other than Charles Stuart. When they adorned their books with frontispiece-portraits of Charles that had mottoes such as "Look, Love, and Follow" or "Look strictly and you'll quickly guess my Name," his chroniclers were drawing on theorists of divine right who had proposed that majesty was a self-evident quality, that the majesty of Charles II (for Jacobites, great-uncle to the newest Stuart) had been visible to those who loved him even when, disguised, he was concealed in an oak tree. Young Charlie's chroni-

clers were proposing, by analogy, that Britons had only to see his picture to
be instantaneously convinced of his legitimate claim to the throne. For these
mid-century creators of Jacobite memorabilia, political allegiance was the
product of an extraordinarily effective recognition scene. In pledging their
faith in Bonnie Prince Charlie's supposedly unmistakable family resemblance
to Charles I, they were insisting on identifying the transmission of the British
Crown with the transmission of a distinctive set of facial features.[18]

The odd thing, though, is that these chroniclers also register the appeal
of the model of characterizing that was being implemented in the narratives
that valued their gentleman protagonist's undistinctive *typicality*, valued it as
the license that authorized him to oversee the social world's diversity. In
fact, chronicles such as *The Wanderer; or, Surprizing Escape, Ascanius; or the Young
Adventurer, Young Juba: or, the History of the Young Chevalier* tend to exploit what
is potentially novel-like about the wanderings that took Charlie across the
Highlands subsequent to his defeat at Culloden. They show him enjoying a
universal conversation and (like the King of the Beggars) making "Application . . . to all sorts and Degrees of Persons and that in all Guises and Characters." Few of these narrators can resist retelling the story of one such guise
and character: the cross-dressing—as Betty Burke, maidservant to Flora
MacDonald—that enabled a fugitive Charlie to escape the Western Isles.
In slightly unseemly ways, considering that as Jacobite narratives these are
committed to the Stuarts' status as the authentic royal family, these chronicles
seem fascinated with scenes that reveal the Pretender pretending—that reveal him "making Merry with our Disguises, while [he] himself personated
by Turns, the various Ranks and Characters of the Highlanders of both
Sexes." The fictional Joseph Andrews and Roderick Random do not seem so
far away when Charlie's peregrinations across the Highlands' social divisions
make him the object of amorous attentions from maidservants or when he
takes to spending time smoking his pipe and ruefully sharing a pot of porter
with a jovial landlord.[19] Indeed, the distinctiveness of those otherwise magically recognizable features compromised, Charlie *could* be anyone and everyone.

In the mid-eighteenth century, Catherine Gallagher has proposed, fictional nobodies first came into their own—beating out those we call real
people to become the most respectable kind of narrative protagonist. Then,
for the first time, she asserts, there was a real "cultural imperative" to use
the conceptual tools, in themselves dating back to Aristotle, that differentiate
fictive from other sorts of narrative. It was then that readers began to feel

for characters who have no extratextual existence, and feel for them because of their fictiveness, not despite it. At a point when reading was beginning to be valued more for affording the reader opportunities for practice at feeling than for acquainting the reader with good examples, "nobody's story" was valuable precisely because its abstention from referentiality guaranteed that it was never about anyone else. By not referring to anyone, it could incite the sympathies of anyone and everyone. Gallagher's description of the mid-century discursive environment suggests one way to understand the conversion of political propaganda into play that unfolds through Fielding's and Smollett's references to Bonnie Prince Charlie or through Bampfylde-Moore Carew's or Charlie's chroniclers' allusions to Fielding and Smollett. Thinking about Gallagher's "nobodies"—fictional characters who do not represent anyone in particular—can suggest that what mid-century texts did with the pretender, that "suppositious" being, and especially with the pretender who pretended, was to play with the meanings of fictionality as such.[20]

It is not my intention here to make a point about the mid-century novelists' political allegiances. Rather than outing crypto-Jacobites, I want instead to underline that a pretender to the throne would have seemed an apt vehicle for the negotiations that made it possible to take the fictiveness of characters for granted. According to the conceptualization of bastardy outlined in Blackstone's *Commentaries on the Laws of England,* James II's progeny was a *filius nullius.* His illegitimacy rendered him, that is, the son of nobody. At the same time, even if considered, as he wants to be, in his guise as a king, a pretender still would not end up being kin to any one in particular. A pretender who is "really" royal is, as such, a "child of the nation," a term that is at once suggestively close to an alternative legal term for the bastard, *filius populi,* and that also aptly figures his status as a type of the nation, an everyperson, a "character" with whom anyone and everyone could sympathize.[21]

Like the Jacobite chronicles of a heroic Charlie, the more familiar narratives about the *fictive* pretenders play up the pledge of sociability and representativeness that was embedded in the term *filius populi.* I have already suggested that the touring gentleman who is the premier protagonist of many eighteenth-century narratives aspires to typicality, to the kind of blankness that would allow him to be anyone and everyone. He is supposed to occupy a position where he might say, wherever the WORLD is, I am.[22] For all her interest in nobody, Catherine Gallagher shows little interest in the studious impersonality and aspirations to generality that distinguish much mid-eighteenth-century fiction. In her book, fiction that is self-aware about its status as fiction tends to be fiction that has got over its neoclassical ambivalence about the circumstantiality of formal realism; it tends to be fiction that has become personal, that features protagonists who are individuated in the way we know real people to be individuated. "The more characters were loaded with circumstantial and seemingly insignificant properties, the more readers were assured that the text was at once assuming and making up for its reference to nobody at all. . . . The very realism of the new form . . . enabled readers to appropriate the stories sympathetically."[23] Bereft of the "properties" that would at once make him someone in particular and make up for the fact that he referred to nobody at all, bereft of the properties that would, in short, make him sympathetic, the gentleman of universal conversation I've focused on so far fails to fit this bill.

In my fourth section I will investigate in precise terms the ways in which Roderick Random, who is intended by Smollett to be prepossessing, deviates, in part *because of* his aspirations to a genteel characterlessness, from Gallagher's profile of the most likely candidate for sympathy. (Roderick deviates from her description of the particularized "realistic" character to such a degree, in fact, that he has difficulties being recognizably Roderick.) For now I wish to suggest that, such deviation notwithstanding, it might be helpful to extend Gallagher's analysis of nobody so that it would encompass a pretender or, better still, an impostor pretender—a protagonist of Smollett's or Fielding's. To complicate her account in this manner can suggest how the era's meditations on the fictionality of characters and on fictions' incitement of the social passion of sympathy could double as forums for reexamining inherited forms of social integration and social division. In the middle of the eighteenth century, to think about nobody is also to think about a cartographic instrument made to map the social order from its lower depths to the very heights to which a would-be royal pretender could aspire. To *play* with nobody, with nobody's unrecognizable facelessness especially, is to begin to renegotiate the identity of the gentleman and to begin to reconsider the particular forms of inequality that authorized this figure, forms that rested on the neoclassical identification of high culture with what was general and abstract and low culture with what was particular and circumstantial.

FACELESSNESS: THE PHYSIOGNOMIES OF MONEY

In treating the transformation that saw fiction get personal, Gallagher construes sympathetic identification, the exercise of compassion, as the principle that mandated the personalizing of character, as well as a process enabling each reader to become her own person—be all that she could be emotionally. To remember, however, that the blank-faced Apollo Belvederes of mid-century narrative are supposed to match the profile that aesthetic theory drew up in conceptualizing "general nature" or a "form belong[ing] to human kind at large," is to be reminded that in the moral philosophy of the period sympathy is often defined in terms that redirect us from the personal to the impersonal. What, for instance, interests David Hume about sympathy is that it can guarantee social harmony by rendering people copies of one another—and, in one particular instance in the *Treatise of Human Nature* (1739–40), by operating as a mechanism enabling all to share in (what remains private) wealth:

> In general we may remark, that the minds of men are mirrors to one another, not only because they reflect each others emotions, but also because those rays of passions, sentiments and opinions may be often reverberated. . . . Thus the pleasure, which a rich man receives from his possessions, being thrown upon the beholder, causes a pleasure and esteem; which sentiments again, being perceiv'd and sympathiz'd with, encrease the pleasure of the possessor; and being once more reflected, become a new foundation for pleasure and esteem in the beholder.[24]

As we proceed through this passage, personal feeling (the pleasure that belongs to somebody in particular) slips away. It gets lost to view as Hume turns our attention to the impersonal system—the miscible reflections and reverberations—that personal feelings construct. Hume takes pains to construct a perspective from which the particularity that makes a person into a gentleman—his fortune—doesn't count for much. Sympathy, as he describes it and as Adam Smith describes it in *A Theory of Moral Sentiments* (1759), socializes and redeems particularity. Through exchanges of fellow feeling, as well as through exchanges of wealth, particular interests are rendered commensurable within an economy structured by reciprocities and correspondences.

Consideration of the company the gentleman protagonist keeps in the booksellers' warehouses tells us even more about the rerouting from particular to general interests that exercised the moral philosophers. The 1760s and 1770s witnessed a number of immensely popular narratives in which the protagonist's place is taken by a piece of money: in 1760, for instance, Charles Johnstone published *Chrysal, or, The Adventures of a Guinea*, supplementing it with two additional volumes in 1765; in 1770 Thomas Bridges published two volumes of *The Adventures of a Bank-Note*, and, presumably encouraged by popular demand, added another two the next year; in 1782 Helenus Scott published *The Adventures of a Rupee, Wherein are interspersed various anecdotes Asiatic and European.* In these first-person narratives, it is money that talks, and to some degree, it talks in ways that would remind readers of money's status as a marker of social agreement. Money stands for people's consent to a standard of value, their selection of the general equivalent that (as classical political economy enjoyed pointing out) enables the buttonmaker to buy cloth and the weaver to buy buttons. Money memorializes the convention that draws persons into a community of mutual dependence—into a social space.

The coin's or banknote's adventures closely resemble those of the gentleman who knows what it is to enter into sociable exchanges with all and sundry. (Conversely, it is the possession of these coins and banknotes that expedites the gentleman's exemplary mobility.) Money is, after all, an appropriate vehicle for a narrative form organized to enable readers to collect the characters of experience by collecting characters in the other sense of the term: money, as Hume wrote in the *Treatise,* "implies a kind of representation of objects, by the power it affords of obtaining them." The resemblance between money's career and the touring gentleman's also derives from how the former invariably illustrates an observation that Adam Smith made in *The Wealth of Nations:* "The same guinea . . . [that] pays the weekly pension of one man today, may pay that of another tomorrow, and that of a third the day after."[25]

So, like a Tom Jones or a David Simple, Bridges's banknote collects characters for our delectation. He begins existence in the possession of a hack poet who deposits the cash to acquire an "Esquire" to affix to the end of his name. (The poet's muse tells him, "After the Bank has dubb'd you an esquire, no man will dare to say a word against it.") The poet changes the note to pay for his lodging, which gives our hero the opportunity to finish off his portrait of a poet and acquaint us with a grocer. The next day the banknote finds his way into an old woman' snuffbox, then the day after that a silk-mercer's drawer, and so on, without showing signs of ever wishing to stop.[26]

From one perspective this substitution of currency for the person who would otherwise act as our chief protagonist humanizes an economic system that, in an era marked by greater financial risk-taking in business and estate management, by an increasing dependence on credit arrangements, and by more and more bankruptcies, made English men and women uneasy. We can see this humanization at work when we think about how *Tom Jones* supplies a shadowy counterpart to the narrative that traces Tom's travels, a narrative, never quite fleshed out, that would recount the peregrinations of Squire Allworthy's banknotes. At the moment in book 18 when Allworthy "recognizes" the money he had given to Tom—which the latter had lost, which had been picked up by Black George, and which the latter deposits with Allworthy's financier friend, Mr. Nightingale—both this pecuniary narrative and to a degree *Tom Jones* itself are brought to a close. This double resolution exemplifies the proposition that, as James Thompson puts it, nothing stays lost. With the recognition of the money, Fielding moves readers back into a romance universe in which the foundling is always found out and his good character reclaimed, and in which banknotes, as well as long-lost relations, can be the subjects for narratives structured by moments of anagnorisis and conducted "in good Aristotelian fashion"; they too can be recognized because they too have "origins" to which they can be re-connected.[27]

Prior to 1797, when passage of the Restriction Bill created an anonymous paper currency in Britain, it would not have required much mental effort to individualize or humanize a banknote in this way. A bill of exchange was issued by a particular bank as a promissory note made out to a particular bearer, who could countersign it over to any third party, who could in turn countersign it over to another, and so on: thus the history of a bill's passage from hand to hand could be read off from the multiple endorsements it bore.[28] The narratives that see the world from money's point of view work a bit differently from Fielding's, in ways we might illuminate if we think about how in the mid-eighteenth century a coin would differ from a banknote. At the mint coins would be imprinted with the king's head, but, after leaving the mint, they would be imprinted no more: unlike banknotes with their personalized histories, coins would not be marked up—they would not, in one sense of the term, be characterized—by their errancy. The contrast, which underlines the fact that, as a typical product of mass production, one coin is virtually indistinguishable from and interchangeable with another, also indicates that the money-centric narratives of the 1760s and 1770s are not necessarily interested in availing themselves of Henry Fielding's strategy for stabilizing money's lability. Certainly, the prosopopeia that endows a rupee or a shilling with a point of view does give it a personal character (though contemplation of any coin's dimensions indicates that it must certainly be a flat one). But before we account in this way for the appeal of the money-centric narratives, before we content ourselves with the claim that these narratives made money into a "character," we need to recall the analogies between coin, character, and countenance discussed in the previous chapter and recall that personal character was also conceptualized as if it were a piece of money. One modern reader of the money-centric narratives has commented on how there is something eerie about how they, along with equally popular narratives such as *The Adventures of a Cork-screw, in which the vices, follies and manners of the present age are exhibited* (1775) or *The Adventures of a Black Coat as related by itself* (1760), subordinate "the individual . . . to impersonal patterns of circulation" and propose that only objects "can explain society as it really is."[29]

At the same time, the narratives that put money's mobility center-stage may well have afforded their readers a kind of comfort. This scheme of characterizing is geared to the demonstration of the adage that what goes round comes round. The banknote is eager at the end of his second volume to point out to the reader that he is back in "the clyster-pipe of the little apothecary that in my first volume got so tumbled about by the blind man and his dog" (2:204). Unlike Tom Jones or Roderick Random, both foundlings who are found out, the banknote's wanderings do not take him home to the landed estate that inspires eighteenth-century writers' fantasies of permanent residences and absolutely private properties. The banknote moves on, into the pockets of persons in high life. Yet, as his momentary return to the little apothecary suggests, the banknote's travels can make circulation seem more tidily circular. As late as 1820, this project retained its appeal: in *Buy a Broom: An Interesting Moral Tale for Children*, the talking broom that passes through a succession of owners also returns to the hands of its maker, although only long enough to be refurbished and resold. Like Asmodeus, the limping devil who knows how to maximize the city's visibility, such circulating protagonists give readers the wherewithal to conceptualize society as a whole. They assuage fears that the social is of unlimited and hence inapprehensible extension. Like the conversible gentleman, the protagonist in this style acts as broker of differences. His social work demonstrates how people are connected.

While making those connections apparent, the money-centered narratives tend, in contradistinction to *Tom Jones*, to make much of currency's impersonality and facelessness. Even the banknote says surprisingly little about the endorsements he bears, his distinguishing features and the registers of those moments, fleeting to be sure, when he was the personalized property of someone. To say much would detract from his status as a rolling stone. Characters such as this gather no moss. They do not want to be found out, as foundlings are, so much as they want to find out others. In this respect the money-centric narratives illuminate what the mainstream of eighteenth-century narratives are up to when they cast their foundling protagonists in the mold of Apollo Belvedere or make them exchangeable men who can put themselves in anyone's place. At the same time that they play knowing objects against the humans who do not know their properties' histories, the money-centric narratives play up the social opposition that in the mainstream of eighteenth-century narrative divided those who characterize from those whose very bodies tell tales—divided, that is, the would-be gentleman, a faceless observer, from the emphatically embodied, hypervisible subjects whom he observes and exposes.

Helenus Scott's talking rupee, for instance, is able to trump Ferdinand Count Fathom's skills in physiognomy. (Fathom's "penetrating eye" [326] and skill in reading the passions are exercised throughout his narrative, especially when Fathom takes to impersonating a physician and so to practicing a science rooted in the observing and weighing of bodily signs.) The rupee does not pause to note the irony of a situation that sees money, decried as a cause of the social fluidity that provided sharpdealers and confidence tricksters with opportunities to misrepresent themselves, offer a physiognomical expertise that could accurately measure these persons' creditworthiness and detect what they really "had in mind."[30] Instead, after naming the "spirits" ("foolishly" called "qualities") that are present in all gold pieces, the rupee tells his audience of how, after he encountered a young lady customer at the pawnbroker's office where he had been deposited, he dispensed his spirit of ductility to follow her home. Not only can this spirit travel astrally, as it were, but he also has the power to read the brain of this young lady or of any person. From the spirit's privileged vantage point, brains are (as readers of Locke would anticipate) "marked with impressions, like the figures on a celestial globe": "These impressions are nothing but the scratches made by objects which have been presented to the senses. . . . By reading these we can discover all the transactions of any consequences in which a man has been engaged."[31]

Unable to read human brains, the protagonists of Fielding and Smollett novels are determined nonetheless to compensate for nature's lapses in supplying the characters that convert the person into the sign of himself. These heroes do it themselves. Their pugilism deposits identifying marks on other men's bodily surfaces. Tom Jones's "handwriting" is visible on Thwackum's breast, "very legible in Black and Blue" (235). At Oxford, Peregrine Pickle sets out to expose his tutor for assuming grave airs: he gets Mr. Jolter drunk and leaves him to get involved in a brawl. When Jolter comes to his young charge for advice about how to conceal his bruises, Peregrine equips himself with a paintbox. He confers on Jolter "such a staring addition to the natural ghastliness of his features, that his visage bore a very apt resemblance to some of those ferocious countenances that hang over the doors of certain taverns and alehouses, under the denomination of the Saracen's head" (116). The social surveys that are the stake of both these modes of mid-century narrative aggressively pictorialize those to whom the privilege of bearing a labile, representative identity is not accorded.

These surveys make wry faces, grimaces, and lined countenances the lot of the men and women of the laboring classes and inhabitants of the outlying regions of the nation. In a certain sense, furthermore, visibility is the lot that the mid-eighteenth-century narrative assigns to women in general. It is no accident that the rupee exploits his physiognomic powers to follow a young woman, nor that the banknote seems so proud of the fact that his small size enables him to be especially intimate with women and especially adept at spying out their secrets: one epoch in his adventures begins, for instance, when he gets tucked inside a milliner's stomacher. To the extent that the narratives of social circulation critique the commercial capitalism that they also exemplify, it is, as Aileen Douglas observes, by implicating the female members of trading families in scandal. The woman who, encouraged by her father's or husband's financial success, aspires to social mobility almost invariably gets it, but she gets it in the form of a sexual fall into prostitution: her virtue lost, she becomes "at different times the property of the peer, the squire, the tradesman and others."[32] The piece of current money or the circulating commodity resembles the woman of the town whose tale he relates, in that her relations with others are, like his, entirely commercial. At the same time, however, no moral opprobrium attaches to *his* wanderings across the social order. The gendering that organizes the narratives makes female characters the targets of the narrative's drive to unmask and expose: it precludes female characters' functioning, as would-be gentlemen do and as (male) money does, as the agents of characterization.

By emphasizing the ways that her *History of Miss Betsy Thoughtless* (1751) rewrites Fielding's *Tom Jones*, Eliza Haywood slyly directs her audience's attention to the negative charge that the conversibility that Fielding celebrates acquires as soon as there is a lady in the case.[33] As an attentive reader of the narratives of social circulation, Haywood knew that what was impersonal in mid-eighteenth-century discourses of character was also, ironically enough, what was gendered. Betsy Thoughtless is like Tom, who begins his story as a "giddy Youth, with little Sobriety in his Manners, and less in his Countenance" (106) and whose imprudence gives opportunities to the envy and malice of a Blifil or a Thwackum. Betsy too has problems with image management: she is, for instance, rumored to be the true mother of the little love child whose fostering she pays for out of the fortune she inherits from her merchant father. But in Betsy's case, this heedlessness is considered to be of a piece with, rather than incidental to, the fact that she is enrolled in a narrative patterned on exchanges in the marketplace. The universal conversation that Tom enjoys—in getting acquainted with "every kind of character from . . . the dutchess at her drum, to the landlady behind her bar"—is also a feature of Betsy's history, which unfolds in London, that "Babel of mixed company": Betsy's lack of enthusiasm for the confined society of the marital tête-à-tête means that she suffers "herself to be treated, presented, and squired about to all publick places, either by the rake, the man of honour, the wit, or the fool, the married as well as the unmarried, without distinctions and just as either fell in her way." This character could be, as this passage suggests, the book's means to demonstrate social connection. She could be a means of subordinating evidence of social diversity to a postulate about social unity and the existence of a general interest, for, like a piece of money—repository of everyone's desire—Betsy is "generally admired." Haywood's point in rewriting *Tom Jones* is precisely this: that Betsy could serve all these ends, but does not. The sociability that makes Tom and the narrative that focuses on him public-spirited makes Betsy "cheap"; in her agreeableness as well as in the choosiness that prevents her from marrying the first man who asks, Betsy "cheapens" herself. Money need never cease circulating: as the additive logic of the money-centric narratives of mid-century suggests, it loses nothing of its attractiveness over time. But unlike the piece of money, unlike the conversible gentleman even, Betsy might all too easily "outstand her market." She does not move unscathed from social exchange to social exchange; she has a limited shelf life.[34]

When she pointedly puts a heroine who is committed to "agreeableness" center-stage, Haywood writes against the grain of the conventions that mid-eighteenth-century culture developed to make character usable for a commercializing society. With their compulsion to reinforce and dissolve, by turns, the boundary dividing the character who sees from the character who is seen, the one who travels from the one who is displayed, Smollett's narratives might provide the most explicit illustrations of the aspects of the mid-century project of characterizing that Haywood's gender-switching contests.

Peregrine Pickle, for female readers the most troubling of Smollett's books, also has the most to say about what Betsy discovers in her inability to both display her person and, controlling others' interpretations of appearances, successfully claim ownership of it: the fact that women's bodies are not really their own. Standing up for their status as gentlemen, Peregrine Pickle and his brother rake Godfrey Gauntlet at one point punish a farmer's wife for her presumption in betraying Godfrey to the farmer just when he was anticipating the pleasures of her seduction. Their plan of revenge involves "fixing her a monument, with her posterior thrust out at a window, for the contemplation of her spouse when he should return in the morning" (169). The two men make the woman's person a picture: framing the picture so that it isolates and displays a single body part, Peregrine and Godfrey mime the ostensible self-assertion with which the lower-class woman has upended the social hierarchy. From this adventure Peregrine goes on to assemble a veritable archive of female sexual transgressions, assisted by an ally, Cadwallader Crabtree, whose habit of feigning deafness permits him to become master of the secrets that ladies whisper in his presence. For Peregrine, Cadwallader represents a secret weapon, a means "to penetrate not only into the chambers but even to the inmost thoughts of the female sex" (388): like the banknote tucked in the milliner's stomacher, Cadwallader is a device the narrative uses to compile a " 'secret history, [which] exhibit[s] a quite different idea of characters from what is commonly entertained' " (387). Betsy Thoughtless's story suggests that rather than unmasking women, Cadwallader and Peregrine or Godfrey and Peregrine could be understood to be otherwise engaged: they could be seen as imposing on women masks of a manmade culture's designing. As Bruce Robbins writes, "Character [can be] the mask people [are] expected to don in the face of power; it [is] a way of making them hold still and be judged."[35]

"ONE FEATURE MAKES NOT A FACE": RECOGNIZING RODERICK RANDOM

In *Roderick Random,* the hero's manservant, Strap, repeatedly demonstrates that he too subscribes to that logic of the example which is implemented whenever characters are held up to infamy. He too is an advocate for unmasking women—removing the obfuscatory layer of appearance and exposing women's true nature to the light. Strap warns his master away from feminine wiles: he has an armory of references to "painted sepulchres" put aside for this purpose (260). Ever ready with quotations, proverbs, and other commonplaces that suit his employer's circumstances, Strap is associated with the storehouse of the already written (the *copia*) on which rhetoric depends. According to Quintilian, whose *Institutes* were invoked in early modern Europe to authorize a pedagogy centered on the discipline of copying and to authorize the value compilers of commonplace books placed on their reading matter, "It is writing that provides that holy of holies where the wealth of oratory is stored, and whence it is produced to meet the demands for sudden emergencies."[36]

That literary servants—eternally returning, eternally chatty, and ever faithful retainers—personify the stock character is reinforced by their connection with a stock of words that are transcribed and imprinted over and over again. Remembering proverbial wisdom is as much a servant's duty as remembering the location of the keys to the cellar or of the lost codicil to the master's last will and testament. Bruce Robbins has commented on the uncanny fidelity with which such conventions have been reiterated over the generations, noting how we are always in the position of having heard the witty servant's gags before. If servants in Western literature are, as Robbins avers, instantly recognizable types, the gentlemen who employ servants in mid-eighteenth-century British narrative are both types in their turn and yet, as I have argued, typically unrecognizable: we are concerned, in fact, with two distinct sorts of typicality or characterlessness. In *Roderick Random*, Smollett uses the device of the chattering, quoting, and quotable servant as a means of reinforcing exactly this division. By making Strap that much more of a legible "character," by connecting him to the filler that hack authors pillage from their commonplace books and so associating him with written words or characters in the graphic sense of the term, Smollett reinforces the line of separation that sorts out those of fluid from those of fixed identity. That line is reinforced in additional ways. As I have already suggested, Strap's physical appearance—his grimacing and gaping—is at issue repeatedly in Roderick's narration in ways that work to make character an unproblematic matter of visual evidence. Indeed, throughout his narrative, Roderick is fond of allowing Strap's body to tell a tale, even though one nugget of proverbial wisdom that Strap cites when he considers Roderick's quest for universal acquaintance and Roderick's acquaintance with women particularly is that "*Fronti nulla fides*"—"People's faces should not be trusted" (260).[37]

Strap's person operates to the same effect as his proverbs—as his proclivity for language in a display mode, for the quotable quotes that in the 1740s would be inscribed on the plinths of statues or would supply the epigraphs for chapters.[38] Strap's language and body make him a picture in an exhibition. Roderick is supposed to be the exhibitor and, as such, the public-minded character who can deliver a disinterested, comprehensive view of society. Yet Smollett's characteristic writing also seems to seek out the fissures in the divisions that separate gentlemen from those who are the objects of their sociological pigeonholing: so much is indicated by the way that Strap's dialogue, in the instance I have just quoted especially, provides an ironic counterpoint to Roderick's first-person narration. *Roderick Random* can be read as a text that, entertaining a different structure for sorting out the meanings of character, seems at moments to view characterlessness as a problem. Smollett not only sets Roderick up to achieve typicality—the representativeness and freedom from singularity that make a hero a gentleman—but he also seems to savor his hero's eccentricity. When Smollett wavers between undercharacterizing and overcharacterizing his gentleman hero, we see an instance of the flexibility that made characteristic writing useful at a period when established forms of social integration were being reexamined and when the forms of social inequality were being renegotiated—in part through a new insistence on making personal effects personal. For this reason, *Roderick Random* merits examining in some detail.

The arbitrariness of the division between the characterless, mobile gentleman and the excessively charactered and fixed world is all the more evident in this narrative because Roderick's title to the status of a gentleman is so patently fictional. It is the product of his determination that whatever he does, he continues to support "the dignity of his character" (136), by which he means his character as a gentleman. John Barrell describes Roderick's personal mythology in these terms: "Whatever he may be forced to do, [Roderick's] true character is to do nothing, to be disengaged from the fixed identities assigned to those whose destiny it is to work for a living."[39] This narrative motivates the scene-shifting that is necessary to a gentleman's inventory of the characters of life by having its hero progress pell-mell through an awe-inspiring number of trades. Orphaned (or so it seems until the eleventh-hour reappearance of his father with a fortune in his hands), disinherited by his rich grandfather, Roderick begins his story with a chronicle of his sojourn at a grammar school, where, not incidentally, Strap is a fellow student. Then for a short time Roderick attends university in Glasgow, where he cultivates the belles lettres. Next he becomes assistant to an apothecary, travels to London, and is press-ganged onto a battleship, where he gains the post of surgeon's mate; after a shipwreck, he turns footman, then becomes a soldier in the French army and runs away from the Battle of Dettingen, and so forth. Recounting this narrative, Roderick makes retrospective sense of his adventures by filing them under the category of education. Thus the narrative's prostitute with a heart of gold, Miss Williams, observes of Roderick that "altho' some situations of my life had been low, yet none of them had been infamous; . . . that the miseries I had undergone, by improving the faculties, both of mind and body, qualified me the more for any dignified station" (342).

When he passes on Miss Williams's observation to his reader, Roderick is shamelessly justifying his entitlement to gentility, as well as puffing the method of mid-eighteenth-century narrative. His shamelessness is the more remarkable because, during the interval that succeeds his time at grammar school with Strap, while Roderick is first at sea, then in service, and then on the Continent, Strap successfully beats Roderick to the romance ending. During this interval Strap inherits a stock of money and clothing from a former employer. For a large portion of Roderick's narrative, it is Strap's inheritance that bankrolls Roderick's appearances in the polite world as, by turns, fortune-hunter, political place-seeker, and gambler. When Strap worries about wily adventuresses and about Roderick's tendency to trust a pretty face (*Fronti nulla fides*), he is concerned with preserving his own stock of wealth. The simplest definition of *gentleman* one can devise is that a gentleman is someone who keeps servants (whereas the "picaro" of picaresque narrative was a kitchen boy): yet it is Strap who keeps Roderick.

The oddity of this last part of Smollett's narrative is that we find ourselves, so convinced are we by Roderick's belief in his own gentility, watching a gentleman impersonating a gentleman. I don't only mean to suggest that Roderick's adventures render "gentleman" an empty sign, that—perhaps registering the shift in social organization that saw fixed status positions, like gentility, replaced by modern notions of class—these adventures call into question the identity of the exemplary overseer of eighteenth-century practices of characterizing. The reader who confronts the way that Roderick manages at the same time both to *be* a gentleman and *act as* a gentleman is pressured into taking it as a given that there is a difference that separates a character from the social role. When we understand Roderick as a gentleman who must impersonate a gentleman, our enterprise of reading the character comes to focus on the difference distinguishing what is contingent from what—as an intimate, intensely personal property of identity—is essential.

Roderick's adventures render him at once more and less than someone.

Almost each time that fortune reunites Roderick with an acquaintance from whom he has been long separated—his maternal uncle, say, or Strap, or a brother officer from the battleship—the scene of recognition that a reader anticipates does not quite come off.[40] Roderick is able to identify his uncle Bowling, despite "the alteration of dress and disguise of a long beard" (232), but is not recognized in turn. When Roderick is first press-ganged aboard the battleship, he discovers an old friend, who is now serving as first mate to the ship's surgeon: "If I knew him at first sight, it was not so easy for him . . . I asked him if my misfortunes had disguised me so much, that he could not recollect my face? Upon this he observed me with great earnestness for some time, and at length, protested he could not recollect one feature of my countenance" (143). Roderick seems to possess a perfectly generic body, which, if it is nobody's body in the foregoing examples, is also everybody's. He exhibits, for instance, an uncanny capacity to fit the clothes that go with the jobs he takes. When he is shipwrecked on the English coast and enters into service in the wealthy household in which he meets Narcissa, his future wife, Roderick finds that the livery that had belonged to the footman who preceded him "fitted me exactly, so that there was no occasion for employing a taylor on my account" (218). Further on in the narrative, we learn that the wardrobe Strap inherited from his former master—"five fashionable coats . . . twelve pair of white silk stockings, as many of black silk, and the same number of fine cotton . . . three dozen of fine ruffled shirts, as many neckcloths" and so forth (256)—fits Roderick as well as it did its original owner. The tailors are once more cheated of business.

That this lack of distinguishing, resolutely personal and durable properties has, despite its convenience for our hero, troubling implications for eighteenth-century ideas of the man of property is underscored by the fact that on these occasions and others Roderick fills the place of the dead. His predecessors in the posts of apothecary's assistant (chapter 7), surgeon's mate (chapter 24), and footman (chapter 39) are all recently deceased. Arranging for the happy close to Roderick's adventures to include marriage to a woman named Narcissa feels like an eleventh-hour measure: it seems that Smollett needs a way to confirm that Roderick *has* a self. Narcissa must be a reflection of the hero, so that the hero can cease to be everyone's second self. The fact that, once married, Narcissa quickly gets pregnant and the fact that, from the moment of her introduction into the narrative, she is associated with the retirement of the country estate also suggest Smollett's concern with preserving Roderick. Smollett exploits the stability and aura ascribed to patrilineal kinship networks and to inherited real estate—the "personality-sustaining property" that was idealized for its imperviousness to the vicissitudes of the market economy—in order to preserve his hero *as* Roderick.[41]

When Miss Williams tells Roderick the story of her ruin and subsequent turn to prostitution, she speaks approvingly of the good looks that distinguished the man who first seduced her:

> He was . . . among the tallest of the middle-size; had chestnut coloured hair which he wore tied up in a ribbon; a high polished fore-head, a nose inclining to the aqualine, lively blue eyes, red pouting lips, teeth as white as snow, and a certain openness of countenance,—but what need I describe any more particulars of his person? I hope you will do me the justice to believe I do not flatter, when I say he was the exact resemblance of you. (119)

As yet another testimony to Roderick's exchangeability, the revelation that Roderick has a double somewhere in England should perhaps be dismissed as a gratuitous detail. But if this duplication of Roderick's person plays no part in what ensues in the narrative, it does end up duplicated in its turn. William Thomson, another genteel surgeon's mate, and one of the few characters in the text (besides Miss Williams) whose proper name does not stereotype him according to his occupation, also has a double. The day after Thomson assumes his post on the battleship,

> another William Thomson came on board, affirming that he was the person for whom the warrant was expedited, and that the other was an impostor.—My friend [Roderick reports] was grievously alarmed at this incident. . . . [T]o acquit himself of the suspicion of imposture, he produced several letters written from Scotland to him in that name, and recollecting that his indentures were in his box on board, he brought them up, and convinced all present, that he had not assumed a name which did not belong to him. (145)

Thomson's misadventure leaves the reader wondering about the extent to which the proper name really does belong to the individual. To put these two episodes of duplication together makes visible a web of connections that links questions about the indeterminacy and the representativeness of the gentleman to questions about resemblance and imposture and pretending, and to questions about personal effects and private property—about whether the most private of properties, a body or a proper name, can ever be private enough. In creating this associational circuit Smollett may well have been reworking, and consciously *fictionalizing*, some of the versions of heroism developed in the narratives of Jacobitism. The year following Charles Stuart's flight from the field of Culloden saw a number of stories of men who died as doubles of the Pretender, saving their prince by misleading his enemies about who they were and pretending to be the Pretender.[42] It also saw these stories of what might aptly be called self-sacrifice strangely parodied in the biography of another pretend pretender, Bampfylde-Moore Carew. After getting caught during an escapade that had involved his impersonating a Newfoundland planter, Bampfylde-Moore Carew was committed to a prison in Taunton, where some time before "there had been one of his Profession there, who with great Confidence stiled himself *Bampfylde-Moore Carew;* . . . under this Name he received Visits and Kindnesses from several Persons."[43]

In fact, as if to prepare readers for a narrative in which too many people either share too few names or look too much alike, the fourth and subsequent editions of *Roderick Random* open with a question about the minimum conditions for exact resemblance—for recollecting a face as a gestalt that one has beheld before. In 1754 Smollett supplemented the preface to his text, aiming to atone for the fact that his Scottish acquaintances had thought themselves intended as the originals for the book's (ostensibly defamatory) portraits. The apologue he added contains this admonitory address to the reader: "If thou should'st meet with a character that reflects thee in some ungracious particular, keep thy own counsel; consider that one feature makes not a face, and that tho' thou art, perhaps, distinguished by a bottle nose, twenty of thy neighbours may be in the same predicament" (xxxviii). In marking in this manner the difference between particular and general satire Smollett makes moves that would be familiar to his first readers. In her preface to *The Cry,* Sarah Fielding insisted, similarly, that proper readings of "characteristic writings" were those that abstained from "fixing them down into personal libels."[44] In an analogous manner, Henry Fielding refined his definition of what was involved in copying from the Book of Nature: he assured readers of *Joseph Andrews* that, far from being a libelous representation of one of their contemporaries, of the sort that had been purveyed by Manley and Haywood, his lawyer had been alive these "4000 years" (168). Moves such as these contributed to a sanitizing process: in the mid-century, vindicating the consumption of characters involved dissociating novel reading from the consumption of scandals involving real people. The playfulness about referentiality that marks Smollett's apologue is a feature it shares with many contemporary texts, all intent on teaching readers to mark out fiction as the ground of the respectable reading experience.[45]

Still, there is something remarkable about the way that Smollett's apologue concludes by observing that twenty-one people can share the same bottle nose and that one such feature does not make a face. Returning to the apologue's observations on the protocols of recognition after we finish *Roderick Random*, we cannot help but notice how oddly they introduce a narrative that is marked by failed recognition scenes and that attaches a lot of anxiety to the ways that personal effects such as names and bodies are not necessarily a single person's property. In the apologue, Smollett is begging just that question about the economy of character, about the legibility of fleshed-out representations, that (my previous chapter suggested) readers of characteristic writing wished to see answered: At what stage in the particularization of a character will the reader be justified in recognizing a likeness?

The oddity here suggests that Smollett is not only trying to ensure that the signs composing a literary character do not implicate actual individuals. Smollett also has to go through some fussing—has even perhaps to entertain a new set of terms for relating characters and countenances—to make those signs refer to one and only one identity. However ready he is to take on the fictionality of the fictional character, it does not come naturally to Smollett to have his fiction treat of nobody *in particular*. By the same token, at a period when the arts were valued for enabling an understanding of the grounds of social affiliation, when characteristic writings' depiction of the idiosyncracies that made people individuals could be decried for targeting a debased taste, it did not come naturally to readers aspiring to respectability to do what Gallagher says they were doing: valuing particularization in their fiction— valuing, in the language of the period, strongly marked characters. On the one hand, then, *Roderick Random* acknowledges the attractions of impersonality and abstraction: the narrative centers on a well-traveled gentleman who is able to put himself in others' places, and, through this protagonist, it animates a principle of generalizability. On the other, if we are prepossessed in Roderick's favor, as Smollett in his preface suggests we should be, it's because the state of not being peculiar only inconsistently does Roderick any good: in those scenes of failed recognitions, we *pity* Roderick for his difficulties in getting himself acknowledged as somebody in particular.

Modern readers' difficulties in positioning Smollett's fiction in relation to notions of "the" novel can shed some light on the ambiguities in his characterizing. Critics have wondered aloud whether *Roderick Random* ought to be considered a satiric survey of the nation's diverse stock of characters, a survey for which the protagonist is a mere vehicle, or whether Smollett's book is really about "the satirist as character type." Ronald Paulson supplies one way of specifying how Roderick crosses the line that separates the faceless exhibitor from the characters he displays when he suggests that *Roderick Random* should be read as an investigation of the satirical temperament—of the bad temper and the thirst for revenge that Roderick keeps as salient features even as he divests himself of all other particularities. Paulson suggests, too, something about Smollett's dexterity: to the extent that he gets worried about the place of typicality and generality in his characteristic writing, Smollett presses into service the remarkable characters whose foibles fascinated his contemporaries. He turns, that is, to the print market's rum fellows, characters whose egregiously individual ways of being themselves seem to withstand civilizing processes such as the Grand Tour, and he rewrites his protagonists along those lines.[46] Perpetually disgruntled, as a square peg in a round hole is expected to be, Matt Bramble, the hypochondriacal, misanthropic protagonist of Smollett's last fiction, is not only somebody in particular, but somebody to be marveled over as a real character. Notably, Smollett effects an elegiac tone in recounting Bramble's story, as if to atone for the sacrifice of the gentleman's polite abstractness by implying that this real character is the last of his prickly breed. Roderick Random, for his part, is a person whose nativity is heralded by a supernatural portent, the way the births of monsters were heralded when prodigies were discussed in eighteenth-century broadsheets: Mrs. Random dreams during her pregnancy that the devil supplies the place of a midwife and delivers her of a tennis ball. Similarly, although the narrator of *Peregrine Pickle* declares that his hero is at seventeen the image of the Apollo of Belvedere (108), the chapters preceding this declaration have chronicled the longings that assail Mrs. Pickle while she is pregnant with her firstborn, movements of the maternal imagination that, medical theory of the period feared, would mark the unborn child's body and cause a monstrous birth. The prepartum chapters of Peregrine's biography prepare us not for "beauty" and not even for "character," but instead for the excessive individualization Joshua Reynolds termed "deformity."

Two new editions of Smollett's fictions were published in the first decades of the nineteenth century. This was a decisive moment for the fortunes of the novel: when, buoyed by the changes in copyright law that made reprints a feasible enterprise, institutions of national canon-formation began to dignify novels as components of the cultural heritage and effectually extricated a singular, adamantly fictionalized entity called "the British novel" from the vast diversity of writing practices represented by characteristic writing. As illustrators of editions that, typical products of this moment, recast Smollett as the author of novels, the artists Thomas Rowlandson (in 1793) and George Cruikshank (1831) were each confronted with the task of determining how Roderick Random should look. It is telling that they resolved the ambiguities in Smollett's characterizing differently. Rowlandson's Roderick is drawn in the idealized style of history painting. With regular features and a long slender body, he looks like the Apollo Belvedere. (Everyone else that Rowlandson portrays is endowed with the bulbous, lumpy shape that he favors for his grotesques.) Pictured in his nightcap, Cruikshank's Roderick, by contrast, can come across as a real character.

Interestingly, a feature that both Rowlandson and Cruikshank (or those who hand-colored their plates) represent, though Rowlandson does so prominently only in the plate that portrays Roderick as a child, is Roderick's hair color. As a new arrival in London, yet another Scot who has traveled the road of ambition, Roderick makes, he confesses, "a very whimsical appearance": "I had dressed myself to the greatest advantage; that is, put on a clean ruffled shirt, my best thread stockings, my hair (which was of the deepest red) hung down upon my shoulders, as lank and streight as a pound of candles; . . . my hat very much resembled a Barber's bason in the shallowness of the crown and narrowness of the brims (62)." At the start of his adventures Roderick is eminently particular, and among his particularities are, to his shame, these "carroty locks," which, a fellow Scotsman counsels him, Roderick must conceal with a periwig, for they are "sufficient to beget an antipathy against [him], in all mankind" (67). We are reminded of these carroty locks in a subsequent episode: when Miss Williams relates her life story to Roderick and describes to him the person of her seducer, Roderick's exact double, we find that the sole truly distinctive feature among the many features Horatio and Roderick are said to share is their "chestnut-coloured" hair. Miss Williams's description could otherwise be a digest of eighteenth-century conventions of male beauty: it comes close, for instance, to matching point for point Fielding's description of Joseph Andrews.[47]

Replacing "carroty" with "chestnut-coloured," Smollett palliates his hero's offense against the bodily decorums of middling culture. He nonetheless cannot forget the red hair of his Scottish hero, the sign of Roderick's origin in a society that (in the era that witnessed the suppression of the Highland clans) had every reason to insist on its peculiarity. Roderick's red hair remains, as an impediment to the gentleman's social circulation, as a characteristic sign that obdurately resists abstraction.[48]

CURRENCY AND CHARACTER

To better understand the difference between Roderick with red hair and Roderick in a genteel periwig, we might think back on the difference distinguishing Mr. Allworthy's banknotes, marked up and recognizable, from the money-narrators of mid-century fictions, who are perpetually incognito. Alternatively, we might draw on our own experience of money and contrast our coins, which each possess an intrinsic value of sorts and have a palpability and solidity that make each an object in its own right, with our modern paper currency, which is more transportable, more pliable, and more indeterminate, and which is perhaps better at representing objects, in the way David Hume described, because it is only tenuously an object itself. This contrast between metallic and paper currency foregrounds the divergence between what is material and what is abstractly representative about money. I mention these contrasts and draw these analogies with Roderick's changing manifestations because as I conclude this chapter I want briefly to consider the particular ways in which the sentimental fictions of the mid-century map characterization onto cash. Smollet works out the tensions in characteristic writing between under- and overparticularization on the persons of his protagonists; his contemporaries the novelists of sentimental masculinity interrogate these tensions in a set piece that dramatizes the double character of money. This little scene, whose outlines can be traced in *Joseph Andrews*, *A Sentimental Journey through France and Italy*, and *The Man of Feeling*, gives me ways to anticipate the personalizing of character that transpired in the last decades of the eighteenth century, when (as the next chapter will argue) characterization accrued psychological meanings as novel readers found new ways to render their property in characters a more personal property.

The scene I have in mind works out the relations between money's currency and its quiddity—its intrinsic nature. It adjudicates between, on the one hand, the powers to generalize that we ascribe to money—insofar as money represents both "the infinite number of objects" for which it may be exchanged and the monarch, the *filius populi*, whose image it bears—and, on the other hand, the particularity that we can ascribe to any one coin, which is made of a specific amount of metal and which is stamped with certain characters.[49] At the same time, this scene balances between allying character with exchange and allying character with proprietorship.

Henry Fielding's readers engage with this balancing when Fielding arranges for the episode that sees Joseph Andrews sick and starving at the Dragon Inn to have a double focus: both Joseph's fortunes and the fortunes of the "little piece of broken gold" Joseph has with him. Because it is a token of his love for Fanny, broken in two when they pledged their love, Joseph refuses to give this little gold piece up: it will not be produced in evidence against the thieves who assaulted him and, though it is the sum total of Joseph's capital, it will not be spent. He resists pressures to send the gold back into the social world, onto the market. Instead Joseph "hug[s] it in his bosom" (83), a gesture that invites us to identify this piece of metallic money with the strawberry mark that is imprinted over his heart and that will at the end of the narrative effect the recognition of Joseph's true identity. As Joseph's gold was once linked with Fanny's gold, the longing mark palpably registers how the infant Joey was once linked to his mother's body.[50] Joseph's gesture—his incorporation of the money—also invites us to remember the tradition of comparing coins to characters, comparing the legends that are inscribed on coins' surfaces and that grant money value to the traits or characteristics that make persons into themselves.

Sterne continues Fielding's investigation of what it means to ascribe sentimental value to the medium of exchange and to convert a social instrument such as money into a personal effect. In *A Sentimental Journey,* he has the fille de chambre with whom Yorick shares a tender moment sew up a purse for the sole purpose of enclosing the money that the English traveler has bestowed on her: with her purse, she pledges that she will not lay the crown out in ribbons, or, presumably, spend it at all (93). In *The Man of Feeling* an old gentleman who has impressed Harley with his talk of benevolence is discovered to be in possession of ten shillings, although shortly before he had lacked change to donate to a beggar. When a game of pool is begun and the gentleman "produce[s] [the shillings] to serve for markers of his score," Mackenzie's ever-optimistic hero explains away the incongruity by observing that "inanimate things" (including money) will create affection in an individual "by a long acquaintance": " 'If I may judge from my own feelings, the old man would not part with one of these counters for ten times its intrinsic value.' " Harley continues by reminding himself that he too has his personal talisman: " 'I myself have a pair of old brass sleeve buttons.' "[51]

Assessing such scenes, we need to remember that the narratives do more than reinstate the connections between character and numismatics that I discussed in my first chapter; they do not merely map characterization onto cash; they also map characterization onto the transactions in which cash changes hands. Like much mid-century narrative, the fiction of sentimental masculinity prefers protagonists whose adventures take them into the hubbub of the marketplace, where they can prove their civility by proving their exchangeability. As much as the money-centered narratives, these sentimental narratives are propelled by moments of exchange. Think of how at Calais Parson Yorick and the Franciscan monk exchange snuffboxes, and think of how for eighteenth-century readers in the know this moment would have racy undertones suggesting the exchangeability of women. It was notorious that Parson Sterne kept a miniature portrait of Eliza inside *his* snuffbox.[52] Think of how the text of *The Man of Feeling* falls into its editor's hands when he and the curate arrange, one day when they are out shooting, to trade the manuscripts they have been using for gun-wadding. Think of the many teary-eyed moments of borrowing and alms-giving that punctuate the narratives of sentimental masculinity, when the man of small means gives his little mite to a man of smaller means still and receives in turn the blessings that accrue from charity.

This is why these moments when a coin is *withheld* from exchange are so odd. We could anachronistically use the language of the elements of fiction and say that, generally, the narratives of sentimental masculinity, as much as a hyper-episodic Smollett narrative, indulge plot at the expense of character. At moments such as these, however, they seem to hover on the brink between plot and plotlessness. Frequently in the narratives of sentimental masculinity, the protagonist, who is the prime mover of the narrative and the medium of the fiction's characterization, appears to partake in the dilemma afflicting his money: rather than entering the transactional space of commercial society and embarking on the project of character reading, he looks to be stalled. The discussion of Grand Touring near the start of *The Man of Feeling* suggests what is potentially appealing about such impasses: "It will often happen that in the velocity of a modern tour, and amidst the materials through which it is commonly made, the friction is so violent, that not only the rust, but the metal too, will be lost in the progress" (4). In the episode of *A Sentimental Journey* titled "Character: Versailles," Yorick, who while in France is for three weeks together "of every man's opinion [he meets]"

(112), waxes nostalgic for the alternative to his social fluidity and rapid rolling:

> A polish'd nation, my dear Count, said I, makes every one its debtor; and besides urbanity itself, like the fair sex, has so many charms; it goes against the heart to say it can do ill; and yet, I believe, there is but a certain line of perfection, that man, take him altogether, is empower'd to arrive at— . . . should it ever be the case of the English, in the progress of their refinements, to arrive at the same polish which distinguishes the French, if we did not lose the *politesse de coeur,* which inclines men more to human actions, than courteous ones—we should at least lose that distinct variety and originality of character, which distinguishes them, not only from each other, but from all the world besides.
>
> I had a few King William's shillings as smooth as glass in my pocket; and foreseeing they would be of use in the illustration of my hypothesis, I had got them into my hand, when I had proceeded so far—
>
> See, Mons. Le Compte, said I rising up, and laying them before him upon the table—by jingling and rubbing one against another for seventy years together in one body's pocket or another's, they are become so much alike, you can scarce distinguish one shilling from another.
>
> The English, like antient medals, kept more apart, and passing but few peoples hands, preserve the first sharpnesses which the fine hand of nature has given them. (90)

In the scenes that wishfully reimagine money along these asocial lines as, in effect, "antient medals, kept more apart," the sentimental narrative comes momentarily to be structured by a strange suspense. Such scenes oblige us to recognize that money by its very nature leaves the person who has it in a condition that is suspended between proprietorship and exchange. I can spend my coin. (In this case this money is no longer my property.) Or I can refuse the spending power that money gives me and keep my coin out of circulation. (In this case my cosseted coin preserves its properties, either the rust or "the first sharpnesses" nature gave it, but this coin is no longer money.)

Modern accounts of sentimental fiction have foregrounded comparable impasses. Sentimental fictions are said to downplay possibilities for moral action, instead privileging moral discrimination, the "analysis of morally intricate and perplexing situations." Positioning their readers as adepts in negotiating moral arcana, they "do not so much recommend correct conduct . . . as assume virtue in the reader[s'] capacity to understand."[53] The moments at which action is perplexed, when the narrative seems to pause and meditate a retreat from the public world, supply the sentimental audience with a breathing space that is really a kind of crying space: readers get the chance to prove themselves virtuosos of sentiment, and the tears that transport them into "the exceptional reaches of sympathy" level the hierarchies of the public world—lovingly quantified, these tears "establish their own distinctions based on expenditure."[54] Under these circumstances, the narrative project of collecting and collating the characters of life and regaling the reader with examples of conduct seems beside the point, since readers are being invited to please themselves with the example of their own sensitivity—their own capacities for fine feeling. Thus Barbara M. Benedict identifies in the sentimental narratives of the 1760s and 1770s a friction between two modes of reading: that exemplified by the third-person narrators, which enacts a program of satiric realism and aims to discover the discrepancy between appearance and truth; and that exemplified by protagonists such as Harley, Goldsmith's Dr. Primrose, or Sheridan's Sidney Biddulph, a reading that aims to illuminate the reader, the self, and a reading in which meaning resides not in the object but in the observer's responses. In the chapter of *The Man of Feeling* to which I've already referred—and which, not incidentally, carries the mischievous title "Physiognomy"—Harley is in error to take the poolplaying old gentleman's professions of benevolence at face value, and yet Harley's distance from social meanings and worldly ways of seeing proves his purity of heart. Because he "see[s] himself in the other," he sees virtuously.[55] My interest lies with how, in assembling this alternative model of what it means to read a character, mid-century sentimental fictions seem to look ahead. In Victorian literature classrooms as in ours, reading will be valued as the medium of self-revelation. The pleasures of the imagination will be valued for contributing to the endeavor to form a personalized interiority: literary characters will acquire depth as readers learn to use their interactions with characters to plumb the depths in their selves.

As they suspend us between possession and exchange and between the coin's currency and its quiddity, scenes such as the one in which Harley observes another's sentimental attachment to his shillings could be said to allegorize the situation of the sentimental style of writing character. Gesturing toward a rejection of the style of character reading that is manifested by welltraveled gentlemen physiognomists, the narratives of sentiment seem to hover on the threshold of new uses for character. Certainly, the romantic ways of writing character to which I turn in part 2—the new critical genre of the character "appreciation" and the novels of manners developed by the so-called Burney school of novelists—gave readers suggestions about new ways to reuse these mid-century characteristic writings. In some ways, the moments when sentimental narratives seemed momentarily to suspend the logic of exemplarity and the logic of exchangeability elicited the romantic rereadings that would eventually reinvent mid-century fiction and, personalizing and psychologizing it, recast it in explicitly novelistic forms. In his monumental *History of English Literature* (1873), Taine, for instance, is able to appropriate Sterne's numismatic metaphor in *A Sentimental Journey* to describe the English novel as a tradition that is defined by its concentration on character: "All these novels are character novels. Englishmen, more reflective than others, more inclined to the melancholy pleasure of concentrated attention and inner examination find around them human medals more vigorously struck, less worn by friction with the world, whose uninjured face is more visible than that of others."[56] We should note the elegiac undertones that imbue Taine's definition of what the English novel is and render it a description of what the English novel may imminently cease to be: it is a mere matter of time before the wear and tear of the world will take a toll on these human medals too. (At its inception, the "character novel" is already in its twilight years. That the very possibility of character is always menaced, that the "individual" is always at risk in "society," is an important element in how character is redefined, individualized, and psychologized.) By ignoring what Sterne did not, that *social* convention gives even an English coin its value, Taine developed a sentimental way of recasting the eighteenth-century text of sentiment. What Taine did not account for is that, even as it gives readers the sense that they are intimate with the most exquisitely private feeling, sentimental fiction's affirmation of public perspectives is such that personal feeling is expressed "impersonally." Tears copy tears, and tears in this context are always stylish, in keeping with the spectacular artifice of eighteenth-century manners.[57]

Still, the personal effects—little knickknacks such as snuffboxes and hankies and lockets—that clutter the house of sentimental fiction do tell us something important about the new uses of character registered when Taine borrowed from Sterne. Quintessential consumer objects (remember the things that those remarkable characters the Pinchbecks marketed), these little knickknacks nonetheless look special. Valued in ways that are supposed to be distinct from the common ways of valuing objects, their thinghood is transmuted. Sentimental possession, we might say, personalizes and decommodifies property by detaching it from the marketplace's system of objects, as new ways of reading and writing character would personalize character by detaching it from the social text. We must note, however, what tends to happen to these little objects. I have commented on the oddity of the scene in which sentimental people refuse the spending power their money gives them: if we track the exchange destinies of the personalized objects we find in mid-century narrative—Sophia Western's muff, for instance, or the engagement ring that the female Bedlamite received from her poor, dead Billy and that she gives in turn to the Man of Feeling (23)—we witness this scene's equally odd inversion. Objects of sentimental value are surprisingly prone to wandering. Parson Yorick's starling, for instance, is featured as the crest to his coat of arms, and yet, as *A Sentimental Journey* is at pains to show, the bird is only tendentiously "his." It is set adrift on the seas of civic finance. Yorick's valet buys the bird for a bottle of burgundy, and then Yorick passes it to Lord A, who trades it away to Lord B, and "so on—half round the alphabet" (74). Zeroing in on the stories that these objects can tell about their transfers and about the social world compromises the glamor of personal effects, because it compromises the personal: it depicts owners, in Marx's phrase, "merely as the representatives" of their hyperexchangeable things.[58] When Yorick charts the starling's movement through the marketplace, he chronicles the circulation of a sign that, as a component of a heraldic signature, the public sign of personal identity, really ought to stick close to his person. We are returned to the condition in which we left Roderick Random, whose excessive circulation, whose characterlessness, was such that he could not claim even Roderick's body as his exclusive possession but instead seemed fated to share it with other pretenders.

In the chapters that follow, I will trace how novels' depictions of a protagonist's plight with property that is not personal enough operate to "round" character—to suggest an inner consciousness that seems to exist independent of exchange relations. I will propose, in addition, that novels of manners have served as sites where people, and perhaps women readers especially, have managed their relations to their things.[59] Our sympathetic identification with the fictional character, with someone who is nobody, Catherine Gallagher asserts, gives us a way to be "acquisitive without impertinence." Gallagher uses this phrase to emphasize how eighteenth-century conceptualizations of sympathy were bound up with conceptualizations of ownership, how feeling with another was thought of as a process that aggrandized the self and its properties. Gallagher's account, which we could align with Wordsworth's description of acts of the imagination as "Possessions . . . that are solely mine/Something within which yet is shared by none," requires supplementing.[60] We need to note that readers have been invited to understand this proprietary relation with the character as one that takes shape against a backdrop of other, imperfect and compromised sorts of possession. In chapter 3 I move forward in the history of character and explore the connections between the consumer revolution of late-eighteenth-century Britain, the new, round character, and a new project of taste. I suggest that readers who are invited to imagine the inner life of the complex character, a character wronged by appearances, are tantalized with what, as consumers who are troubled by luxury yet in thrall to the world of goods, they most fervently seek—a way to be acquisitive and antimaterialist at once.

Inside Stories

"Round" Characters and Romantic-Period Reading Relations

Readers may be divided into four classes.
1. Sponges, who absorb all they read, and return it nearly in the same state, only a little dirtied.
2. Sand-glasses, who retain nothing, and are content to get through a book for the sake of getting through the time.
3. Strain-bags, who retain merely the dregs of what they read.
4. Mogul diamonds, equally rare and valuable, who profit by what they read, and enable others to profit by it also.
—Samuel Taylor Coleridge, *Lectures* (1811–12)

STORIES OF PROGRESS

When one moves forward in the history of character into the romantic period, as I do in this chapter, it often seems a mandatory part of the routine to engage a particular question, one that is designed to produce a romantic answer. Were round characters inside flat characters all along, signaling frantically to get out? In addressing this question, literary historians who chart the passage from the eighteenth-century novel to the nineteenth-century novel or from neoclassicism to romanticism have often found themselves drawing on a romantic-era story about the spirit of the age. When they have written up change as a triumphal story of "development" and cast history as the story of a return to nature and oneself—plotted it as a romance—they have recycled turn-of-the-nineteenth-century models for identifying the form and content of the period's history. Equipping themselves with notions of unrealized potential and intrinsic meaning, they have come to an agreement about the whereabouts of the round characters in eighteenth-century writing: they were indeed inside flat characters all along.

In *The Rise of the Novel*, for instance, Ian Watt concludes his critical narrative with confidence as soon as he turns to the nineteenth century. When he arrives at the era of Jane Austen, he is certain that the novel has arrived at its historical rendezvous with psychological depth. Nineteenth-century characterizing, Watt asserts, realizes the potential for "a full and authentic report of human experience" that is "implicit in the novel form in general." According to *The Rise of the Novel*, the rounding of character occurs when writers at last do in earnest what should have come naturally to them as exponents of the novel form. Characterization progresses, that is, as soon as novels come to be full participants in the history of freedom and democratic revolutions, an overarching story of progress that sees the state ultimately acknowledge the claims, worth, and singularity of the individual. When the novel's rendezvous with this history takes place, the inner truths of individuality that were latent in the characterizing of an eighteenth-century ancien régime are liberated from the impediments to expression that had held them in thrall. In romantic-period culture, the individual character and the novel each finds its true voice. The timing is perfect—as the founding text of canonical romanticism, Wordsworth's preface to the *Lyrical Ballads*, instructs us, this era also sees systems of allegorizing and stereotyping, didacticism, literariness, and "gaudy phraseology" lose their grip; for a liberal and romantic history, it is this era that sees the rise of the self-expressive language of man.[1]

In my first two chapters, I remarked on the problems with economy—with the overloading of characters—that mid-eighteenth-century practitioners of characteristic writing both fostered and decried as they presented persons as reading matter. In this chapter, I turn to the last decades of the eighteenth century and the first decades of the nineteenth, when, as we shall see, "swelling figures" are once again at issue in discussions of literary character, but at issue in a new way. In the literary-historical explanations that began to crystallize in the romantic period and that were mobilized to new ends by Ian Watt's Cold War generation, the diseconomy of the novelistic character has a new status. The excess that makes a character more than the sum of its parts is in this context valued as a proof of the novel form's liberal veneration for freedom. Realistically rendered, "round" characters have, so Robert Langbaum maintained in 1957, "a residue of intelligence and will" that exceeds the requirements of the plot and that cannot be accounted for by it.[2] For Langbaum, the significance of really round characters escapes attempts to pigeonhole them; it exceeds the names by which characters are publicly known. Thirty years earlier E. M. Forster had been less confident than successors such as Langbaum or W. J. Harvey would be about whether there was indeed an exact correspondence between particular kinds of characters and particular liberal (or illiberal) epochs and worldviews. But in the course of the most famous critical meditation on the distinctions separating round characters and flat, Forster made a claim resembling Langbaum's. A great novelist such as Jane Austen, he wrote in *Aspects of the Novel,* may well "label her characters 'Sense,' 'Pride,' 'Sensibility,' 'Prejudice,'" but such labels would be found insufficient; her characters "are not tethered to those qualities."[3]

Often when early-nineteenth-century critics bore witness to contemporary novel writers' newly acquired enlightenment, they too equated truth in characterizing with a freedom-loving flouting of abstractions and a consequent profusion of particulars. Take, for instance, the outline of novelistic history that begins the *Quarterly Review*'s 1814 review of Walter Scott's *Waverley.* Here literary history is a story of developing mimetic facility. Development is presented as a process of refining, and ultimately dissolving, general classifications or types. Characterizing in fiction changed, the *Quarterly* claims, when "the great mass of mankind" learned through "a nearer intercourse" with one another about "the real course of human life": "theory . . . was improved into a *generic* description, and that again led the way to a more particular classification—a copying not of man in general, but of men of a peculiar nation, profession, or temper, or, to go a step further, of *individuals.*" Prefacing a projected 1823 reissue of Clara Reeve's *The Old English Baron,* first published in 1777, Scott himself assumes a comparable progressive model as he distinguishes his literary generation's characters from their imperfect precursors. "The general defect in novels of [Reeve's] period," Scott declares, was the "total absence of peculiar character"; "every person [was] described [as] one of a genus [rather] than as an original, discriminated, and individual person." Scott thought differently of the "new style of novel . . . arisen within the last fifteen or twenty years" that he delineated in his review of Jane Austen's *Emma*—a review in some measure repeating earlier notices that had identified "the Burney school" of novelists with the modernity of a "new era." This new style of novel did appear to have space for original, discriminated individuals. It eschewed the flashy excitements composing earlier narratives—other novels' incidents of banditry, bankruptcy, and other "uncommon events." It eschewed adventures, the category of experience that is the common lot of Roderick Random, Betsy Thoughtless, and banknotes alike. The new style of novel unfolded, instead, in "ordinary walks of life," through "such common occurrences as may have fallen under the observation of most folks."[4] Under this new dispensation, what was taken away from plot was given to character. Incident was transmuted into inner experience in these new novels of manners.[5]

In this chapter my aim is to supply an alternative to this narrative, which has been taking shape since the romantic period, about when and why the novel rose and about how particularized, rounded characters evolved out of eighteenth-century flat ones. Behind that narrative, I want to show, lies a history of material and affective practices, a history in which changes in the retailing of novels and changes in what novel readers *did* with characters, play as important a role as democratic ideals. Because of the persistence of mimetic models of character and the persistence of "the rise of individualism" as an all-purpose explanation for political and aesthetic change, when we have looked at the era that gave the world democratic revolutions, the romantic movement, Austen, and Scott, we have seen the characters in novels take on depth and become more like real, "well-rounded" individuals. We have seen fictional characters seem to become more like their readers. By contrast, the narrative I assemble in this chapter rests on the claim that at the turn of the nineteenth century characters became the imaginative resources on which readers drew to make themselves into individuals, to expand their own interior resources of sensibility. The expanded inner life of the literary character—the psychological depth of the "new style of novel"—will be read here as an artifact of a new form of self-culture and as the mechanism of a new mode of class awareness.

There is more than one way, in other words, to understand the project that engaged participants in the turn of the century's reading revolution; I want to argue that they were doing something besides honing the novel's powers of mimesis and coaxing deep characters out of shallow ones. In large measure, character changed in the romantic period because the project of these readers and writers also involved rendering reading an occasion when readers got to know themselves and their feelings. It changed because literacy represented to many readers and writers a preferred field within which to administer the individuation of the individual and to govern populations that were being organized in new ways. In this respect, the sensitive reading that plumbs the depths of a character in a novel—the enterprise of "appreciating" the inner lives of beings who cannot possibly be taken at face value—can be ranged alongside other, cognate technologies of the self that came into use in the romantic era: the viewing of a picturesque landscape, for instance, or, as we shall see, the act of window-shopping.

At the same time, the reading revolution that produced new ways of making books matter (through new linkages to emotional practice) also registers the incipient codification of the opposition between high art and popular culture that makes some "good" books matter more than others. From the outset, round characters in novels contribute to the project of taste, the concept of cultural competence that was reenergized in the romantic period to assuage anxieties provoked as the increasing availability of books—more and more of them with the words "a novel" on their title pages—seemed to threaten social hierarchy.[6] Thanks to the boom in the novel business, turn-of-the-nineteenth-century culture no longer seemed one in which ways of writing and reading could be legislated from above. The expanded inner life of the literary character was, among other things, the cushioning that helped reading audiences get comfortable with this experience of a broadened, and somewhat democratized, book market. Character depth became a possible object of discussion at the turn of the century, then, not only because the quest for *égalité* and *liberté* assisted the rediscovery of the whole, well-rounded "man," but also because other "revolutions," in methods of marketing and distributing books, gave rise to a new insistence on distinguishing between styles of reading and on propagating the decorums that separate one reader's refined receptiveness to literary meanings from another, vulgar reader's avid following of fashion. Indeed, the "full and authentic report of human experience" realized in the new style of novels is inseparable from the other principal activity of these narratives: the way they seek out infractions of taste, exposing the ludicrous inability of some followers of fashion (Burney's Branghtons, say, or Austen's Thorpes) to convert their money into value and convert their possessions into self-enhancing signs of moral probity.

The social offices that literary characterization performs are historically contingent. That this contingency is difficult to acknowledge has much to do with how ideas of progress and of a uniform, continuous history have ordered literary historians' dealings with change. Histories that chronicle "rises" lend plausibility to the claim that the occasional all-but-round character can be found at particularly prescient moments in eighteenth-century fiction. Conversely, they also make it hard to find anything worthwhile to say about nineteenth-century writers' recapitulation of the impersonal perspectives of characteristic writing or nineteenth-century writers' fascination with remarkable characters—those topics become inaccessible to interpretation. Such histories' intertwining makes change in characterizing look inevitable: it is a bit too neat how the narrative about characterization's development dovetails with the narrative about culture's long-postponed recognition of the intrinsic significance of the private individual. Analyzing the social production of that individual's significance is difficult, as well, because it can be hard to step outside the parameters of a psychological culture, parameters that were established by an apparatus of reading that recast the knowledges characterization produced as private and personalized knowledges.

In *S/Z* Roland Barthes remarks that, from a "classic," "psychological" viewpoint, the "precious remainder"—the individuality—that makes character more than the sum of its parts is something "qualitative and ineffable"; as such, it "escapes the vulgar bookkeeping of compositional characters."[7] The irony in which Barthes indulges as he ventriloquizes the psychological viewpoint invites us to understand the particular economy—the "precious remainder"—that facilitates the psychological character's escape from bookkeeping in conjunction with a real economy. It invites us to delineate the historical surface on which psychological depth becomes recognizable as a space of commercial transactions—where goods with prices change hands. I am suggesting that the reified aesthetic value that is the *terminus a quo* of the stories of character's progress (stories in which change is invariably described in qualitative terms) should be aligned with exchange value in the marketplace. We know that value in the quantum form of the price is not a self-evident fact; it is not determined by consensus. Instead, as Marx insisted in his riposte to eighteenth-century and romantic-era political economy, value is a "hieroglyphic" that inscribes agonistic social relations of exchange.[8] Likewise, the aesthetic value realized in the round character is not innate. It is the product of conflictual social relations of reading.

In contrast to approaches to turn-of-the-nineteenth-century writing focused on how literary characterization and the novel form each realized its intrinsic worth, this chapter emphasizes those conflicts. It proposes that readers learned to enter into the inner lives of characters while they learned, as participants in such value-generating conflicts, to lay claim to a particular interpretive identity. In the mid-eighteenth century the proliferation within the market of new things to see and buy gave rise to a crisis of legibility. The production of characters—via the peripatetic gentleman physiognomist's reading of the face of the nation, via his documentation of "specimens of characters"—simultaneously contributed to and attempted to redress that crisis. By the nineteenth century, by contrast, the most influential figuring of literary character was one that served as a means of restaging market stratification. An ordinary-looking heroine, possessing an extraordinary, indescribable soul, presided over romantic and Victorian fiction. The psychic depths that this heroine concealed beneath her public reticence were central, as I shall demonstrate at the end of this chapter, to a new understanding of literary experience, one that doubled as a new means of locating oneself in social space. The advent of new techniques for reading—the silent scanning involved in the "close reading"—and of new motives for the reading experience—the notion that sharing a space of sensibility with a fictitious character could occasion a therapeutic recovery of one's real feelings—are crucial events in the history of literary change.

Assessing the history of psychological meaning as a history of reading, and so as a social practice, will necessitate, first of all, accounting for the changes that reshaped the romantic book market and for the contradictory effect that the new modes of disseminating reading matter had on the prestige of novel readers. The literacy rate in England soared following the Evangelical movement's foundation in 1780 of Sunday schools targeting the laboring poor. It is well established that the following decades saw England's new readers turn their literacy to some frightening antiauthoritarian uses. (Historians estimate, for instance, that two hundred thousand copies of Tom Paine's *The Rights of Man* were in circulation within a year of its publication in 1792.) The turn of the nineteenth century was also crowned in the English book trade by transformations that represented another sort of menace to the propertied classes' privileges and their monopoly on text. In the 1790s, in a London store reportedly identified by a sign that read "Cheaper than any Bookseller in the World," James Lackington pioneered the sale of remaindered books. Another book market entrepreneur was busy in this period. Known for engineering the Gothic publishing phenomenon of the 90s and for exploiting a popular taste for novelties in fiction, William Lane was busy creating that popular taste by creating a new readership. In 1784 Lane began to franchise a network of circulating libraries: he published a prospectus promising shopkeepers that at "a few days notice" they could obtain from his Minerva Press collections of some five thousand volumes. Previously it was only would-be novel readers in London and the resort towns who could hire novels from circulating libraries, but in the 1780s and 1790s these establishments appeared in "the previously untouched fastnesses of the provinces." Thousands of perfumists, tobacconists, engravers, and picture framers concurred with Lane's suggestion that they should increase business via an "employ both respectable and lucrative."[9] In 1774 the landmark legal case *Donaldson v. Becket* had, by abolishing perpetual copyright, increased the number of texts in the public domain and encouraged cheap reprints and enterprises such as the *Novelist's Magazine:* a protesting pamphleteer worried that the decision would in the long term render reading matter " 'the Property of any Person.' "[10] The retailing innovations that Lane and Lackington undertook in the 1790s built on this alteration in the property relations of the book market. In a sense, they made it conceivable that novels might become the property of *every* person.

The outcome of the retailing revolution was, in general terms, an accelerated print market. I emphasize in this chapter one particular aspect of that transformed market: the new insistence on making reading itself an object of observation—on devising criteria that might distinguish good uses of "every person's property" from bad and that would make *some* persons' relations to their properties more personalized. In order to apprehend the ramifications of this interest in what Coleridge calls the "classes of readers," we might consider, for instance, how when Ann Radcliffe in *The Romance of the Forest* (1791) identifies the silver lining in her heroine's misfortunes, it has to do with the singular interpretive identity Adeline's Gothic sufferings procure for her, one that converts her relationship to books into a mode of sentimental possession. For most of *The Romance*, Adeline is the helpless dependent of strangers who, fugitives from the law, have made a domestic refuge for themselves in the ghostly ruins of an abbey in the forest of Fontanville. Radcliffe not only has us recognize Adeline as an exemplar of the domestic virtues, of a disciplined inwardness, by having us recognize that she is well-read; she also seems to suggest that the admirable thing about Adeline's literacy is its necessarily contracted field of operation. She dissociates the quality of well-read-ness from promiscuous consumerism and from desires for novel stimulations. "From books indeed, she had constantly derived her chief information and amusement: those belonging to La Motte were few, but well chosen; and Adeline could find pleasure in reading them more than once."[11]

Pride and Prejudice (1813) also promotes rereading. Austen devotes two chapters to accounts of Elizabeth Bennet's second readings of the letters she receives from her sister Jane and from Darcy—second readings that in supplementing and redressing the first are meant to be adequate to "implicit significations," "silent purposes," and "obscure contents." (The latter terms are those that the new novel of manners could easily deploy to figure the knowledges its protagonist must master to negotiate the restrictions of drawing-room culture. But, as their appearance in Foucault's "What Is an Author?" suggests, these terms also designate the motivating forces of a specific regime of reading, one functioning historically to install writing within "the confines of interiority.")[12] As many readers of Austen have noted, Elizabeth finds happiness when she learns not to estimate others at face value. Happiness proves a function of the second looks that correct "first impressions" (Austen's original title for the novel). A matter of the most serendipitous timing, Elizabeth's reunion with Darcy at Pemberley, for instance, occurs only because, when Elizabeth and the Gardiners walk away from his house, she turns "back to look again," and because before this, during the tour of the house, she decided to take a second look at his portrait—the second of two that were on show. Elizabeth lingers over the sight of Darcy's pictured face not, Austen stresses, because she sees an altered or new Darcy (the portrait depicts him with "such a smile as she remembered to have sometimes seen"), but rather, because the past that she shares with him is, on "reperusal," permeated with new meanings.[13]

The significance that the narrative attaches to this scene of the heroine's introspection—for the episode at Pemberley is arranged so that in sightseeing Elizabeth discovers her own desire—explains its centrality to critics who trace the consolidation of psychological meaning in romantic fiction.[14] I want to suggest in addition, however, that Austen's concern with her readers' well-being matches her concern with her heroine's: this is why I've juxtaposed Elizabeth's rereading with Adeline's particular form of bookishness. *Pride and Prejudice* is in this respect typical of the fictions that mediated the experience of the expanded book market: Austen identifies to her readers the proper means of and motives for literary experience when she demonstrates that the truth of a letter is situated beneath or beyond the face of the page and when she demonstrates that character cannot be known at first sight. The scenes of "reperusal" establish Elizabeth's development and character depth while they present her close reading as an impetus to revision, as the prelude to a love more valuable than that ostensibly "[more] interesting mode of attachment" that "is so often described as arising on a first interview with the object."[15] (To celebrate true love Austen celebrates the activity of interpretation.) But these scenes also present novel readers with instructions in fashioning an individualized interiority. Given the opportunity to certify their powers of taste, mental discipline, and sympathetic identification, Austen's readers are able to affirm their *individual* distinction. They can deny their participation in what was, thanks to figures such as Lackington and Lane, rapidly becoming a *mass* market.

The practice of reading character changed when it came to serve as a means of self-culture and, congruently, a means of confronting the problem posed by this ebullient commercial society—the problem of the promiscuous circulation and universal exchangeability that eroded the differences defining the self and its belongings. Political economy, Brian Doyle observes, must negotiate the problem of "ensuring popular acceptance of exchange as a rational basis for all value." The solution that romantic-period readers and writers tried out was the now-familiar construction of culture as the repository of a value that is valuable in the absence of relations of exchange—as, in Doyle's words, an "apparently self-sustaining transcendental . . . ground for *all* use and exchange values."[16] The solution was, as many scholars maintain, the modern formation of literature: the romantic-period displacement of a rhetorical culture in which words served pragmatic, social ends by a culture of consumption that gave precedence to the pleasures of the imagination. The life of its own that the round character leads off the page, the "residue of intelligence or will" that enables it to transcend the requirements of plot, are in context quintessential signs of the literary.[17]

Characteristic writing, we saw in chapters 1 and 2, attempted to achieve universality through addition. The transcription of more characteristics or specimens of human nature made (ideally) for more adequate and more valuable representations. At the turn of the nineteenth century, by contrast, the writing and reading of a now *literary* character assist the processes of individual and class formation by virtue of a very different relation to enumeration and evaluation. Literature is hyperbolically constituted; literature pivots on an idea of infinity insofar as its initiates have, since the romantic period, assumed that nothing that is said about the literary work says enough. The conditions under which good readings and really round characters are conceptualized rule out the possibility of an adequate accounting. In romantic aesthetics we don't terminate interpretation. Like Radcliffe's Adeline and Austen's Elizabeth, we reread and reread again. The discussions that follow engage this insistence on never terminating interpretation by engaging first with the reading and rereading practices mobilized in the new character "appreciations" and then with those practices as they were mobilized in and by the new style of novels, novels that were starting to count *as* literature. I will engage this romantic faith in unsoundable depths in an effort to explain why a reconfiguration of the character's status as reading matter came to be so intimately involved with the social struggles that effected the transition from gentry to middle-class hegemony. Restyled, the reading of character could serve as a pretext for endless moral invigilation and self-revision. It could also serve as the pretext for the games of distinction that establish an "aristocracy of culture" as they make cultural capital something more than mere money can buy.[18]

FINDING ROUND CHARACTERS

In attributing aesthetic consequences to changes in retailing, legal decisions about copyright, and novelists' hints about what readers should do with their literacy, I have been underlining the provisionality of the codes organizing the narratives of character's romantic progress. Nothing as orderly or inevitable as "development," I have been arguing, can account for the reconstitution of literary character between the publication of *A Patch-Work Screen for the Ladies* and the publication of *Emma*. The eighteenth century and the nineteenth century are not analogous fields on which the same cultural object can appear and reappear in differing positions. Literary character has no essence, or, better, its "essence was fabricated in a piecemeal fashion from alien forms."[19]

Still, even though I'm arguing against an idealist pursuit of origins, I can't resist the opportunity that presents itself when I confront an early example of reading as ethical exercise, Maurice Morgann's *An Essay on the Dramatic Character of Sir John Falstaff* (1777). It is inviting to claim that the *first* really round character in literature (or the first to get his due in the eighteenth century) was William Shakespeare's fat knight—a "form," Morgann declares, of "roundness and integrity."[20] It seems appropriate that Morgann's account of this notoriously rotund character should provide this chapter with its first example of the character appreciation—the critical exercise that teases out the complex meanings composing a character's interiority and that thereby reanimates a being who never really was, of course, alive at all. The critical genre that Morgann founds merits consideration for another reason: it is linked in important ways to the novel's elaboration of psychological meaning.

Morgann's *Essay* predicts a daily ritual in the twentieth-century literature classroom: the discussion of the protagonist's psychology, of what she or he

is *really* like. So do similar essays by Morgann's contemporaries Henry Mackenzie (the author of *The Man of Feeling*), William Richardson, and Thomas
Robertson. At times these writers also cast Shakespeare's Falstaff as the recip-
ient of their efforts of reanimation. Quite often, however, the round character
who receives the homage of their character sketches is Shakespeare's Hamlet,
who, it bears remembering, resembles Falstaff in at least one respect: Hamlet
is "fat, and scant of breath" (V.ii.27).[21] And indeed the fleshy excessiveness
that Hamlet and Falstaff share might well serve as a metaphor for the new
genre of character criticism that these two inspired beginning in the 1770s
and 1780s.[22] The character appreciation often deploys an overnourished
style. Intent on a thorough presentation of a psychological subtext that is
nowhere stated in print, it is, by definition, excessive with respect to its subject
matter. The most egregious instance of this excess is usually said to be Mary
Cowden Clarke's *The Girlhood of Shakespeare's Heroines, in a Series of Tales* (1851),
anticipated almost twenty years earlier by Anna Jameson's *Characteristics of
Women, Moral, Poetical and Historical* (1832). (For readers of the Victorian period, the Shakespearean *heroine* is the paradigmatic prop for commentary,
taking over the function that Falstaff and Hamlet exercised for the last quarter of the eighteenth century.) However, the same over-the-top effect and
purple prose that distinguish Clarke's panegyrics to heroines' lives of their
own may be encountered in both Morgann and Mackenzie.

Mackenzie, for example, is capable of sentences such as this one: "Falstaff
is the work of Circe and her swinish associates, who in some favoured hour
of revelry and riot moulded this compound of gross debauchery, acute discernment, admirable invention and nimble wit"; Mackenzie continues, adding three more subordinate clauses.[23] When Morgann describes Falstaff—
who is bulky, he writes, "as if his mind had inflated his body and demanded
a habitation of no less circumference" (170)—he attempts to cast his own
self-indulgence in verbal excess as, in this case, an effect authorized by its
object. At the turn of the nineteenth century readers of Shakespearean character seem suddenly to have determined that such expansive interiority
needed more room than the envelope of language had hitherto supplied for it.
Coleridge suggests, for instance, that Hamlet's mind is given to "superfluous
activities." Mackenzie asserts, similarly, that, being a melancholy man, Hamlet must feel "in himself . . . a sort of double person"—"one that . . . looks
not forth into the world nor takes any concern in vulgar objects or frivolous
pursuits; another, which he lends . . . to ordinary men, which can accommodate itself to their tempers and manners."[24] In this period, conversely, readers

seem suddenly to have taken issue with previous essayists' restrictive concentration on form and fable in Shakespeare. And they retooled their critical prose, making it into a capacious medium tailor-made for these swelling figures, who were, accordingly, rounded by their efforts.[25]

Thus the character appreciation works to draw out the deep meanings that the text on which it comments both implies and withholds. It pursues the slightest implication and expatiates on the sketchiest connotation. The energies invested in it affirm character's semantic plenitude. And in deferring complete explication, the character appreciation *produces* the depth that needs explicating and with it the textual effects that signal the psychological real. Maurice Morgann's special importance as an inventor of immaterial, psychological meaning lies in the deliberateness, and downright audaciousness, with which he elaborates this characterology that has more to it than meets the eye. He rewrites the truth of a character as a function of "latent motives and policies not avowed" (62). Morgann's appreciation of Falstaff has a perverse aim. He wants to vindicate Falstaff's valor from charges of cowardice laid by the critics whom this character encounters inside and outside the play text. It turns out, Morgann avers, that while "cheating the eye with shews of balefulness and folly," Shakespeare actually "stole . . . upon the palate a richer and fuller gout" (149); and it turns out that Falstaff is in "reality" (as it were) a character of much "natural courage and resolution" (15).

A comparison with a text from thirty years before the *Essay* illuminates the novelty of Morgann's notion that the truth of a character lies beyond the page or stage, resides somewhere other than in the visible marks by which characters are signified. Touting the cognitive advantages accruing to gentlemen from Grand Tours and universal conversation, Fielding asserted in *Tom Jones* that "on the real Stage, the Character shews himself in a stronger and bolder Light, than he can be described." In order to elucidate this assertion about character's obviousness under the right conditions, Fielding used an instructive analogy: "after the nicest Strokes of a Shakespear [*sic*]. . . some Touches of Nature will escape the Reader, which the judicious Action of a Garrick . . . can convey to him."[26] In 1777, by contrast, Morgann dismisses the "mummery" (21) of stage performance, along with the notion of the visible as a register for telltale signs. A finer optic than that of the playgoer is needed if one is to apprehend the "Falstaff of Nature" as well as the "Stage Falstaff" (172) and so apprehend the "secret Impressions . . . of Courage" Shakespeare has "contrived" to make on us (13).

Closer to life than rival dramatists, Shakespeare produces "forms of roundness and integrity." They produce characters who can be seen and who exist in *parts* only.[27] Whereas the other dramatists invent an action and leave character to be inferred from that action, Shakespeare, Morgann argues, begins with "first principles of character"; Shakespeare introduces a seeming incongruity between character and action (between Falstaff's real valor and his actions, which *look* as if they proceed from cowardice). This incongruity is one that searching readers such as Morgann may then explain away. ("We are compelled to look farther, and examine if there be not something more in the character than is shewn; something inferred, which is not brought under our special notice" [153].) The proposition behind Morgann's indictment of *most* "novels and plays"—his assertion that "the union of character and action [is] not seen in nature" (9)—is a means of separating essences from accidents and character from the exigencies of plot. It serves to extricate a grand, freestanding psychology from the surrounding textual medium. "Shakespeare had no particular plan laid out in his mind for Hamlet to walk by," Thomas Robertson asserted in a rewriting and repowering of character comparable to Morgann's; "Shakespeare rather meant to *follow* [Hamlet]; and like an historian, with fidelity to record how a person so singularly and marvellously made up should act."[28]

Out of the legal wrangling over literary property that culminated in the *Donaldson v. Becket* decision, a new notion that Shakespeare, not the booksellers, was the "owner" of his words came to be articulated. With this notion came a new emphasis on how language, which might otherwise be considered a social, transactional medium, enshrined the self-expression of the individual. Margreta de Grazia demonstrates how these developments underwrote the tactics late-eighteenth-century commentators adopted to manage the incongruities in the Shakespearean play texts and how the postulate of psychological complexity—the notion of roundness that dissociates meaning from what the player says and what the printer prints—was a consequence of this management. For instance, some of Hamlet's lines in act 3, scene 3 had left generations of eighteenth-century commentators at a loss as to how to align Hamlet's character and his speech. His decision, taken when he comes upon Claudius at prayer, to spare his uncle at that moment in order to ensure the latter's damnation contravenes the neoclassical concern for the "preservation" of character;[29] the nasty words Hamlet uses as he mulls this decision over contravene the neoclassical conviction that noble characters should speak and act decorously, in ways conformable with their rank. The late eighteenth century, de Grazia argues, had a novel solution to the problem of preserving Hamlet's integrity and ensuring his "presence in language"— ensuring that even nasty words could nonetheless be seen as Hamlet's own. In 1783 William Richardson returned to this crux in *Hamlet:*

> You ask me, why he did not kill the Usurper? And I answer, because he was at that instant irresolute. . . . His sense of justice, or his feelings of tenderness, in a moment when his violent emotions were not excited, overcame his resentment. But you urge the inconsistency of this account with the inhuman sentiments he expresses. . . . In reply to this difficulty, and it is not inconsiderable, I will venture to affirm that *these are not his real sentiments.* . . . on many occasions [do we not] alledge those consider-ations as the motive of our conduct which really are not our motives? Nay, is not this sometimes done almost without our knowledge?

De Grazia comments: "Interpretation delved below, mining the text for a justification concealed from and mystified by its surface. Inaudible and im-perceptible, the essential meaning of [Hamlet's] words was stifled within the postulated inner regions of his soul."[30]

With the alteration of property relations within the book market, the con-ditions of character's legibility changed. The now-urgent pursuit of charac-ter's essential meaning opened up depths in texts. In the last quarter of the eighteenth century, Hamlet thus acquired inner regions of selfhood. In a related development he also acquired a youth. He began, that is, to exist not only within the expanse of time delimited in the play but also in a happier epoch, before the death of his father.[31] In the same period, similarly, Falstaff acquired a house in the country and a house in town: these domiciles, to which Shakespeare himself never alluded, became indices of Falstaff's social standing that Morgann could invoke as he pieced together evidence of the persistent misunderstanding of the character. Falstaff too acquired in *his* youth the "bad habits" (19) that led him into the circumstances in which he might wrongly be seen as a coward.

Character expanded in an inward direction, and also an outward. Late-eighteenth-century readers pledged their belief in a "true" character and so accommodated possibilities extending beyond the boundaries of the play text. The full-bodied character sustains speculation about what he would have been like had circumstances been otherwise. For Morgann, Falstaff is, with "so much of the invulnerable in his frame," a "game-ball" who will withstand

FIG. 5. *A Fancy Sketch to the Memory of Shakespeare*, from G. M. Woodward,
Eccentric excursions: Literary and pictorial sketches of character and countenance.
Courtesy of the Grosvenor Rare Book Room, Buffalo and
Erie County Public Library, Buffalo.

baiting through a hundred plays (176). In 1797 the illustrator George Mou-
tard Woodward's "poetic offering" to Shakespeare was a sketch of Falstaff,
Ariel, and other Shakespearean characters gathered mournfully around their
author's tomb (fig. 5). By the close of the eighteenth century literary characters have moved out of time. Immortals, they survive, surpass, and in some
sense are realer than human authors.[32]

INTERIOR DECORATION: READING AT HOME

Secretary to the politician-magnate the earl of Shelburne, his special charge
the affairs of British North America, Maurice Morgann participated in a
transition in ruling-class styles. He did this not so much by pulling political
strings as by importing new norms into the reading of character. Signifi-

cantly, many contemporaries of Morgann, and of Richardson, Robertson, and Mackenzie, were hard-pressed to identify the *utility* of their investigations into the psychology of Shakespearean character. They refused to take character for granted. One reviewer marveled that Richardson could be so sure that "fictitious personages can really provide insight into the workings of the human mind." Another commentator, Richard Stack, disapproved of Morgann's essay on the grounds that "dramatic characters are not drawn for speculative ingenious men in their closets, but for mankind at large." The puzzlement in these criticisms points up the historical significance of the late-eighteenth-century rereadings of Falstaff and Hamlet, which is not that Morgann and his peers looked harder and so found out the deep truths of Shakespearean representations but that they were doing something new with the Shakespearean text. They brought it into alliance with a new set of procedures for constituting selves and constituting social relations. This new alliance between texts and modes of social and subjective organization is evident, above all, in the way in which these character appreciations enclosed *dramatic* characters in *narrative* and made them in fact novelistic (as Shakespeare scholars habitually complain). And indeed, at the turn of the nineteenth century, the primary site of that alliance began to shift from Shakespearean commentary to reemerge in the novel, a migration that simultaneously assisted the generic consolidation of "the" novel and helped make that now-literary genre's special access to round characters' inner lives possible.[33]

In his response to Morgann, Richard Stack refuses to take into account the "speculative ingenious man in his closet," but that man's cognitive practices and his pleasures *can* be located within a historical series of regimens of character reading. The closeted man's practices and pleasures mark an intermediate point between a model of the reader as the roving gentleman of characteristic writing and the modern regimen that, increasingly since the early nineteenth century, has organized our novel reading by linking it in an expressive relation to the desires and the sympathetic capacities that constitute the private truths of our individualities. We have only to consider a text such as George Stubbes' 1736 *Some Remarks on the Tragedy of Hamlet* to realize that we are separated from Stubbes' moment by, as Ian Hunter argues, the emergence of "a new form of looking." For example, rather than asking what the characters are like, Stubbes subordinates them to a scene-by-scene account of how Shakespeare organizes his exposition. He skips the

"To be or not to be" soliloquy because "every *English* Reader knows its Beauties." Since Stubbes, Hunter remarks, there has been an alteration of "the
historical surfaces on which the content of a text can appear":

> If character in the eighteenth-century reading is primarily a rhetorical
> object emerging from the iteration of a set of rules/norms determining
> what counts as an appropriate or plausible representation, then it is pos-
> sible to say that character in the nineteenth-century practice of reading
> is primarily a moral object. Which is to say that character [in the nine-
> teenth century] appears in a space opened by a set of techniques and
> practices whose object is not "character as an element of a dramatic
> representation" but rather "character as a projection or correlate of the
> reader's moral self and personality."[34]

The place formerly assigned to the interpretive power that uncloseted gentlemen derived from their extensive acquaintance with "mankind at large" is
now the site where reading individuals find a means to reflect on the state
of their own sensibilities. In 1883 Anne Thackeray Ritchie, a particularly
canny commentator on nineteenth-century "women's fiction," outlined this
aspect of modern self-culture and pleasure when she portrayed the ideal
novel reader as the man or woman who learns, by rereading, to "love" characters, to make friends with signs. For Ritchie, the virtue of having Austen's
Fanny Price and Anne Elliot for friends is precisely that they're *old* friends,
and so "we seem to find our own selves again in their company." The
nineteenth-century novel "requires us to meet its characters as equals ('Your
homes the scene, yourselves the actors, here!' was Dickens's early choice for
an epigraph to *Martin Chuzzlewit* [1843–44])."[35]

The practices and pleasures of the "speculative ingenious man in his
closet" are so much evidence that the means by which individuals form themselves as subjects of aesthetic doctrine are not constant. The techniques that
assisted the literary formation of gentry identity—culling the classical authorities and retrieving their words of wisdom and elegant turns of phrase at
moments of oratorical need—have little in common with Morgann's practice
of the self. (Richardson's Clarissa Harlowe is exemplary not least for the ways
her correspondence is shaped by these older techniques: in a letter stuffed
with proverbs, Lord M. writes admiringly to Lovelace of how he has heard
that the lady's writing is also "full of sentences.")[36] Morgann's essay is a
blueprint for an alternative set of techniques—an apparatus for producing
and accrediting literacy and literary value—that was to be formalized in

nineteenth-century middle-class culture, the schoolroom particularly. In the nineteenth century, to appreciate a character as an "old friend," to activate moral norms common to oneself and the character, and to construct and identify with the character's point of view were means of probing one's receptiveness to literature and so of constituting a moral self. (Schiller's description of what it meant to *really* read is more celebrated, as a canonical instance of German romanticism, than Anne Thackeray Ritchie's, though this statement from *On the Aesthetic Education of Man* [1795] prescribes the same program she did: "If he [who judges the work of art] is too tense or relaxed, if he is used to apprehending either exclusively with the intellect or exclusively with the senses, he will, even in the case of the most successfully realized whole, attend only to the parts, and in the presence of the most beauteous form respond only to the matter.")[37] These techniques for producing new depths in readers simultaneously helped to produce those depths distinguishing the characters of the "new style" of turn-of-the-nineteenth-century novels; each new reading ensured their intensification.

By the late nineteenth century state institutions underwrote those depths, as well as the pleasures that readers took in their discovery. When "English" emerged as a school subject, when the romantic-period reader's strategies for ethical individualization found a place within the supervisory machinery of public administration, the character appreciation became a device for forming the student's character and for exposing the student's sensibility to invigilation by a sympathetic inspector-teacher.[38] It helped to bring student-subjects within the domain of government, which set out to manage masses of people by promoting and monitoring subjectivities and by making self-expression the stake of social regulation. In these circumstances, the literature that—in its pleasure-giving capacities—individuated also purveyed assurances about human homogeneity, those captured in Wordsworth's definition of the poet as a man "carrying everywhere with him relationship and love": precisely by virtue of calling forth readers' "best selves," as Matthew Arnold phrased it later, by humanizing and fitting them for membership in an ideal interpretive community (versus the real reading public), imaginative literature could define itself as the groundwork of society.[39]

How did literature perform this function? No matter how sensitive it was, no character reading could ever exhaust the meanings of an interiority (that "within which passeth show") which, it was understood, had slipped beneath the surfaces of words. This postulate of a depth that could never finally be sounded ensured that aesthetic dispositions would receive repeated and regular workouts: and so such "infinitization of Literature" made the character reading all the more useful a device for governmentality. From the late nineteenth century on, the literature teacher's "*permanent* care" was (as Henry Smith, author of "The Education of the Citizen," wrote in 1917) "to liberate the possibilities of character in his students."[40]

As he opened his essay on Falstaff, Maurice Morgann made no secret of the fact that the Shakespearean character offered him a means to develop a relationship with his self: "The vindication of Falstaff's Courage is truly no otherwise the object than some old fantastic Oak, or grotesque Rock, may be the object of a morning's ride. . . . The real object is Exercise, and the delight which a rich, beautiful, picturesque, and perhaps unknown Country, may excite from every side" (4–5). When he delves below the textual surface to find a Falstaff of nature concealed within the stage Falstaff, Morgann is keeping fit. He is doing what is good for him: he is engaged in an athletic exercise that puts his literary health to the proof. Here Morgann also casts himself as a traveler who quests after the picturesque. This role was becoming increasingly popular in the late eighteenth and early nineteenth centuries, as Britons grew warier of Continental travel and Continental fleshpots, and as, conversely, an alternative practice of domestic tourism and an alternative way of seeing reenchanted the rural landscape of Britain. Conforming to the precepts of eighteenth-century associationist psychology, the cult of the picturesque made "old fantastic oaks" and "grotesque rocks" into the props of a perceiving mind that could discover its own individuated and interiorized contents as it pulled those unlikely objects into aesthetic unity. The picturesque presumed a new sort of beholder of landscape at the same time that it created a landscape capable of fixing the eyes of travelers who might otherwise range too far and so forget domestic virtues and themselves. In these respects the cult of the picturesque can be seen as a cultural technology that functioned alongside the "new style" of novels with which it was contemporary, and to the same ends. Its insistence that nature be dilated through subjectivity points to an important aspect of the ethico-political context that shaped the other "new form of looking" in the era—the new reading of character.

In 1807 William Gilpin articulated the moral program that underpinned his catalogs of picturesque beauty and that also underpinned the novels of manners, with their devotion to "ordinary walks of life" and their particular mode of negotiating the private and public, outer and inner experience. Gilpin maintained that *"learning to stay at home* is a great point of education."[41] His statement points to how, at the turn of the nineteenth century, progress (individual and national) was pegged to new techniques of the self that allowed one to appreciate what was close at hand and that privatized and quite explicitly *domesticated* cognition. The idea of progress to which John Locke subscribed in *An Essay Concerning Human Understanding* hinged on a better labeling of the world—on achieving a closer match between language and phenomena, between names, bodies, and identities. Accordingly, the farther the gentleman traveler of characteristic writing traveled, the more progress there was. The stakes differ, however, as soon as we turn to the practices of domestic tourism and picturesque seeing touted by Gilpin and carried out by the heroines of numerous romantic novelists. They resemble the pleasures that Maurice Morgann's speculative ingenious man takes "in his closet."

That is, at the turn of the nineteenth century, progress happened because the would-be reader of character stayed at home, with his or her self for company. And, whereas neoclassical epistemology supposed that truth was instantaneously transmitted in the eye's encounter with its object, in this period temporality was introduced "as an inescapable component of observation." The rejection of a model of the observer as a passive receiver of sensation, someone well-traveled but characterless, coincided with a new insistence on protracting the act of reading or seeing, on understanding perception as a multilayered, temporally dispersed event. After the turn of the nineteenth century, discerning the truth of a picturesque scene or a literary work also meant experiencing "the shifting processes of one's own subjectivity" through time. It meant fashioning a personalized interiority through that experience.[42]

In her patriotic conduct book *The Women of England* (1836), Sarah Stickney Ellis praised the reading that Englishwomen did above that performed by other nationals, not on the grounds that Englishwomen read widely, but because they read well. (The rereading that occupies Adeline in *The Romance of the Forest* would have met with Ellis's approval.)

> It was not with them a point of importance to devour every book that was written as soon as it came out. They were satisfied to single out the best, and, making themselves familiar with every page, conversed with the writer as with a friend, and felt that, with minds superior, but yet congenial to their own, they could make friends indeed. . . . [A]n acute vision directed to immediate objects, whatever they may be, will often discover as much of the wonders of creation, and supply the intelligent

mind with food for reflection as valuable, as that which is the result of a widely extended view, where the objects, though more numerous, are consequently less distinct.

In another sign of the priority that romantic-period culture ascribed to getting familiar with one's books, the early nineteenth century witnessed the apogee of the library within the English country house. Darcy has one at Pemberley: early in Austen's novel he states, in response to some flattering prodding by Miss Bingley, that he " 'cannot comprehend the neglect of a family library in such days as these.' " The new architectural prominence of the library in the home registered how it had become de rigeur among the propertied classes to number books among one's personal effects. It also suggested, as did the contemporary marketing of elegant reprints of "standard novels," how rereading had emerged as a fashionable rite of ownership. Being good and being English—really experiencing pleasure—now meant protracting one's reading and becoming *at home* with one's books.[43]

In accounts of romanticism, the post-Kantian aesthetic of "subjective vision" that one might associate with Ellis's proper reading is most frequently the subject of commentary when the critic defines what made the romantics romantic: their acknowledgment of the constitutive role that the mind plays in perception. It's not necessary, however, to associate the shift from mimetic pictorialism to interpretation—the shift from the model of the mirror to the model of the lamp—with a handful of poets exclusively and to dissociate it from the knowledges, pleasures, and practices that accommodated large groups of people to new norms of conduct and new economic requirements.[44] As noted above, the interiorization of the truths of texts and the new scrutiny of the individual's reading habits could be numbered among the conditions not only for a psychologizing of literary character but also for the nineteenth-century emergence of the literature classroom and of a new technology for human resources management. When Colin Campbell analyzes the development in Georgian England of a consumer market of unprecedented size, such new hermeneutics of the self are likewise given center-stage: Campbell's *The Romantic Ethic and the Spirit of Modern Consumerism* proposes that those techniques of ethical self-fashioning—organized by churches at the start of the early modern period, reemerging in the late eighteenth century in the secular domain of the marketplace—thoroughly reorganized national finances, class relations, and relations within the bourgeois household. This study of the "consumer revolution" maintains that the role that supply (production or technology) played in Britain's industrialization and commercial growth has been overemphasized; Campbell focuses instead on the historical effectivity of "home demand"—a demand identifiable with women's consumer choice and women's compulsory if sometimes pleasurable involvement in the unpaid labor that accompanies "home-making."[45] Campbell is explicit about how, in ascribing historical consequence to home demand, he aims to revamp Weber's thesis about the Protestant ethic and the spirit of capitalism. The individual's formation of a secular conscience, a disciplined, deep self, is identified here not with the irrational rationality of frugality but with her luxury spending.

Campbell's discussion casts consumerism as a kind of emotional practice—and so akin, I would suggest, to the character appreciation. For him, the acceleration of luxury consumption and of rates of product obsolescence pivots on eighteenth-century changes in affective practice. In this psychology of consumerism, commodities provide the individual with the means of symbolizing the qualities of her distinctive inner life. The diversified consumer marketplace that is in place by the end of the century is, Campbell hypothesizes, both an effect and a cause of the change that occurs when a doctrine of signs in which individuals scrutinize themselves and others for the advertisements of grace gives way to a doctrine of signs in which they scrutinize indications of consumer preference. That individuals with disposable income became readier to buy in excess of "need" is a function of a new structure of longing that Campbell identifies as he argues that pleasure in consumer culture has less to do with the consumption of products and more to do with "the self-illusory experiences" that individuals construct out of the meanings that the imagery of the advertiser links to the products.[46] Within consumer cultures interest lies not so much in objects as in their effects. While they practiced at feeling feelings, eighteenth-century Britons began to value consumer goods for their suggestive potential, and they began to accumulate them as stimuli with which to manipulate emotional highs and lows.[47] A figure who first appears in the late-eighteenth-century retail scene—the window-shopper, who is, for the moment, only looking and who daydreams in the interval—is thus Campbell's chief candidate as the model for "another Protestant ethic." Window-shoppers are exemplary in the way they dilate the time of desire. They resemble Weberian captains of industry in their willingness to defer gratification and organize their pleasures according to a developmental logic of fulfillment.[48]

Buying—or, as in window-shopping, the mere contemplation of buying—began in the late eighteenth century to form a common field with other techniques of self-culture, among them the picturesque tourist's redesigning and personalizing of the landscape and the reader's sympathetic identification with the deep psyches of characters. Indeed, these practices of the self—which were also practices that magically invested mass-marketed commodities with personal meanings, "reenchanted" the scenery of Britons' homeland, and endowed characters in books with lives of their own—were mutually reinforcing. Literally or figuratively, we are in all these cases concerned with modes of interior decoration.

READING IN THE MARKET: CHARACTER, "EVERY PERSON'S PROPERTY," AND CULTURAL CAPITAL

These convergences suggest another reason to consider the rounded character as one of the commodities of the consumer revolution, despite the scheme that would make only second-rate characters subject to "vulgar bookkeeping." As an endeavor to claim "taste," the self-culture that was at stake in the character appreciation doubled as an endeavor to position oneself in the economy of prestige. Amassing intellectual wealth—the treasury of meaning buried deep within the literary work—brought real returns for readers who were negotiating the transition from eighteenth-century status awareness to nineteenth-century class consciousness. When they responded to the hints about proper interpretive identities tendered them in the new style of novels, as much as when they chose muslin over brocade, readers were adapting to how "being" middle class was becoming a function of "an extremely anxious production of endless discriminations between people who are constantly assessing each other's standing."[49] In experiencing through the text of character the contours of their own ineluctable individualities, readers classified other readers. The pleasures of social calculation were inextricable from, in the characteristic coinage of the romantics, the pleasures of the imagination. We return here to how, in a different sense than usually assumed, the inner life of the character is a historical marker. Not just an expression of how, in the age of revolutions, history was at last obliged to acknowledge the *individual*, that inner life is also an artifact of the processes of class formation portrayed as "the making of English reading audiences."[50]

The psychological depths that served to round romantic literary characters exercised this historical effectivity: they offered each reader the opportunity to distinguish himself or herself as the sole audience possessing the temperamental resources necessary if one aspired to *really* sound those depths. Since *deep* truths can so easily be represented as knowledge inaccessible to all but a few, the private reading could supply a means of restaging the stratification of society. The act of sympathetic rereading, of constructing and identifying with a character's point of view, could appear a means of forestalling the process whereby the mass circulation of elite culture threatens to turn it into its opposite. (Compare how Elizabeth Bennet, the British novel's most famous picturesque tourist, only half-ironically portrays her visit to Derbyshire as an opportunity to display the superior taste of the class fragment with which she identifies herself: " '[W]hat hours of transport we shall spend! And when we *do* return, it shall not be like other travellers. . . . Let *our* first effusions be less insupportable than those of the generality of travellers.' ")[51] In this respect, the new understanding of interpretation as interior decoration—as an enterprise that responds to the individuality configured in the text and expresses the individuality of the interpreter—registers the "struggles in social space that guide and block the passage of signs among historical writers, readers, and audiences."[52]

A passage in William Richardson's essay on Hamlet suggests the social ends served when the authors of the character appreciation proposed that the meanings of character were latent and not patent. Just after Richardson declares that Hamlet is not expressing "his real sentiments" in the episode in which he catches Claudius at his prayers, and just after he gazes *within* the text for the truth, he sums up the difficulties of Shakespearean depth: "The lines and colours are indeed very fine, and not very obvious to cursory observation. The beauties of Shakespeare, like genuine beauty of every kind, are often veiled; they are not forward nor obtrusive. They do not demand although they claim attention." Richardson brings to view the differential logic from which deep characters and deep reading derive their significance. To distinguish itself, genuine beauty must summon forth the meretricious beauty that delimits and defines it. Beautiful depth, similarly, can be apprehended as such only through a contrast with "forward" and "obtrusive" beauties that "demand attention." (That language reappears in an early use of the term *flat character*: a favorable review that happily reports the absence in *Pride and Prejudice* of characters "flat in appearance," who "obtrude themselves upon the notice with troublesome impertinence.")[53] Good reading has to be juxtaposed with bad reading ("cursory observation"). The reader who is sensitive to Hamlet's hidden motives doesn't only opt *for* this one set of interpretive protocols but also refuses another. Richardson's procedure here suggests how "audiences are not simply distinct sectors of the cultural sphere" but instead "are mutually produced as an otherness within one's own dis-

147

course."[54] In this sense, the transactions between the singular, sensitive reader, the great writer, and the character with a life of its own are more mediated—more pressured by contrary, fractious readings—than Stack's reference to the "gentleman in his closet" suggests. The private recovery of the truths of character turns out to be a social production.

Through such turn-of-the-century discussions of character, differential patterns of consumption (increasingly visible in an era marked both by mass literacy and by the fracturing of the public institutions of textuality) were rewritten as indices of moral disposition. This rewriting transpired within a scheme that set out the ways of reading and the dispositions expected of each social class. In the first decades of the nineteenth century, Wordsworth's prefaces and Coleridge's essays testified frequently to this need to make distinctions and safeguard distinction. Their writings exemplify how in the critical discourse of the period the consumption done by *some* readers was sanitized and rewritten as imaginative desire. At the same time they show how this critical discourse was haunted by the figure of "the other reader." Wordsworth's preface to the *Lyrical Ballads* drives a wedge between the meaning-making work of reception, on one hand, and the brute appetites of consumption, on the other (it is the "craving for gross and violent stimulants" that impels other readers to the circulating library). Coleridge matches the preface with testy comments on addict-readers who won't read closely or deeply, who can't tell the difference between deep works of genius and the flimsy works churned out by a hyperactive press. When he claims that the difference between those textual categories would elude the "mass of readers," even though it is not less than that "between an egg and an egg-shell," the gulf that the modernist movement and the literature classroom would establish between aesthetic subjects and the subjects of mass culture is easy to foresee.[55]

Nonetheless, even as we link character reading to the romantic-era formation of class awareness, we should also acknowledge the volatility of the cultural categories generated by these acts of audience-making and -regulating and the difficulties that attended these efforts to correlate symbolic capital and social worth. This is not to deny that, for some—the new readers whom reviewers of the period slighted with their references to the "millinery misses and aspiring apprentices of our country towns"[56]—the poets' "classing" of readers must have made the injuries of social class hurt more. To a degree, that was the poets' point. But the scheme that differentiates good readers from bad, or Coleridge's eggs (round characters with interiority?) from Coleridge's eggshells, was, for a start, a scheme that could be deployed indiscriminately to articulate *both* the differences ordering a nascent class society *and* the more tenuous differences dividing fragments of Britain's power bloc and so dividing the culture of the professions from the culture of fashionable beaux and bucks, dividing merchant-nabobs from gentry and also—in some attempts to legislate reading—dividing men from women. This suggests the difficulty of assigning a sociological referent to that other reader whose superficiality haunts the proper reader's encounter with the depths of characters and with her self. The other reader is not simply the bearer of social difference but is a complex fantasy, produced out of the ambivalent attempt to exclude from the domestic scene of reading the traces of the marketplace and of the individual's implication in the promiscuous comminglings of commodity exchange. As one might expect, misreading was cast in the reviews, as in the novels that dropped hints about proper reading, as the failure to read through the book's materiality to the meaning within. Bad readers judged books by their covers; they got hung up on the commodifiable body of the text. What is notable, though, is the sexual charge to this discourse's renditions of print, paper, and ink. The objects singled out for their aphrodisiac effects on the other reader were "beautiful type," "paper wire-wove and hot-pressed," and the assault on the book's uncut pages with a "long, smooth, white paper-knife."[57] Such a language of fetishism reveals how the making of English reading audiences also unfolded at the level of the fantasy life of the English reader.

Along these lines, it is good to keep in mind that the very readers interpellated by the critical rhetoric about rereading and close reading—readers who were *meant* to view their interpretive activity as a support for self-invigilation and meant to find in the complexities of the literary character a site of "exercise" and discipline, where social norms would surface as personal pleasures—could also experience their reading as a support for transgression. Definitions of good reading also formalize new possibilities for misbehavior: textual slumming. To glimpse this aspect of our own techniques of self-culture, we have only to consider how "page-turners" are the object of semisecret rites of hedonism within the subculture of late-twentieth-century literature professors (a group who in other guises profess the Wordsworthian creed of "looking steadily" at one's object).[58] Our academic subculture, after all, can boast both good and bad ways of *re*reading. When I have a hard day, and decide to reread *Jane Eyre* and make myself cry, my motive in returning to Jane is not to continue my pursuit of the hidden meanings lodged in the character or my pursuit of the unconscious structure of the text. Under such conditions, I don't take pleasure in repetition with a difference; I take pleasure in repetition without it.

There is no historical record of such insubordination by the proper readers of the Regency, at least none that can be compared with the reveries over round characters: that particular reading practice can easily, as current pedagogic procedures indicate, be converted into a way of writing. Nonetheless, evidence of the props for bad reading exists. Auxiliary stacks of twentieth-century libraries are jam-packed with annuals and forget-me-nots, characteristic sketches of the picturesque lower orders, anthologies of remarkable characters, microcosms of the city such as Pierce Egan's *Life in London*, physiologies, and physiognomies—exhibitionary forms that rendered characters, classes, locales, and bodies adamantly visible. That literature came to organize the field of writing in this era has much to do with the boom affecting these other modes, which constituted in a sense the limit-case that enabled literature's self-recognition. *They* typified texts eliciting a reading that was an act of the body, where literature elicited reading that was an act of the mind. Their high production values and conspicuous costliness suggest, however, that these ancestors of the coffee-table book addressed the same public that sought to make literature its exclusive property and to meet deep characters as old friends. In ways I will examine more fully in the conclusion, we are concerned with the recto and verso of the same configuration of character reading.

VEILED AND FORWARD BEAUTIES: TASTE AND WOMEN'S FICTION

Something like this ambivalence in the constitution of literature—manifested as discriminating initiates were invited to navigate reading practices marked as other, as they engaged with literature's representations of contrary forms of writing—inflects the construction of femininities within women's fiction of the turn of the nineteenth century. To figures such as Coleridge, the conjunction "women-and-fiction" looked like the worst product of the spread of literacy and luxury consumption: "a whole field of writing and reading outside critical order and literary control."[59] Women's fiction was not (yet) romantic literature. But notwithstanding the feminine novel's status as critical outsider (already in Coleridge's lifetime being amended by the welcome reviewers extended to the "new style of novels"), there are close connections between, on the one hand, the techniques for accrediting one's literacy and producing literary value that I have associated with the changes in character and, on the other, female novel reading, novel writing, and heroines with deep souls. To suggest these links, I want to return briefly to William Richardson's essay on Hamlet.

When Richardson refers to the "veiled beauties" who differ from "obtrusive" and "forward beauties," the language he uses to designate depth and the superficiality providing a foil to depth sounds like language from a novel. He could be echoing one of the many women's fictions that prescribed the tricky terms for female visibility and female modesty. We could be reading a passage in which a narrator makes an example of the fashion maven who crosses the line between being dressed and being overdressed.

The resemblance is not surprising. If we associate the emergence of the character's inner life as a recognizable kind of fictional content with the domestication of cognition that cast education as the process of "learning to stay at home"—and with the development of techniques of self-culture that hinged on the difference between conspicuous and inconspicuous meanings—it makes sense that this depth should have been understood in feminine terms. Heroines, whose stories end when they find a home or learn to stay in one, were center-stage in novels of the turn of the nineteenth century. Veiled beauties abounded. Pioneers of one of the novel's chief resources for depth effects, the free indirect discourse that seems to voice the character's mental life, it was women novelists who were in the forefront in writing to the period's new techniques of reading.[60] The character system that structured many of their novels was one of the chief mechanisms by which inner meaning became recognizable and desirable. The manner in which the novelists divided attention between reticent heroines and forward, overdressed beauties helped to reorganize romantic-period reading as an experience in exercising personal preferences—in choosing not only among texts, but also among characters and ways of regarding them. And it is women readers who have had perhaps the most compelling reasons for enthusiastic participation in these new reading relations, which are centered on the things about the reticent heroine that the reader knows but the other characters do not and cannot. (Jane Austen positions her reader in this manner, for instance, when she arranges in her third volume for Elizabeth Bennet's discovery of her desire to occur without her father or sister or aunt being aware of her transformation. Only the reader knows how Elizabeth suffers in silence when her father jokes about the rumors that identify Mr. Darcy as his future son-in-law, because only the reader knows that Elizabeth wants the gossip to be true.)[61] Taking part in a reading situation in which true knowledge of character was cast as personalized, intimate knowledge, inaccessible to an outside world, women readers could enjoy the idea that they were turning necessity into a virtue. They were turning their social deprivation, their exclusion from many forms of public discourse and their full-time experience of the secrecy and subterfuge of family life, into aesthetic advantage.

The opacities of character and the pleasurable difficulties of character reading had been signaled in the Shakespearean character appreciations when Falstaff and Hamlet were recast as, above all else, the victims of others' misunderstanding. "Nay," Coleridge wrote of Hamlet, "even the character sees himself through the medium of his character and not exactly as he is."[62] In many of the novels contemporary with the character appreciations, such opacities and difficulties converge on disguised, disfigured, or undersized female bodies. In the female Gothic fiction of the 1790s, as in the fiction of "the Burney school," the heroine is misunderstood by everyone but the reader, whose powers of discrimination are thus flatteringly ratified. Such a heroine's story is often one in which the relation between the visible and the knowable is confounded. A heroine doesn't look right. Her public appearances, too often with the wrong people or in the wrong places, regularly misrepresent the reality of her motives and morals. Certainly, the various victims of propriety and of prejudice who populate works such as Regina Maria Roche's *Children of the Abbey* (1796) cannot be described as psychologically complex; the historical point is, instead, that romantic-period women writers developed the particular form of reading relations that made the postulate of depth possible and necessary. They had the forms for interiority.[63] Discriminating readers of that fiction, those who are privy to the novel's true text of free indirect discourse and who share a space of sensibility with the heroine, quickly learn to discredit as mere appearance the appearances that the supporting characters see when they look at her. Discriminating readers will accept the invitation to sympathy the text tenders each time it asks them to contrast their powers of discernment with those of the misjudging characters within the fiction, and as they do so they will locate the true meaning of the person beneath the surface, in an indescribable soul.

As the novels of the turn of the nineteenth century established the inevitable unknownness of female identities in a repressive social world, and as they pitted psychology against society, they established their feminist interest. Yet in drawing up divisions distinguishing one sort of interpretive identity from another, one constituency of readers from another, this style of novel also played to the status insecurities of an upwardly mobilizing subject. A class strategy for negotiating the experience of the expanded and democratized book market conditions how women's fiction cast the shapes of female subjectivity.

With similar results, chronicles of heroines' "entrance into the world"—initiated by either their first ball or (in Gothic depictions of the terrors of sociability) their first abduction—frequently became occasions for writing off heroines' looks. As they assembled this plot of socialization, novelists often eliminated the props that conferred social visibility and readability on the person: they made it impossible for their female protagonist to use her family name, or they put her at the mercy of slanderers. Invariably, when we are concerned with Frances Burney's and Charlotte Smith's social nobody heroines or with Gothic orphans such as Radcliffe's Adeline or Eliza Parsons' Matilda (heroine of the 1793 *The Castle of Wolfenbach*), the rumors of their obscure parentage are in the end converted into proofs of irreproachable pedigree. But for most of their stories these heroines have nothing but their subjectivity to entitle them. However menaced, the selfhood of such a heroine appears all the more deep and dense with individuality *because* of the embarrassments of her situation and her estrangement from the courtship plot. Unable to communicate the truth of who she is, in limbo accordingly as to whose she will be, she manages (though only for a while) to have character, and have it without partaking of any form of partitive identity.

Profundity of character was in this context, I am suggesting, an effect produced by a heroine's difficulties with image management. It was produced when circumstances "wrapped" her in "mystery" or forced her to "wear the appearance of infamy" (*Northanger Abbey*'s way of describing Catherine Morland's fate once she becomes a heroine);[64] alternately, it was produced as the novelist concealed or marred her heroine's face. Radcliffe's *The Italian* (1797) begins with the hero's curiosity about the countenance hidden beneath the heroine's veil. Thanks to a timely gust of wind, Vivaldi's curiosity is soon satisfied, but this inauguration of the romance plot serves only to underscore the consistent insufficiency of vision in this novel. Vision fails to provide the ground for meaning or identity. The text of appearances in *The Italian* is hyperlegible—we are told about the "characters"—of sadness or demoniac evil—"stamped" on characters' brows, and we meet a man "who had 'villain' engraved in every line of his face"—but it is also bizarrely inconsequential.[65] Inside the convents in which the heroine Ellena is confined, as in the dungeons of the Inquisition, where Vivaldi is imprisoned, whenever nuns remove their veils or monks lower the cowls that shroud their faces, the action does

not *unwrap* the mystery that envelops them. For the witnesses to these unveil-
ings, the lineaments that are revealed hold no significance.[66] Radcliffe's play
with anagnorisis makes the character's face a site where she uncouples knowing from seeing and legibility from visibility. The third chapter of Burney's
The Wanderer (1814) supplies another version of this uncoupling. The heroine,
who has been dwelling incognito among the other characters, strips off the
bandages that have to this point concealed her features. Her unmasking does
not reveal the birthmark or scar that those who behold her anticipate. The
onlookers expect, in fact, one of those telltale tokens from recognition plots
and family romances—something to hide. But instead, what shows when the
Wanderer's face shows is nothing at all.[67]

The enterprise of writing off the heroine's looks can be literal as well as
figurative. When a heroine's body is presented to view for the first time it
is often shown as marred—by, for example, the languor that alters Laura
Montreville's gait as she leaves her mother's sickbed on the first page of Mary
Brunton's *Self-Control* (1811)—or otherwise different from itself—Roche
opens *The Children of the Abbey* by drawing attention to what is on the verge
of disappearing, writing that the luster of Amanda Fitzalan's eyes is "fled"
and the "rose upon her cheek" is "pale."[68] Similarly, in Austen's *Persuasion*
(1818), what shows in Anne Elliot's "ruins" of a face is the disappearance of
what once was visible; what marks Anne's countenance is a curtailment of
the apparent. Almost by definition a heroine's beauty is "faded." In Susan
Ferrier's *The Inheritance* (1824), the heroine's looks acquire "a character of still
deeper interest" because their "brilliancy" has been "dimmed by the blight
which had fallen upon her."[69] If a rounded character promises a fund of
meanings, one infinitely generative of second looks and speculation, that
promise is made in romantic-period fiction by a seemingly self-effacing heroine, modest-looking, plainly dressed, someone who *looks* as though she were
fast dwindling into invisibility and *in*significance.

One might suppose that the premise that underwrites turn-of-the-
nineteenth-century characterization is that declarative sentences do not suit
a heroine: they say too much. When the hero of *The Children of the Abbey*
confronts Amanda Fitzalan with " 'proofs' " of her sexual guilt, she both describes herself as bearing " 'the appearance and stigma' " of crime and insists,
nonetheless, on the truth of her innocence. Such truth is different in kind
from truths that are available to public apprehension. That much is indicated
by Lord Mortimer's response, in which he spells out the crucial point about

these novels' epistemology of inner life: " 'You would almost convince me against the evidence of my own senses.' "[70]

When Roche first describes Amanda—when she asserts that although "sorrow has faded her vivid bloom," Amanda is therefore, "if less dazzling to the eye, more affecting to the heart," and when she proposes that "hers was that interesting face and figure which had power to fix the wandering eye, and change the gaze of admiration into the throb of sensibility"—she avoids direct statements. Instead she proceeds by first articulating and then setting aside alternate modes of embodiment and modes of observing a body. Roche's description requisitions a foil for the heroine, in the absence at this early stage in the narrative of any minor characters who might fulfill that function. A heroine's retiring, deep femininity is meaningful only in relation to femininities constructed according to other specifications, and she is usually presented alongside a supporting character who, in contrast to the perpetually misrecognized heroine, really *is* just another pretty face—someone who exists for the "sole purpose . . . of catching the eye and captivating the sense," to cite the damning description of one such character in Susan Ferrier's *Marriage* (1814). Even if heroines do not avoid making an appearance altogether they avoid "the appearance of finery," a maxim that will be familiar to anyone who reads more than one novel by Regina Maria Roche. Finery, the trashier the better, is for a heroine's foil. When Amanda Fitzalan attends a ball, her attire, "a robe of pale white lutestring [with] no appearance of finery," is pointedly contrasted to the "painted tiffany" and "trains of at least two yards" donned by other women of showier but tasteless charms.[71] By 1790, the character system dividing the showy from the plain, first impressions from second looks, was already well enough ensconced in the culture of the novel to have been wickedly parodied by a teenaged Jane Austen in "Frederic and Elfrida: A Novel." Visiting some recent additions to their neighborhood, and shown into the Fitzroys' drawing room, Elfrida and her companions are instantly "struck with the engaging Exterior and beautifull outside of Jezalinda":

> [B]ut e'er they had been many minutes seated, the Wit and Charms which shone resplendent in the conversation of the amiable Rebecca, enchanted them so much that they all with one accord jumped up and exclaimed.
> "Lovely and too charming Fair one, notwithstanding your forbidding Squint, your greasy tresses and your swelling Back, which are more

frightfull than imagination can paint or pen describe, I cannot refrain from expressing my raptures, at the engaging Qualities of your Mind, which so amply atone for the Horror, with which your first appearance must ever inspire the unwary visitor."[72]

In *Woman; or, Ida of Athens* (1809), Lady Morgan's novel promoting the cause of Greek liberation, the role of the woman whose "first appearance" *does* impress is assigned to a Turkish character named Jumeli. Even Jumeli's way of wearing her veil is an element to be installed in the binary opposition that divides being and looking between the heroine and her foil. When Jumeli and Ida present themselves at a festival, Jumeli "coquettishly let fall her veil, and affected a confusion that resembled nothing less than modesty; for her wandering eye refused its testimony to her blushing cheek. Ida wore no veil, but the always chaste and delicate pudicity of her look shed over her retiring graces the air of a consecrated vestal!" Jumeli's efforts to prevent her body from showing betoken her status as a character who is all body and mere show. In this manner, true womanliness—for Morgan, Greece is where "the character of woman" may be observed in "its natural state"—is cast as an identity that exceeds the plane of visible information.[73] Flawed womanliness is associated with the very material of signification and publicity: for a heroine's foil, character is not a substance but a means of appearance. Jumeli's false modesty helps to secure the claims on interiority Morgan makes on behalf of her heroine. Roche, through the idiom of understatement that tells us how Amanda *once* appeared and how she does *not* look, manages to place her heroine in a space beyond description. She makes Amanda's body into a figure for how character eludes definite characterization. In similar fashion, Morgan suggests in *Ida of Athens* that the best veil, the best barrier to the body's visibility, is one that itself does not appear.

The necessary part that figures such as Jumeli play in this character system suggests how the new modes of reading and writing that ushered in round characters were defined through representations of the residual categories—the category of patently significant ("flat") characters, as well as the category of superficial readers who could be counted on to overvalue those characters.[74] As literacy was redefined at the turn of the century, and as literary value came to be located in a dependably discreet subtext of meaning, the flatness of characters lost the social, horizontal complexity it had possessed in the characteristic writing of the mid-eighteenth century. Reclassified, this complexity became a superficiality that was irrelevant to interpretation.[75] This reclassification transpired in part through the mobilization of a hierarchical opposition between the ornamental and the essential—a distinction that often divides a popular aesthetic from the "taste" founded on the refusal of sensual pleasure. The disqualified idiom of characterizing was written out of significance by being written into the feminized semantic domain of the superfluous detail, the ornament, and the accessory. Thus the other reader figures in reviews as someone who tastelessly cruises the text searching for "minute descriptions" of "elegant drapery," turning characters into fashion plates. In a similar way, in taking an indecorous interest in the pattern of her bonnet or the price she pays for muslin, the secondary characters of women's fiction seem to stall the heroine's narrative. They put the inside story on hold as they force her body into the text.[76] When, as the compiler of *Blackwood's Novelist's Library*, Walter Scott assembled a canon meant to equip the new style of novel with a history, he included *Clarissa* but, envisioning a defeminization that would make the book less appealing for the wrong readers, he expressed the hope that someone might work on cutting Richardson's "trivial details of dresses and decorations, which relish . . . of . . . mantua-makers' shops."[77]

When the romantic-period novel of manners introduces the heroine's foil, that fashion maven who sports "painted tiffany," it invites readers to implement the piecemeal procedures that were elicited by the blazons and the verbal portraits of the seventeenth-century character book. Such procedures had been the norm when readers officially read for detached episodes and discrete passages—for "images" or "pictures" or "little touches of nature." In the mid-eighteenth century, reading had been a matter of disassembling characters and texts into catalogs of so-called beauties and blemishes: a telling phrase in its linkage of composition and cosmetology and in its implication that semantic wealth is located on and not beneath the face of the page. (The narrator of *Tom Jones* describes aesthetic judgment as a matter of balancing beauties—which should, "more in Number, shine"—against faults: "All Beauty of Character, as well as of Countenance, and indeed of every Thing human is to be tried in this manner.") By contrast, after the turn of the nineteenth century, the moral fitness of the reader who was fixated on parts, the "beauty-monger" who could manage only "little snatches of ornamental reading," was deplored; so was the unofficial literacy of the laboring poor, whose schooling was haphazard and whose reading, often confined to the moments when they paused from work or paused before a bookstore window, was fragmentary and improvisatory.[78] In *Marriage*, Susan Ferrier goes out of her way to portray the heroine's mother, that woman educated for the sole purpose of "catching the eye, and captivating the sense," as an improper reader, someone who has no compunction about scrambling the volumes of circulating-library novels and reading them out of sequence.[79]

In some measure, reading in parts, reading distracted by superfluous details, was as integral a component of the novel's production of inner meaning as the heroine's foil who elicited such reading. To experience what the close reading of a subjectivity profligate with meaning was necessitated experiencing what it wasn't.

INCONSPICUOUS CONSUMPTION

The stories of progress that have been assembled since the nineteenth century have presented the "inward turn" taken by the new style of novels as a reconstitution of characterization that liberated the real meanings of the individual. In this chapter I have suggested, however, that, instead of being considered according to criteria grounded in a concept of realistic representation, the effect of psychological verisimilitude might be considered a kind of fictional content that became legible only when certain techniques of self were attached to the pleasures of reading and consumption and when these techniques were redeployed in a reshaped, expanded book market. The changes in characterizing that have been narrated through a plot of emancipation could, furthermore, just as usefully be described in terms of a struggle between signifying practices. From one angle this struggle appears as a never wholly achieved *narrowing* of the concept of the fictional character. The literary status of novels, their distinction from mass entertainment, hinges on that circumscription of possibilities according to which entry into the minds of characters is *the* activity that defines "the" novel. But such a narrowing is not equivalent to (although it can be redefined as) a return to intrinsic truth, a return that makes the novel or the character more like itself. This is not the fundamentally peaceful process that is at issue when Ian Watt talks about how nineteenth-century characterizing realizes the potential latent in the novel form. Despite what the received historiography of characterization tells us, the transition from one set of norms for character writing and reading to the other is not to be understood as a completed, coherent process. The traces of old canons of representation unsettle the new configuration of character. The staging of misreading that underwrites the novel reader's sense of distinction makes it impossible to grasp the deep reading of a heroine's complexities in isolation from the social forms in which people become subjects of and subject to power. If one grants these premises, one can begin to see turn-of-the-nineteenth-century literary culture as ambivalent and different from itself, and so available to alternative, postpsychological uses.

William Hazlitt implicitly took issue with other people's accounts of the "new style of novels" when he proposed in 1815 that the breakthrough in novels' representation of persons had occurred in the reign of George II, a half-century before the genre fell into decline in the hands of the women novelists who were popular in Hazlitt's own day. Nonetheless, Hazlitt shared other reviewers' presuppositions about what the criterion for literary progress might be—as is evinced in his assertion that by the mid-eighteenth century "[i]t was found high time that the people should be represented in books as well as in Parliament." In concluding this chapter, I want to show how the conflict edited out by stories organized by "development" becomes visible if we look at another story about the "progress . . . made in taste and elegance" that Hazlitt promoted three years after "Standard Novels and Romances." In 1818 Hazlitt's subject was clothing, not character:

> A very striking change has . . . taken place . . . [T]he monstrous pretensions to distinctions in dress have dwindled away by tacit consent, and the simplest and most graceful have been in the same request with all classes. The ideas of natural equality and the Manchester steam-engines together have, like a double battery, levelled the high towers and artificial structures of fashion in dress. . . . It would be ridiculous . . . for the courtier to take the wall of the citizen, without having a sword by his side to maintain his right of precedence; and, from the stricter notions that have prevailed of a man's merit and identity, a cane dangling from his arm is the greatest extension of his figure that can be allowed to the modern *petit-maître*.[80]

Hazlitt relays a story about the return to nature that succeeds an era of "monstrous" pretension and about the collapse of the classificatory system that formerly differentiated and separated men from each other. In its confidence that history was progressive, this story of the overthrow of the dictatorship of fashion resembles and reinforces similar turn-of-the-nineteenth-century narratives about romantic poetry's recovery of humanity's authentic voice or about the refinement of characterizing.

The triumphal narrative of fashion to which Hazlitt's essay contributes is usually recounted like this. Over the last decades of the eighteenth century, refined Englishmen renounced the rainbow assortment of satins, silks, and laces that had hitherto supplied them with flowered waistcoats, shirtsleeves and collars frothing with ruffles, and coats edged with braid and cut in expan-

159

sive proportions to ensure that the fabric would drape with the wearer's movements. Leaving off dressing up, the better sort of Englishman began to dress down. Adopting a look of buttoned-down earnestness, the gentleman garbed himself in coats and breeches of dark wool, cut close to the body as if his tailor had economized on cloth. He gave up his wig and stopped powdering his hair; he replaced shoe buckles with utilitarian shoelaces. The dress of choice became an abstraction of dress: the prototype for the soberly colored business suit of the twentieth century.

In *The Psychology of Clothes* (1930) J. C. Flugel called this change of wardrobe the Great Masculine Renunciation. What gentlemen renounced through this fashion statement was self-display: Beau Brummel advised would-be emulators that "[i]f John Bull turns round to look after you you are not well dressed." The gentility of the protagonist of mid-eighteenth-century characteristic writing was a function of how much he saw in the course of his peregrinations across the social order. At the turn of the nineteenth century, however, the gentleman came to be defined more by his refusal to be remarkable than by the opportunities for overseeing that this inconspicuousness facilitated.[81]

There is a portrait of Sir Brooke Boothby, painted by Joseph Wright of Derby in 1781, that outlines in a preliminary way the ideological parameters of this change in male apparel. The volume of Rousseau that Wright put in the hands of his sitter proclaims the latter's putative commitment to a civility that would be faithful to nature. That political message is doubled by the drably colored woolen suit, everyday working dress rather than court dress, that identifies Boothby (despite his lounging posture) as an agrarian capitalist who has work to do. For many historians of costume, the portrait records the displacement of a social semantics in which extravagant finery had provided legible signifiers of social rank. Since Hazlitt's era the elimination of that sartorial sumptuousness has been read as a sign of progress. This is because in its uniformity, "serving to integrate not only male members of the same class, but male members of different classes," menswear ostensibly reveals men as they really, naturally, are—equal.[82] As this narrative of progress maintains, men were, when thus reclothed, free to deal with each other as individuals. (What Manchester engines and ideas of equality meant, by contrast, for the clothing customs and social relations of *women* has not become a subject for the clichés of costume history to nearly the same extent.)[83] Thus, in France, where the project of sartorial leveling was explicitly connected to revolutionary politics and was carried out with an Anglophiliac inflection, conservatives were enraged as the overcoat became a "must": they saw in this shapeless garment that concealed the clothing and body beneath it "the ne plus ultra of egalitarian clothing—a veritable uniform for the phalanstery."[84]

The specter of men in uniform may have suggested Fourierist socialism to some, but the gentleman's new clothes were just as often construed as a means of emptying out prior systems of classification and class and so as a means of articulating an individuality that was utterly antecedent to social forms. Turn-of-the-nineteenth-century fiction often assembles an analogous story about personal meaning in which, as the example of the misrecognized, veiled, nameless heroine indicates, character can only legitimately be evaluated in itself. The truth of character in novels such as *The Wanderer* or *Persuasion* is only apprehensible apart from the social codes that misrepresent it and apart from the extraneous decor of the body's looks. The reformed gentlemanly body, purified by the Great Masculine Renunciation, is also meant to be complete in itself. This body of blank surfaces does not owe its meanings to a code of appearances that correlates ornament with social rank. It sets up shop independent of those fetishistic extensions of the figure that (as Hazlitt implies) had hitherto been supplied by the cane or periwig or the ruffle that dangled from a lordling's shirtsleeve.

As I have implied, however, there is a problem with this story about progress and the decline of the "artificial structures of fashion in dress." The same problem afflicts the story of literary progress that casts nineteenth-century fiction as the site for realism's long-delayed encounter with the individual's inner life. Both stories make us forget that these two avatars of a rising individualism—the round character and the gentleman who had dissociated himself from the body language of the ancien régime—were the effects of networks of social relations. Those narratives take the effects of intrinsicality and integrity out of history. They pass over the extrinsic conditions for the creation of those effects. The historical effectivity of the business suit, the leverage it offers me in thinking about individuality as a social practice, does not consist in the way that its unremarkability underscores Marx's point about the contentlessness of the individual who orders classical political thought. It consists in the fact that these clothes only *apparently* stopped speaking about class—they only stopped speaking about class *apparently*.

The plain style had in fact been an option for the English country gentleman since the late seventeenth century, a means for him to bear witness to his civic virtue. The innovation of the turn of the nineteenth century was, first, the new prestige that was accorded to custom-tailoring as English tailors exploited the pliability of woolen cloth and as they made fit the hallmark of style, and, second, that with the tailors' complicity, men's apparel became less a medium through which the individual's public appearances could take a recognizable and legible form and more an idiom in which secrets could be both kept and half-betrayed. What was kept secret was the knowledge that the triumph of the harmonizing, homogenizing business suit in the late eighteenth century mandated not a renunciation of social difference but, more precisely, a renunciation of graphic, overstated difference.

At the moment when the "real" meanings of character came to adhere in inside stories that were presented as the exclusive property of the discerning few, the Great Masculine Renunciation likewise reordered the articulation of difference. This reform turned articulation inside out. It transposed rather than erased the sartorial markers of social stratification. It shifted them from the ornamented façade of the aristocrat's clothes—clothes that in the mid-century had been constructed as if for the stage, to dazzle but not to bear close scrutiny—to insides of costly construction.[85] The signs of social hierarchy were reinscribed in interior decorating, as it were: in underclothing, in finely stitched and sometimes splendidly colored linings, or in extra buttons positioned demurely out of sight on the inside of a cuff. "One could always recognize gentlemanly dress because the buttons on the sleeves of a gentleman's coat actually buttoned and unbuttoned, while one recognized gentlemanly behaviour in his keeping the buttons scrupulously fastened, so that his sleeves never called attention to this fact." The gentleman's mode of knotting his cravat—his engagement in a quasi-spiritual exercise in which a bit of white cloth that anyone could own was magically transformed as it was submitted to the gentleman's individuality—was another such elusive marker of distinction.[86]

Stripped of his former opulence, the gentleman continued to derive support for his narcissism from the fact that only those who had clothing of equal price and commanded an equivalent amount of leisure could properly appreciate the little extras that distinguished his dress. Where well-dressed gentlemen were concerned, it took one to know one. As I have argued, a comparable epistemological demand is crucial to psychological fiction's presentation of deep characters. And psychological fiction and the reading relations that underwrite it were also sites for a comparable politics of fine distinctions and inside stories. Anne Thackeray Ritchie wrote in 1883 of how Jane Austen and Maria Edgeworth made a "simple discovery, that of reality, that of speaking from the heart" and how they thereby reinvented the experience of novel reading and made it an encounter with "new selves." The story Ritchie tells about how reading had become a practice of the self could also relate how the self produced in that transaction occupied a particular social space—one that was defined just as much by what and whom it sought to exclude.[87]

☞ F O U R ☜

Agoraphobia and Interiority
in Frances Burney's Fiction

In the liveliest London streets, the shops press one against the other, shops which flaunt behind their hollow eyes of glass all the riches of the world, Indian cashmeres, American revolvers, Chinese porcelains, French corsets, Russian furs and tropical spices; but all these things promising the pleasures of the world bear those deadly white labels on their fronts on which are engraved arabic numerals with laconic characters—£, s, d (pound sterling, shilling, pence). This is the image of commodities as they appear in circulation.

—Karl Marx, *Zur Kritik der politischen Ökonomie*

During tea, a conversation was commenced upon the times, fashions, and public places. . . . It began by Sir Clement's enquiring of Miss Mirvan and of me if the Pantheon had answered our expectations.

We both readily agreed that it had greatly exceeded them.

"Ay, to be sure," said the Captain, . . . "Whatever's the fashion, they must like of course;—or else I'd be bound for it they'd own, that there never was such a dull place as this here invented."

"And has, then, this building," said Lord Orville, "no merit that may serve to lessen your censure? Will not your eye, Sir, speak something in its favour?"

"Eye," cried the Lord, (I don't know his name,) "and is there any eye here, that can find any pleasure in looking at dead walls or statues, when such heavenly living objects as I now see demand all their admiration?"

"O, certainly," said Lord Orville, "the lifeless symmetry of architecture, however beautiful the design and proportion, no man would be so mad as to put in competition with the animated charms of nature: but when, as to-night, the eye may be regaled at the same time, and in one view, with all the excellence of art, and all the perfection of nature, I cannot think that either suffer by being seen together." . . .

"Aye, aye," cried the Captain, "you may talk what you will of your eye here, and your eye there, and, for the matter of that, to be sure you have two,—but

164

we all know they both squint one way. . . . I should be glad to know what you
can see in e'er a face among them that's worth half a guinea for the sight."
—Frances Burney, *Evelina*

FASHION VICTIMS

When Frances Burney dispatches her heroine to London's Pantheon, a prime
tourist attraction of the 1770s and 1780s, and when she positions Evelina
against the backdrop formed by the building's statues of gods and goddesses,
she puts her heroine's selfhood at risk. A prescient commentator on the emergence of a culture of consumption in Britain, and like the builders of the
Pantheon someone who capitalized on that emergence, Burney habitually
depicts the scene of consumption as one in which things and individuals
(especially female individuals) seem to change places. In such a scene objects
become animated—in Cox's Museum, featured in an earlier episode of *Evelina* (1778), musical instruments play themselves, and clockwork birds are
set singing.[1] People for their part assume the characteristics of objects of
consumption: commodities' hypervisibility, their abstract comparability
through the medium of money, and, by extension, their asubjectivity. The
fops and fine ladies of Burney's fiction may enter public places as sightseers
and consumers, but the goal of such an exercise of agency is the erasure of
agency in conspicuousness. The fop Mr. Lovel puts himself to considerable
expense to display his fashionable body at the theater (rather than *watch* the
play, rather than *do* anything), because if he goes out of sight he will no longer
exist: " '[I]t costs you five shillings a night, just to shew that you're alive' "
(80). At moments in Burney's narratives it appears that such objectification
will also be the fate of her heroines. In these narratives, which recount how
a heroine claims her identity, the ballroom is often where she comes to know
her heart, but the codes of politeness regulating that site allocate the signs
of personhood as if they were a scarce resource. In the ballroom, the attributes of motion and stillness that normally distinguish individuals from things
are divided along gendered lines. Waiting for dancing partners and obliged
to accept the first who ask, the polite young ladies take on the characteristics
of commodities, which, Marxist philosopher Alfred Sohn-Rethel observes,
"are under the spell of one activity only, to change owners": "[T]hey stand
there [in the marketplace and shop windows] waiting to be sold."[2] In the
meantime, as Evelina reports, the polite young gentlemen "pass and repass,
look[ing] as if they thought we were quite at their disposal"; "they [saunter]

about, in a careless indolent manner, as if with a view to keep us in suspense" (28).

In the passage in which Evelina chronicles how she and Miss Mirvan "did" the Pantheon, *their* activity is conspicuous in its absence. The trope of personification that is deployed by the gentlemen they encounter at the Pantheon, a trope permitting "eyes" to "speak" and to "find pleasure," underscores the silence and depersonalization of the female persons who listen in on this exercise in connoisseurship (104). In the act of comparing "the lifeless symmetry of architecture" with "the animated charms of nature," Lord Orville aligns rather than distinguishes the lifeless and the living. One may be more valuable than the other to the connoisseur because its appearance has more of the *lifelike* about it, but both the woman and the Pantheon are sights.

This scene of fashionable consumption outlines the manner in which heroines' public appearances and social exchanges are presented throughout Burney's fiction. Those occasions invariably render the woman conspicuous only to make the "real" woman disappear. They entail an experience of excessive embodiment, of being misrepresented as someone who is all body. Simultaneously, they entail an experience of the abstraction that Marx details when he tells of how the distinguishing attributes of furs, cashmeres, and corsets, the individuating differences that identify things, disappear behind the "image of commodities as they appear in circulation" and behind the common measure of the money form. To enter into the world is to be confounded with the body's representations—with what one looks like from outside. It is, furthermore, to be so thoroughly inscribed by the marketplace's mandates that the relationship between the "laconic characters" that put one's worth on paper and any other sort of character becomes tautological. These are the agoraphobic theorems illustrated by the scene of fashionable consumption.

Such warnings sound familiar for a reason. The passages demonstrating persons' reduction to commodified still lifes also impart an often-repeated lesson about the value that we should accord to the *novelistic* presentation of personhood. While staging a scene of reification, the text defines its enterprise as that of supplying a reanimating remedy to reification. Its recovery (more precisely, its production) of an inner life is also its claim to literary capital. In this passage from *Evelina*, others see the heroine as just another pretty face. They value her at "half a guinea for a sight." The readers whom this novel solicits look deeply and they value differently. For good readers, it is not so much that Evelina is silenced in the Pantheon episode, her self effaced

and her story turned into a still life. Instead, the contrast in Evelina's epistolary account between her verbatim quotation of the connoisseurs' discourse
and the reticent indirect discourse she uses to relay her own speech calls
attention to what she is not saying. The internal hierarchy of discourses
within the journal-novel creates the illusion of psychic resources in reserve.

The passages from *Evelina* that recount the merchandising of women actually perform an additional function, then: they also serve as passages of novelistic self-promotion. They remind readers of what fiction is for. I want to
argue that it is in dramatizing the reification attendant on a female character's public appearances and her social exchanges that the novel of manners
produces an inner consciousness that seems to operate independent of exchange relations. Rather than casting the objectification that attends appearances in the fashionable "world" as antithetical to the cause of female subjecthood, rather than opposing matter and mind and condemning the way
that the fashionable female body misrepresents the interior self, I want to
suggest how depictions of consumer society could function in the romantic
era as *the* literary venue for the production of a brave new world of female
interiority.

Few readers would dispute that Burney's marriage plots unfold in a marriage *market:* this is the manifest, not the latent, meaning of *Evelina* and the
novels succeeding it.[3] As a matter of course, Burney's fictions juxtapose erotic
desire with economic need and juxtapose the project of individual self-
definition with the "objective" account of persons generated as the market
orchestrates disparate determinations of value. This chapter is motivated,
however, by my sense that the handy label "marriage market" has discour-
aged interpretations of the way that Burney insistently arranges for those
ostensibly opposed terms, commodification and self-definition, to be brought
into relation. The text I will concentrate on for much of this chapter is Burney's most detailed investigation of her era's new retail culture and of the
confusions between shopping and courting this culture facilitates. In *Camilla,
or, A Picture of Youth* (1796), we encounter one of those romantic-era heroines,
introduced in my previous chapter, whose worth is forever being misesti-
mated by those who reckon in worldly terms. Camilla Tyrold is also a heroine
who is so identified with the marketplace, so intent on reproducing herself
in the image fashion mandates, that she literally shops until she drops. The
self-inflicted pain that Camilla incurs through her debts is hopelessly entan-
gled with the pain that the hero inflicts on her whenever he tells her she is
no longer herself. What *Camilla* suggests in its agoraphobia is the cooperative

relation that links the marketing of beautiful exteriors to fiction that privileges the invisible "wonders of the Heart" (7). *Camilla* suggests that the reductive logic that Burney's portrait of consumer culture critiques (the logic according to which women are reduced to their bodies, and characters are reduced to economic indicators) is not the cancelation of psychological complexity but simply the state of its operations.

The story of Burney's critical fortunes includes an agoraphobic element also. Within the *Oxford English Dictionary* it is a quotation from her diaries that illustrates the earliest use of the noun *shopping*. Feminist critics who have rehabilitated Burney's aesthetic reputation over the last decade have had to liberate the novelist from the reading that the lexicographers' use of the diaries indexes—one that made her a fixture inside the emporia of late Georgian England. Before critics reread Burney's fiction as anticipating Charlotte Brontë's examination of the subtexts of feminine subjectivity, and before we revalued it for pioneering the free indirect discourse that gives the novel reader access to the inner consciousness of character, Burney novels were stock in trade for readers of an antiquarian bent, who doted on the charming commodities and diversions—the visits to auctions, toy shops, and other commercial meccas—that they catalogued. Before she was prized, as in Margaret Doody's work, as the originator of a "new kind of mimesis, an imitation of the mind in flux," Burney had the dubious distinction of being, for early-twentieth-century chroniclers such as Austin Dobson and Constance Hill, the chief local colorist of the Georgian retail scene.[4] I propose that we challenge the assumption that makes these two depictions of Burney's enterprise appear antithetical to each other: the assumption that the psychological is one thing and the realm in which economic transactions take place is another. We can challenge it by apprehending interiority as an effect of public and social discourses. In particular, we can attend to how the very dynamic of individuation was modified as luxury consumption came to function as an occasion on which one made the self an element of reflection. So far, identifying the Frances Burney who gives consciousness a narrative has meant disregarding the Burney who describes the spectacle of consumption. Here I want to identify the relationship between those two constructs.

Returning to the epoch when Englishwomen first learned how to conduct themselves in shops will help to historicize the inner life that Burney gives to her heroine. It can also help to complicate the all-or-nothing terms that still come too quickly to hand when we consider women's fortunes in consumer society. Often, in contemporary critiques of consumerism, the self is conceptualized as a presocial, prediscursive entity located well outside the marketplace. Conversely, individuals who seek opportunities for self-production within the market are portrayed as consumer culture's unwitting products. They are ascribed bodies that re-present the market's meanings— a portrayal that effectively endorses advertisers' promise that clothes will make the woman. (In my epigraph, Captain Mirvan takes an analogous view of consumer society's female insiders when he expects Miss Mirvan's and Evelina's desire to mirror market values back to the market: " 'Whatever's the fashion, they must like of course' " [106].) The first part of this account, the part that concerns the subject, seems optimistically to assume that the market has a place and can be kept in it and that under some social arrangement that we have not yet attained, the individual will likewise be able to keep to herself. That optimism is belied by the thoroughgoing culturalism of the second part, in which we talk about the object and, with some regularity in feminist critiques, about woman as object of male exchange. Structured by a subject-object split, this consumer theory leaves us ill prepared to consider the historical mutations that Igor Kopytoff points to when he observes that "the conceptualized boundary of individualized persons and commoditized things is recent, and, culturally speaking, exceptional."[5] It leaves us unable to deal with the possibility that the late-eighteenth-century transformation of consumption patterns might actually have been accelerated as people began to insist on the radical disparities separating what the person is and what the market affords, as people learned to claim their subjecthood by turning down the commodity's invitation and demurring, "It's not me."

For similar reasons, it is only so helpful to use this consumer theory when we assess the device that Burney uses to foreground the incommensurability between what the heroine's self is and how her transactions in a consumer society make it appear: the vignette that makes the heroine vulnerable by positioning her as the sole animated being in a crowd of immobile things and of immobile people who, oversocialized, are becoming things. We need to ask whether Burney's readers might not have found in this way of writing character, this way of playing subjecthood against objecthood, resources for managing the newly intimate relations between their selves and commodities. As I shall argue in the next two sections, *Camilla* is less an exposé of women's objectification in a female flesh market than a guide to the peculiarly *double* logic of the culture of consumption: a logic that at one moment foregrounds the visible female body and at the next foregrounds a female self whose embodiment is suspended, who, by repeatedly making herself over, is (in the Wordsworthian terms of the period) "ever more about to be."

The scene of stilled life Burney stages and restages—where the heroine's subjectivity shares the limelight with the objects of her consumption—has had an influential afterlife in the aesthetic discourses of feminism. It informs these discourses' ways of speaking for an authentic selfhood. Think of Jane Eyre's uneasiness as she faces the trunks filled with the finery she will wear as Mrs. Rochester, "a person whom as yet I knew not." Or think of how Jane's earlier reluctance to visit silk warehouses and jewelers with Rochester and her discomfiture with those sessions of costume-fitting serve to certify her alienation from *any* socially scripted identity (" 'I will not be your English Céline Varens,' " she says). By virtue of its reinscription in *Jane Eyre,* the scene of reification in the Burney novel has provided feminist criticism with the imagery by which it recognizes itself. Studies such as *The Madwoman in the Attic* identify the mission of feminist fictions and criticism with the release of "the real [female] self" from the "immobilized" state to which a patriarchal system of society and of representation condemns it. Such characterizations of what feminist writing and reading does with the real self—rescue it from "objectification"—resemble Burney's description of the project of *Camilla,* which was, the novelist wrote, to put "*sketches of Character & morals*" into "*action.*"[6] In my last two sections, where my discussion of Burney's self-conscious treatment of "animation" in *Camilla* will suggest the equivocations that can be built into such a project, I want to comment on the fantasies of self-possession that underpin this definition of feminism's aesthetic mission. Making "objectification" the recurring reference point of feminist assessments of characterization may invite an overvaluation of private subjectivity. It may numb our sense of the claims of the social.[7] In my conclusion, keeping just this possibility in mind, I shall turn to Burney's presentation of the market in her last novel, *The Wanderer, or, Female Difficulties* (1814). I shall read it for something different: for another story about what it means to enter "the world" and for another use of character.

BURNEY'S SHOWROOMS

When things happen in *Camilla*—to any one of the many characters who enters into the world and embarks on her romantic career—that narratability is nearly always a function either of an increase or decrease in the woman's monetary worth or of an alteration in her appearance. In each of its subplots

Camilla rings the changes on the marriage-market maxim that a woman's face is her fortune. The interlinked fates of the protagonist, Camilla Tyrold, her younger sister, Eugenia, and her cousin Indiana Lynmere diagram how female faces and fortunes are substitutable objects belonging to a single system of currency. They demonstrate that those assets are incompatible (as are the desire for beauty and the desire for money) by making it axiomatic that if a woman has one she lacks the other. A summary of the early stages of the plot of *Camilla* will begin to clarify what bearing that axiom has on Burney's project of converting female objects into female characters.

On retiring to the Hampshire countryside and becoming acquainted with his brother's second daughter, Camilla (then ten years old), Sir Hugh Tyrold makes her his heiress. This decision about the disposal of the Tyrold fortune leaves Camilla's cousin, Indiana—an orphan and the baronet's ward—without prospects, but, appraising this ten-year-old ex-heiress's "already exquisite beauty" (19), Sir Hugh reassures himself that when Indiana comes of age she is sure to be looked on favorably by the eligible Edgar Mandelbert, the adolescent heir to the estate that borders on Sir Hugh's. Sir Hugh dislikes distinctions and likes happiness to be distributed in a fair and square way: his confidence in Indiana's attractions leads him to think that she and Camilla will end up equally fortunate. His attempts at calibrating individual and collective good (social engineering on a domestic scale) are nullified, however, by mishaps that occur during the festivities the baronet sponsors to proclaim those plans to the world. Despite the rumor that there is smallpox in the neighborhood, he begins the festivities by absent-mindedly taking the children to a country fair, initiating their careers as consumers. Then, on the party's return home, the giddiness that has so far characterized the baronet's conduct is made literal. Riding on one end of a seesaw that he has set up for the children, he is overcome with dizziness; he upsets the balance.

The consequences both of this accident and of the earlier misrouting of the family excursion fall entirely to eight-year-old Eugenia Tyrold's share. "Born with a beauty which surpassed that of her lovely sisters" (50), she is left crippled by her fall from the seesaw and also disfigured beyond recognition by the smallpox that sets in afterwards. Another round of redistribution ensues. As compensation to Eugenia for her loss of looks, Sir Hugh arranges for his fortune to fall to her share rather than Camilla's—" 'a guinea for every pit in that poor face' " (30). Camilla gains in countenance here—Edgar Mandelbert observes the nobility with which the girl learns of her financial loss and thinks that she has grown "a thousand times more beautiful" (32)—

171

and this gain occurs precisely *because* it is now Camilla's turn to be disinherited.

Cramming this flurry of sudden transformations into the first of the ten books of *Camilla*, Burney inaugurates a narrative that is preoccupied with speculation and credit because it is preoccupied with the irresolution of identity, the mutability of the social indices on which selfhood is propped. According to the reductive account of female character and value current in the market, a woman (is her face) is her fortune. It follows, therefore, that when faces and fortunes have the capacity to disappear and reappear, female identity is suspended. Under these circumstances, then, female identity is defined as that which thwarts definitive determination. The difficulty of pegging the rumored existence of an heiress to a specific female body or name eventually occasions a series of misidentifications and miscalculations among the would-be suitors of Eugenia, Camilla, and Indiana (and, in addition, among the moneylenders who are willing to grant credit to heiresses). Typical is the situation of a certain Mr. Dubster, who invests in a pair of gloves so that he may dance with Camilla at a ball. When he finds out that her current relation to Sir Hugh has been misrepresented, he finds he has made a bad gamble.

In book 1, the Tyrold fortune circulates among the novel's three female principals—but it would be as accurate to say that, mimicking money, Eugenia, Camilla, and Indiana are themselves set in motion by the mutable terms of Sir Hugh's will and his desire. This is particularly true where Camilla and Eugenia are concerned. Each is shuttled back and forth between her parents' house and Sir Hugh's, her "home" being a product of his whim. Similarly, when the novel shifts to Camilla's seventeenth year and to the trials that she, Eugenia, and Indiana undergo when they enter the social scene, the three women seem, in each subplot, to resemble exchangeable property in the frequency with which they are conveyanced between one man and another. One subplot gets under way when Indiana's brother, Clermont, disinherited along with his sister in book 1, returns to Hampshire and thwarts Sir Hugh's plan for compensating his nephew for his disinheritance: Sir Hugh had hoped to marry him off to Eugenia and thereby merely defer Clermont's accession to the Tyrold fortune. Clermont's contempt for the plan and for her body gives Eugenia the space for desire: that sends her into the world and into exogamous and more complicated circuits of exchange. When Eugenia's love for the penniless Melmond (an acquaintance contracted at a public place) becomes known within their social circle, he takes advantage of the evident opportunity and agrees to enter into a mercenary marriage with her. After Eugenia discovers that Melmond has longed for her cousin all along, she renounces her desire, designates Indiana as her substitute, and sweetens this exchange of her fortune for Indiana's face by promising a portion of her inheritance to the engaged couple. Vain, vacuous, and imprudent, Indiana ends up following the standard career path for the romantic-period heroine's foil: she elopes with an Irish officer in book 10 of the novel. Eugenia then replaces Indiana and marries Melmond.

These exchanges are by no means smooth. *Camilla* evokes the fantasy about women as moveable goods that organizes Claude Lévi-Strauss' theories of kinship.[8] But where in that structuralist-functionalist account the exchange of women is a guarantee of social cohesion and the very type of communication, *Camilla* is by contrast concerned with the unaccountable. The romance plot that involves Camilla Tyrold and Edgar Mandelbert begins, like the romances referred to above, with the substitution of one woman for another. When Edgar returns to his estate as an adult, he finds himself, contrary to Sir Hugh's design, in love with Camilla and not with her cousin Indiana: the two women trade places therefore, as they did following Sir Hugh's first alteration of his will. However, the problem that arises is that Edgar both can and cannot tell Camilla and Indiana apart. He knows which of the two he loves. But he doesn't know whether he should love her, since, as if he were perversely determined to ascribe meaningfulness to the anthropologist's merely formal account of the two women's exchangeability, Edgar comes to suspect that, deep down, his current choice really *is* like her cousin: that Camilla too is a material-minded coquette. The exchangeability that is the catalyst for their love story doubles, then, as an obstacle to narrative fulfillment, because Edgar construes it as an index of the secret truth of Camilla's identity. Similar exchange in another form—the return of love for love—also fails to secure a happy resolution to the romance plot. Camilla loves Edgar back; midway through the novel she accepts his proposal of marriage. But her acceptance merely encourages Edgar to give heed to the reports, which Indiana's vengeful governess helps to disseminate, of this heroine's secretly mercenary motives.

I have already noted that, bested by the tentative way in which social identities appear in the world of the novel, Mr. Dubster—the poor sap who bought new gloves so as to dance with an heiress—has no idea of what to make of Camilla. Edgar also complains that he cannot read her. In the first half of the novel, the illegibility that is the consequence of his own mind games is compounded by the prevailing codes of female modesty, which stimulate the perverse pleasure he takes in second-guessing Camilla. Designed, as the conduct book writers of the era made clear, to augment the value of the woman on the marriage market, those codes of modesty enjoin Camilla to suppress her feelings for Edgar, or, more precisely, not to feel first. If she fails in that project, she is to "shut up every avenue by which a secret which should die untold can further escape you" (360).[9]

As others have commented, *Camilla* indicts the way "desire-based relativism" makes courtship another version of commerce. In private life, as in public, Burney seems to be saying, fixed standards of value are eroded as both conduct book writers and the women whom they advise scramble to adjust to shifts in male demand. What eludes commentary is how the counterdiscourse that Burney promotes to set off her social critique, her affirmation of the intrinsic and immeasurable value of the self, is as embedded in social history as the commercialization she deplores.[10] By contrasting Burney's depiction of women's fortunes in retail culture with that of her contemporaries, we can start to specify how the stock-in-trade of her novels—a character who is unaccountable—itself does cultural work. This is also a way we can start to specify the cooperative relation that links psychological fiction's promise of self-recovery to consumer culture's promise of reembodiment and links psychological fiction's inside stories to consumer culture's carbon-copy images of bodies beautiful.

From the moment Eugenia contracts smallpox, *Camilla* could be read as a lecture on how female mobility, compounded by what the narrator calls "the contagion of example" (93), endangers self-possession and individuation. Certainly, the novel appears to cast the force of example as the motor of the consumer economy. Camilla's ill-advised habit of referring to what other women do when she's judging how much to spend (for example, 406), and the comic ways in which the dramatis personae of the novel repeatedly pile one after another into the same increasingly crowded store, suggest how Burney equates shopping with copying. And this social disease of consumption, spreading from woman to woman, does seem to make each one sick. Thus, echoing Eugenia's fate after her visit to the fair, Camilla's entrance into the world ultimately leads her to a sickbed. Just before the multiple marriages that give the novel its happy end, during a period when Mr. Tyrold has been temporarily imprisoned for his daughter's debts, and when she has been temporarily abandoned by Edgar, Camilla ends up in an inn where no one knows her—where she has no credit. There, ashamed to rejoin the family she has ruined, she falls so ill of remorse that she cannot identify herself. Burney seems to suggest that her characters would have the best chance of remaining characters—rather than fading into the background (like female visitors to the Pantheon), rather than being reduced to anonymous types—if they stayed still, outside the market and inside the home.

However, if the survey of the fashion centers of Tunbridge, Southampton, and London that occupies eight books of *Camilla* promotes the same moral program as the antimarket vindications of domestic privacy that abounded in the 1790s, it does so only in a limited way. For instance, Hannah More's *Strictures on the Modern System of Female Education* (1799) indicts the roaming, conspicuous consumption, and promiscuous commingling that arise because the gentry settles its domestic affairs in public places. More campaigns in particularly interesting terms against courtships being conducted in public assemblies, arguing that, whereas the connoisseur who selects a picture from "among all its exhibited competitors" can be sure of fixing it in his house, the man who finds a wife in a public place has to expect that she will "escape to the exhibition-room again, and continue to be displayed at every subsequent exhibition, just as if she were not become private property."[11] More is vexed by the mobile woman's lack of resemblance to the picture, which unlike the woman does not claim to be anything other than a "passive" object. She is vexed by the world of commercialized leisure for fostering opportunities for female mobility. Burney's argument is not with mobility. Instead, Burney faults the fashionable world largely *because* it makes the woman appear as a picture—as a still life.

What harms Camilla in the marketplace is not so much participation in fashionable dissipation or acquaintance with bad examples. These are effects in Burney's narrative, not causes. Instead, what harms Camilla is the misrepresentation and self-estrangement that result when one must represent oneself in the public arena and accommodate other people's accountings. Camilla's problem is that she is answerable to others' interpretative frameworks, others' power to analogize between physical and moral being. The point is underscored by the role that accident plays in Eugenia's afflictions. After visiting the fair, Eugenia tumbles from a seesaw and nearly dies of smallpox: such is the aftermath of her very first excursion into the consumer economy. In this case, however, the project of reading a moral meaning into bodily contingencies seems grotesque. It is the more thoroughly discredited, precisely because Eugenia's story at once calls on readers to mobilize the sexual allegories usually embedded in accounts of women who have fallen or contracted the pox and (since Eugenia has no history before her accident, and since there is really no explaining her body's fate) it makes that allegorizing seem a bad joke.[12] In *Camilla*'s primary plot, Edgar, who recoils from Indiana's superficiality and who values Camilla's capacity for deep feeling, also perversely longs for her transparency, for what Camilla seems and what she is to be the same. Edgar's project of heroine-watching is premised accordingly on the proposition that Camilla *should* be morally accountable for how she looks—for appearances, which throughout the novel are against her. And Camilla's near-undoing in money matters and affairs of the heart result from the contortions she has to go through, and the parts she has to play, in order to make Edgar recognize her as the same person "inside" as she has always been.

Edgar's uncertainty as to whether she is worthy of his love leaves Camilla wavering between a single and an attached state. She has to wait him out. Since modesty prohibits Camilla from simply asking Edgar why he sometimes appears partial to her and sometimes appears indifferent (to have "precisely . . . the same sentiments for my sisters as for me" [338]), she has in effect been saddled with the task of *acting* as if she believed he had no intentions, and as if she had none either. Camilla has to "*prove* herself . . . unmortified and disengaged" and make a "*display* of her indifference" (290–91; my emphasis): little wonder, then, that the "exhibition rooms" Hannah More decries become her destination. Camilla accepts the fashionable Mrs. Arlbery's invitation to pass part of the season with her at Tunbridge Wells.

These are the circumstances under which Camilla embarks on what in *Evelina* would be called her "entrance into the world," and this is how Burney revises *Evelina* and her earlier, more straightforward rewriting of the mid-eighteenth-century narrative that traced the gentleman physiognomist's travels. It is Camilla's compliance with Edgar's agenda (or lack of agenda)—and not Camilla's own desire—that takes her into the marketplace. And if such an itinerary does retrace that of the possessive individual of mid-century fiction, who entered the world so as to see things and "purchase experience," Camilla's opportunities to look about her en route are much more limited. She has not only to submit to Edgar's moody surveillance, but also, at a great cost, to outfit herself *for* the world. She purchases clothes, she visits public places, because in the world one conforms to the social and socializing demand that an individual display her identity. Camilla adapts to the codes of recognition requiring some one who wishes to *count* as a lady to *look* like a lady, and, in that sense, to make a scene. (In much mid-century characteristic writing, by contrast, the gentleman surveyor's image is not at issue: *Roderick Random* represents the exception insofar as Roderick has to work at appearing to be what he is or at being what he appears.) Yet the criteria Edgar sets for Camilla's presentation of self conflict in some respects with those the social world sets. Even after they become engaged, Edgar invokes a logic running along these lines. The more Camilla appears in public, the less she looks like herself, and the more—apparently unworthy of his love—she resembles women like her cousin Indiana or like those who initiate her into fashionable society: "confirmed coquettes" (681), the overdetermined figures who are at once designing manipulators of appearances and, as merely stylish women, far too apparently the products of a mercenary society's designs.

For Edgar appearances are consistently significant, though in a flexible way. Either they document how the fashionable world has altered Camilla or they reveal her latent likeness to worldly women. Sometimes Edgar invokes a principle of guilt by association, concluding *this* Camilla to be different from the woman he had formerly loved because she must be like her new acquaintance. "Untoward contrariety of circumstance" (679) also contributes to the paradox according to which Camilla "seems 'unworthy' because—and when[ever]—she tries to act 'discreetly.' "[13] When she visits the Tunbridge assembly rooms, for instance, Camilla promises Edgar the first dance of the evening, and the promise soon proves an embarrassment; Mrs. Arlbery wishes to leave the assembly early, and, so as to be able to keep faith with Edgar, Camilla must discreetly arrange for a recent acquaintance to chaperone her in Mrs. Arlbery's stead. This show of intimacy with one of the leaders of Tunbridge fashion provides Edgar, who is ignorant of how Camilla "had been circumstanced" (446), with new reasons for mistrust. Observing how this woman's notice "raise[s] Camilla higher and higher in the eyes of the bystanders," how "Camilla, thus distinguished, became now herself an object of peculiar notice" (443), Edgar sees in Camilla's conduct tokens of social ambition and immodesty.

Camilla's apparent determination to escape to the exhibition room, rather than dwell in the domestic obscurity commended by social commentators such as Hannah More, provokes doubts in Edgar that stall the courtship plot. At the same time, Edgar's doubts—and, behind them, his determination to judge Camilla—at once occasion and prolong Camilla's sojourn in the world. The program of moral surveillance Edgar undertakes so that Camilla will no longer be unaccountable merely implements in another form the fashionable world's demand that the individual *display* who she is.

Spectacle in *Camilla* thus suspends story, though not exactly in the manner that exercised the historians who cast Burney as the local colorist of the Georgian leisure class. As I have indicated, moments of arrested motion, when heroines become still-life pictures of themselves, are frequent in Burney's novels: Burney regularly arranges for Camilla and her sister heroines to be "petrified" (719) by trauma and for their images to be magnified in the lenses of their interlocutors' lorgnettes and "near-sighted glasses" (86). Even as he strenuously opposes Camilla's entry into the public spaces of the gaze, Edgar is complicit with this exposure. His complicity suggests that within Camilla's story a lot is riding on the interference of spectacle with story; and there is a sense in which the novel operates so as to convert these moments of awful physical conspicuousness into the achievements of a psychologized identity. These moments are equally significant for the work that psychological fiction does in culture. This interference of spectacle with story aligns the novel reader's demand for psychological verisimilitude with the desires that have made a complex, ineffable selfhood a primary asset for consumer capitalism. That is the social significance of the novel reader's personal involvement in the problems Camilla has with image management and the problems, to which I now turn, she has when she goes shopping. Our willingness to grant Camilla an inner self different from what appears is not defined against, but constituted on, Camilla's exposure—as shopper and as commodity—in the marketplace.

CAMILLA'S SHOPPING

Feminist scholars have often commented on a duplicity in the way the fashion and beauty industries address the female shopper: she is interpellated as both an agent and an object of commercial exchange, both invited to look at the clothing and the cosmetics on display and reminded of the requirement that she be eye-catching in turn.[14] Burney's most extensive account of Camilla's shopping exemplifies this tautological relation between women and the commodities they buy. Indeed, the shopping trip that Camilla takes when she arrives in Southampton with Mrs. Arlbery confirms feminisms' most agoraphobic reckonings of the costs of women's participation in the market. As Camilla and her companion for the day, a certain Mrs. Mittin, stroll together down the High Street of Southampton, a trio of shopkeepers involved in the beauty industry—a perfumer, a linen draper, and a haberdasher—begin to shadow the two women and to speculate aloud on their sanity and morality. Becoming uncomfortable but not yet realizing that she is the object of the men's pursuit and their wagers, Camilla, like many romantic protagonists, seeks consolation in nature. She finds refuge in a bathing house on the beach. As an especially commodified version of nature, the Southampton seashore is, however, crowded with other tourists, and Camilla's efforts to sightsee from this vantage point finally coincide with her metamorphosis into a framed image that performs its own sort of consumer address. While Camilla sits at the window, "all eyes" are drawn "to the bathing room; and new bets [are] soon . . . circulated" (611).

Recounted in this way, the story of this excursion into the market not only portrays shopkeepers as sexual harassers; it also seems to imply that the merchant operates in this guise inside as well as outside his shop. To put it bluntly, the story depicts the harm shopping does to women shoppers. (The sexual menace gets compounded as Burney's narrative continues: their interest piqued by the shopkeepers' speculations, two predatory aristocrats force their way into the bathing house on the quay. It takes the intervention of another male outsider, and belatedly Edgar's intervention too, for Camilla to escape their insults.) In that the episode correlates a woman's consumption of beautiful images with *her* visualization and victimization, it readily evokes some familiar arguments that link women's situation as spectacle to the social repression of female subjectivity and agency. It seems, too, to ratify the arguments that cast women's desire for fashionable beauty as a symptom of a false consciousness operating to the sole benefit of a patriarchal economy. (And it should be noted that Camilla, at this point in the novel, has already learned something about the monetary costs of reproducing her self in the image that fashion mandates: before departing for Southampton, Camilla racked up a large debt with the milliners and shoemakers of Tunbridge Wells.) However, attention to the history of the built spaces and learned practices that have mediated women's relations with the world of goods brings to light other less familiar ways of reading this story of shopping.

That Southampton's High Street is not just a thoroughfare but itself an attraction for visitors is, for a start, testimony to the romantic-period transformations that moved the accent in retailing onto lavish display techniques. Rosalind Williams's description of the Victorian department store—as a site of visual allure, where "consumers [were] an audience to be entertained by commodities, . . . and where arousal of free-floating desire [was] as important as the immediate purchase of particular items"—is equally applicable to the spas and seaside resorts of late Georgian England. There the proprietors of permanent shops had begun, early in the century, to assume functions in the economy formerly filled by traveling peddlers and by the stallholders of the old fairs: in the last quarter of the eighteenth century, a time of increased domestic tourism, boulevards had been broadened, gas lighting had been introduced (1792), and the shops had acquired plate-glass show windows (1786).[15] When city streets across England became in this manner showcases for commodities and, as prototypes for today's pedestrian malls, sites for holidaymakers' leisurely spectatorship and strolling, women of the propertied classes acquired new opportunities and arenas for public mobility. In regarding the Regency woman, therefore, we might well be seeing a forerunner to the ambiguously empowered figure that historians have associated with the Victorian department store: this is, in Anne Friedberg's words, "the female flâneur[, who] . . . was not possible until she was free to roam the city on her own. And this was equated with the privilege of shopping on her own."[16]

That last sentence suggests, as Camilla's misadventures do too, that this new itinerancy came with a price. It is, nonetheless, worth postponing the agoraphobic analysis, backtracking, and noting, in light of the history of Georgian retail spaces, precisely why the Southampton shopkeepers made Camilla the object of their speculations in the first place. Camilla suffers not so much because she enters the market but because she and Mrs. Mittin have engaged in behavior in the vanguard of consumer practice. They have engaged in conduct that, in slightly altered circumstances, would express what recent cultural criticism identifies as a new consumer subjectivity. At Mrs. Mittin's instigation, the two women have in succession stepped into each store on the High Street, inquired at the counter about the town's tourist attractions, and then, rather than acting on the recommendations, moved on to the next establishment.[17] Adapted to Mrs. Mittin's desire to "take a near view of the various commodities exposed to sale," this bizarre mode of *not* sightseeing scandalizes the burghers of Southampton. They construe the women's conduct as a pretext for " 'routing over [rummaging through] every body's best goods, yet not laying out a penny' " (611). The perfumer, the linen-draper, and the haberdasher assume they are dealing with either shoplifters or escaped lunatics: their wagers pivot on which of these explanations of the women is true. But the real story is how thoroughly Mrs. Mittin has, in response to the cues emitted by the aestheticizing of the High Street, muddled sightseeing and marketing.

Apparently, the retail principle of the *entrée libre*, which would have legitimated Mrs. Mittin's pastime, is not yet entrenched among Southampton shopkeepers. In that they were "just looking," as we would now put it, Camilla and Mrs. Mittin have jumped the gun on one stage of the consumer revolution. They have anticipated the era of obligation-free browsing. Camilla's and Mrs. Mittin's timing may be bad. Yet to supply a counterweight to the agoraphobic narrative that we have constructed out of their adventures, it might be important to note that the novel in which Camilla and Mrs. Mittin appear still offers ample evidence of the pervasiveness in Burney's culture of that itinerancy, physical and mental, which is at stake in "just looking" and which was crucial to the eighteenth-century takeoff in rates of luxury consumption. Such evidence is to be found precisely in Burney's representation of her protagonist's inner life.

The emergence in Georgian England of new retail spaces like the gaslit, showy high streets of the watering places or the arcades of the capital (opened in 1818 and 1819) did more than facilitate the mobility of the formerly housebound lady. Anne Friedberg speculates about the psychic consequences of the consumer's new itinerancy. She proposes that when the itinerant looking abetted by the new spaces converged with the way of looking that was called up by the new protocinematic entertainments such as the panorama (patented in 1787) and the diorama (1823), a new subjectivity came into being. Those turn-of-the-nineteenth-century architectural forms and the social behaviors they facilitated changed the relation between sight and bodily movement. Making possible a "mobilized 'virtual' gaze," they also helped produce a new kind of "virtual" subjectivity, one that was not bound by any one particular mode of embodiment, that shifted fluidly among subject positions. The female flâneur perambulating down the new High Street, like the audience member transported out of herself by the panorama's simulations of other spaces and times, could try on and discard a variety of identities, and without obligation.[18]

It is through something like this notion of a virtual subjectivity that the Frances Burney who describes the spectacle of consumption joins forces with the Frances Burney who narrates the ineffable psychological subtexts of selfhood. Perhaps the insistence in *Camilla* that the heroine is not only an accidental tourist but also an accidental consumer may seem to controvert this account of the conjunction of self-making and consumerism. Burney indeed goes to great lengths to depict the articles of personal property that Camilla accumulates as she rushes toward ruin as articles of *impersonal* property. Camilla's first acquisition on entering into the world is a locket offered as a prize in a raffle—a raffle from which, or so she believes up to the moment when the prize is put into her hands, she has withdrawn her name (105–8).

Even if it had been the object of Camilla's desire, this lottery prize would still be as such an odd personal effect since, in the interval between the purchase of the tickets and the draw that selects the winner, it has, potentially, been anyone's and everyone's locket.[19] Even though she has aimed to give the cost of the lottery ticket to the poor, in this episode Camilla still appears to gain more than her fellows from participation in sociable exchange, and likewise, in a second raffle, for earrings (474–77), she again makes the best bargain. First, acting as the proxy for her friend, Mrs. Berlinton, she throws the dice and loses; then, acting for herself, she throws and wins: once again, it is just when Camilla conforms to the consumer desire of everyone else that she acquires property—and also appears singularly lucky, singularly acquisitive, and so alarmingly conspicuous. In a sense, then, Camilla's possessions are scarcely hers. And at the point when she first arrives in Southampton, it is, the narrator indicates, the demands of decency—and not those of vanity nor even of fashion—that keep Camilla buying. "[A]fter a very short time, the little wardrobe exhibited a worse quality than that of not keeping pace with the last devices of the *ton;* it lost not merely its newness, but its delicacy" (689). Camilla rarely takes her own desire into the market; she takes other people's.

But, finally, no one gets what she wants in the market. Our agoraphobia—and our agoraphilia—have to do with the fact that property acquired there is never personal enough. Indeed the momentum of the consumer economy is a function of those moments when someone stands in front of a dressing-room mirror, or contemplates the layout in a fashion magazine, and says, "It's *not* me." It is a product, that is, of precisely that resistance to a determinate representation of the self, and that insistence that there is more to the self than meets the eye, that underpins the psychological novelist's expression of irreducibly personal truths. Considering the scene that finishes off Camilla's sojourn in Southampton can illuminate the convergences between these models of selfhood and help to clarify how a consumer culture is a psychological culture. In this scene, Camilla returns to her lodgings after a ball that she has attended in vain on the chance that Edgar might be there and that she might at last convince him that he has misunderstood her (721). Depositing her ornaments on the toilette table, she sees in the mirror the virtual image of the ball gown that has plunged her into her most desperate condition of indebtedness yet, a ball gown whose menace to her self-possession is underlined by the fact that it is the "uniform" required by the host of the ball. Duplicates of this dress have just been worn by almost all the female characters in the narrative.

In a peculiar manner, meaning in this scene migrates between the self and the body. The signs by which we recognize the fictional character with an inner life—this scene of private introspection is a textbook instance of what Bakhtin called "psychological time"—are here joined to what Kristina Straub has dubbed "a bit of eighteenth-century fashion copy," since we are given through Camilla's eyes an exhaustive inventory of her purchases:[20] "Her robe was everywhere edged with the finest Valencienne lace; her lilac shoes, sash, and gloves, were richly spangled with silver, and finished with a silver fringe; her ear-rings and necklace were of lilac and gold beads; her fan and shoe roses were brilliant with lilac foil, and her bouquet of artificial lilac flowers, and her plumes of lilac feathers, were here and there tipt with the most tiny transparent white beads, to give them the effect of being glittering with the dew" (721). Yoking this description to a passage of free indirect discourse, the narrator continues by quoting the heroine's "reflections." Encountering in this spectacle "glaring" evidence of the extravagance she shares with the most worldly of women, Camilla identifies with Edgar's reproachful way of seeing—of glaring at—her (721). She half-accepts his reproaches as identifying hidden aspects of her self and half-thinks of herself as *being* in addition to *appearing* "erring" and "unequal," without integrity or steadiness. Of course, as a uniform, this ball gown literalizes the logic of guilt by association—the theory that Camilla must be like the women who have initiated her into fashionable consumption—that Edgar has mobilized ever since Camilla's entrance into the world.

In one respect, then, this is a moment where the self is misrecognized, alienated, lost. In a manner something like that at stake in the most pessimistic accounts of the objectification that befalls women in the market, Camilla's clothed body seems to have the last word on Camilla's identity here. But it is Camilla herself who orchestrates this moment, in which she becomes a representation, an image, to herself. So, in another respect, the moment when the heroine sees herself as she is seen, when the view from inside and the view from outside are juxtaposed, also establishes the self-difference—the distance over which "self negotiates with self for self"[21]—that we think of as the hallmark of psychological complexity.

Camilla does not simply look in the mirror, behold the ball gown, and say, "That's me," but most indictments of the socially indoctrinated consumer pivot on that declaration. They portray contented receptivity of that sort as the female consumer's standard response to the world of goods.[22] To endorse that social constructivism and grant the market such inexorability is not only to reproduce the misogyny that Edgar voices when he supposes Camilla ruined by the world because the female character is "often so unstable, as to be completely new moulded by every new accident, or . . . associate" (594), or that Captain Mirvan expresses when he says of Evelina, "Whatever's the fashion, [she] must like of course." To forget that consumers can withhold their assent is also to efface a distinction crucial to the ethos of consumer capitalism: that between the old marketing and the new shopping. As Friedberg explains, marketing "means simply buying items in the marketplace, 'stocking up.'" Shopping, on the other hand, "is a more leisurely examination of the goods; its behaviors are more directly determined by desire than need. To shop: as a verb, it implies choice, empowerment in the relation between looking and having, the act of buying as a willful choice."[23] If we think about the practice of window-shopping and the institution of the *entrée libre*, we realize that behaviorist discussions of consumer society occlude precisely what defined the new shopping: the suspension of purchasing power. But this was perhaps what made the new shopping into the opportunity that some women had for what Foucault, studying how men in Greek antiquity turned themselves into subjects, called "work upon the self." The new shopping was, that is, a chance to negotiate and transform the ready-to-wear modes of subjectification provided by commercial society.

In this account, shopping doesn't so much substitute a fashionable female body—a culturally mandated image—in the place of a "real" woman as it fosters a notion of the self as different from the body and separate from culture—the same notion at stake in Burney's fiction. What is at stake in the reader's conviction that Camilla's ball gown is "not her"—and that the woman Camilla observes in the looking glass isn't her either—is a notion of a self that is dislocated from the body and that is the object of a purely private act of intellection: precisely the fluid, virtual subjectivity ready to try on and discard identities that Friedberg's account of the female flâneur describes. In this respect, Burney's presentation of the familiar image of an unhappy woman before her looking glass complicates the behaviorism inscribed in the myth of the female shopper who responds to every fashionable image with the declaration—"It's me." In the scene that unfolds after the ball, Camilla goes to her glass, looks at her clothes, and sees a disguise. And in a similar episode in *The Wanderer* Burney seems to sum up the conditions of representation defining psychological fiction and defining consumer culture: she does so through the declaration of a country girl who has given up the finery bestowed on her by a rakish aristocrat—" '[W]hen I go to the glass . . . to see what sort of a figure I make, I could break it with pleasure, for seeing [myself] such a disguise' " (464).

Considering Evelina's account of her "Londonizing" makeover in tandem with Burney's diary reports on her own wardrobe crises, Kristina Straub describes, in comparable terms, the notion of the real self that Burney's narratives mobilize. Straub describes an elasticity of consciousness that manifests itself in a double and contradictory attitude toward female dress as "both a 'paltry duty' and as a necessary aspect of femininity." In her journal, Burney complains of the time she loses to dealing with "caps, hats, and ribbons" in tones that evoke, as Straub suggests, "the modern bumper stickers that announce 'I'd rather be running' or 'I'd rather be reading Jane Austen' ": "Burney's statement says what she would really rather be doing, and, by implication, being."[24] It makes sense, then, that Camilla goes into debt for a uniform, that she acquires personal effects against her will, in a manner that makes them impersonal. When one can try on and discard identities, and when, accordingly, the image one confronts in the mirror, or the body one is inside, can at any given moment be regarded as misrepresenting one's real self, then one's properties—one's things or one's attributes—will never be personal enough. Burney's image of an unhappy woman before her glass also tells us something about the cooperative relation that links psychological fiction's promise of self-recovery to consumer culture's promise of reembodiment. My decision as I stand in front of the mirror that it's "not me" ultimately fuels the high rates of product turnover and product obsolescence that define consumer capitalism; for something that *is* me today may very well *not* be me tomorrow. The shop window and the fashion plate are sites where the self constructs itself but also—because I inevitably do accept substitutes for the personal properties that *really* would be me—where it loses itself. This dynamic finally enlarges the sphere of subjectivity. It renders "being" oneself an occasion for, again recalling Foucault's discussions of the care of the self, the exercise of agency and ethical choice.

Throughout *Camilla* Burney's inscription of interiority operates by reminding us of the compulsory nature of a clothed and a socialized identity. Our frustration with Camilla's predicament in representing herself leads Burney's readers to wish that the meaning of appearances—the meaning of Camilla's appearance—might be something that this one woman alone might legislate. However, much as the personal property one acquires in the consumer marketplace can never, since it *is* exchanged on the market, be quite as personal as one wants it to be, the text of appearances, like all texts, inevitably gives rise to readings different from the individual's own. It matches with external associations and social identifications not of the individual's making. Our wish for an isolate, incomparable self is frustrated. Yet that frustration becomes the site for the mixed feelings—for an identity suspended between the me and the not-me—that are basic to a novelistic consumer culture's modeling of complex selfhood.[25]

"SKETCHES OF CHARACTER . . . PUT IN ACTION"

Mark Seltzer's writing about still life painting alerts us to another means by which Burney endows her characterization with depth effects and alerts us to the complexity of the desires traversing Burney's account of the pretty finishing touches on Camilla's ball gown. What attracts us in the still life, Seltzer suggests, "is the reminder of the difference between what has the ability to move and what doesn't. . . . the attraction to the still life, like the attraction to the still life of commodities, instances the perpetual recovery of the more-than-appearance that allows one to set oneself in motion: the reaffirmation of agency itself."[26] The affirmation of the difference between motion and still life, between persons and their things, Seltzer states, projects the subjectivity of the subject.

In prompting novel readers to acknowledge this difference, in insistently making Camilla's "animation" the measure of her worth, Burney replaces one of her period's ways of sorting out femininities with another. *Camilla* downplays the dualistic rhetoric of the eighteenth- and nineteenth-century literature of conduct, which, as Nancy Armstrong has taught us, pitted the aristocratic lady, with her ornamented, flashy body, against an "ardently undazzling" domestic woman and pitted this domestic woman's deeply felt attachment to private life against the other woman's participation in public spectacle. In a pinch, the roles in this system of character might be assigned to Camilla's cousin Indiana and Camilla. There is no disputing that Indiana could be pigeonholed as a member of what moralists decry as "the large class of superficial women." Indiana is "from the first glance . . . brilliant and alluring" (61); in perfect keeping with the animadversions that Hannah More makes about women overaccustomed to exhibition, she deserts her fiancé and runs away to a Gretna Green marriage. Tellingly, when Indiana's admirers blazon her beautiful eyes, mouth, and nose, and especially when, almost as an afterthought, they commend her "inside" as altogether worthy of her "outside," they seem hard-pressed to counter the reading in which the brilliance of her bodily surface would actually betoken an underlying emptiness. They too seem half-convinced by the axiomatics of domestic hero-inehood, in which, in Armstrong's terms, "outward and visible signs of value" count only as manifestations of "emotional lack."[27] Thus the complimentary speeches Sir Hugh makes about Indiana soon turn defensive: " 'Indiana, my dear, you really look prettier than I could even have guessed; and yet I always knew there was no fault to be found with the outside; nor indeed with the inside neither, . . . so I don't mean anything by that; only, by use, one is apt to put the outside first' " (59). Lieutenant McDersey, the Irish officer whom Indiana ultimately marries, also protests too much: "[H]er outside is the com-pletest diamond I ever saw! and if her inside is the same, which I dare say it is . . ." (250).

But whereas the scheme for sorting out bad women from good that in-forms passages such as these splits body from soul, Camilla's fate seems rather to exemplify the ways that consumer culture reorganized body and soul to-gether. It is not so easy to pigeonhole Camilla as playing domestic woman to Indiana's aristocratic lady, as representing the soulfulness that is the coun-terpart to Indiana's egregious carnality. Because of the way Edgar's doubts send her into the "exhibition-rooms," Camilla's story is primarily one of her finding herself inside a body. Coinciding historically with the conduct book writers' efforts to strip power away from sumptuary display, the consumer revolution's address to moneyed Englishwomen presupposed the value of a bodily style founded on visibility and publicity.[28] Burney's account of the travails her heroine undergoes to appear herself could be read as an allegory of the costs of the difficult *collaboration* between the conduct book and the fashion magazine. Camilla's problems with credit testify in multiple ways to how women pay once the "natural good looks" ascribed to those who are heroine material become something to be acquired in the marketplace. In order to sport a "natural look," to be socially recognizable as herself, even the most domestic woman may find herself queuing up at the cosmetics counter.

For Burney, making Camilla recognizable as a heroine involves displacing the conduct book framework for differentiating good women from bad and adapting in its stead the terms in which late-eighteenth-century aesthetic dis-cussion privileged variety over uniformity, motion over stillness, and narra-tives over pictures. This enterprise involves pitting Camilla's motion and live-liness against other women's lack of "animation." If anyone in Burney's novel could match the description of the domestic woman who is all soul, it would be Eugenia. As women of interiority should be, she is associated with the enclosed space of her "book-closet" and private practices such as reading and writing. To be valued solely for her subjectivity is the only mode in which Eugenia, with her scarred face and misshapen person, *can* be valued; ultimately Melmond learns to regard and to love her with "mental eyes" (794). If Eugenia's story amplifies the way that appearances misrepresent inner feeling in the main plot of the novel, it is also true that Burney projects through this character an asocial ideal of integrity, a potential transcendence of the world of appearances. And yet, though they are cast as the text's deep and superficial women respectively, Eugenia and Indiana occupy the same devalued position vis-à-vis Camilla. Eugenia is associated with immutability, endowed with a selfhood that transcends change in ways that liken it to the "epitaphs and inscriptions" and dead languages she loves to read (127). Indiana is endowed with picture-perfect looks (84)—a significant association with the pictorial in a novel that echoes texts such as Lessing's *Laocoön* or Burke's *Enquiry into . . . the Sublime and the Beautiful* while it decries the fact that a picture "appears to us today [as] it will appear again tomorrow and tomorrow" and that a picture "tell[s] you only the present moment" (307, 538). Thanks to this campaign against stilled life, Indiana is also associated with the monotony and insipidity of what is pictured.

Neither Indiana nor Eugenia, that is, can attain the standard extolled in the narrator's descriptions of Camilla, who, we are told, embodies "variety," whose character is "elastic" (a neologism in the eighteenth century) and whose spirits are "volatile" (52). While Eugenia is devoted to the written word, the mercurial Camilla fails dismally as a letter writer, never managing once in the novel to set a feeling down in writing. While to those who witness her debut in the ballroom Indiana is "from the first glance . . . brilliant and alluring" and has only to be seen to be known, "to the observant eye" Camilla is "captivating upon examination" (61).

> Indiana was a beauty of so regular a cast, that her face had no feature, no look . . . on which admiration could dwell with more delight than on the rest. . . . The beauty of Camilla, though neither perfect nor regular, had an influence so peculiar on the beholder, it was hard to catch its fault. (84)

In Camilla we see a character who is tailored to desires shaped by the new apparatus of reading. The animation that endows her with a body to be narrated, not pictured, also invites onlookers to look twice. (Tellingly, social success is hers not on the occasion of her first ball but at the breakfast held the morning after.) As I suggested in chapter 3, when onlookers protract the act of perception in this way, they put their sensibilities to the proof. They certify their distinction—the discernment that individuates and dissociates them from, in this case, the "general voice" (84) that acclaims Indiana as the belle of the ballroom. The fact, conversely, that initially enthusiastic onlookers grow "sated with gazing" at Indiana (715)—that Indiana's image doesn't elicit a second look—reminds us of why eighteenth-century aesthetics grew dissatisfied with beauty, why, as the revival of the category of the sublime instances, the consensus developed that the beautiful object did not adequately further the tasteful man's quest for distinction in and through his relations with cultural goods. For Burney's friend Edmund Burke, the bad thing about beauty is that it doesn't require "any work" from the observer. To experience sublimity, by contrast, is to exercise the faculties, an imperative for participants in the romantic project of taste. As Tom Furniss has observed, Burke's *Enquiry* develops a new trope of middle-class identity in defining the sublime as an escape through "strenuous action" from the stasis of beauty—the stasis of the picture that will look the same again tomorrow as it does today. The sublime in Burke's book becomes a "means through which bourgeois thought establishes itself . . . as the locus of individual effort."[29] That rearrangement of class identities is also projected in the value scheme Burney deploys while she compares Camilla, Indiana, and Eugenia and while she refashions the heroine's person to make room for a new idealizing of the subject in action. I am concentrating on Camilla's "animation" for that reason: when she insists on situating her animated heroine in a world of stilled lives, Burney tells us something about the social meanings that are produced by fictions' production of psychological selves.

Burney's way of writing Camilla's body has that effect in two respects. By stressing the animation of her person and the challenge it poses to the beholder, the "peculiar influence" it has, Burney rewrites the knowledge of character as a process or as a story. Because Burney arranges for her protagonist to negotiate the conjunction of body and soul, because she doesn't follow the conduct book writers in dividing the one from the other, the possession of character gets rewritten along the same lines. While she theorizes the fate of body and of soul in the eighteenth century's new retail culture, Burney helps us see how, in the market, "having" a body while "being" oneself becomes a dynamic activity. The goods in the milliner's shop and the patterns in the *Lady's Magazine* simultaneously solicit and thwart the shopper's efforts to produce a perfect unity between what she looks like and who she believes she is. In pointing up the discrepancies between the self and its embodiment—and between the body one has and the body one might acquire— the market also increases the scope or the jurisdiction of subjectivity, because it gives the self more to *do* with the self. Within *Camilla*, this key postulate of both a psychological and a consumer culture—that self-identity is not a given, but a project—also regulates how Edgar views Camilla. It therefore has the consequences I delineated earlier when I noted how his hesitations send Camilla into the "world" in the first place. Burney portrays Edgar as someone who gives too much credit to the appearances that testify against Camilla (he is too prone to think that because she can appear as Indiana does she must *be* like Indiana). But it's worth acknowledging the mixed feelings that motivate Edgar. The infuriating policies of prudence he pursues in courtship also amount to an admission that Camilla's body and mind, and what she appears to mean and wants to mean, might well be at odds. For he adopts the policies out of worry that possession of Camilla's "hand" will not guarantee "possession of her heart" (163). Edgar further collaborates with the novel's rewriting of character as a course of action, a phenomenon in time, when he scrutinizes Camilla for signs of the coquetry that may be "incipient" in her character (291). The model of personhood at stake in this conviction that the investor in the marriage market needs to do more than worry about the real character of his elected spouse, that he should also consider what that character might become, complements the model that sustains the new retail culture, in which a woman must never stop shopping for the look that would really be her. Within the marriage market model, correspondingly, there is no end to the work that a woman must do to make good on (what Burney's male characters call) the "pledge" of her "countenance."

In casting both knowing and having a character as occasions for work, *Camilla* attests to how, in Clifford Siskin's words, labor was transformed in romantic culture from "that which a true gentleman does not do to the primary activity informing adult identity." The fact that Burney thought of *Camilla*, as she says in a letter, not as a mere "novel" but as "*sketches of Character & morals, put in action*" registers both the centrality of "animation" to her project and the middle-class rewriting of identity and activity to which Siskin refers.[30] I have been aiming here to revise in my turn a familiar proposition about the roundness of round characters—to rewrite that truism of a psychological culture which maintains that real characters have stories. We value characters' roundness for what it says about our own capacities for self-contained privacy. The self looks natural in psychologized characterization when it looks detached from the social text. But as Burney rewrites character as a course of action, she also advances the shift in which society was reenvisioned not as "an arrangement of orders" but as "an arrangement of production."[31] The same oppositions between animation and still life on which she draws in order to endow character with interiority, and that interiority with a narrative, also register the psychological character's engagement with the social circuit of production and consumption.

There are, of course, tensions in that engagement. They become most apparent if we inquire into the other identities that began to be circulated once labor assumed a privileged space within middle-class identity politics. In thinking about how living women and lifeless things switch places in the Pantheon scene in *Evelina*, and in considering Captain Mirvan's claim in that scene that "whatever's the fashion, [women] must like of course," we have already encountered versions of one of these alternative identities—that of the idle woman. If Burney looks defiant and even feminist when she argues with how the marriage market allocates the signs of personhood, when she ascribes an inside story to a *female* protagonist, this is in part because of the gendered terms that political economy deployed to link individuals' selfhood with individuals' occupation or vocation. Within political economy, the feminization of *inactivity* was a crucial element of the transition from gentleman to professional that Clifford Siskin describes. Naturalizing the figure of the productive, active man involved minimizing the role that women workers played in the economy, and it involved minimizing the extent to which consumption—increasingly imaged in feminine terms—might itself represent an exercise of enterprise. Instead, agreeing with Captain Mirvan that whatever women are offered, "they must like of course," political economy portrayed consumption as an automatic and passive reaction to stimuli. It left consumption without a story.[32]

As I have argued, Burney recovers that story, by depicting the mixed feelings her heroine has in finding her self inside a fashionable body and by depicting the labor of female leisure. Where political economy finds idleness and inertia, where it paints a still life, so to speak, she finds activity and sets the pictures in motion. In this manner her novels give middle-class women guidelines as to how, like men with careers, they might understand their lives in narrative terms, as their projects of self-fulfillment. But from inquiring into the ways in which Burney's project of "animation" might further feminine access to new stories about interiority and individualism, I want to move now to the anxieties about social control that it registers. When Burney thinks about bodies in motion she sometimes thinks too about what it means for the self to be subject to the imperatives of the outside world.

To show this, I turn here to another figure who served as a foil to productive man—the automaton. The underside of the effort to understand the self as work and work as self-expressive was a fascination with the labor of the machine and machinelike. Since Burney attended the shows where mechanical wonders such as the singing birds of *Evelina* were displayed, since her father commissioned one of the first player pianos, and since the papers she left behind her at her death included a celebrated sketch of a female steam engine (fig. 6), she was well placed to report on this fascination.[33] Seeming to work by themselves, but not working for their selves, automatons emblemized the ambiguities built into that new insistence on conjoining identity and activity. So did the so-called mechanical orders, increasingly represented as automatons. Like his descriptions of preternaturally active "hands" and their operations, Adam Smith's discussions of the alienating effects of the division of labor—of work that consisted in nothing but the repetition of a single simple gesture—anticipated the Victorian factory inspectors' tales of selves "mutilated" by their bodies' occupation.[34] Such automatized bodies transmitted a compelling spectacle of activity severed from agency. They displayed the vulnerability of the self-made individual—how the work of self-making could be work outside the self's control. And, conversely, the spectacle of their *impersonal* labor provided a ritual reaffirmation of the beholder's *personhood*, enabling that vulnerability to be both monitored and disavowed. This may be why, in its definition of *character*, the *Oxford English Dictionary* stages a confrontation of person and machine and cites John Stuart Mill's declaration that "One whose desires and impulses are not his own, has no character, no more than a steam-engine has a character." Members of a middle class who wished both to define themselves through work and to distinguish themselves from a working class found a coping mechanism in the automaton. At the same time the automaton called attention to the very tensions over self-dominion and agency it was meant to relieve.[35]

Automatons permit a kind of equivocating, then. Entering this cultural colloquy on persons and machines, peopling her fictions with characters who appear as automatons, enables Burney to open up possibilities foreclosed by the value scheme that otherwise governs her characterization. Burney is interested in animated, bouncy heroines with a spring in their step, but she

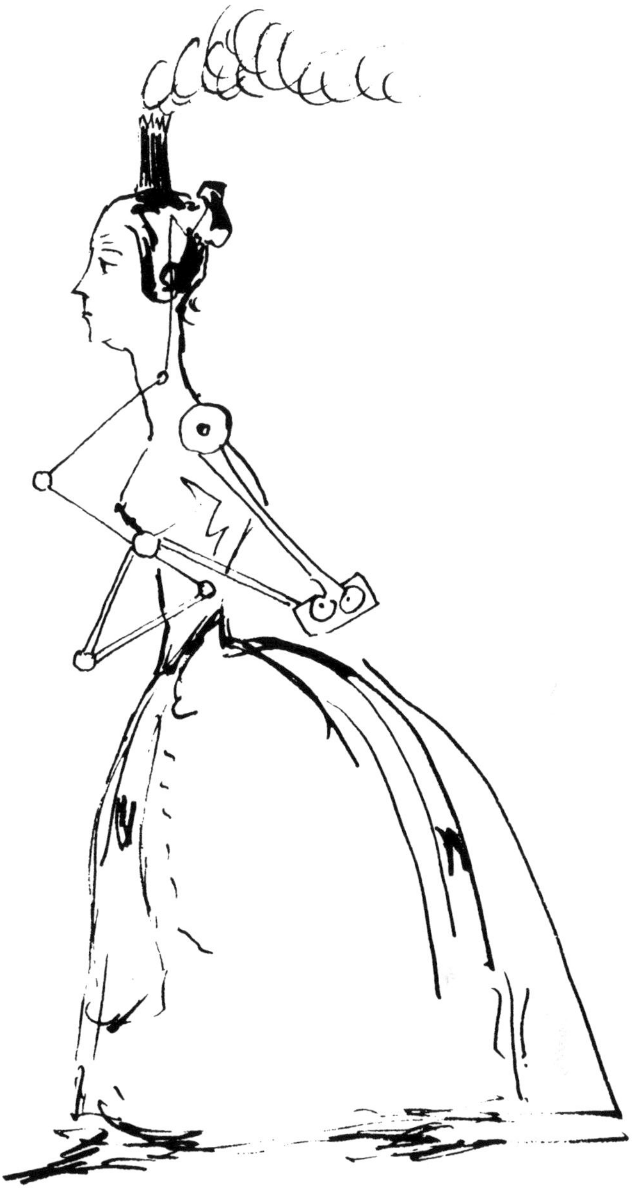

FIG. 6. Ink drawing of a mechanical woman by a member of the Burney family. Courtesy of the Berg Collection of English and American Literature, The New York Public Library, Astor, Lenox, and Tilden Foundations.

is also interested in bodies whose compulsive motions make them look subjected to remote control.[36] In her depictions of fashionable consumption, especially, she is interested in bodies that disrupt basic definitions of selfhood and agency in that their locomotion looks to be compelled from the outside, not by persons' will, but by commodities. A stroll past the shop windows in Tunbridge Wells, the narrator informs us, "afforded some amusement to Camilla," but, tellingly, when the narrator turns to the effects that the wares in the windows have on Camilla's companion, Miss Dennel, the narrator ups the ante. She describes something resembling a hysterical seizure, depicting the power that things have to keep the girl's "mouth open, and her head jerking from object to object, so incessantly, that she saw nothing distinctly" (394). It doesn't come as a surprise to readers accustomed to this passage's way of sorting out characters that Indiana, insipid and pretty as a picture, is similarly described as a "beautiful machine" and an "automaton" (191). But at moments Burney makes not only Camilla's foil but Camilla too look machinelike, not just to the outside world (Edgar) or to herself, but also to us.

This crossover between rhetorical registers that have been set up as opposites feels like so much fiddling, and of course the sheer length of *Camilla* testifies to its author's attraction to gratuitous complications, her unwillingness to leave well enough alone. Yet, as Claudia Johnson has asserted, Burney's "defamiliarizing excess discloses the . . . oddness of the exemplary."[37] Accordingly, it might even be worth exaggerating the significance of those moments, which unsettle the polarities—between self-control and social control, between animation and reification—that since Burney's day have made the novel of manners a site where people have managed their relations to their things. These moments also provide a useful way of reassessing that emancipatory narrative which has a talismanic status in feminist criticism of novels and which, in its concerns with pictures and stilled lives, *Camilla* predicts: the narrative of reanimation that sees the "real self" as a Sleeping Beauty who must be released "from the glass coffins of the patriarchal text."[38]

BURNEY'S MACHINES

It is a given of *Camilla* and the ways of reading that Burney teaches that it is "animation" that endows Camilla with more selfhood, more personality, than any other character in the novel. In Burney's rewriting of character as a narrative process, animation is what separates her heroine from Indiana and Eugenia, neither of whom is really a character who moves or who develops. But animation is also part of what is equivocal about the automaton. Automatons are animated *things*. Representations of automatized movement unsettle the polarities between narratives and pictures, animation and objectification, that underwrite Burney's elaboration of interiority and her agoraphobic take on the marketplace. In the context her automatons create, to make "animation" the measure of personhood is to link Camilla's liveliness and the machine's lifelikeness, not distinguish them.

The strangest episode in *Camilla*, a set piece in the novel's meditations on the relation of body and identity, exemplifies this elision while it recounts an " 'experiment' " (310) in setting pictures in motion. In this chapter, titled "Strictures on Beauty," Mr. Tyrold schools Camilla and Eugenia in how little value the deep-feeling individual should place on physical charms: the lesson is designed to reason the two women out of their grief over society's incapacity to see the real Eugenia, to look any further than her disfigured body. Instruction begins during a family walk, when their father has Camilla and Eugenia take a look at the beautiful girl who stands in a window of the house they are approaching. Training his own gaze on the " 'perfect face' " of the fair unknown, Tyrold muses aloud on the difference that distinguishes the contemplation of a picture from the contemplation of a countenance. " 'We look at a fine picture . . . with an internal security that such as it appears to us today, it will appear again tomorrow and tomorrow and tomorrow,' " he maintains, making the remarks on the stubborn fixity of pictures that others in the novel repeat; but, he continues, in our examination of a fine face " 'there is always . . . some little mixture of pain; the consciousness how short a time we can view it perfect, how quickly its brilliancy of bloom will be blown, and how ultimately it will be nothing' " (307). The plot of animation that organizes this aesthetic argument effects what it describes. In Tyrold's discourse, the fine picture becomes a fine face. It comes alive (but only to perish), and, likewise, the girl on cue moves out of the window and the house, leaving the frame in which she has been pictured. After she reappears in the front garden of the house, this transition from still life to movement is repeated several times, each transition more "abrupt," "hasty," and shocking than the one before. When she starts into motion for the fourth time, it is to "begin turning round with a velocity that no machine could have exceeded" (309). Her language, a formulaic stammer, seems similarly unhuman: "[S]he perceived them, and, coming eagerly forward, dropt several low courtesies, saying, at every fresh bend—'Good day!—Good day!—Good day!' " As his daughters cower behind him, Mr. Tyrold asks the girl whether she lives in the house she has just left. " 'Yes, please—yes, please—yes, please,' she answered, twenty times following, and almost black in the face before she would allow herself to take another breath" (309). The girl has manners: she speaks in the requisite formulae of social interaction—what *Cecilia* identifies as "the insignificant click-clack of modish conversation" (27). But like the Energizer bunny this girl just keeps on going. As Burney opens the throttle and cranks up their rate of iteration, these Ps and Qs—the social niceties that are supposed to be repeated, because characters in a novel of manners can never cease to pay their social dues—become gibberish, impertinence.

The punch line of Mr. Tyrold's lurid bit of pedagogy is, of course, that the beautiful girl proves (in the parlance of the age) an idiot. Though Mr. Tyrold begins the lesson with commonplaces on the way of all flesh, the edifying message that Eugenia is supposed to derive from the spectacle of the other's "shocking imbecility" concerns her own particular good fortune: she should count herself lucky to have a mind inside her deformed body. The beautiful girl also proves a machine, grinding out lessons on the inadequacy of the body's signs to self's truths. Her animation is not expressive. Nor is her activity a mode of self-making. It makes a spectacle of her self.

The difference that this encounter between person and automaton hammers home—which is the difference separating the imbecile's mindlessness from Eugenia's inner life—is also the difference determining Indiana's place in the novel's value scheme. Superficial Indiana " 'has really no head' " either (47). And the automated politeness of the beautiful imbecile seems to literalize Indiana's vapid conformity to the social script. Since Indiana fills the role of the heroine's foil, it is a matter of course that mechanical imitation will be her forte; in Indiana's case it *is* true that "whatever's the fashion, [she] must like of course," and, furthermore, when situated in the context of a tradition of women's fiction, Indiana looks thoroughly conventional. Her type always copy one another. Most modern readers will, for instance, recognize Indiana's affinities with the troop of "negative role-models" that *The Madwoman in the Attic* musters to show off Jane Eyre's "independence": the troop that, for Gilbert and Gubar, not only includes the showy Blanche Ingram and Céline Varens, but is also, they aver, headed up by "a clockwork temptress invented by E. T. A. Hoffmann."[39]

But it is not only Indiana who has a body double in the beautiful imbecile. Mr. Tyrold sets up the beautiful machine in order to define interiority against vacancy, but the "experiment" also targets Camilla. The girl's pirouettes parodically mirror the vivacity of the "little whirligig" (80)—to cite Uncle Hugh Tyrold's epithet for his favorite niece. And, later in the text, when Burney turns from pedagogy unfolding in the family circle to sightseeing in the fashionable world, we are treated to another demonstration of how a picture may be animated. In an episode that takes place during Lord Pervil's yachting party at Southampton, Burney exhibits a Camilla revivified by her sudden conviction that Edgar must have been convinced at last of the purity of her motives: "[S]he . . . ran up to the deck, with a renovation of animal spirits, so high, so lively, and so buoyant, that she scarce knew what she said or did, from the uncontroulable gaiety, which made every idea dance. . . . Whoever she looked at, she smiled upon; to whatever was proposed, she assented; scarce could she restrain her voice from involuntarily singing, or her feet from instinctively dancing" (705). That this staging of Camilla's animation does not in the end prove a prelude to the long-postponed scene of renewed mutual understanding only adds to the tension it produces. Burney's enthusiasm, already noted, for her heroine's "form and mind of equal elasticity," for the expressiveness of her countenance, is taken too far here (15). All those dancing spirits, all that blushing and quivering, are meant to affirm the power inner feeling has to alter (to animate) the condition of the body, but in its excessiveness this passage has the reverse effect. With its copious annotations of all this body is up to—on its own, "involuntarily," unconsciously—the passage all but effaces the inner consciousness to which it attests. The resemblance Camilla bears here to the beautiful imbecile who turns "in circles with a velocity that no machine could have exceeded" is the product of this weird conjunction of animation and the self's vitiation, of the resemblance between the signs of psychological plenitude and the signs of absence of mind.

For this reason, this gratuitous-feeling depiction of hysterical frenzy embarrasses us. Our embarrassment also derives from the way that, in both this episode and the scene with the beautiful imbecile that overshadows it, we seem to glimpse the novel's own machinery, the author's machinations. In restaging and displacing the hierarchies of depth/surface and animation/inertia that structure *Camilla*'s writing and reading of character, these exhibitions of mechanical motion also display Burney's reflections on the contrivances of characterization. Because it blurs the lines between a person and a thing, between intentional and coerced action, automatized motion sets in relief what is equivocal about literary character, made particularly equivocal after real or "round" characters are thought of as animated, as escaping the discursive conditions of their meaning and acquiring lives of their own. Automatized motion highlights the difficulty of saying where literary character ends and the contriving author begins. For even the most animated characters neither express nor create themselves, but are instead constructed from the outside in, controlled and created by narrative exigency and authorial designs.

This is why Mr. Tyrold's experiment reminds us of what Burney does in setting her sketches of character in motion. The resemblances that make multiple figures in *Camilla* appear as mechanical women highlight the "coercive logic of the [conventions] . . . through which literary character is rendered."[40] At the same time, they depict the formal predicament of textually determined characters as a version of the plight that befalls women in the marketplace, the place where, at Burney's most agoraphobic moments, identities seem most socially determined, where the dues individuals pay to the social seem most costly.[41] And this is why, as the idiot's repetitive courtesies or Miss Dennel's frenzied window-shopping indicates, the antics of Burney's automatons also seem to amplify the performances mandated by the social script. More so than other doings, these antics—shopping, minding one's manners—can't be "personified," can't be brought back into the purview of the individual person.[42] The difficulty of conceiving of the literary character as both "real" and legible, and the difficulty of conceiving of the individual as both an autonomous agent and a participant in social exchange, are each rehearsed when the novel confounds the animation of people with the animation of machines.

Because they look and move in ways that are, equivocally, both the same as and different from the ways persons look and move, automatons serve at once to explain and explain away the individual's irrevocably social condition, the incursions that the outside world and the others in it make on the inner sphere of selfhood. This statement is, in addition, a fair description of the explanatory and consolatory powers that, increasingly after the turn of the nineteenth century, will seem to characterize the tradition of "the" novel. I have been exploring Burney's interest in what can be im-personal and machinelike about the literary character in order to discover the limits of those powers. In this chapter's concluding remarks on the imagining of the self and the market in *The Wanderer, or, Female Difficulties*, I want to finish up that exploration by thinking about how in her last novel Burney juggles an interest in subjectivity with a new interest in society. In *The Wanderer* Burney moves back and forth between rendering the inside story in which a heroine is most her self and rendering the impersonal, societal perspective from which that story looks to be subsumed by the mechanical operations of the system. At moments the novel seems as interested in "the world" as in the heroine who "enters into it." It seems as interested in the samenesses that make the world, the social order, hold together as in the differences that make the heroine her self.

Within *Camilla*, animation serves as the marker of Camilla's subjecthood: it is the trait that makes her more three-dimensional than other characters. At the same time animation emblemizes subjugation to others—it makes the beautiful imbecile the dummy that speaks someone else's script. Animation, as we have seen, unsettles the boundaries between self-expression and self-objectification. The interplay between personal and impersonal perspectives in *The Wanderer* has similar effects. It effaces the difference between what belongs to the self and what falls under the purview of the social. Burney marks the labors that the Wanderer undertakes as the means by which this heroine fulfills her guardian's (and, presumably, her author's) injunction as to what "the motto of [her] story" should be: "[T]hose, only, are fitted for the vicissitudes of human fortune, who, whether female or male, learn to suffice to themselves" (220). At the same time, however, that she chronicles the Wanderer's efforts to earn a wage and support herself (as a music-mistress, a seamstress, a milliner), Burney stresses her membership in a face-less workforce that is being slotted into and retired out of the labor market in conformity with the booms and slumps of the business cycle. The vagaries of supply and demand—the surplus of female labor (290), the end of "the season" at the watering places (410)—animate and paralyse, compelling and terminating the performance of labor regardless of the individual laborer's will or need. "The market" (like "the workforce," an abstract entity that overruns direct apprehension) makes people start into motion. Then it converts these working bodies into still lives.[43]

Positioning its heroine at the point of connection between *Camilla*'s mechanical women and the mechanical orders, *The Wanderer* makes the work that sustains the self look like what Mr. Tyrold seems to do to the beautiful imbecile, or what authors seem to do to characters. Burney's last novel thus registers a certain self-consciousness about the social exchanges and the communicative mechanisms that underwrite the value and intelligibility of the "work" of literature: the work, that is, of animating characters and demonstrating that the self may be redeemed from social constraints and appear as it "really" is.

REMOTE CONTROL AND SOCIAL EXCHANGES:
The Wanderer

The Wanderer recounts the "female difficulties" encountered by a refugee who escapes incognito from Robespierre's Reign of Terror and who arrives in England penniless and obliged to conceal her name, descent, and even nationality in order to protect those she has left behind in France. This elusive personage, whose name is withheld not only from other characters but also, for multiple volumes, from the reader, has been cast as Exhibit A in many discussions of how the social order as Burney renders it reduces woman to a nobody. (The Wanderer shares this condition of nonentity with Evelina, who at one point, despairing over *her* lack of a patronym, describes herself as a "cypher, . . . to nobody belonging" [340].) However, these discussions of a character without an identity, one with whom, perversely, the reader nonetheless "identifies," discount what is alluring as well as tragic about figuring the self in negative terms. In one respect, the heroine's wanderings across England trace the same romantic route as the peregrinations of an outcast Childe Harold or Melmoth. Demonstrating that she belongs nowhere, they certify that she has no social self, only an inner identity that transcends social determination. In the state of anonymity, the self is left without the protection provided by the definitions, classifications, and evaluations that attach persons to social meaning and yet, for this reason, is also invulnerable to other people's readings.[44] This is the source of the nameless character's seductions for a psychological culture.

The protagonist's wanderings cover familiar ground in another way. Even while striving to keep a low profile, she must, like Camilla before her, negotiate the tricky codes of female self-display. At moments when this heroine is simply trying to be, she too can look as if she is trying to be *looked at*, as if she is pandering to the public eye and struggling "for occasion to exhibit character; instead of leaving its display to the jumble of nature and of accident" (630). In some episodes, her face is her fortune, and her beauty secures her credit as the gentlewoman she will ultimately prove to be. In other episodes, her body betrays her. For the last third of the novel, her projects of self-preservation are repeatedly thwarted when those she must depend on read a notice in the newspapers that offers a reward in exchange for information about her whereabouts and that describes her face and figure. Even when the people whom she encounters have not read this "advertisement" (663), the discrepancy between her ladylike looks and her evident neediness exposes her to the notice she is trying to elude. As in *Camilla*, the notice she gets is the kind directed towards objects for sale.[45] When the Wanderer finds employment in a milliner's establishment, the proprietor exposes her and the other pretty assistants to public view along with the ribbons and caps, attracting custom by misleading her clients about what it is the shop has for sale (429). Still, an indication of how *The Wanderer* diverges from the novels preceding it is that here Burney eventually subjects her protagonist to "exposure with a vengeance": when this heroine's flight from her persecutors takes her along the routes that the rural poor also travel, "she meets this population *as one of them,* on foot, meanly attired, physically exhausted, sometimes hungry and thirsty, and almost without resources herself."[46]

In articulating the relations between some women's shopping and others' work, in telling the commodity's story from the vantage point both of the shop and the workplace, this novel trumps *Camilla* as a testimonial to the market's powers to efface the self. Yet at the same time, *The Wanderer,* like Burney's preceding novels, fuels the fantasy of an inner self that might operate independent of relations of social exchange. *The Wanderer* couples an instrumentalizing account of the self in which the individual person is a means to a social end with an emphasis on what in the person is most impervious to social contingency.

Its heroine's associations with circulating goods and with money are signs of how the narrative sets her up as a catalyst for a sense of the social. What holds the book's numerous characters together and makes them a society is that each is this stranger's creditor: each lends her money, and she is what other people have in lieu of a social contract to lend to the nation and so to themselves. Her narrative function is to be a perambulating personification of the national debt.[47] In this novel Burney seems interested in issues that concerned the political economy of her era.[48] Her preoccupation here with the mechanisms of social integration ("public opinion"; "the general circulation of money" [218, 305]) also dictates the functions that the Wanderer assumes when the aristocratic household in which she finds refuge amuses itself with private theatricals. The Wanderer is the amanuensis who copies out the lines for the individual players and the prompter who knows all the parts without (at least initially) having one herself. Her mediation converts the acting that individuals have rehearsed in private into something approaching an ensemble performance. Her credentials for this "social work" are made evident by the way that the description of how she sounds as a prompter recalls most descriptions of third-person narrative. Like Burney's narrator, like the general consciousness that broods over a realist narrative, negotiating social divides and orchestrating multiple points of view, she fills in the silences between the actors' speeches. She does it in a voice that "varied, with the nicest discrimination, for the expression of every character, changing its modulation from tones of softest sensibility, to those of archest humour; and from reasoning severity, to those of uncultured rusticity" (80). To think, however, about the multiple occasions on which the Wanderer, acting as go-between, confidante, or looker-on, has no "personal" interest in what transpires (164, 191) is also to see Burney locate subjectivity precisely where it seems to have least room to maneuver. Burney's interest in impersonality, that is, also registers her interest in making personality the stake of narrative. That the heroine so often denies her personal stake in the narrative's events revalidates and repowers the category of the personal: it makes this character's personal affairs more personal, more uniquely differentiated, and harder to read than others'. For all her work in staging the social, this heroine—her family, class, and nationality mystified—has no social context. This is what is indicated in the last paragraph of the novel, when, enumerating the proofs of her heroine's independence, Burney invokes a treasured middle-class myth of self-sufficiency and value prior to exchange and characterizes the Wanderer's story as that of "a female Robinson Crusoe" (873).

These relays between the social and the personal also shape the sequence of episodes near the end of *The Wanderer* in which Burney abandons the overcrowded public rooms that are the settings for the novel of manners and moves the narrative from the town to the rural scene. At this point, Burney's recourse to a romantic language of sublime vision supplies additional corroboration of the richness of her heroine's interior life. Accounts of the psychic transformations that transpire when the individual is left alone with majestic nature, when he finds a refuge from the pressures of other people, and when this seclusion calls forth his deep self, were the romantic era's privileged vehicle for rendering what was individual about the individual. There is something odd, however, about the way Burney uses the discourse of the sublime to rewrite character, and I want to conclude this chapter by thinking about what it is in this sequence in book 8, besides prospects evacuated of the traces of other people, that occasions the Wanderer's moments of "soul-expanding contemplation" (676).

Those moments are for the most part occasioned—much as one supposes they would be for an antisocial Crusoe—by scenery whose majesty is best represented in negative terms: "Here, far removed from 'the busy hum of man' . . . [there was] not even a beaten path within view; not a sheep walk, nor a hamlet, nor a cottage to be discerned . . . to announce the vicinity of mortal habitation" (675). One moment in this sequence of views of the landscape of the New Forest works differently. Burney uses the sequence as a whole to lead up to the denouement of her plot, the point at which this heroine's individuality finally receives the social backup offered by the conjugal tie and a legacy of landed property. It is significant, then, that at the moment inaugurating this final phase of her narrative of self-recovery the Wanderer accedes to a God's-eye view, not (as would be customary) of the natural scene and her place within it, but rather of the economic processes in which her individual story has been absorbed. This is what she sees: "Carts, waggons, and diligences, were wheeling through the town; marketwomen were arriving with butter, eggs, and poultry; workmen and manufacturers were trudging to their daily occupations; all was alive and in motion; and commerce, with its hundred hands, was every where opening and spreading its sources of wealth, through its active sisters, ingenuity and industry" (666–67). The heroine's flight from her persecutors gets absorbed into the traffic patterns produced as workers and commodities move around the economic system.

The agoraphobia Burney is so good at inciting might invite us to read this as a moment when the market subsumes or even consumes the individual. This reading, however, would have to ignore how it is at this moment, after volumes of harassment, and even as crowds seem to gather and disperse, that the Wanderer is left alone and at peace. She finds her place in the state of circulation.[49] For a brief respite she has "nothing more to apprehend" (666). When they catch sight of "the deep care in her countenance," this society of marketwomen, workmen, and manufacturers see "but an air of business" (667). She looks like one of them.

And, of course, from the pointedly impersonal perspective adopted in this passage, the Wanderer *is* one of them. Burney here aligns her heroine's point of view with the "extensive views" that Samuel Johnson ascribed to the men [*sic*] who wrote good books on "trade." In this rewriting of the sublime, such "extensive views" rescript the expansive vistas contemplated by the protagonist whose "summons to self-consciousness" happens when he is stationed on a wilderness promontory.[50] What can be said about the self-consciousness that is recovered in contemplating not nature but commerce? The sociological language that enables one to speak about what marketwomen or manufacturers are doing *in general*—about the operations of "society" at large—

dislocates individual experience. Though in this instance the Wanderer is on the run from her enemies, she has brought her labor to the market before, and overall it is of little significance if one person on the road to the market does not *mean* to go there, just as it is of little significance that no individual is particularly conscious of her contribution to the system's total organization. This passage thus underlines what is uncanny about our involvement in vast, impersonal structures such as "society," "the economy," "the workforce," or "commerce with her hundred hands." It underlines how that involvement is as much an illustration of the haplessness of the individual in society— her entrapment in a role of mechanical imitation—as it is of her agency. In ways that parallel the effect of *Camilla*'s accounts of beautiful machines, the view of the market economy that the Wanderer attains makes visible the gap between what we think we do and what we really do.

Like Burney, the practitioners of political economy also used the image of the machine, and of the individual's instrumentality within the "workshop" of society, to capture those discontinuities. In his *Essay on the History of Civil Society*, for instance, Adam Ferguson wrote of individuals as "tools . . . ignorant of the system in which they are themselves combined." He remarked on how government functionaries "are made, like the parts of an engine, to concur to a purpose, without any concert of their own; and equally blind with the trader to any general combination, they unite with him, in furnishing to the state its resources, its conduct, and its force."[51] Getting ready to wind up her story about how an individual becomes her self, Burney rewrites the sublime in a way that joins the romantic story of animation—the Wanderer's contemplation of the prospect of commerce coincides with her "refreshment" by a revivifying breeze that comes straight out of the romantic lyric (667)— to a disquisition on social motion. The moments when the Wanderer's geographical mobility grants her an expanded vision include a moment when she sees herself as a moving cog in political economy's social machine.

The discourse of political economy used the image of the machine for an additional purpose—to expound a theory of social cohesion. To occupy the panoramic vantage point from which the entire machine could be seen to be moving, from which "the parts of the engine" could be seen to "concur to a purpose," was to apprehend a vast and diffused society as a whole and apprehend apparently divided labors as a unity. The philosophical histories penned by figures such as Hume, Smith, and Ferguson—whose disquisitions on public credit and public opinion Burney echoes throughout *The Wanderer*—claimed such a perspective. In its vindications of the market economy, political economy recounted the history of economic expansion, industrialization, and increasing occupational specialization as a story of social cohesion, of the coming together of individuals in communities. The moral which that history exemplified was that when "each of us produces only one thing, or has only one service to offer, we are obliged to depend on each other for every other service and product that we need." In this scheme, the mere existence of market society could be pointed to as edifying, socializing testimony to how, as Adam Smith put it, the individual "stands at all times in need of the co-operation and assistance of great multitudes."[52]

As I have suggested throughout this chapter, Burney's ways of representing women wronged by the market's reckonings continue to guide twentieth-century literary critics, both when we tell stories, very different from Smith's, about the market as a place of social exchange, and when we tell stories about literary character. We value the characters who, as we say, have taken on lives of their own, even though our faith in their singularity and autonomy is difficult to reconcile with our knowledge that a character exists to be read, that the legibility of the literary character makes it a social experience. At the same time, the plot of animation on which we draw to discuss character in these terms indexes our wish to make our novel reading the occasion for our own romantic escapes from the social.

Burney's accounts of victims of fashion and of prejudice are also the origin of this plot of animation. Her novels, with those of the "Burney school" generally, prepared the ground for the novel reader's persisting preoccupation with recovering inside, untold stories. They anchor a tradition that has valued psychological fiction for its enshrinement of a real self misrepresented by its appearances in the social realm and objectified by society's commercial arrangements. In a psychological culture, this privatized notion of the self is the telos of novel writing and reading. Conversely, the subject who is utterly explained by her social context—a character who can yet be rescued from her automaton-like state if the feminist critic, speaking for her and "giving [her] life with another look," affirms her independence[53]—provides the starting point for most assessments of women's fiction's critical relation to consumer capitalism. Accordingly, it is not surprising that, in these assessments, discussion of social determination crowds out discussion of social participation, of the collaborative relations that link "great multitudes." What thinking of characterization as animation leaves unresolved is the question of "how social transformation can take place in a communal or collective sense."[54]

In this respect, *The Wanderer*'s provokingly agoraphilic inscription of the

sublime poses two challenges: to think about how the subject is already socialized, rather than external to the world she enters, and to think about how
the market is, for better or worse, a social site. In one way, this novel's shifts
between the absolutely personal and the absolutely impersonal are a bravura
demonstration of the lengths to which readers will go to "identify" with a
faceless nobody. At the same time, those shifts between anyone and everyone
suggest that the reading of literary character can involve more than recovering the occluded depths of selfhood. "Character" can be a device for pursuing lines of analysis that extend from one self on to others.[55]

Jane Austen and the Social Machine

CIRCULATION AND PERSONAL EFFECTS

In 1786 the German novelist Sophie von LaRoche kept a travel diary recording her journey to and around London. Her itinerary was determined in part by her crush on her sister novelist Frances Burney and her determination to put a face to her mind's-eye image of the genius behind *Evelina* and *Cecilia*. A female Boswell, engaged in a literary pilgrimage, Sophie von LaRoche was a missionary for the author function, the institution that has made sense of texts by privileging the meanings of the literary work that seem to pertain to the author's psychological profile. Along with literature, LaRoche's most pressing concern while in London was shopping: she was an inveterate window-shopper. From her diary's catalog of the contents of the city's show-windows and shop interiors, its reports on research into the retailing of women's shoes, lapdogs, and "liqueurs of every brand," two typical passages, which encapsulate two distinct propositions about the value of the consumer's pleasures, may be extracted. I want to use these two consumer reports to outline in a preliminary way the complex response that, two decades later, Jane Austen—another fan of Burney's—would make in assessing her contemporaries' new uses of literary character.

In the first of LaRoche's consumer reports, the discovery of an Oxford Street lampseller's stall excites the sightseer's Anglophilia. This entry in the diary praises a progressive nation in which commodities' travels across social space bespeak the glory of the constitution that guarantees the equality of citizens, at least on the shop floor. The Bill of Rights secures Britons the freedom to exercise their individual preferences and to choose their bill of goods. "The highest lord and humble labourer may purchase here lamps of immense beauty and price[,] or at a very reasonable figure, and both receive

equally rapid and courteous attention." The story about the circulation of
goods that this diary entry recounts reiterates the sociable fictions of political
economy. According to the moral philosophy of the mid-eighteenth century,
the expansion of commerce creates an impersonal public sphere—one in
which citizens of various income brackets are universally incorporated and
which endows each of them with an identity. While arguing against the
French Jacobins' plans to confiscate church lands, Edmund Burke, who
loathed the Jacobins' political activity and heartily preferred moral philosophy's assurances that the market would eventually take care of questions of
distributive rights all by itself, restated this argument for LaRoche and Austen's generation. A passage from his *Reflections on the Revolution in France* (1790),
a text in which Burke addresses a member of the French national assembly
but keeps one eye on his own nation of shopkeepers, defends the contribution
to the commonwealth that is proffered by lazy monks and even by "those
who sing on the stage." Pursued to its logical conclusion, this vindication of
the social contributions made by those who do not produce economic wealth
would also ascribe value to the activities of Burke's female readers: through
exchange, Burke proposed (recycling a phrase of Adam Smith's), each one
helps to turn "the great wheel of circulation."[1]

Sophie von LaRoche does not seem to have had the great wheel of circulation on her mind, however, when, visiting Josiah Wedgwood's showroom,
she did some shopping in propria persona: "I bought a seal really expressive
of my present mood and past fortune; namely, a female figure leaning on a
ruined pillar, looking back along the road she had come." This passage, the
second of the consumer reports that interest me, makes the commodity a
vehicle for a personal narrative rather than a social fiction: LaRoche suggests
how a writing desk accessory can be serviceable in the interior decoration
of the self. Made on a miniature scale, her knickknack is—like the diminutive
thimble cases and snuffboxes and perfume flasks that are to be found in our
museums' eighteenth-century galleries—a natural for inconspicuous consumption. Because, like the various collectible containers that I've just listed,
it articulates a boundary and defines private space (before the mid-nineteenth-
century introduction of envelopes, seals closed up the folds of letters), the souvenir LaRoche acquires can be the sort of personal effect that testifies to and
intensifies the individual's secret life. "The souvenir," Susan Stewart writes,
"contracts the world in order to expand the personal."[2]

This souvenir's provenance in one of the *public* spaces Josiah Wedgwood designed to sell his china produces ironies we would do well to engage, however. In the history of mass production and mass marketing Wedgwood figures as a pioneer. "Common Wedgwood" was by the end of the eighteenth century in the reach of the "common people," and its use, the manufacturer boasted, was "spread over the whole Globe." Wedgwood also pioneered techniques that enhanced the imaginary singularity of any one piece of goods and encouraged the customer to develop especially intimate relations with his wares: LaRoche's reverie over her Wedgwood seal bears witness to his success. He made the client's acquisition of his stock a matter of seemingly exclusive privilege and a marker of individual distinction. Thus, while Wedgwood built canals and promoted turnpikes to improve his distribution, invented the advertising blitz, canvassed his associates for suggestions for new methods of displaying his wares, and filled his showroom with mock-ups of the dining tables of the titled aristocracy, he also, by contrast, appears to have studied the protocols of secrecy as well as the protocols of showmanship. He limited the number of articles from his popular line of jasper tea services that would be accessible to the public eye at any one time. He told King George a fib about how the ingredients necessary in the manufacture of that jasper china ware had been used up, in the hope of starting a rumor that might make the cups and saucers that he marketed seem rarer still.[3]

When we put them together, LaRoche's reports on her Wedgwood seal and on the crowd at the Oxford street lampseller's also confront us with ironies. Taken in tandem, they suggest a paradox of which Jane Austen was well aware, as her novels' cagey presentation of the fashionable snobberies of tourists and circulating library subscribers attests: the perturbing sociability of the act of private consumption. LaRoche pivots between personalizing her property—identifying her self in her (decommodified) things—and valorizing "the great wheel of circulation"—the mechanism of social integration that could make her personal effects any person's property. Extrapolating, we can identify in her consumer reports a fable about how, even in reading by and for oneself, one reads in a crowd. In the inside stories of the novel of manners, the romantic reader finds the means to sound the depths of her own special self and manifest her distinctive sensibility. In an age of steam-powered printing presses and circulating libraries, however, the silent reader's intimate transactions with the inner meanings of literature are public-spirited in a couple of senses: from such pursuits of individual distinction a public sphere is composed, and such pursuits of individual distinction are haunted by the murmuring spirit of mass consumption. The treatment of Austen's characterization that this chapter offers will double as a discussion of how Austen registers novel readers' need to navigate ironies of this kind.

Appreciation of this irony, this chapter will demonstrate, underlies Jane Austen's response to her era's reorganization of reading: her insistence on articulating the individuated language of the heroine's psyche with the impersonal language of the commonplace. This chapter builds on the previous two in treating the particular uses of the literary character that developed in tandem with the expansion of the book market. In order to complicate the history of romantic reading that I've already laid out, I aim here to demonstrate how Austen's novels position interiority at a relay point that articulates the personal with the mass-produced.

Compare the mental life of an Elinor Dashwood (*Sense and Sensibility*) or an Anne Elliot (*Persuasion*) to that of Burney's Wanderer, a misunderstood loner. The comparison casts into relief one measure Austen adopts to register her insight into the embarrassing sociability of her readers' rites of introspection and to give us the wherewithal to manage that embarrassment. In contrast to Burney's protagonists, an Austen heroine is never precisely in a position to be a "female Robinson Crusoe" and have her thoughts as her sole companions. Characters who are rarely alone with their thoughts—characters who instead are perpetually anxious about keeping the lines of communication open and the wheels of conversation turning—are precisely those whom Austen chooses for her heroines. At the same time that Austen mobilizes the hallmarks of literary psychology to endow her heroine with an inner life, she also depicts her (to adopt a locution the novelist favors throughout her oeuvre) as conscientiously "mindful" of "the feelings of others." Her "mind filled," this heroine has a head supplied with emotions that belong to other people, a mental life that unfolds in what accordingly is at once an interior and a social space. In *Sense and Sensibility* and *Persuasion* especially, Austen handles point of view so that listening in on the self-confirming language of depth that endows a heroine with an inner life consistently involves hearing in the background the murmurs of a crowd.

In this chapter I will, accordingly, treat not just Austen's interest in individualizing her characters and readers; I will also treat her interest in crowding. Even as Austen equips novel readers to participate in a psychological culture's rites of distinction, she also has us contemplate copying as she archly goes through the motions of writing women's fiction and as she adds more texts to an overcrowded novel market, and she makes us contemplate how a commercial culture renders people copies of one another. In the latter vein, she offers crowd portraits of the sort that the narrator of *Persuasion* puts together as she introduces the women who are Anne Elliot's neighbors for volume 1, Henrietta and Louisa Musgrove. Thinking about these particular two young ladies prompts the narrator to think of vast numbers and so dislocate the question of individual particularity: "Henrietta and Louisa, young ladies of nineteen and twenty, . . . had brought from a school at Exeter all the usual stock of accomplishments, and were now, like thousands of other young ladies, living to be fashionable, happy, and merry."[4] The Misses Steele are installed within the society of *Sense and Sensibility* in similar fashion. Their kinsman promises Elinor Dashwood the acquaintance of " 'the sweetest girls in the world,' " but, his superlative notwithstanding, they are introduced as faces in the crowd: "Elinor well knew that the sweetest girls in the world were to be met with in every part of England, under every possible variation of form, face, temper, and understanding" (102). Such portraits of copycats, whose characterization is exhausted in a single sentence, indulge novel readers with the pleasure of instant legibility—the pleasure of character *types*. Another way to say this, one I will elaborate on in this chapter as I chart the developments in graphic technology that underlay this repowered notion of the "type," is that throughout her work Austen is concerned not just with the sound of the round character's inner voice, but also with noise. She concerns herself with the noise emitted by what I will call her culture's copy machines—a label I use to underline how frequently Austen confronts us with the mechanized aspects of social life (and of literature). In Austen's novels, complying with fashion and the demands of what the Dashwood sisters call "general civility"—writing bread-and-butter letters, talking about the weather—involves recycling the commonplaces that everybody uses and accommodating oneself to customs and linguistic forms that, machinelike, have an impersonal logic of their own. Thus to depict social transactions such as epistolary exchanges and polite conversations—transactions in which, as with the character type, meaningfulness is sacrificed to repetition—Austen will use language we more often associate with a machine and its clatter. In *Persuasion*, rooms filled with people are experienced by Anne Elliot as stages for unintelligible sound: the fashionable world's "nothing-saying" (178) is apprehended less often as an aggregate of distinct voices, more frequently as a "ceaseless buzz" or a hum (173). Elizabeth Bennet's traveling companion to Hunsford Parsonage, courtly Sir William Lucas, regales her with civilities that are "worn out like his information," and that, since Sir William has "nothing to say that could be worth hearing," are "listened to with about as much delight as the rattle of the chaise" (136). Austen's unfinished novel *Sanditon* features a frenzy of epistolary activity in which one letter generates another, without any ever making sense. The character who sets up this "circuitous train of intelligence" (367) caps her admiring description of the clamor of this correspondence with the words "Wheel within wheel" (343)—casting herself as the engineer of a sort of white noise machine.

Noise in Austen registers the ubiquity of the social.[5] By directing attention to it, Austen reveals the mechanisms of transmission that compose a society and the networks for mechanical repetition that sustain mass communications. She directs attention to the circuits of exchange that underwrite the inside stories of romantic fiction—that give that fiction's deep meanings their currency in the book market. Paying attention to the busy, prosy hum of her crowds dislocates our sense of what Austen's priorities are. Customarily, Austen's position within histories of the novel is pinpointed by relating her to a concept of "romantic individualism." Either she is against it, as we are told by the scholarship associating her with an anti-Jacobin recoil from the cult of sensibility and the moral claims of individual feeling,[6] or she finds in her novels the means—specifically, her use of free indirect discourse—of bringing about an ideal blend of the individual and the social, rehabilitating sensibility for the nineteenth-century novel's sociocentric world. As *The Rise of the Novel* put it in a now somewhat notoriously androcentric statement, Austen combines into "a harmonious unity" the subjective narrative mode cultivated by the domestic Samuel Richardson and the objective mode cultivated by the public man Henry Fielding and thereby makes Henry James possible.[7] These ways of relating Austen to literary history converge insofar as each preempts consideration of how a self-society opposition is constructed and how it is naturalized. They preempt consideration of how Austen's novels, in bringing impersonal discourses into dynamic exchange with the feeling-filled language of inside views, help to establish the staging and management of that opposition as the special social office of "the" novel, an office that endows the genre with its authority among the disciplines.[8] As I analyze crowd noise and interior feeling in *Sense and Sensibility*, *Persuasion*, and *Sanditon*, I will show how Austen stages and manages that exchange between the impersonal and the personal in ways that recast the emergent romantic protocols for reading: she supplements the opportunities her readers have for practice in sympathetic feeling by inviting them to partake in lighthearted games of stereotype-recognition and cliché-busting. I also will suggest that for Austen self-expression and the rites of self-culture prosper truly only when sheltered by the whir and hum of the run-of-the mill.

READING AND REPEATING

Earlier, in the remarks on *Pride and Prejudice* and *Persuasion* included in my third chapter, I suggested how Austen's ways of writing character furthered the reorganization of romantic-period reading and how her novels contributed to positioning audiences and defining literature in new ways, so that "good" books were no longer those proclaiming standards of conduct but instead those supplying readers with practice in feeling.[9] It is easy to see how in characterizing Elinor Dashwood and Anne Elliot, the two heroines I focus on here, Austen recapitulates in some measure the techniques for producing psychological depth—the use of free indirect discourse, for instance—that were developed by Burney and Burney's "school." After all, as we read in the blurb that the Oxford University Press uses for its edition of Austen's early work *The Watsons*, the novelist's preferred story line features a "heroine . . . outstanding for her sense and goodness, virtues notably lacking in the other characters." Arranging for this heroine's isolation in her moral and cognitive individuality—arranging it so that no other character in the novel feels or sees as she does—Austen is making sure that her readership knows this protagonist in a way that the heroine's world cannot. Austen's distinction lies with the way that, reiterating the psychological story line that the novelists of her youth had begun to make familiar, she is especially self-aware about what is at stake in its reading, to the point that in *Persuasion* particularly— a novel that deemphasizes plot, concentrates on inward feeling, and reads like a transcript of Anne's inner consciousness—this language of self-expression is presented as a reader's language. To engage with the way Austen treats reading, I begin by addressing the manner in which, like Burney and her contemporaries, Austen moves the meaning of character into the inward territories of the unavowed.

This is where the meaning is in Austen's characterization of Elinor Dashwood. For the entirety of volume two of *Sense and Sensibility*, Elinor does not impart to her mother or her sister the knowledge that the reader shares with her in private, that Edward Ferrars has engaged his self if not his affections elsewhere. "She was stronger alone" (121). Neither Elinor's speech nor her conduct indicates that she has a strong claim—indeed, one equal to her sister Marianne's—on the role of abandoned woman and on a story line of romantic disaster. Marianne, by contrast, stakes her claim to the position of sentimental heroine through a by-the-book adherence to a program of debility, letter writing, and tears. While she pursues her program, following Willoughby's departure from Devonshire, she makes no secret of her belief that feeling separates her from her sister and that she must suffer alone. Marianne assumes that Elinor is " 'happy' " in Edward's love (160), hence unable to feel with her in her agony. The tension that drives *Sense and Sensibility* is rooted in the fact that Marianne's assumption is mistaken: grief and abandonment constitute the sisters' common ground. At the same time, however, that Austen arranges for there to be a real "resemblance in their situations" (227), she is also staging the conflict between Elinor's and Marianne's ways of seeing. She establishes Elinor's isolation so as to establish her inwardness, and *Sense and Sensibility* is in the final analysis very precise about how the two sisters are divided—which is in another manner than Marianne thinks. In conformity with the codes of inner meaning, it is through not displaying that she is a heroine that Elinor qualifies as one. Through free indirect discourse Elinor's inner life is delivered into the safekeeping of an impersonal narrator, who takes up the burden of that language of sentiment and self-expression which, with near-fatal results, Marianne has clamorously made her own.[10]

"Marianne restored to life, health, friends, and to her doating mother, was an idea to fill [Elinor's] heart with sensations of exquisite comfort, and expand it in fervent gratitude;—but it led to no outward demonstrations of joy, no words, no smiles. All within Elinor's breast was satisfaction, silent and strong" (275). *Sense and Sensibility* in its own way follows a policy of eschewing outward demonstrations. By this means, it frames its real story—this narrative of Elinor's interior experience—as arcane knowledge, imparted in confidence.

In *Persuasion,* the "little history of sorrowful interest" (31) that relates how in 1806 Anne Elliot was persuaded out of her engagement with Captain Wentworth is framed in similar ways: the framing renders it the basis for a similar reading situation, in which readers can measure their sympathies against the characters' and in which the true story, played against a publicly apprehended story, seems more possessible because it seems possessed exclusively. When in *Persuasion* the action of the novel proper begins, as peace turns the navy ashore and Anne and Wentworth find themselves reunited by chance eight years after their first separation, no one but the reader is aware of this prior narrative. This "little history of sorrowful interest" is, in effect, off the record. At this point, Anne, at Uppercross with her younger sister Mary, is separated from Lady Russell, Sir Walter Elliot, and her elder sister Elizabeth, who are the "only three of her own friends in the secret of the past" and who have buried the episode in "oblivion" (33–34). Her consciousness of the past isolates her. Free indirect discourse reveals to readers how Anne copes alone with the shock of this reunion with Wentworth. Repeatedly following Anne as she retreats into the spaces of privacy that offer her intervals for reflection, it suggests that she savors this revival of bygone pains and pleasures, in the way that one savors a secret indulgence. Reading *Persuasion* is an experience of reading a narrative that, focusing on second chances even more than the other Austen novels do, frames itself as "a second novel"—a successor narrative to that first novel that is off the record.[11] What enhances readers' intimacy with Anne is that the experience of living *Persuasion* feels like that too. Adela Pinch remarks that "Anne's early experience is like a text which she is repeating with renewed feeling." It is not just that Anne is a bookish heroine, whose expressions of desolation take the form of repeating "to herself some few of the thousand poetical descriptions extant of autumn" (82), whose mind is occupied with recollections of Wentworth *and* remembered quotations. It is also, as Pinch observes, that "there is something literary in the temporal structure of *Persuasion*" itself, which "produces an isomorphism between the doubling of the first courtship and the second courtship, *and* the doubling of Anne's experience and a reader's experience."[12]

Participating in Anne's point of view means being privy to another, secret story in a way that generates a constant awareness of the lacunae in what is being narrated. In such a context, innocuous-sounding statements—" 'We are expecting a brother of Mrs. Croft's here soon; I dare say you know him by name' " (51)—are laced with ironies for the initiated reader; polite conversation has unsuspected depths. Anne's absorption in her memories of how she formerly stood with Wentworth, her engagement with the story inside her head, has the effect of making her both thought-full and wordless. She and Wentworth share the past but share it separately. As a participant in the public life of the nation, Wentworth *can* revert to the year of their engagement: "His profession qualified him, his disposition led him, to talk; and '*That* was in the year six;' '*That* happened before I went to sea in the year six,' occurred in the course of the first evening they spent together" (63). By contrast, remembrance of the past—which for her is wholly defined in terms of a private life spent either with or without Wentworth—seems to bar Anne from speaking. Thus the interior animation that makes *Persuasion* into the record of the "dialogue of Anne's mind with itself" is also manifested as a

215

form of privation, as if interiority had as its necessary consequence an impassive, incommunicative exterior.[13] *Persuasion* makes this dissociation between inner and outer worlds into a principle of characterization. Describing the reactions that Wentworth elicits from his female listeners as he recounts his somewhat macho stories of disasters at sea, the narrator separates Anne from the others: "Anne's shudderings were to herself alone: but the Miss Musgroves could be as open as they were sincere, in their exclamations of pity and horror" (66). The negative distinction here ascribed to Anne registers how Austen accommodates her psychological culture's protocols for characterization. She is enabling readers to practice feeling along with Anne, with a sympathy that feels more authentic, like a more immaculately personal effect, because nobody within the novel, with the eventual exception of Wentworth, is conscious of her story. With their exclamations, the Misses Musgrove make too much noise for any one to notice it.

As is suggested by the echo of the language of Aristotle's *Poetics* that we hear in that mention of the Misses Musgroves' "pity and horror," Austen casts the women in this novel as Wentworth's readers. Soon after his arrival at Uppercross, Louisa and Henrietta acquire their own copy of the navy list and sit down together "to pore over it, with the professed view of finding out the ships which Captain Wentworth had commanded" (64): at the start of the novel Anne's ability to identify the rank and squadron of the Admiral Croft who wishes to rent her father's house indicates that she too possesses a navy list to pore over. Austen uses these examples to propose that to occupy one's mind with Wentworth means occupying one's eye with a book.[14] This analogy, and the passages that depict Anne withdrawing from company and casting a retrospective glance over events as if she were retiring with a book, suggest in their turn how the treatment of social matters and treatment of reading matter coincide in *Persuasion*. This is the case in the novels generally: as I shall demonstrate in the next section, Austen's commentaries in *Sense and Sensibility* on what Marianne Dashwood does with her reading matter are anything but a gratuitous addition to the courtship narrative. As a whole Austen's writing is about social relations—the relationship between, say, domestic life and public life—*and* about reading relations—about the textual conventions by which audiences are formed and distinguished. Her narratives weave together the processes of romantic choice and cultural discrimination.

Hence *Persuasion*'s mobilizing of the question of taste. Austen's characters adopt a language of judgment and appraisal to talk about courting: as characterized by Lady Russell, Wentworth is someone who "at twenty-three had seemed to understand somewhat of the value of an Anne Elliot" (119). As we gather, at thirty he is someone who will understand that value again. But Wentworth's and Anne's second chance at happiness is postponed until Wentworth in his turn discovers how better to read other people. Anne and Wentworth's separation appears irrevocable and Wentworth remains angry over the events of 1806 so long as he thinks that those events brought to light a fatal flaw in Anne's character, so long as he thinks that "character" is something that can be deemed decided or proved once and for all. Austen suggests the trouble with Wentworth's theory of character by delineating his attitude to Anne in words that hearken back, anachronistically, to early-eighteenth-century ways of relating character and writing. His conviction that Anne is unworthy because she has been and, as he supposes, continues to be susceptible to persuasion is described as an " 'indelible, immoveable impression' " (230). Similar terms occur when, conversing with Louisa Musgrove on the path to Winthrop, Wentworth suggests that such persuadability is to be deplored because it represents a falling away from an ideal of legibility and indelibility:

> It is the worst evil of too yielding and indecisive a character, that no influence over it can be depended on.—You are never sure of a good impression being durable. Every body may sway it; let those who would be happy be firm.—Here is a nut . . . To exemplify,—a beautiful glossy nut, which, blessed with original strength, has outlived all the storms of autumn. Not a puncture, not a weak spot any where.—This nut . . . , while so many of its brethren have fallen and been trodden under foot, is still in possession of all the happiness that a hazel-nut can be supposed capable of. (86)

The underlying metaphor of Wentworth's speech to Louisa recalls Alexander Pope's "Epistle on the Characters of Women"; it depicts Anne, whom Wentworth is here faulting for inconstancy, as "matter too soft a lasting mark to bear."[15] In place of this faith in the value of the mind that is made up, or, this faith in the character that is stabilized because it will take no more than a single mark (preferably Wentworth's own), what Wentworth must discover is something like romantic reading practices. He must learn to read in the manner in which, in *Pride and Prejudice*, Elizabeth Bennet learns to read. As I suggested two chapters ago, Austen's account of how Elizabeth comes to realize the inadequacy of "first impressions" not only bespeaks the value

Austen places on human complexity and capacity for change through time[16] but also incorporates lessons in literary experience. With the happy ending that rewards Elizabeth for her reperusals of letters and second looks at Darcy's portrait—rewards her for rereadings that uncover inner meanings and acknowledge that "character" is something that can never be definitively deciphered—Austen reinforces her proposals to her readers about what it means to *really* read. The Austen novel often associates love with the processes of interpreting a text, processes that are (to quote a pertinent passage in *Persuasion*) "ceaseless in interest" (227). This association underlies Austen's characteristic conclusion: the Austen novel's penultimate chapter often features a vaguely giggly conversation between the newly engaged couple in which, in the manner of Sophie von LaRoche's description of her Wedgwood seal, they "look back over the road they have come," reading their own story and repeating passages from it in the way Anne Elliot "repeats" elegiac verse. Thus the penultimate chapter of *Pride and Prejudice* begins: "Elizabeth's spirits soon rising to playfulness again, she wanted Mr. Darcy to account for his having ever fallen in love with her" (262).[17] With her customary tact, Austen frequently keeps her readers at a distance from these exercises in reminiscence, but, we might infer, the conversation must be not only about laying the groundwork for an interpretive partnership devoted to the appreciation of "our love-story," but also about finding out the latent significance in events that formerly seemed known. In these chapters, the lovers' activity and the readers' are aligned—which is also to say that these endings align the processes of remembering a lived experience and reassessing a text we have read. Austen might there be saying of the experience of being in love what romantic aesthetics said in making "the classic" into the prop for exercises in which individuals prolonged the act of interpretation and thereby probed their sensibilities: that the classic must be "never entirely comprehensible. But those who are cultivated and who cultivate themselves must always seem to learn more from it."[18] In *Sense and Sensibility*, Elinor Dashwood and Edward Ferrars model this aesthetic attitude as they talk about their story: "[T]hough a very few hours spent in the hard labour of incessant talking will dispatch more subjects than can really be in common between any two rational creatures, yet with lovers it is different. Between *them* no subject is finished, no communication is even made, till it has been made at least twenty times over" (319).

When *Persuasion* concludes with the conversation that absorbs a newly engaged Anne and Wentworth, it makes a similar claim: "They could indulge in those retrospections and acknowledgments, and especially in those explanations of what had directly preceded the present moment, which were so poignant and so ceaseless in interest. All the little variations of the last week were gone through; and of yesterday and to-day there could scarcely be an end" (227). Wentworth at last arrives at an understanding of Anne that is readerly in the approved manner this passage from chapter 23 commemorates. Clearly, it is Anne's attempts to understand Wentworth once again— "Now, how were his sentiments to be read?" (61)—that supply the chief episodes in the novel's drama of reading. But that drama also pivots on the particular, reader-centered manner in which *Persuasion* rewrites the Cinderella narrative, as it shifts the fairy tale's emphasis from the heroine's transformation into a beauty to the prince's second look at her face. This second look magically undoes the effects of the seven years whose passing faded Anne's complexion, robbed her of her bloom, and left her "wretchedly altered" (62).

The interest in interpretation that this rewriting of the Cinderella narrative indexes—an emphasis on revising and repeating, on spinning out the act of interpretation—also in 1818 represents an interest in conduct that garners cultural capital. It is time to remind ourselves that Austen's concern throughout her work with readers' relations to texts is a response to historically new uses of reading matter in which, as I have noted, literary response could serve as a mode of distinction and in which the pleasures of the imagination and the pleasures of social calculation were mutually enhancing. The second sort of pleasures are certainly on display in *Persuasion*'s description of the romantic environs of the seaside resort in which Anne Elliot's fortunes first take their turn for the better. "[T]hese places," the narrator comments, "must be visited, and visited again, to make the worth of Lyme understood" (94). Austen published in an era when the tourist trade was heating up on England's south coast and when, as a character in her own *Sanditon* points out, " 'Every five years, one hears of some new place or other starting up by the Sea, and growing the fashion.—How they can half of them be filled, is the wonder! . . . our Coast is too full of them altogether' " (325). *Sanditon* proposes a less-than-romantic reading of *Persuasion*'s paean to Lyme: it makes it look as though *Persuasion*'s narrator is impersonating someone who (in a buyer's market) attempts to solicit the custom of the discriminating traveler. ("[T]hese places must be visited, and visited again, to make the worth of Lyme understood": What tourist in quest of the picturesque would not like to be addressed as somebody who prefers the less showy sightseeing available off the beaten track?) Recast along those lines, this statement suggesting that

219

Lyme's unostentatious attractions "blush unseen" operates as a useful reminder of the context of social classification and contest in which Austen makes Elinor's and Anne's narratives into inside stories and exclusive property.

Perhaps it could also provide a reminder of the pedagogic context in which the cultural dispositions equipping readers to take pleasure in those secret, inside stories are formed. Like the attractions of Lyme, round characters "must be visited and visited again" for their worth to be understood. That effort of understanding transpires in the literature classroom especially, where we conscientiously reperuse texts and year after year debate questions such as "Emma Woodhouse—a Heroine no one can like?" or "How sensible *is* Elinor Dashwood?" Austen's round characters are visited again: she herself supplied the terms in which those debates about her characters, a staple of literary pedagogy and a basic mechanism of literary depth, are managed. The very title *Sense and Sensibility* invites us to remind ourselves that the personalities of real characters exceed moral abstractions. It commends a program of author-ized character reading. So does Austen's prediction in correspondence that no one could like Emma but herself. This prescience on Austen's part about how to keep readers talking is not surprising: as I have suggested, while they meditate on what it means to repeat an experience or a story with renewed feeling, her novels vividly annotate the practices of romantic readers.

"WHEEL WITHIN WHEEL": READING AND WRITING MACHINES

On the evidence of that annotating, Austen should be seen as a self-aware contributor to the practices and protocols of aesthetic self-cultivation. She knows exactly what she is doing when she writes in support of the romantic premise that the interiority of the literary character represents for the reader a repository of significance not exhausted by commentary and of intellectual wealth not exhausted by consumption. At the same time she gives every evidence of intending to manage her characterization in ways that will put interiority in its place. She deliberately locates the reading of character at the edge of the polemical field in which her romantic contemporaries negotiated the relationship between literariness and literacy and pitted literary meaning against the bestselling meaninglessness of the stereotype and the cliché. What relation can there be between the "new editions," the repetitions of old impulses to which Freud alluded in assembling his romantic portrait of the intricacies of individuality, and the new editions that worried many romantics because—in a period when a ten-thousand-copy edition of a Waverley novel could be bought up in three weeks—all those books made novel reading the activity of a crowd? The repetitions that are a component of romantic reading practices coexist uneasily with the repetitions of mass communications, which were stepped up in Austen's lifetime as presses began to be driven by steam engines and as printers began to employ the molds called "stereotypes" (invented in 1798) and "clichés" (introduced in France in 1809).[19] They coexist just as uneasily with the repetitions that define the economic cycles of a commercial society, uneasiness compounded in that when romantic commentators think about money as "a financial instrument that can reproduce itself through interest without reference to any actual exchange," they often seem, by an association of ideas, to think about how the production of literary works can proceed through "the purely technical manipulation of conventional forms and images."[20] This uneasy coexistence is precisely Austen's subject.

Round characters, who disavow outward demonstrations, are accomplices of discourse. They keep us talking, much as the complexities that lovers can discover in each other and in each other's stories keep Austen's couples talking. By contrast, a revoking of self-expression seems incorporated into our notion of flat characters. The fact that *cliché* and *stereotype*, the terms we use in designating substandard characterization, have their provenance in the history of printing registers a fear of repeating and copying the word that intersects, paradoxically, with a fear of wordlessness. The antiprint romanticism that wields those terms reacts to the frightening prospect that, in an age of mass communications, the signs producing personal effects—the depth effects that we identify with personality—can belong to everybody. Books might become "every person's property"—and for this very reason these signs might as well belong to nobody in particular.

Austen's reading would have made her acquainted with the rhetoric that conduct literature and critical reviews such as the *Gentleman's Magazine*, the *Edinburgh*, and the *Quarterly* mobilized to defend the aesthetic and defend the self against this dispossession. Her contemporaries' efforts to preserve literariness as an exclusive property resonate throughout her work. The hallmarks of their antiprint rhetoric were an emphasis on excess and an emphasis on the mechanical. The diatribes against popular literature are troubled by its apparent proliferation: in this context, presses are with regularity "inundated," "deluged," or "groaning" under the weight of too many novels that are too much alike. In Austen's *Sanditon* Sir Edward Denham complains about the " 'mere trash' " of the " 'common circulating library' " but also borrows books from the Sanditon library by the armful (357), an episode suggesting how Austen has both picked up on the reviewers' implicit contention that bad books are those that come in bulk and recognized the self-aggrandizing ends to which the reviewers' ultra-repeatable rhetoric can be turned.

Conduct book writers and critics are also wont to imply—if only through their fondness for borrowing technical terms from printers—that it is now machines that are doing the writing and the reading. Hence Coleridge in his *Biographia Literaria* (1816): "Now, partly by the labours of successive poets and in part by the more artificial state of society and social intercourse, language, mechanized as it were into a barrel-organ, supplies at once instrument and tune."[21] Confronting what was apparently a bad epic poem commemorating the English victory at Waterloo, a critic for the *Quarterly Review* chose to assess the text as if it were a specimen of the mechanical genius of one M. Didot, a French printer, who was, "if not the inventor, at least the introducer of that mode of printing called *Stereotype*," and who was also most recently, according to the reviewer, the designer of a "verse engine": "It was not, indeed, to be expected that the machine, however ingenious, could always place the words in intelligible order or work out anything like sense or meaning, but . . . the lines of the pamphlet look as like real bona fide verses, as if they had been written by the hand of man, and printed by the ordinary process of the press."[22] The hackneyed novel is likewise presented in the reviews as a product stamped out by a press rather than created by an author. As the *Edinburgh* suggested in 1803 in an indignant review of Germaine de Staël's *Delphine,* the hackneyed novel's heroine is a creature of prefabricated language: she is made not of sugar and spice, but of "customary phrases, *union of souls* . . . &c. &c. &c., the types of which Mr. Lane of the Minerva Press very prudently keeps ready composed, in order to facilitate the printing of the Adventures of Captain C— and Miss F—, and other interesting stories." The anxiety informing this Luddite mode of literary criticism is that books' (and characters') roles in the rites of privacy and private ownership are mitigated by the iterability and predictability that associate them with machines. This is because, for a start, the machine's promiscuous availability to all users suspends the individuality of any one user. (The *Edinburgh* reviewer in fact goes on to equate that availability with a sexual threat. To demonstrate that the "vulgarity" of the ready-made language of *Delphine* ought to "diminish [the novel's] value," he cites the latest statistical study on the surplus of prostitutes in the London streets: "Mr. Colquhoun . . . reckons up above 40,000 heroines of this species, most of whom . . . have at one time or another reasoned like the sentimental Delphine.")[23]

In some measure the role circulating libraries played in facilitating new readers' reading accounts for the frequency with which they appear in the negative descriptions of modern mass communications. But arguably the commentators' tendency to dwell on what was "circulating" about these institutions derives from the ways in which, to early-nineteenth-century observers, books resembled money, not necessarily by partaking of money's desirability but rather by mimicking its ubiquity and characterlessness. Books from circulating libraries are represented in the reviews as a form of circulating specie. They move with rapidity from hand to hand: one book resembles another as one penny resembles another penny. Thomas Carlyle thus referred to "the legal coins of the Minerva Press" in an 1820 review that delineated a kind of literary Gresham's law as Carlyle complained that the "critical Assaying-house" had allowed Goethe's *Wilhelm Meister*, "a German *Friedrich d'or*," to slip unnoticed among "new and brilliant British brass Farthings." There may be a second reason, however, why commentators dwelt on the circulating. It is worth acknowledging that to modern ears the phrase *circulating library* (used where we would expect to hear of a lending library) doesn't necessarily describe exchanges of books so much as it suggests a building that is in motion. That is, the phrase itself suggests some sort of a machine, a bibliopolic form of Burke's "great wheel of circulation" or Coleridge's "barrel organ." Certainly, commentators deployed images of the mechanical in ways that suggested "circulating" as a possible description of the condition of the library's users. Reading on automatic pilot, bad readers can look like giddy cogs in a whirling machine. Impelled by the "demand for the same adventures, the same language, and the same sentiments," the novel addict portrayed in the *Gentleman's Magazine* and the like, who moves back and forth and back and forth from sofa to circulating library, is herself engaging in a kind of mechanical circulation.[24] In the dystopias of antiprint romanticism, female reading, "for all its self-indulgence, . . . is oddly impersonal."[25]

Together with *Northanger Abbey*, *Sanditon*, the novel Austen was writing at the time of her death, represents an exploration of what Coleridge's "barrel-organ" might sound like: each is an experiment in mobilizing the authorless, impersonal hum of a ready-made language. *Northanger Abbey* is a tour de force demonstration of the repeatability of the codes of novel writing. Catherine

Morland's excursions to Bath and Northamptonshire take her down a generic beaten track. Like a Burney heroine, Evelina having her hair frizzed
or Camilla catching up with fashion, Catherine finds that a "heroine's entrée
into life could not take place till after three or four days had been spent in
learning what was mostly worn" (7); she is even abducted as Radcliffe's Adeline and Emily are, although the villain in the case is merely a boorish John
Thorpe intent on bullying Catherine into carriage-rides at unsuitable moments.[26] All that is out of the ordinary, finally, about Catherine's adventures
is that Austen has transposed them to the register of the commonplace: "Every thing indeed . . . was done, on the part of the Morlands, with a degree
of moderation and composure, which seemed rather consistent with the common feelings of common life, than with the refined susceptibilities, the tender
emotions which . . . [a heroine's story] ought always to excite" (6).

Critical consensus has it that *Northanger*, published posthumously in 1818,
was written in the 1790s and revised for the last time in 1803. However, a
later date suggests itself once we note how neatly its concerns lead into *Sanditon's*.[27] Allusions to Burney, Richardson, and Scott make *Sanditon* read, as
Northanger does, as if Austen's fun in writing it consisted partly in going archly
through the motions of writing a novel. Not only novel reading but also
advertising, the fashion trade, quack medicine, and picturesque tourism are
at issue here: in the town of Sanditon—at its circulating library especially—
these practices flourish in their most conventionalized, inane, and excessive
forms. It is the desire to copy strategies for seduction from novels and to
learn to talk "a good deal by rote" (353) that takes Sir Edward Denham
to Mrs. Whitby's circulating library. Charlotte Heywood visits it to examine
its stock of fashionable accessories: "new Parasols, new Gloves, and new
Broches" (331), "all the useless things in the World that could not be done
without" (345). When he wishes to investigate Sanditon's financial fortunes,
Mr. Parker visits the library and inspects the library's subscription list, which
to his disappointment proves "but commonplace" (344). It is fitting that all
roads in the town Mr. Parker has "planned and built, and praised and
puffed" (328) seem to lead to the circulating library, because Sanditonians
like Parker, who has built on sand, seem immensely willing to invest in empty
convention—in signs in the place of substance. The healthy people at the
watering place invest in the signs of rakishness, which is here precisely a kind
of speaking rather than doing, or they invest in the signs of fashion. The
invalids advertise their genteel refinement through the signs of sickness and
also, as consumers of "Tonic Pills" in which their friends have a financial

interest (374), purchase the signs of health. The Minerva novels with which William Lane stocked his network of circulating libraries were notorious for repeating one another: more precisely, rumor had it that often one Minerva novel was a replica of another and that, in the effort to augment his inventory, Lane merely simulated the differences between them. He shuffled chapters, played "tricks . . . with title-pages," and so escalated the fictionality of his fictions by cavalierly marketing the trappings and not the substance of novelty and by making pretense an element of his retail practice.[28] Fiction plays a parallel role in Sanditon's speculative economy.

In a fitting exemplification of the circularity that fascinates Austen in this novel, *Sanditon*—which was never finished and never gets around to launching a courtship plot—ends up being about the puffing of Sanditon. The twelve chapters we have are largely devoted to the efforts that Mr. Parker, his sister, and his partner-in-speculation, Lady Denham, make to add names with élan to the library's undistinguished subscription list and to fill up the resort's lodgings with invalids who require salubrious sea breezes. For Diana Parker, the novel's hypochondriac, selling Sanditon is a matter of selling sickness or imaginary complaints in order to sell health or imaginary cures.[29] Putting his faith in mimetic desire, Mr. Parker, for his part, is confident that fashion will attract fashion to Sanditon—will attract, in the impersonal, generic terms that passages from Parker's point of view regularly adopt, more harps heard through "upper casements" and more "Females in elegant white . . . to be seen with [the] books and [the] campstools" that mark them as chic devotees of the picturesque (338). *Sanditon*'s account of puffery reveals the picturesque tourist, the female in elegant white, the novel reader, and the hypochondriac to be copy machines. While it does so, the reading machines and writing machines of Austen's lifetime seem to be humming in the background.

But there are additional ways in which this novel can seem an examination of the mechanized aspects of social life. The codes that shape the Sanditonians' speech and action seem impersonal, not only because they are codes—and as such inherently transferable—but also because they operate according to a logic that bypasses or mutates human intentions. Puffery in the form of inflation works like this as it demonstrates that economic indicators (for example, the increases in the cost of meat that so exasperate Lady Denham) are dissociated utterly from real values and needs. Dependent on the letter-writing of acquaintances of acquaintances, the intricate epistolary machine ("Wheel within wheel") that Diana Parker mobilizes to drum up business for

Sanditon likewise takes on a life of its own. It giddily spins out of Diana's control, "vaporis[ing] reality and generat[ing] purely verbal 'facts.' "[30] Under its influence she thinks she has persuaded two large families to take lodgings in Sanditon, but "the subject had supplied Letters and Extracts and Messages enough to make everything appear what it was not" (372), and only one family (a *little* family of four) arrives.

In general, writing is immensely productive of absurdity here, print especially so. *Sanditon* begins when two newspaper clippings—advertisements in the *Morning Post* and the *Kentish Gazette* (323)—send Mr. Parker off on a wild goose chase for a surgeon who will let himself be lured from Willingden to Sanditon. That there are two advertisements in Parker's pocket seems to speak to the inherent excessiveness of print. There are also two places called Willingden (and Parker goes to the wrong one), just as there are two Sanditons, old Sanditon and the new town Mr. Parker has developed. Parker has left his old house vacant and built a second one, which, unable to resist a cliché, he has named Trafalgar Place, replicating other Trafalgar Places popping up like mushrooms across England.

No doubt, one stake of the recurring celebrations of the "economical" nature of Austen's prose is the consolatory service these celebrations do in a climate in which, like the one she satirizes in *Sanditon*, mechanical reproduction is perceived to be operating overtime and running amok. In this climate, interpretation—readers' intimate transactions with psychological inside stories and their experiments in repeating and revising their readings with renewed feeling—operates as another, equivalent sort of defense mechanism. The exercises in interpreting that Austen writes into her characterization offer readers a way to salvage what is personal and personalizing, rather than mechanical, about their reading. But it is characteristic of Austen's even-handedness that she also invites readers to analyze the social machinery of distinction, the maneuvering that occurs when we claim, while we interpret, to be *in* a print culture's crowd of readers but not *of* it.

Even Mr. Parker, a creature of replication, is capable of making the moves that support a claim to distinction. When Mr. Heywood reminds him that the south coast is overcrowded with fashionable bathing-places, Parker agrees that " 'those good people who are trying to add to the number, are . . . excessively absurd, and must soon find themselves the Dupes of their own fallacious Calculations' "; yet somehow, for Mr. Parker Sanditon does not add to the number, though the recent " 'attempts of two or three speculating People about Brinshore' " do (326). Austen's interest in such crowd-repelling strategies also lies behind the irony we hear in the third chapter of *Northanger Abbey* when the narrator describes how Catherine Morland and her friends visit the pump-room at Bath. They stayed "long enough . . . to discover that the crowd was insupportable, and that there was not a genteel face to be seen, which every body discovers every Sunday throughout the season" (19). With the words that underscore the commonplace nature of their discovery (it is everybody's discovery on every Sunday), Austen underscores how her characters are contributing to the crowdedness of the crowd, even as they lament it and establish their own distinctive gentility through that lament. Their pursuit of personal distinction is what makes the figures in this crowd portrait into run-of-the-mill types. Every one goes through these motions. The process that this passage in *Northanger Abbey* describes is like the one we replay whenever we drive onto the freeway, are brought to a halt by bumper-to-bumper traffic, and proceed to marvel over the number of cars and marvel over why "people" simply cannot stay home. The sequel of the chapter, which ushers in *Northanger Abbey*'s famous vindication of novel writing and reading, makes it clear that the process the passage describes is likewise akin to the one Austen's fellow novelists replay whenever they degrade "by their contemptuous censure the very performances, to the number of which they are themselves adding." Mindful of the cramped conditions in their shared generic territory, the narrator of *Northanger Abbey* draws a moral for fellow novelists. They have responded to the crowding by "scarcely ever permitting [such works] to be read by their own heroine[s], who, if [they] accidentally take up a novel, [are] sure to turn over its insipid pages with disgust." The advice of Austen's narrator is: "Let us leave it to the Reviewers to abuse such effusions of fancy at their leisure, and over every new novel to talk in thread-bare strains of the trash with which the press now groans" (21).

There is no gainsaying the pleasures Austen supplies when her characterization enables us to watch the characters turn into types. One astute definition has it that the stereotype is an already-read text.[31] This description suggests the affinities that link the pleasure that we feel when we begin to think that we've really got Mr. Parker's number to the pleasure that we reap from Austen's intertextuality. We can see the first of these pleasures as a variant on the parlor game of allusion-spotting that Austen initiates whenever, flirting with conventionality, she regales us with "novel slang" or rewrites quotations from Pope. This game, in catering to the comfortable pleasures of recognition (the pleasures of seeing again a figure that "Adam saw in the first novel he opened"), is not so different from the game that the characters of *Emma* play with the little Knightleys' box of letters.[32] The enjoyment afforded by the already-read text of the stereotype is also like one form of the enjoyment afforded by gossip, an activity Austen's readers have frequently alluded to when they have defined the nature of her comedy. Rumor mills too—as, with its suggestions of mechanical reproduction, the very term *mill* implies— thrive off the reiterative pleasures of the code, and the interest that the hackneyed narratives of gossip arouse depends partly on "the very familiarity of [their] form."[33]

THE PERSONAL AND THE PRO FORMA

Austen's comfort with the paradoxes that attend the mechanical reproducibility of personal effects shapes not only her novels' comedy but also their concern with the cultivation of feeling. To get a sense of that comfort, one might start by recognizing how the Dashwood sisters' enthusiastic participation in commercialized print culture contributes toward *Sense and Sensibility*'s creation of "a new arena for personal feeling in the novel."[34] Margaret, the youngest Dashwood, engages her elders in a game of speculation when, "striking out a novel thought," she wonders aloud what they would do " 'if somebody [gave them] all a large fortune apiece.' " In response Edward Ferrars predicts that the Dashwoods would shop: " 'What magnificent orders would travel from this family to London . . . in such an event! What a happy day for booksellers, music-sellers and print-shops!' " (79). Edward's suggestion that the sisters' shopping spree would encompass the sister arts—literature, music, and graphic art—indexes the degree to which Austen identifies both Marianne and Elinor with the project of "taste." Both are committed to developing their aesthetic sensibilities. When he continues, however, Edward lingers on the mixed motives that would inform Marianne's particular share in this shopping: " 'Thomson, Cowper, Scott—[Marianne] would buy them all over and over again; she would buy up every copy, I believe, to prevent their falling into unworthy hands' " (79). Marianne, Edward suggests, would not only buy for pleasure, but would also buy to make poetry into a controlled substance, property reserved for those few who could consume it appropriately. The desire Edward attributes to Marianne—for a property of a rigorously personalized kind—seems to motivate the dissatisfaction she expresses later with the codes of picturesque description: "It is very true . . . that admiration of landscape scenery is become a mere jargon. Every body pretends to feel and tries to describe with the taste and elegance of him who first defined what picturesque beauty was. I detest jargon of every kind, and sometimes I have kept my feelings to myself, because I could find no language to describe them in but what was worn and hackneyed out of all sense and meaning" (83). Unlike Anne Elliot, who, as I have noted, is a quoting heroine and who in this capacity *does* repeat what others have uttered, Marianne, uncomfortable with being numbered among "every body" and being a face in the crowd, wants language to herself. " 'I abhor every common-place phrase' " (38). The fact that language circulates, and the possibility that words—like coins traveling from hand to hand—may be "worn" in their passage from mouth to mouth, bother her.[35] Marianne takes pride in how her self-fashioned ethical program gives preference to the authentic over the imitative, real feelings over pretended feelings, and self-expression over conformity to " 'common-place notions' " (45). But here this scheme leads Marianne into a logical quandary. To describe her rapturous feelings about the countryside around Barton Cottage involves, simultaneously, expressing herself *and* immersing herself in the conventional and commonplace: Marianne is almost tempted therefore to conform to what she identifies as Elinor's overcautious self-restraint and so fall silent.

Despite her best intentions, Marianne copies. In this instance, she is almost tempted to copy her sister's silence. Austen arranges for repetition and for convention to prove crucial to Marianne's fate. For instance, that complaint about the hackneyed jargon of the picturesque echoes any number of literary reviews that, in equally programmatic ways, lamented the repetitive propensities of the travelers who published accounts of their journeys in quest of the picturesque. "Next to novels," the most "fashionable kind of reading," according to one rather jaded reviewer, the descriptive tour, another reviewer observed, soon makes us "sensible of that disgust, which attends the frequent repetition of the same remarks." These tours, it was said, could place the reader "in an unvaried reverie, like that produced by the constant and uniform repetition of any heavy sound."[36] Willoughby, who at the start of the novel devotedly copies out pieces of piano music for Marianne (72), goes on to betray her with copying in the novel's second volume. The insulting letter he sends to her in London turns out in some sense not to be his own: " '[he] had only the credit of servilely copying' " what his fiancée dictated to him (288). Noting the resemblances that affiliate Marianne with Colonel Brandon's two Elizas, other readers have speculated that, in creating Marianne, Austen gave herself a means of examining her genre's sentimental investment in repeating the stereotypes of female suffering.[37] Marianne is a new edition of a half-century's worth of betrayed heroines. The fact that she's taken a page (or more) from sentimental fiction's book alters how we assess her claim to possess an inner uniqueness that would be compromised by association with other people's commonplaces. In her cultivation of individuality (*because* of her cultivation of individuality), Marianne may be recognized as a type—a victim of convention in more than one sense.

If Austen slyly arranges for Marianne, the sister with sensibility, to be read like a book, it does not follow that she wants the inner life of the sister with sense to be identified in any simple way with notions of deep meanings too personal to be articulated. When Elinor Dashwood describes personal responses—even so personal a response as her attraction to Edward Ferrars—her language is at once impersonal *and* self-betraying. This is the language that Elinor uses to Marianne at the moment when she does not " 'attempt to deny . . . that [she thinks] very highly of [Edward]—that [she] greatly esteem[s], that [she] like[s] him' " (17):

> Of his sense and his goodness, . . . no one can, I think, be in doubt, who has seen him often enough to engage him in unreserved conversation. . . . upon the whole, I venture to pronounce that his mind is well-informed, his enjoyment of books exceedingly great, his imagination lively, his observation just and correct, and his taste delicate and pure. His abilities in every respect improve as much upon acquaintance as his manners and person. At first sight, his address is certainly not striking; and his person can hardly be called handsome, till the expression of his eyes, which are uncommonly good, and the general sweetness of his countenance, is perceived. (16–17)

Barbara M. Benedict has called attention to the "mannered parallelisms, abstract diction and passive phrasing" that make this little speech curiously evocative of the moral essays that Mary Bennet in *Pride and Prejudice* parrots and copies into her commonplace book. Benedict proposes that what we are hearing from Elinor is a version of the dispassionate language of a third-person narrator, a version of novels' language of communal judgment and social authority. Indeed, the description of Edward that Elinor offers could be one that such a narrator would use to introduce a heroine, a character whose worth, in conformity to the program of the period, could not be judged at "first sight." Oddly, the phrasing that allies Elinor with the faceless narrator of *Sense and Sensibility* also characterizes and personalizes her. For all its stilted formality and impersonality, this passage of description tells us more about Elinor's caution than it does about Edward's worth. It suggests Elinor's curiously distanced relation to her own feelings: how Elinor's resolve is not so much *to* judge objectively as it is *not to* let desire sway her.[38]

That the passage points in two directions invites us to think further about how, with Elinor, the language of private feeling, which gives readers an inside view, is articulated with the language of commonplaces and crowd portraits. Austen's handling of point of view and use of free indirect discourse, I have suggested, render the real story of *Sense and Sensibility* the story of Elinor's inner experience. Yet Austen makes us work if we want straightforwardly to correlate psychological effects with individuality or to correlate what is most private with what is most personal. In talking of her love, Elinor places herself in a crowd and re-cites what everyone says and feels. (" 'No one' " can doubt Edward's abilities; the sweetness of his face " 'is perceived,' " perhaps by all the world, certainly not by Elinor in particular.) In *Emma*, Jane Fairfax (at least when she is seen in company in Highbury) adopts a similar habit of speech. The transcript of Emma's attempts to pump Jane for information about Frank Churchill, with whom Jane was ostensibly "a little acquainted" at Weymouth, reads like this: " 'Was he handsome?'—'She believed he was reckoned a very fine young man.' . . . 'Did he appear a sensible young man; a young man of information?'—'At a watering-place, or in a common London acquaintance, it was difficult to decide on such points. Manners were all that could be safely judged of. . . . She believed every body found his manners pleasing' " (151). The conversations that engage Highbury socialites (like the shopping excursions in *Camilla*) seem to have encouraged recent readers, whenever they talk about character, to mobilize an opposition between self and society and an opposition between what separates individuals and what connects them. Civility for Austen, accounts of her "conservatism" have proposed, exacts a heavy but necessary toll from the self because it demands a perfect conformity between personal and public opinion: the conventions of drawing-room culture have the power to make Austen's most adamant individualists fall into line.[39] This seems a simplification. Manipulating such demands that the personal be aligned with the public, Jane Fairfax echoes what "every body" thinks of Frank's looks and manners in ways that safeguard her personal opinions and her private life (including her private life as the woman to whom Frank is secretly engaged). If we were to draw our conclusions from her responses to Emma, it would appear that for Jane the voice of the world is protective of feeling—affording a kind of camouflage—as much as it is restrictive.

This may also be true for Elinor Dashwood: Elinor's distinction from Marianne, and from the heroines of the Burney school of novelists, lies with the fact that she never occupies a victim position vis-à-vis a censorious, gossiping world. After Willoughby rejects her, Marianne's feelings *are* exposed as material for the world's rumor mill, a consequence of the value she placed on sincerity and openness from the very start of her acquaintance with him. That exposure compounds her wretchedness. Elinor's situation is different. As early as the first volume of *Sense and Sensibility* Elinor's vexation when Sir John and Mrs. Jennings tease her about the beau she must have left behind her in Sussex is not so acute that Marianne, who "felt for her most sincerely," cannot augment it, doing "more harm than good to the cause, by speaking . . . in an angry manner" (53); "Elinor was much more hurt by Marianne's warmth than she had been by what produced it" (206). Here it is not the collective consciousness of the world (that abstract entity that recognizable vulgarians such as Sir John and Mrs. Jennings incarnate) that poses a problem for the self but instead one's intimates, not public exposure but what transpires in the apparently safe zone of semiprivacy. Daniel Cottom's nod toward Marianne as he examines love's "commonness" in the Austen novel suggests one way to assess what Austen might value about Elinor's—or for that matter her readers'—relation to the impersonal: "[T]he only persons liable to be ruined by love are those who are ashamed of how essentially impersonal and insignificant it is and who therefore try to exaggerate it into some realm of sublime transcendence."[40]

Extrapolating from Barbara Benedict's account of Elinor's language, one could conjecture that by virtue of her alliance with the narrator of *Sense and Sensibility* Elinor avoids being the lead character in a novel about being ruined by love. One way Austen makes her characters deep is by reworking what her contemporaries did in juxtaposing a self-effacing heroine with her overdressed foil. In Austen's novels, relations between women—the relations between Marianne and Elinor; between Jane and Elizabeth Bennet; between Fanny Price and Mary Crawford; between Jane Fairfax and Harriet Smith, on the one hand, and Emma Woodhouse, on the other; or even between the Misses Musgrove and Anne Elliot—also involve two sorts of characters. These relations involve secondary characters who lead their romantic lives in public—who are "out," who "can act," who, like Jane Bennet, "are the only handsome girl[s] in the room" (9), or whose appearance, like Harriet Smith's in *Emma* or Clara Brereton's in *Sanditon*, which I quote, suggests "the most perfect representation of [a] Heroine" (346)—and they involve heroines to whom these statements will scarcely apply.[41] "No one who had ever seen

Catherine Morland in her infancy, would have supposed her born to be an heroine" (1), the narrator of *Northanger Abbey* declares as she bemoans her fate in being saddled with such unpropitious material. Within the Austen canon, Catherine has a lot of company. Austen does more, however, than comply with the fictional convention that locates authentic subjectivity with the woman who is *not* favored by the public voice; she also casts her protagonists as the silent and sympathetic observers of other people's stories and the repositories of their secrets.

Their participation in situations of spectatorship and secret-sharing endows Anne Elliot and Elinor Dashwood, in particular, with the qualities that novel readers in Austen's lifetime were learning to associate with third-person narrators; likewise the capacity that each has for a self-possession that seems to numb her sense of self-interest. Anne and Elinor each partake of something like a narrator's invisibility, omniscience, and capacity to enter into others' feelings and coordinate and harmonize others' perspectives.[42] Believing herself to have outlived the age for dancing and blushing, Anne takes almost too easily to a role requiring her to sympathize with Captain Benwick one moment and Henrietta Musgrove the next, and to be "as ready to do good by entering into the feelings of a young lady as of a young man" (100). At Uppercross and Lyme she is everyone's confidante (even Wentworth's for the brief interval that succeeds Louisa Musgrove's accident), and she is "privy" accordingly to the "general inclination" of this community (116). Anne has access to the vantage point—which is also that of the narrator of *Persuasion*—from which discrepant individual interests will appear as the same social interest. If Anne's services as a mediator, laboring for and producing a common good, ally her with the narrator, in *Sense and Sensibility* this alliance takes shape while Elinor (whom I wish to linger over a bit longer) acts as a clearinghouse for information, handing over letters, forwarding Colonel Brandon's offer of the living to Edward, and transmitting Brandon's story of the Elizas and Willoughby's story of copying to Marianne. It is in Elinor's consciousness that the subplots of *Sense and Sensibility* come together.

The suspension of individuality that Elinor's performance of this quasi-institutional office entails is also a requisite part of being a sister to Marianne: it is part of acting as Marianne's stand-in in conversations with Colonel Brandon (who in volume 2 comes almost daily to Mrs. Jennings's "to look at Marianne and talk to Elinor" [145]) and with Willoughby and, in the episode in which she tells Marianne about Edward's engagement to Lucy, part of acting as "the comforter of others in her own distresses, no less than in theirs"

(227). Arguments for recognizing *Sense and Sensibility*'s centrality in the history of the novel often proceed by applauding Austen's use of free indirect discourse and her reworking of the form of the epistolary novel and by suggesting that the language of inward experience these innovations produce is capable of conveying what is most authentically individual about the individual. These ways of valuing the characterization of Elinor, I would suggest, need to be qualified along the lines of the formulation that Eve Sedgwick offers when, adopting the language of codependency that is mobilized in late-twentieth-century family analysis, she highlights Elinor's self-forgetting attentiveness to her oblivious sister: "As far as this novel is concerned, the co-dependent subjectivity simply *is subjectivity*."[43]

The content of the rich inner life Austen grants to Elinor is a mindfulness of others. The strategy Barbara Benedict pursues to demonstrate the distinction between the impersonal language that Elinor adopts in speaking of her own feelings—the language of a narrator's general moral lessons—and the internal language that presents Elinor as a "heroine" is illuminating in this regard. To supply a contrast to the passage in which Elinor gives her opinion of Edward Ferrars by giving everybody's opinion, Benedict chooses a passage from the third volume of *Sense and Sensibility* in which the narrative "employs the punctuation and syntax of sentimental impressionism: exclamation points, fragmented sentences, italicized words."[44] The passage of free indirect discourse that Benedict describes unfolds as Elinor awaits the arrival of her mother, who, with Colonel Brandon, is rushing the eighty miles from Barton Cottage to Cleveland in order to be, as she thinks, beside Marianne's deathbed. (Mrs. Dashwood does not yet know that Marianne's sickness has suddenly abated.)

> Never in her life had Elinor found it so difficult to be calm, as at that moment. The knowledge of what her mother must be feeling as the carriage stopt at the door,—of her doubt—her dread—perhaps her despair!—and of what *she* had to tell!—with such knowledge it was impossible to be calm. All that remained to be done, was to be speedy; and therefore staying only till she could leave Mrs. Jennings's maid with her sister, she hurried down stairs.
>
> The bustle in the vestibule, as she passed along an inner lobby, assured her that they were already in the house. She rushed forwards towards the drawing-room,—she entered it,—and saw only Willoughby. (277)

The energies of this passage derive from Elinor's capacity for sympathy—for feeling in another's place. And, tellingly, it is succeeded immediately by a conversation between Elinor and Willoughby that offers the sole example in the novel of an intimate tête-à-tête between a woman and a man, in which Willoughby " 'open[s] [his] whole heart' " (279) and in which, accordingly, Elinor again plays the role of confidante.[45] As the passage and its sequel suggest, what transpires in the interior space that the text hollows out for Elinor is the vicarious experience of another's feelings.

What transpires in that space is also, however, the unceasing mental activity involved in acting as Marianne's minister of the exterior, smoothing her run-of-the-mill transactions with the outside world. The exercise of covering up Marianne's failures to "tell lies when politeness required it" (105) and of giving social countenance to Marianne's wool-gathering and her gift for becoming "insensible" of others' presence make Elinor a mistress of the pro forma. Devoted to making the "usual inquiries" about other people's health or the usual compliments to one's host, and so reiterating the customary phrases that pass from mouth to mouth in polite circles, Elinor's language is often language on automatic pilot. On a visit to Barton Park, she reiterates (in only a slightly different key) the politely fatuous exclamations of the Misses Steele over Sir John, Lady Middleton, and the little Middletons' "charm" (105). On arriving in London, Elinor writes the letters home that are the currency of filial duty and, as such, contentless—we know without getting the chance to read them the little they will say. (As if to point the contrast, Marianne, for her part, writes at the same time her sister does, but those letters to Willoughby are feeling-filled *cris de coeur*.)[46] The language of inward experience that makes Elinor a mind-full heroine is articulated with language that, "worn and hackneyed out of all sense and meaning," brings to view an Elinor mindful of maintaining the forms of common courtesy. By such means, the heroine's interior monologues are set off by the noise of automated communications.

Persuasion is distinguished by similar conjunctions. In one of the many scenes that Austen sets in a crowded public place, Anne, who finds herself in Molland's, a confectioner's establishment in Bath, catches sight through the shop window of Captain Wentworth. While others consume, chatter, and gossip (about the Elliots eventually), Anne both battles her inclination to observe Wentworth as he passes down the street and battles her inclination to second-guess the motive that impels her toward the shop door: "She now felt a great inclination to go to the outer door; she wanted to see if it rained. Why was she to suspect herself of another motive? Captain Wentworth must be out of sight. She left her seat, she would go, one half of her should not be always so much wiser than the other half, or always suspecting the other of being worse than it was. She would see if it rained" (165–66). In this passage of free indirect discourse, in which Austen deliberately takes as her subject the interior conflicts that individuate the psychological subject, talk about the weather also has a part to play. That most hackneyed, because the safest, of topics (one notoriously capable of generating idle chatter) gives Anne the means of diverting her consciousness into channels other than that of the language of her heart's desire.

If, in delineating such moments, we confine ourselves either to commenting on how the socializing effects of "propriety" repress a heroine's self-expression or to equating a heroine's civility with the appeasement of male power, we tell half the story. As I suggested earlier, the heroine's adherence to the codes of manners—her association with safe topics and the usual inquiries—can as easily be viewed as a manipulation that makes manners into a cover for privacy. Frequently, it is at the junctures when the presence of company requires Elinor to conform to a " 'plan of general civility' " (81) that the novel reminds us that she has an interior life that can be engaged "elsewhere" (90). Elinor and Anne, as well as Fanny Price and even (given the pleasure she at least *thinks* she takes in putting her own life on hold and in supervising the lives of others) Emma Woodhouse exemplify in various ways a logic according to which self-effacement secures self-possession. The tensions between social forms and self-expression not only constrain, but also create, novel readers' sense that the depths of character exceed what is sayable (and in this sense that tension is self-*enhancing*). And it is by administrating those tensions that novelists of manners define and legitimate their narrative authority and social office.[47]

After all, Austen too is a mistress of the pro forma. Her forte is in part her ability to play with the compulsoriness of forms: her capacity to take the overcoded, or overcrowded, conditions of modern novel writing in her stride. Take, for instance, her ways of winding up her novels' marriage plots. Austen's endings tend to call attention to the tension between the forms for expression and the creative imagination that uses those forms. When Edward Ferrars, providentially jilted by Lucy Steele, can at last honorably declare himself to Elinor, the narrator of *Sense and Sensibility* deals with his declaration by resorting to the impersonal language of the crowd portrait: "[In] what manner he expressed himself, and how he was received, need not be particularly told. This only need be said;—that when they all sat down to table at four o' clock, about three hours after his arrival, he had secured his lady, engaged her mother's consent, and was not only in the rapturous profession of the lover, but in the reality of reason and truth, one of the happiest of men" (317). Austen can be delightfully perfunctory when she gestures in this manner toward satisfying run-of-the-mill demands for closure—when, as here, she echoes what other novels in the circulating-library swarm talk about ("the happiest of men"), and when she arranges for her characters to be subjected to the common fate and lost in the crowd. (Thus this passage with its generic terms reveals Elinor as a lover's "lady," much as in the proposal scene of *Emma* "all that need be said" about the dawning of our heroine's nuptial bliss is that, in her response to Knightley's proposal, "[Emma] spoke, on being so entreated.—What did she say?—Just what she ought, of course. A lady always does" [391].) When in this knowing manner Austen hints that her pen is hardwired with the novel-writing engines that obsessed romantic reviewers, she is both catering to our pleasure as convention-spotters in being *knowing* ourselves, and encouraging us to apprehend this recourse to the pro forma as the very sign of a meaningfulness that resists formalization.[48]

Something else besides the revelation or even production of psychological meaning is going on here. Austen takes the mechanical part of novel writing, as well as the mechanical aspects of social life, as a conscious object of study. For this reason she is as interested in the banalizing of meaning that accompanies the reiteration of novel slang and the empty formalities of common civility as she is in the intensification of meaning that produces the inner lives of characters. Whereas Austen's modern readers have emphasized the free indirect discourse she uses (1) to supply the illusion of entry into a character's consciousness and (2) to suggest a zone of meaning too deep to sustain direct utterance, they have not often remarked on how her style in fact orchestrates *two* modes of reported speech. Austen's style coordinates free indirect discourse of the sort I have been discussing hitherto—the narrator's rearticulation of an individual character's point of view—with the narrator's rearticulation of everyone's thoughts on the matter. Here I have in mind the commonplace-seeming locutions that sound as if we should be able to render them as direct quotations but are neither attributed nor enclosed in quotation marks: whenever she announces something like "Every neighbourhood must have a great Lady" (the opening to the fifth chapter of *Sanditon*) or, most famously, "It is a truth universally acknowledged that a single man in possession of a good fortune must be in want of a wife," the narrator seems to hand over her text to the voice of the cultural context. The narrator moves over to make room not only for a rendering of subjective consciousness in its own idiom, but also for a rendering of the secondhand idiom of a vox populi—the murmurings that issue from the impersonal and insipid semantic domain of "received ideas" or "what everybody says." That Elinor's mind is full of other people's feelings and the usual civilities suggests how Austen renders interiority as a social space. By extension, the centrality of a second sort of reported speech to Austen's style suggests the sociability of the text. It suggests how in their assembly Austen novels exemplify the belief that "narrative consists not in communicating what one has seen but in transmitting what one has heard, what someone else said to you. Hearsay."[49]

The punctuation of dialogue within novels represents one way that the otherwise slippery or arbitrary distinctions between the personal and impersonal, the individual and collective, are established and naturalized. In much the same way, the fact that I've just used quotation marks to cordon off a passage of Deleuze and Guattari's helps me (as do the pages of notes at the end of this book) to preserve the mandatory distinctions between the *meum* and the *suum*. Yet before these familiar uses of quotation marks were standardized, which was only in Austen's lifetime, this type of punctuation was used to flag an authoritative saying "like a proverb, commonplace, or statement of consensual truth." Quotation marks made it easy for Renaissance Mary Bennets to spot *sententiae* and copy them into the customized commonplace books that were the media of their self-fashioning. They called attention to a discursive zone that was every person's property and was ripe for reproduction.[50] This early usage was governed by an intimate relation between reading and transcription and collection and by the exigencies of a rhetorical culture—exigencies that, even in the first half of the eighteenth century, could prompt Jane Barker to cast one Mr. Dyke's book of proverbs as a prototype for Galesia's patch-work-cum-"novel" or could prompt an elderly Samuel Richardson, along with Solomon Lowe, to assemble a collection of "sentiments" from *Clarissa* (subsequently a rich source of the quotations that were recopied into Johnson's *Dictionary*).[51] The later-eighteenth-century transformation in the use of quotation marks registers the new uses of texts and new technologies of the self that emerged at a moment when language was reconceptualized as appropriable property and when readers pledged their belief in characters' lives of their own. In an oblique way, Austen's orchestration of the varieties of hearsay recalls the ironic prehistory of the punctuation marks that now signal that words belong to and express individuals. For in her novels, as Daniel Cottom notes, a rigid distinction between "empty formalities and meaningful signs" is unsupportable: it is hard to say where self-expression leaves off and repetition begins.[52]

"THERE IS A SORT OF DOMESTIC ENJOYMENT TO BE KNOWN EVEN IN A CROWD"

After all, the routine running of the social machine that the novels portray depends on recycling polite phrases, not on interpreting them. Austen is interested in the nonsignificative aspects of language because she understands the business of common life in the same terms that Lionel Trilling does when, attempting to define *manners* in the broad sense of the term, he uses words such as *hum* and *buzz* and refers to "the voice of multifarious intention and activity . . . all the buzz of implication which always surrounds us."[53] Austen understands social life, as Trilling, her reader, does, in terms of noise. She often positions her heroines so that they are excluded from others' colloquies but unable to avoid overhearing information of unexpected interest to themselves. This measure makes readers conscious of the auditory contingencies that impinge on communications. *Persuasion* particularly, a novel notable for its poignant depiction of impasses in communications, is also a novel of noise. Like the works that precede it, it deals with chatter and records how people trade fatuities and re-urge "admitted truths" (218), but it is also a book, as Adela Pinch notes, in which doors slam (173) and fires roar, "determined to be heard" (127), in which the "bawling . . . newsmen, muffin-men, and milk-men" (128) of the Bath marketplace contribute to the cacophony, and in which individual characters are liable to be distinguished by their "taste in noise" (128).[54] When she stages scenes of overhearing, Austen makes us conscious both of the ambient noise that frustrates the listener's efforts to hear and of the idle chatter that delays her receipt of a crucial piece of intelligence.

Thus *Sense and Sensibility* and *Persuasion* present the language of real feeling as a language of undertone, uttered under a blanket of noise. The sessions in which Elinor serves as someone's secret-sharer have for their accompaniment the drone of Marianne's piano playing: Lucy's romantic difficulties can be communicated because "Marianne was then giving them the powerful protection of a very magnificent concerto" (128); the pianoforte again proves of use when Colonel Brandon, meaning to show his delicacy, but blundering dreadfully, asks Elinor to help him facilitate Edward's marriage to Lucy (245). We do not learn whose compositions Marianne plays, only that at some moments the music is louder than at others: it seems reasonable to view Marianne's piano as a kind of white noise machine. Indeed, given Marianne's association with a commercialized print culture (remember the orders that will go to London music sellers once she gets her thousand pounds), and given the seeming narrowness of her repertoire (for part of the novel, she will play only the songs that she formerly played to Willoughby [72]), her music might be said to possess some of the automated qualities of Coleridge's barrel-organ.

In *Persuasion*, Anne Elliot's place is likewise on the piano bench, and, in this novel too, mental activity has a pianoforte accompaniment. "Her fingers . . . mechanically at work, proceeding for half an hour together, equally without error, and without consciousness" (71), Anne seems to find in her performances—in going through the motions of performances—a means of at once being alone with her thoughts and fulfilling her public duties. Evidence of how, with their "modern minds and manners [and] . . . usual stock of accomplishments," the daughters of the house cannot resist a trend, the piano at Uppercross Hall contributes to the crowdedness of an overfilled parlor (42), but Austen shows how these noise machines give their female operators and auditors the space for private life.

Women's music had its social utility too, of course. The piano in the Musgroves' old-fashioned parlor is a marker of the family's social aspirations. The first manifestation of Anne's efforts as the obliging mediator or social worker of volume 1 of *Persuasion* are her performances on the piano: she will play country dances all night long at Uppercross and so permit Louisa and Henrietta and other younger women to be courted on the dance floor. And yet at the same time, as I have suggested, the musical powers that make Anne and other women socially useful also supply Anne with the means for self-possession. Her piano playing registers the demands of Anne's society *and* it supplies her with the means of parrying the incursions society would make on her autonomy of mind. Austen arranges for Anne's reading to confront us with a comparable paradox, and as I conclude this chapter I want to return to the ways in which Austen annotates the practices of romantic reading and consider how *Persuasion*—in its concluding proposal scene most interestingly—specifies those practices' *social* place. Mary Musgrove's complaint about the bookishness of a certain Captain Benwick conveniently outlines the divisions between social obligation and self-possession, silent reading and noisy social life, that *Persuasion* seems set up to interrogate. Building on her husband's description of how Benwick would willingly " 'read all day long,'" Mary exclaims "tauntingly": "'[T]hat he will! . . . He will sit poring over his book and not know when a person speaks to him, or when one drops one's scissors, or any thing that happens'" (125–26). Captain Benwick's absorption in a book is presented here as an imperviousness to the outside world's demands and noises. (Mary, who whines, may be taken as representative of both of those.)

But Mary's description of Benwick also speaks to the semipublic (and noisy) nature of the scene of reading in this era. The rites of gentry sociability had readers reading in company, in common sitting rooms in which other people were playing at cards or playing the piano or doing needlework and dropping their scissors, and thereby producing, to borrow a much-used locution from *Persuasion*, a buzz of sound. Female reading was particularly likely to have this aural accompaniment. Ladies' transactions with literature had social sanction insofar as they made ladies better company: in the words of Anna Laetitia Barbauld's essay "On Female Studies" (1826), the genteel young woman should read only as many books as would enable her to "give spirit and variety to conversation."[55] For all their pessimism about the female character, the period's depersonalized depictions of circulating library subscribers as so many cogs in a rotatory machine supply a not dissimilar image of women's reading: as an experience that leaves the individual governed by the dynamic of the group.

For *Persuasion*, which responds to these commentaries on women and books,[56] literary experience both manifests the influence of the crowd *and* supplies crowd-repelling strategies. In this doubleness literary experience is like noise. Much as the sounds of the Uppercross piano shelter mental activity, during the walk to Winthrop Anne's recollection of poets' descriptions of autumn functions as a kind of buffer: her "fall into . . . quotation" (83) bolsters her capacity to screen out the world and occupy herself with her thoughts. Indeed, if we often see Anne (as we see Elinor Dashwood) giving "herself up to the demands of the party, to the needful civilities of the moment" (174), we just as frequently see her so thought-full as to resemble Captain Benwick when he has his nose in a book. In the chapter from which I have just quoted, in which the Elliots attend an evening concert at Bath, and in which Anne has a conversation with Wentworth that encourages her to hope that he loves her once again, the narrator is very exact in the way she *places* her heroine's emotion of joy. "Anne saw nothing, thought nothing of the brilliancy of the room. Her happiness was from within" (175). At such moments, what Austen has us hear with Anne is a buzz of voices. Adopting

Anne's point of view means experiencing what the people in this assembly room are saying not as a number of distinct utterances issuing from particular agents, but as a wash of noise. Here, for instance, is how, linking inwardness and noise, Austen records Anne's reception of the words Wentworth uses when he seems to be on the brink of renewing his former feelings. "[I]n spite of the agitated voice in which [his remarks] had been uttered, and in spite of all the various noises of the room, the almost ceaseless slam of the door, and ceaseless buzz of persons walking through, [Anne] had distinguished every word, was struck, gratified, confused, and beginning to breathe very quick, and feel an hundred things in a moment" (173). The process delineated in this passage, as Adela Pinch has argued, is one in which subjectivity has "dominion over the outside world": "the narrator impresses these noises upon us in order to assert that Anne can subordinate them . . . [and in order to affirm] the capacity of the mind, even as it has been traumatized by the rushing in of sensations, to reduce the external world to a blur."[57]

But the dilemma *Persuasion* confronts is that these internal resources—the capacities for thinking, feeling, and listening that enable her to close out the noise of social contingency and hear only words of love—are not enough for Anne. Anne can do things with her books, but Anne's "word ha[s] no weight" (12): her ability to abstract herself from her social environment compels the reader's admiration, but it is easy to see that she could abstract herself into nothingness. *Persuasion* in its second half is preoccupied with the sort of repetitive rounds of polite "nothing-saying" we witness when Anne and Wentworth talk "of the weather and Bath and the concert" (171) largely because it is addressing the question of whether something-saying is possible and whether Anne can say what she means.[58] If Wentworth indeed has a heart returning to Anne, how is the truth about her feelings to reach him? "How . . . would he ever learn her real sentiments?" (180).

In this chapter I have stressed Austen's comfort when she thinks about the social content of interior life—when she contemplates the idea that whatever is most personal about characters and readers is also that which is most by the book. Generally, she finds little cause for pessimism when she considers how the readings with which we repeat one another are also the means by which we each fashion an individualized interiority. But *Persuasion*, more than her other novels, does register a certain resistance to women's association with the new technologies of introspection purveyed by the book market and their association with the inner spaces of feeling. The proposal scene of the novel is famous for two statements Anne makes as she vindicates her sex's constancy to Captain Harville (and to Captain Wentworth, who overhears her words). When Captain Harville proposes that books are filled with examples of female fickleness, she reminds him that literature is not a representation of truth, but a type of rhetoric, a matter of reiterated codes rather than of mimesis: " '[I]f you please, no reference to examples in books. Men have had every advantage of us in telling their own story. Education has been theirs in so much higher a degree; the pen has been in their hands. I will not allow books to prove any thing' " (221). With this statement Anne also reminds us that she is a reader. (Austen's allusiveness, in the meantime, reminds us of what we have read before: overtly "literary," the debate about constancy that occupies Harville and Anne replays a debate Richard Steele's *Spectator* recorded between a lady and a "Common-Place Talker" a century before.)[59] And when Anne refers to social circumstances to explicate the powers of feeling she claims for her sex, her words resonate with statements that Austen's contemporaries made about the introspection of the reader. " 'We certainly do not forget you, so soon as you forget us. It is, perhaps, our fate rather than our merit. We cannot help ourselves. We live at home, quiet, confined, and our feelings prey upon us' " (219). As Adela Pinch notes, commenting on Anne and Harville's debate, "the notion that 'the pen has always been in their hands,' that the true nature of women's feeling falls outside of literature, can only be one moment in what this book has to say on this subject: Austen's ambivalence may have to do as well with its opposite— with a sense that literature has been too much with women."[60] Literature in Austen's period was geared increasingly to facilitating the reader's exploration of her inner sensibilities. And this could only be a mixed blessing for women, who, as Anne reminds Harville, live at home, who are connected only indirectly to the world in which men have " 'continual occupation' " (219), and who, accordingly, know the spaces of interior feeling only too well. Does the secret self that a woman forms through her reading—through the sort of secret indulgence in "the sweets of poetical despondence" that occupies Anne on the walk to Winthrop (83)—merely manifest her acquiescence to the social pressures of gender? " 'Our feelings prey upon us.' "

Of course, these hints of ambivalence about books' role in readers' affective lives do not seem particularly weighty once they are measured against the overwhelming affective power of the messages that pass between Wentworth and Anne under the surface of this conversation. This is, after all, a chapter that makes Austen's readers feel. Indeed, its intoxicating pleasures are in large measure a function of how, despite those reservations about literature's consolatory powers, Austen fulfills readers' desire for a literature that would take into account what is most individual in our individualities, that would be addressed to no one but ourselves. The vehicle with which she does this is Wentworth's love letter, the other much-celebrated feature of *Persuasion*'s penultimate chapter. While Anne and Captain Harville disagree over what literature can prove about men's and women's constancy, Captain Wentworth, like them a visitor to the rooms that the Musgroves have taken at the White Hart Inn at Bath, sits in another corner of the common sitting room and writes a letter. Anne and Harville talk about books and feelings, and Wentworth writes what is apparently a letter of business, reporting on a consumer transaction. (He has been commissioned by Captain Benwick to purchase a new frame for a portrait: this portrait of Benwick, painted for his first love, is now intended as a wedding present for Louisa Musgrove.) Yet Wentworth proves merely to be going through the motions of fulfilling his epistolary duty: the letter to Benwick is a cover. An instant after he leaves the room with Harville, he reenters it and draws "out a letter from under the scattered paper" (223)—an epistle that at a single stroke remedies the characters' inability to move out of the round of nothing-saying and jolts them and us into another time and space.

When Anne sees on the folded paper the direction "Miss A. E.," the narrator supplies these words to document her thoughts: "While supposed to be writing only to Captain Benwick, he had been also addressing her!" The reader shares Anne's shock and elation on finding herself Wentworth's addressee. I intend the ambiguity my use of the pronoun "herself" introduces here: the moment of the letter's delivery and the rupture in the narrative texture that it leads to also startle us—also startle me. From this moment, the particular intimacy that the epistolary form makes possible ensures that readers read with Anne. Then too, although this letter changes everything, it is never subjected to the public rereadings (in Nicola Watson's words, "the verdict of public circulation") that correspondence usually seems to call for in Austen's novels.[61] Invisible to others—Mrs. Musgrove is in the room but occupied by "little arrangements of her own at her own table"—the letter exists only for Anne, Wentworth, and us. The magic of the proposal scene that Anne and Harville's debate about books turns into is partly a product of this privacy.

The scene is magical too in being arranged so as to defuse the doubts that the debate raises about reading's consolatory powers. The scene records a "revolution": "any thing [is] possible" (223). Anne's words have weight here, and the effect is to dissolve the distinctions that separate reading and feeling, on the one hand, from speaking and acting, on the other.

> I can listen no longer in silence. I must speak to you by such means as are within my reach. You pierce my soul. I am half agony, half hope. Tell me not that I am too late, that such precious feelings are gone for ever. I offer myself to you again with a heart even more your own, than when you almost broke it eight years and a half ago. Dare not say that man forgets sooner than woman, that his love has an earlier death. I have loved none but you. Unjust I may have been, weak and resentful I have been, but never inconstant. You alone have brought me to Bath. For you alone I think and plan.—Have you not seen this? Can you fail to have understood my wishes?—I had not waited even these ten days, could I have read your feelings, as I think you must have penetrated mine. I can hardly write. I am every instant hearing something which overpowers me. You sink your voice, but I can distinguish the tones of that voice, when they would be lost on others.—Too good, too excellent creature! You do us justice indeed. You do believe that there is true attachment and constancy among men. Believe it to be most fervent, most undeviating in
> 	F.W.

This is the text (223–24) that Anne reads, but as his phrase "read your feelings" suggests, Wentworth is annotating Anne's text in his turn. The stops and starts in his prose testify to how closely structured on Anne's conversation with Harville his composition is: her statement that "we certainly do not forget you so soon as you forget us" gives him his entry point ("Dare not say that man forgets sooner than woman"); her statement that "I should deserve utter contempt if I dared to suppose that true attachment and constancy were known only by women" compels his reply, "You do us justice indeed." His letter is incomplete without Anne's words. Because the lovers complete each other's meaning, enunciation and reception are thoroughly mingled here.[62] Austen tells us that while Anne reads, she occupies "the chair which [Wentworth] had occupied, . . . the very spot where he had leaned and written" (223).

We cannot but remember too, that while Anne was speaking to Captain Harville, "a slight noise [had] called their attention to Captain Wentworth's hitherto perfectly quiet division of the room. It was nothing more than that his pen had fallen down" (220). Wentworth cannot monopolize the pen, and when he expresses himself in writing, it is, fittingly, in the sort of language of ravishment Austen's contemporaries would deploy to describe the female reader's transport by the text.

Austen uses the noise Wentworth's pen makes when it falls to two different ends. She underlines Anne's complaint about what it means to be a female reader: " 'Men have had every advantage of us in telling their own story . . . the pen has been in their hands.' " The mention of the noise that momentarily breaks in on their conversation also reminds us that Anne and Harville speak in a semipublic space: they are to one side of a room that also holds Captain Wentworth at his writing desk, as well as Mrs. Musgrove and Mrs. Croft, who gossip together throughout the chapter. The dialogues of the scene are dialogue by courtesy only; the language of love takes shape against "the buzz of words" (218) that Mrs. Musgrove's and Mrs. Croft's conversation represents for Anne. The resulting noise adds to the contrast between our experience in this scene and our experience, two chapters before, of the letter that advances Anne's knowledge of William Elliot's character. The latter episode, in which Mrs. Smith produces the letter that illumines Mr. Elliot's villainy, is curiously irrelevant to the novel as a whole: there is never much possibility that Anne will look favorably on her cousin's attentions. This irrelevance testifies to how Austen rejects the mode of apprehending another's "real character" (187) that this somewhat melodramatic scene of revelation exemplifies. Susan Morgan, indeed, has remarked on how, when Mrs. Smith tenders " 'proof' " that Mr. Elliot is " 'black at heart' " (187) and produces one of his old letters out her "small inlaid box" (190–91), Austen seems to be assessing what is at stake in thinking about the knowledge of character as a matter of unmasking. Mrs. Smith's stagey gesture, Morgan notes, reminds us of Wentworth's rhetorical flourish with the hazelnut, and both Mrs. Smith and the Wentworth who thinks he has apprehended Anne's fatal flaw are overinvested in an epistemology in which another's character is something liable to proof, something that can be disclosed once and for all.[63] The contrast between the two letters deciding the fates of Anne's two suitors could also be aligned with the contrast between the privacy of the earlier scene—a scene dependent on enclosed spaces, the "dark bed-room" behind Mrs. Smith's "noisy parlour" (146) and within that room the box in which the letter is housed (191)—and the relatively convivial and noisy surroundings in which Anne reads the letter that manifests Wentworth's better knowledge of *her* character.

The rooms at the White Hart Inn are ones the Musgroves have taken so as to shop in Bath for Louisa and Henrietta's wedding clothes. They are at best a semiprivate site, "a quick-changing, unsettled scene": "One five min-utes brought a note, the next a parcel" (208). The readers in and of the proposal scene are constantly on the verge of being jolted out of the space of romantic intimacy, and back into public; they are on the verge of being made cognizant once again of the social mechanisms of transmission and exchange that govern notes, parcels, and declarations of love alike. Loving and reading and writing are intermingled here, yet at the same time, radically reimagining the novelistic spaces of romance, this chapter finally associates all of these with being in a crowd.

For what remains of the novel, Anne and Wentworth continue to find themselves in a crowd. The conversation in which they return again into their private past transpires in urban space, in the midst of a crowd the narra-tor can only catalog with a series of generic terms: "sauntering politicians, bustling house-keepers, flirting girls, [and] nursery-maids and children" (227). Earlier in the novel, Mrs. Smith, finding that Anne has noticed very little about the evening concert at the octagon room that she has attended, alights on the reason: " 'There is a sort of domestic enjoyment to be known even in a crowd, and this you had' " (182). Potentially a description of the way that Captain Wentworth and Anne must work to make the business of common life accommodate the possibility of intimacy, this statement could double as a comment on Austen's comfort with the crowded conditions of the book market and of her genre. It seems to capture the practice of a writer who made her peace with the impersonality of publication: the novels, potentially any person's property, are dotted with in-jokes about the Austen family's private affairs.[64]

Likewise, the scene of writing that is the proposal scene of *Persuasion* seems reinscribed in the portraits of the artist that Austen's biographers paint when they depict her at work in the "general sitting room, subject to all kinds of casual interruptions"—writing with the obviously bothersome accompani-ment of the slams of a door and the buzz of other people's words.[65] We often hear about this "domestic white noise" because reminders of it expose the contrast between the ineluctably social circumstances of most women writers and the asocial solitariness that Austen's male contemporaries, licensed by their masculinity, made into the hallmark of canonical romantic authorship.

Too often, however, the scholarship that mobilizes this contrast makes privacy into an absolute value: it assumes that the difference between life in a family circle, on the one hand, and romantic solitude, on the other, inevitably worked to Austen's disadvantage. This covertly normative presupposition about writing's relationship to social circumstance has been contested by Deborah Kaplan, who has recently studied Austen's reliance on her network of female supporters and studied the writings that passed like greeting cards among the members of her gentry community.[66] To be sure, acknowledging how Austen's own writings could have functioned as a social currency, and conceding that authorship is sometimes underwritten by community, conflicts with the investment many readers have in Austen's privacy—with many readers' conviction that if she was in her society she was not *of* it. Even if they have trouble getting her out of earshot of her domestic milieu, literary histories, for instance, have tended to set Austen apart from the crowd. Segregated from her merely fashionable female contemporaries in the book market, insofar as their names had been forgotten while hers was remembered, or segregated from them by being cast as the "ironical censurer" who had seen through their pretensions, Austen thus for a long time seemed to have the ladies' room of literature to herself.[67] The efforts that produced that appearance of a feminized romantic solitariness represent a variation on the campaigns against automatic reading machines and writing machines that otherwise engaged Austen's contemporaries. The model of cultural work as the expression and the property of a singular creative personality—a model reinforced in Austen's lifetime by the discourse of literary biography—both reacts and stands in symbiotic relation to the model of cultural pathology that Austen's contemporaries elaborated as they complained about the "shoals of composition" churned out by the presses: too many texts, too cheaply printed, and too given to repeating themselves. Such crowd-repelling strategies also play a role in the history of Austen's audiences: her reception history is punctuated by moments when her readers have, in their urge to make the novels into personalized property, sounded a bit like the caricature of Marianne Dashwood that Edward Ferrars offers when he talks about her plan to buy up all of Cowper. In the nineteenth century it was a critical commonplace that Austen's attractions blushed unseen. Appreciation of Austen was cast as a minority taste, or, as Virginia Woolf put it half-facetiously but a tad nostalgically in 1913, as "a gift that ran in families and . . . a mark of rather peculiar culture."[68]

When in *Persuasion* the customers at the confectioner's shop start gossiping about the Elliots, just after Anne has left the shop with her cousin, one lady says to two others: " 'She is pretty, I think; Anne Elliot; very pretty, when one comes to look at her. It is not the fashion to say so, but I confess I admire her more than her sister' " (168). With these phrases the lady, unnamed and never heard from again, stakes her claim to the chic territory of a minority taste. Refusing to copy others and say what is fashionable, she distinguishes herself by making distinctions. She separates herself from the crowd. In roughly the same way, the bit of heroine description that Austen offers here participates in a tradition of character writing that furthered the reader's projects of self-enhancement. This lady's phrases are not, however, the final word on the subject. Does Austen introduce a hint of irony about what it is and isn't the fashion to say when two more anonymous voices chime in and concur with the first speaker—" 'Oh! so do I' " and " 'so do I' "?

The Real Thing and the "Work" of Literature in Nineteenth-Century Culture

Austen's stories leave readers uncertain about how to separate the meanings that compose the sphere of the self from the meanings that compose the spheres of common life and social commerce. The uncertainty her stories produce put ideas of "the real thing" on the agenda of the British novel. At the same time, the convergences that Austen's novels trace between a language of the self and a language of the world—what it is "the fashion" to say—give us access to one chapter in the history that my study of literary characters' uses has ended up outlining: the history of that strange discursive object called society. When Henry Gally and William Hogarth were debating the economy of character, the term *society* was still used primarily to designate an association, created by a contractual arrangement among individuals, that might, variously, be as small as a club or as large as the Lockean polity. In the early decades of the eighteenth century there could be many societies. By the time Austen wrote, society was an object sui generis, one that seemed to preexist the individuals who did not join but found themselves "in" it. The disconcerting conjunctions of what is original and what is derivative, what has intrinsic worth and what has social currency, that we encountered in Austen's quoting heroines and in Burney's beautiful machines respond, I think, to the disconcerting conjunction of alterity and familiarity in these new ideas of the social. "Society" turned an alien, very often antagonistic, face to "individuals." It did so insofar as it had, by the opening decades of the nineteenth century, its own history and own laws, although this history and these laws—and this is where the productive tension that inhabits romanticism's new fictions of society and of "manners" becomes evident—were made *by* individuals, albeit imperceptibly and unintentionally. Austen's generation was perhaps the first to use characters in ways that did not so much resolve as exploit the tensions engendered by this doubleness in our vision of the social: the tensions arising from one's sense that the relation between individual and society is at once a relation of mismatching and, because individuals may be understood to be thoroughly determined by their social context, a relation of redundancy. Those tensions made the act of appreciating a character's inside story an exercise in emotional keep-fit and even an opportunity for civics classes. It is, for example, an aspect of the "democratic consciousness" of a work such as *Middlemarch* that Eliot's readers should not only be required to acknowledge the authentic individuality of the novel's characters but also be invited to dwell on what these same characters share with thousands of others.[1]

I am interested in how the questions about characters that are raised when "the real thing" finds its way onto literature's agenda are those whose answers are unverifiable. Questions about the contents of the Austen characters' inner lives (about whether a quoting heroine such as Anne Elliot has a real inner life or a socially scripted one; about whether a particular piece of characterization is the real thing or, in Carlyle's terms, merely "painted like") are undecidable. Like the undecidability of connected questions about whether a particular romantic poem is a bona fide product of the poet's sincerity or whether it represents the output of M. Didot's mechanized poetry mill, such undecidability was, after Austen, the order of the day. Ian Duncan writes, for example, about how the achievement of Walter Scott (a student of Burney's and of Austen's) was to cast "the relation between private and public meaning as the moral and formal crux" that would define the social office of novelists.[2] This undecidability is in a precise sense the work of literature. It is the *work* of the literary character, its socially generative task in the pedagogy that unfolds in our classrooms and elsewhere, to be somewhere in between the personal and the impersonal: subsequent to the retailoring of reading that I described in chapter 3, the literary character's way of seeming at once self-made, self-expressive, *and* a product of conventions gives readers something to do. In another sense, which I would like to explore at length in this conclusion, the undecidability that I have just evoked keeps literature at work. It might be seen, that is, as the constitutive element of a make-work project for literature.

One sign of the new ways in which novels mattered in early-nineteenth-century Britain was the emergence, in literary histories and reviews, as well as within some novels, of a rise-of-the-novel narrative: a framework for making literary history that marshaled a diverse assortment of narrative fictions under the unifying and stabilizing rubric, "the novel," and equipped the genre it thereby instituted with a canon of its own. The nineteenth century had numerous story lines that it could use to tell the novel's story as one of progressive development, only a few of them reducible to a story of developing realism. Some charted the increasing morality of novels' characters or charted the increasing Englishness of their style. Other literary histories rewrote *Don Quixote*—and had the requisite movement from romantic frenzy and fabulousness to good sense and probability begin when writers turned for inspiration toward "life" and ceased to rewrite the pages of their predecessors (very often their female predecessors, the précieuses, or England's own scribblers of seduction fictions and scandalous memoirs).

It is noteworthy, however, how often a concept of depth—a concept, more precisely, of *real* depth—provided nineteenth-century literary historians with their organizing and periodizing principle. Admittedly, it is quite probable that the schemes that nineteenth-century people used to organize their writing and reading practices did not involve to any great extent the hard and fast divisions, either between the eighteenth and nineteenth centuries or between "flat" and "round" characters, to which we are accustomed. In the nineteenth century, those divisions—and the concept of "real" depth on which they were based—were productive mainly when they were harnessed to that emergent discourse of canon-making and criticism that contributed to the making of "the" novel, the discourse that constructed that disciplinary object and made it literary. Nonetheless, I do want to emphasize that the engagement with depth within what would become novel studies eventually rearranged the cultural field. The nineteenth century in fact saw an efflorescence of "sketchbooks," books of "remarkable characters," "eccentric magazines," and "caricature portfolios," but in the long term the new way of engaging with literature made the non-novelistic uses of characters to which books like these catered into a topic on which there could be nothing to say. These ways of conspicuously consuming characters became invisible. One can illustrate this transformation by pointing to Dickens's *Pickwick Papers* (1836–7), which started out as a series of "sporting engravings" and which was taken by many of its first readers either to belong with others' "tales and sketches of characters" or to be a sort of magazine or miscellany: laboring under the latter conviction, some wrote letters offering to supply *Pickwick* with contributions.[3] The rearrangement of the cultural field that transpired when involvement with literature became an involvement with "inner" meaning is such that when *we* look back on Dickens's characters—anyone's characters—all that we can see is "the novel."

Before we turn to that rearrangement, let us consider this critical system for distinguishing between (as one nineteenth-century literary history put it) heroes and heroines with throbbing hearts and those who were only so much "figured silk and tamboured muslin . . . [fluttering] about society," an axiomatics that eventually equipped novel readers with their official guides as to which characters should matter and how. In his *History of Fiction* of 1814 John Dunlop casts the loss of popularity suffered by the fictions of Madeleine de Scudery as a turning point in writers' and readers' progress from romances to novels: "Mankind," Dunlop writes, "are little interested in the eyes and eye-brows of antiquated coquettes, and the work in which these were celebrated, soon appeared in [its] intrinsic dulness." In Dunlop's scheme, it is a sign of the novel's imminent ascent that the public grew bored with the woman writer's self-reflexive and self-publicizing fascination with her central character's looks—that at the close of the seventeenth century the bottom fell out of the market for female exhibitionism. In Julia Kavanagh's *English Women of Letters* (1863), Sarah Fielding occupies a position analogous to that which de Scudery occupies for Dunlop. Kavanagh casts Fielding's as a story of wasted talent and deficient Englishness. Seduced by the "southern" or "picaresca" school of fiction, for which "the visible is everything," Fielding betrayed an English school for which character is everything, in which the "human being is almost invariably lord of circumstances," and in which incident is used only to develop character. Such differences between nations are homologous with a difference between epochs. "In the last century," writes R. H. Hutton in the *North British Review* in 1858, "it was . . . thought sufficient to present finished sketches of character. . . . To sound the depths and analyze the secret roots of individual character, after the fashion of the modern school, . . . would never have been thought a legitimate or possible aim."[4]

There are two things to say about how notions of inner, deep-seated meaning are mobilized in instances such as these. First, it is worth noting how the questions about the decorums and protocols of communication that occupied mid-eighteenth-century discussions of the reading and writing of character were being displaced by a mode of engagement that, if it were addressed to real rather than imaginary beings, we would classify as an interrogation of the other's sincerity. By the mid-nineteenth century, even when critics retained the old language and referred to characters who are "overcharged" or "coloured too highly," this terminology no longer applied in any exact way to the *techniques* deployed in drawing a character. Criticism no longer treated the character as if it belonged to the realm of discourse: put otherwise, what became important was not so much the saying but what the saying was said about. Overcharged characters were at this point objects of critical suspicion because of what was in a sense a surfeit of legibility, a quality that was connected in turn to such characters' deplorable lack of individuality. The implicit assumption organizing the critique of characters once the criterion of sincerity came into play was that the quality of a character's meaningfulness is diminished if the meanings are too obviously destined to be shared. Characters shouldn't play too much to their audience, and if they do—if their authors have expended too much time in "finishing" their sketches—this may be a sign that they are merely "painted like."

Furthermore, these ways of narrating literary history—as stories of writers' enhanced intimacy with their characters' inside stories—produced a form for which the ante might always be upped. The emphasis on *real* depth authorizes each generation of writers to detect the spuriousness of the depths purveyed by their predecessors and then to correct for that superficiality: in this scheme, each generation of writers could feel called on to round and reanimate character anew. To focus fiction on deep inner meanings is, then, to stimulate the market for fiction and call for more novels that might continue the rise of the genre to which they belong. In *The Heroine, or, Adventures of a Fair Romance Reader* (1813), a satire on female writing and reading and the expansion of the book market, Eaton Stannard Barrett develops a metaphor that can be useful to us here. Barrett's prologue to his novel, a rather aggressive fantasy about the ultimate fate to be suffered by his readers' reading matter, clarifies how characters' ways of looking simultaneously self-made and made-up, individual and socially scripted, could underwrite a make-work project for fiction. Barrett begins his story of how characters cease to beguile on the moon. Cast as a double and mirror to the earth, as is customary in the satiric tradition, the moon also represents here a kind of lumber room for obsolescent writing. It is a retirement home populated by the characters who are sketched each day in terrestrial manuscripts and who take flight for the moon at "the moment . . . the word End or Finis [is] annexed thereto." The moon, that is, is where *yesterday's* characters are consigned—characters who worked an illusionistic magic when they looked real and "round" but who today are discovered to be paper-thin. I have associated romantic-period Britons' emerging interest in inner lives of characters with the notions of virtual subjectivity Britons encountered in the discourses of fashion, but what Barrett hints at in this description of the rhythm of engagement and disengagement with characters that defines the life of the novel reader is that round characters will always end up as fashion victims: Cherubina first shows signs of being cured of her tendency to find characters *real* and so of her quixotic aspirations to be a heroine herself when she thinks with distaste of "Evelina's powdered, pomatumed, and frizzled hair," absurdly out of style in the new nineteenth century.[5] Barrett's bit of lunar ethnography preserves the memory of the ephemera generated in the course of that open-ended redefinition of desire that distinguishes modern consumer societies. It underlines how, as Colin Campbell observes, these societies are "symbolized at least as much by the mountains of rubbish, the garage . . . sales, . . . and the second-hand car lots, as [they are] by the ubiquitous propaganda on behalf of new goods." Barrett might—as "the sisterhood" of "Radcliffian, Rochian, and other heroines" laments with one voice—have "a design on [heroines'] lives," but sometimes he frames his critique (his character assassination) in terms that encourage as much as prohibit the ongoing production of new and improved characters.[6]

I am suggesting that when we think about the narratives of progress in characterization, we also need to think about how this construction of novels' history in some measure depends on the fact that it is no simple matter to distinguish depth from surface—to distinguish characters who are all inner life from characters who are all outer life (a particular hairstyle, a kind of muslin) and so *of* their time (so many period pieces). Needing to write characters all over again, after finding that their realness and roundness have ceased to convince, is what makes the "character business" go.

The reader of *The Wanderer* encounters the following assessment of Elinor Joddrell, the foil to Burney's heroine: Elinor, one character says, is as well as " 'it is possible for a person to be, who is afflicted with the restless malady of struggling for occasion to exhibit character; instead of leaving its display to the jumble of nature and accident.' "[7] This condemnation of Elinor, no adept when it comes to the programs of image management prescribed by the discourses of female conduct, could double as literary criticism. Certainly, it underlines how discourses of gender (suspicions of female display and conniving) have intersected with the terms in which the inauthenticity of merely fashionable novels or of painted characters has been assessed. As it lays out such distinctions as nature versus artifice or sincerity versus showiness, the condemnation of Elinor resembles the statements generated in the course of romantic projects of canon formation in a second respect. It makes sense that these distinctions strike us as unstable: interpretation would put itself out of work if it *were* a simple matter to distinguish between novels in which the characters spring naturally to life and those in which we encounter an author, or, worse, a set of social commonplaces, deceptively speaking in the characters' guise.

Rather than trying to discern signs of an increasing realism in novelistic characterization, then, perhaps we should try to conceive of an institutionalized instability within the cultural field that the romantic-period reinventions of literariness, literacy, and reading relations brought into being. To that end, we could speculate on how, as some of the nineteenth century's retrospects on its reading habits suggest, a fascination with finding personal feelings in books might, from the start, have been shadowed by a fascination with those feelings' evanescence—a fascination with the slide from the personal to the conventional. We could cite Charlotte Brontë's complaints about how Jane Austen's characteristic concern "[was] not half so much with the human heart as with the human eyes, mouth, hands, and feet," and about how an "accurate daguerrotyped portrait of a commonplace face" was all that she found in *Pride and Prejudice* to point to the utility of such fluctuations in characters' creditworthiness.[8] Brontë's roundabout comment on her own engagement with readers' and characters' "hearts" is the more notable because in making Austen represent devalued surface to her depth, Brontë is (unintentionally) turning the tables on the criticism from two decades before in which Austen had trumped Frances Burney in an analogous manner. Austen's novels had been celebrated for their representation of persons who could be ourselves: "we feel as if we had lived among them." If the Austen hero was *not*, as one reviewer for the *Athenaeum* stressed with decision, "a suit of fashionable clothes," and if her heroine was *not* "a ball-dress," Burney's novels, by contrast, seemed to be excessively concerned with the social life of things. "She has considered so anxiously the figured silks and tamboured muslins which flutter about society, that she has made the throbbing of the hearts which they cover a secondary consideration."[9] In retrospect, characterization in Burney (formerly the expression of a new, improved era in novel writing) looked an almost eerily impersonal matter, or rather personal solely in the older, pre-romantic sense of the term that rerouted attention from the private life to the body or "person" that enclosed it. Capping these discussions from the 1830s, Thomas Babington Macaulay's 1843 essay on Burney likewise represents Austen as commanding the skills Burney lacks. If we know each

Austen character as an individual, Macaulay says, the older writer, on the contrary, has nothing better than the skills of "the sign-painter" to bring to the task of discriminating one person from another. Burney can manage only to paint the "living skeleton, the pig-faced lady or the Siamese twins, so that nobody can mistake them."[10]

I want to stress that I do not reconstruct these distinctions so as to rehabilitate them: I am not concurring with those evaluations of character's history that would cast the movement from *Camilla* to *Persuasion* to *Jane Eyre* as a steady development in writers' intimacy with their characters' inner lives. (After all, to begin my discussion of Burney I emphasized the agoraphobia that she and Brontë shared: each woman, I suggested, insisted on bringing commodification and self-definition into relation.) Instead, I am putting the spotlight on the defining rhythms or boom and bust cycles of the character business and suggesting that these are better engaged if we ponder the pragmatic ends that were secured once the enterprise of recognizing the real thing—recognizing truer, more individuated characterization—became one thing that one *had* to do when professing literary history. Crucially, Brontë's dismissal of Austen is made possible by the same axiomatics (the same oppositions between personal and commonplace meanings) that have also been used to secure Austen's exemplarity.

Still, even if we do not linger over Macaulay's insistence on valuing Austen over Burney—even if we hold back from either endorsing his value scheme or reversing it—it is nonetheless worth dwelling on the language of popular entertainment that his essay associates with Burney. Perhaps building on Edmund Burke's much-cited epithet for Burney, the "little character-monger," Macaulay makes Burney over into a sideshow barker.[11] He situates her in the fair, among flamboyantly odd-bodied folk. When he goes on to say that as "a mere caricaturist" Burney might at best be able to approximate "the squint of Wilkes," he situates her as well in another unladylike sphere, that of a rowdy popular politics of English liberties and English eccentricity.

In 1822, Burney's first novel was republished in a new illustrated edition as *Evelina: or, Female Life in London, being the history of a young lady's introduction to fashionable life, and the gay scenes of the metropolis: displaying a highly humourous, satirical, and entertaining description of fashionable, characters, manners, and amusements, in the higher circles of metropolitan society* (fig. 7). The new title reclassified Burney's novel. It made *Evelina* a feminine counterpart to Pierce Egan's *Life in London.* Published two years before, subtitled *The Day and Night Scenes of Jerry Hawthorn Esq and his elegant friend Corinthian Tom, in their Rambles and Sprees through the*

FIG. 7. Illustrated half-title (above) and title page (opposite) of the 1822 reissue of *Evelina*. Reproduced by permission of the Houghton Library, Harvard University.

EVELINA:

OR

FEMALE

LIFE IN LONDON:

BEING THE HISTORY OF

A YOUNG LADY'S INTRODUCTION

TO

𝕱𝖆𝖘𝖍𝖎𝖔𝖓𝖆𝖇𝖑𝖊 𝕷𝖎𝖋𝖊,

AND THE

Gay Scenes of the Metropolis;

DISPLAYING

A Highly Humorous, Satirical, and Entertaining Description
of Fashionable Characters, Manners, and Amusements,

IN THE

HIGHER CIRCLES OF METROPOLITAN SOCIETY.

EMBELLISHED AND ILLUSTRATED WITH

A SERIES OF HUMOROUS COLORED ENGRAVINGS,

BY THE FIRST ARTISTS.

LONDON :

PUBLISHED BY JONES AND CO. WARWICK SQUARE.

1822.

Metropolis, illustrated with aquatints by Robert and George Cruikshank, Egan's book was at once a novel, a guidebook, a comic strip, and the record of a quasi-ethnographic investigation of London subcultures. It married up-to-date graphic technologies to the conycatching pamphlets and rogue biographies of an earlier period: Egan recapitulated, for instance, some of the inventorying of tricks of the town that had engaged mid-century characteristic writing. When, in 1822, Burney's novel was repackaged to resemble Egan's work in particular and the Regency period's newly fashionable "sketchbooks of characters and manners" in general, *Evelina,* embellished now with pictures of the heroine "at the opera" and the heroine "shopping," became not so much a literature of roguery as a literature of voguery. The crucial point, however, concerns the alliances into which *Evelina* was brought as a result of this repackaging. These alliances joined Burney's book to texts that were devoted to cataloging the picturesque qualities of everyday Englishness and whose projects were unabashedly situated within the field of consumer desires. At the same time, they also curtailed readers' interest in the inner lives and inner meanings that were concealed by the gorgeous spectacle of consumption. This repackaging suspended, we might say, what was novelistic about Burney's novel.

As *Female Life in London, Evelina* joined, in addition to Egan's panoramic collection of London types, books such as James Caulfield's *Blackguardiana: Dictionary of Rogues, Bawds, Pimps, Whores, Pickpockets, Shoplifters, Mail-Robbers, Coiners, House-breakers, Murderers, Pirates, Gipsies, Mountebanks, &c., &c.* (1795); G. M. Woodward's *Eccentric excursions: Literary and pictorial sketches of character and countenance* (1797); R. S. Kirby's *The Wonderful and Scientific Museum: or, Magazine of Remarkable Characters* (1809) (fig. 8); G. H. Wilson's *The eccentric mirror, reflecting a faithful delineation of Male and Female characters . . . particularly distinguished by extraordinary Qualifications, Talents, and Propensities* (1813). These copiously illustrated, expensive books sold what was hard to get. Addressing readers as *buyers* ("hunters of oddities," of rare prints especially), some of their authors made no bones about their intention to exploit the antiquarianism and mania for collecting of their reading public.[12] Above all, through recording the eccentricities and commemorating the marked-up countenances of the great (a nobleman with bizarre views on sea-bathing) and of the vulgar (the peddler Colly Molly Puff, who had a unique method for selling pastry), this character literature sold variety. Its consumers were invited to divert themselves with anecdotes that attest, for instance, to how the cant expressions of "the great vulgar" and "the small vulgar" of England have "a force and poignancy not to be found under arbitrary governments": in England, or at least such is the nation that Woodward exposes to view in his vignettes of manners and "original characters," there can be as many as six ways of carrying a walking stick.[13]

In some sense, then, Burney already occupied the place in the cultural field to which the Janeite Macaulay wished to consign her. In 1822 her novel had already been associated with extraliterary, slightly risqué uses of character, those solicited by an idiom of character writing that was graphic in all senses of the term. Appearances by characters in this kind of writing are by definition cameo appearances. Deviant figures such as Daniel Dance and Jemmy Taylor—notorious misers—or Mother Louse—featured by Caulfield because she lived so long that she was the last woman in England to wear a ruff—exemplify what is finally a distinctiveness for distinctiveness's sake. Within the books of remarkable characters and eccentric excursions, what people actually do (some have trained cats, while others have passed as members of the opposite sex) tends to be effaced by the authors' insistence on the "singularity" and "the eccentric whims" that make them do it. Woodward's and Caulfield's is a view of the nation in which, uniformly, all play what Britons later in the nineteenth century would learn to think of as "character parts." In their mode of presenting character, to postulate social heterogeneity—to insist that the different subsectors of society may be at once mutually indecipherable and easily distinguishable—is actually to say something comforting about the fate of people's projects of self-definition subsequent to the "invention of society." In the typing mobilized by this local colorism, what is distinctive about the person is situated and sheltered.

There is likewise something reassuring, although there may also be something unsettlingly un-human, about the way that these books seem always to have room for just one more character or one more vignette revealing the manners of merry England. On the one hand, undisguisedly eager to accumulate odds and ends, their unifying principle an elaborate and colorful sufficiency, these books of character offered succor to the readers' wishes for a better, fuller life.[14] On the other hand, like still life paintings, with their assault "on the prestige of the human subject," there is something perturbing about the character books' clutter.[15] This perturbing quality is exacerbated by a tendency we can detect among illustrators from the 1820s on. Illustrators tended to image fictional characters—when they designed novels' title pages especially—in the same pictorial idiom that they mobilized when they drew cartoons about hypochondria or hallucination and portrayed the so-called

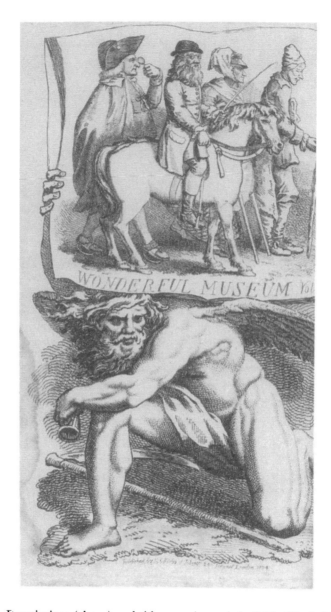

FIG. 8. Frontispiece (above) and title page (opposite) of *The Wonderful and Scientific Museum: or, Magazine of Remarkable Characters.* Courtesy of the Department of Special Collections, Stanford University Libraries.

THE
WONDERFUL

AND

SCIENTIFIC MUSEUM:

OR,

MAGAZINE

OF

REMARKABLE CHARACTERS;

INCLUDING ALL THE

CURIOSITIES OF NATURE AND ART,

FROM THE REMOTEST PERIOD TO THE PRESENT TIME,

Drawn from every authentic Source.

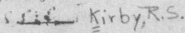 Kirby, R.S.

ILLUSTRATED WITH

Elegant Engravings,

FROM THE MOST SINGULAR AND VALUABLE COLLECTION OF

PRINTS AND DRAWINGS EXTANT.

VOL. I.

LONDON:

Printed by T. KEATING, *Cow-Lane, Snowhill,*
FOR R. S. KIRBY, PATERNOSTER ROW; AND J. SCOTT,
ST. MARTIN'S COURT, LEICESTER FIELDS;

1803.

blue devils, the little demons, and fluttering spectral objects that plagued the human victim of an overactive imagination. Thus, in the context constituted by what some early-nineteenth-century reviewers pigeonholed as "illustrated literature," the imagery associated with characters is frequently an imagery of infestation. Many Regency and early Victorian title pages (those of *Female Life in London* and many of Dickens's novels included) show us *swarming*. This is what the illustrators' pictures of characters or of the unbound pages (fluttering off the writer's desk or out of the bookseller's shop) in which characters are confined do. They swarm—"circle continually," to cite a phrase from R. H. Horne's essay on Dickens and Hogarth—and form "a buzzing world of outward vitality."[16] Miniaturized, yet frenetically energetic in the way they play out their stories, on page one—even before these stories have begun— characters seem, in this style of title page, to be on the verge of escaping out of the book. One has a sense, in confronting such population explosions, that the real, human subject is being crowded out, dispossessed by an embarrassment of riches. The prolific displaces the personal. When they present themselves as collections (museums or rogues' galleries), books such as Woodward's and Caulfield's adopt a display mode, in which social relations fade from view, replaced by the illusion of relations between things.

To take account of who and what Evelina is in the context of these paraliterary ancestors of the coffee table book, the stuff of after-dinner entertainments in family parlors, is just for a moment to read without the guidance purveyed by the disciplinary protocols of novel studies and literary history. It can, I hope to have suggested, be illuminating for just this reason. *Evelina*'s transformation in 1822 points to how the meanings of character, those depths and those signs of the psychological real that discerning readers read for, cannot be understood in isolation from a wider field of social relations— in isolation from the definitions of literacy and literature that readers have mobilized to understand themselves, to understand other readers and, in a rapidly changing, commercializing society, to reinvent the terms of their fellowship. To be sure, the roundest round character may seem—indeed, it will no doubt continue to seem, no matter how successfully I may have argued the contrary—authoritatively transcendent, realistic, magical, and charismatic. The round character may seem to escape the social conditions of its meaning. "In this escape, meaning is indeed liberated, but only in the sense in which we speak of a 'liberated territory' and so indicate a controversy over its rightful possession."[17]

Exploring the new uses that Burney's character-mongering could be put to in 1822 reveals the pitfalls of contemplating texts of the past through the frameworks purveyed by a history of mimesis and a history of individualism. The history of literary characters is not only a mirror in which we catch a glimpse of our own faces. When we reconstruct the history of what we have done to and along with them, it is possible to glimpse something besides earlier versions of what we presently are. We can catch sight, in addition, of alternatives that might once have been.

➳ N O T E S ⤝

INTRODUCTION

1. John Frow, "Spectacle Binding: On Character," *Poetics Today* 7 (1986): 227.

2. "Goethe's Works," *The Works of Thomas Carlyle* (London: Chapman and Hall, 1905), 27:438 (emphasis in original).

3. I quote a phrase of Jean-Christophe Agnew's. See *Worlds Apart: The Market and the Theater in Anglo-American Thought, 1550–1750* (Cambridge: Cambridge University Press, 1986), 194. Throughout my discussion of eighteenth-century market culture I have drawn on Agnew; the other texts I have found particularly useful are J. G. A. Pocock, *Virtue, Commerce, and History: Essays on Political Thought and History, Chiefly in the Eighteenth Century* (Cambridge: Cambridge University Press, 1985); Neil McKendrick, John Brewer, and J. H. Plumb, *The Birth of a Consumer Society: The Commercialization of Eighteenth-Century England* (Bloomington: Indiana University Press, 1985); Amanda Vickery, "Women and the World of Goods: A Lancashire Consumer and Her Possessions, 1751–1781," in *Consumption and the World of Goods*, ed. John Brewer and Roy Porter (London: Routledge, 1993), 274–301; and Adela Pinch, "Stealing Happiness: Shoplifting in Early Nineteenth-Century England," in *Border Fetishisms*, ed. Patricia Spyer (London: Routledge, 1997), 122–49.

4. The entry on "round" in the Supplement to the *OED* identifies E. M. Forster's *Aspects of the Novel* (originally published in 1927) as the origin of the figurative usage of the term that is applied to a character who is "well shaped" or "filled out." This dating can be disputed—a Shakespeare scholar in the eighteenth century will, as we shall see, talk punningly about Falstaff as a "round" character, and R. H. Horne refers to how Dickens's characters have each the "roundness" of "individual reality" (*A New Spirit of the Age* [London: Smith, Elder, and Co., 1844], 1:24). It is beyond dispute, nonetheless, that *Aspects of the Novel* represents the canonical instantiation of the opposition between the round and the flat. Of course, we should not overlook how, over the course of their history, these terms have been mobilized to varying ends. Before Forster, for instance, the value term *round* seems to have been used in ways that called attention to what was complex and unformulaic. Because the afterlife of Forster's scheme for sorting out characters is most visible in the twentieth-century literature classroom—and so in a space devoted to students' "personal growth"—it stands to reason that now, as a matter of course, we match up roundness

267

and "development," an association that is rather more sketchy in pre-twentieth-century discussions of character. The close connections between what readers have done with characters and what consumers have done with consumables become apparent in a suggestion that the *OED* makes about early instances of the term *flat.* In early-nineteenth-century reviews, it would appear, if insipid, lifeless characters are "flat," they are identified in this way because of their resemblance to soda water, too long in the bottle, that has also gone "flat."

5. Michel Foucault, "Truth and Power," in *Power/Knowledge: Selected Interviews and Other Writings, 1972–1977,* ed. Colin Gordon (New York: Pantheon, 1980), 131.

6. Ian Watt, *The Rise of the Novel: Studies in Defoe, Richardson, and Fielding* (1957; reprint, Harmondsworth: Pelican, 1972); compare Michael McKeon's history of the English novel, a dialectical development that sees romance idealism succeeded by antiromance empiricism and sees the latter assimilated in its turn to an aesthetic of conservative skepticism (*The Origins of the English Novel, 1600–1740* [Baltimore: Johns Hopkins University Press, 1986]).

7. Pocock, "The Mobility of Property and the Rise of Eighteenth-Century Sociology," in *Virtue, Commerce, and History,* 109.

8. For statistics documenting these increases in consumption see Peter Matthias, "Leisure and Wages in Theory and Practice," in *The Transformation of England: Essays in the Economic and Social History of England in the Eighteenth Century* (New York: Columbia University Press, 1979), 162.

9. In attending to "economies of prestige," I draw on Pierre Bourdieu's *Distinction: A Social Critique of the Judgement of Taste,* trans. Richard Nice (Cambridge: Harvard University Press, 1984) and his *Language and Symbolic Power,* ed. John B. Thompson, trans. Gino Raymond and Matthew Adamson (Cambridge: Harvard University Press, 1991).

10. For this new work on the trade in novels see, e.g., J. A. Downie, "The Making of the English Novel," *Eighteenth-Century Fiction* 9, no. 3 (1997): 249–66.

11. I quote Bernard Edelman, "The Character and His Double," in *The Real Me: Postmodernism and the Question of Identity,* ed. Lisa Appignanesi (London: Institute of Contemporary Arts, 1987), 36; I also draw on Jane M. Gaines, *Contested Culture: The Image, the Voice, and the Law* (Chapel Hill: University of North Carolina Press, 1991), 212–13.

12. I quote Walter Scott's discussion of the novelist Clara Reeve, intended as an introduction to a volume of *Ballantyne's Novelist's Library,* as well as the review of Austen's *Emma* that Scott wrote for the *Quarterly Review* (*Sir Walter Scott on Novelists and Fiction,* ed. Ioan Williams [London: Routledge, 1968], 99, 227.

13. "Texts, Readers, Reading Formations," *M/MLA: Bulletin of the Midwestern Modern Language Association* 16 (1983): 8. See also Bennett's "The Sociology of Genres" in *Outside Literature* (London: Routledge, 1990), 78–114. For a helpful discussion of why literary history should turn from a concern with the history of genres, conceptualized as so many independent, organic entities, to a concern with generic history, involving the hierarchical relations between kinds of texts, see Clifford Siskin's introduction to *The Historicity of Romantic Discourse* (New York: Oxford University Press, 1988).

14. "Reception seems too mild a word for the Pamela craze that swept through eighteenth-century Europe. . . . A keen Pamela hunter in the 1740s could . . . visit two Pamela waxworks, drop in on Joseph Highmore's studio to see his twelve Pamela paintings and buy the set of his engravings, then see David Garrick in *Pamela, A Comedy*": James

Grantham Turner, "Novel Panic: Picture and Performance in the Reception of Richardson's *Pamela*," *Representations* 48 (1994): 70–71.

15. In thinking about how readers have "working epistemologies," which the cultural historian can reconstruct, I have been much assisted by Nancy Glazener's *Reading for Realism: The Cultural History of a U.S. Literary Institution* (Durham: Duke University Press, 1997).

16. "[W]hat must be described is not a general process or mechanism, but the fact that the use of such and such a procedure is compulsory; that a particular technique has been installed; that children are required to repeat a particular notation; that individuals master a particular technology for . . . confessing their sins or finding their conscience reflected in literary characters' and so on": Ian Hunter, "After Representation: Recent Discussions of the Relation Between Language and Literature," *Economy and Society* 13 (1984): 426. This article, along with Hunter's "Reading Character" (*Southern Review* 16 [1983]: 226–43), has helped me formulate the project of this book.

17. Kay, "Character," in *Political Constructions: Defoe, Richardson, and Sterne in Relation to Hobbes, Hume, and Burke* (Ithaca: Cornell University Press, 1988), 25–32; I quote 26.

18. Random Cloud (Randall McLeod), " 'The Very Names of the Persons': Editing and the Invention of Dramatick Character," in *Staging the Renaissance: Reinterpretations of Elizabethan and Jacobean Drama,* ed. David Scott Kastan and Peter Stallybrass (New York: Routledge, 1991), 88–98.

19. Catherine Belsey, *Critical Practice* (London: Methuen, 1980), 73, 66–67. In the second quotation, Belsey cites Louis Althusser, "Ideology and Ideological State Apparatuses," in *Lenin and Philosophy* (London: New Left Books, 1971).

20. Frow, "Spectacle Binding," 229.

21. Ibid., 238.

22. In *The Care of the Self* (vol. 3 of *The History of Sexuality,* trans. Robert Hurley [New York: Vintage, 1988]), Michel Foucault complained about the lack of rigor cultural historians show in invoking individualism "in different epochs, to explain very diverse phenomena." I have tried to take warning from his comment that "quite often with such categories, entirely different realities are lumped together." Foucault distinguishes 1. "the individualistic attitude, characterized by the absolute value attributed to the individual in his singularity and by the degree of independence conceded to him vis-a-vis the group . . . 2. the positive valuation of private life . . . 3. the intensity of the relations to self." He remarks that "these attitudes can be interconnected . . . but these connections are neither constant nor necessary" (42).

23. See Elspeth Probyn's careful discussion of literary selves in *Sexing the Self: Gendered Positions in Cultural Studies* (London: Routledge, 1993), 33–43.

24. F. R. Leavis, *The Great Tradition: George Eliot, Henry James, Joseph Conrad* (London: Chatto and Windus, 1948), 227; Q. D. Leavis, *Fiction and the Reading Public* (1932; reprint, London: Chatto and Windus, 1939), 60–61. At the start of this paragraph, I quote Ian Duncan's reference to F. R. Leavis in *Modern Romance and Transformations of the Novel: The Gothic, Scott, and Dickens* (Cambridge: Cambridge University Press, 1992), 3; Duncan's comments on the Englishness of English characters—and on how "character was the genius that animated the national literary tradition: its image of the eternal subject" (181)—have likewise been most helpful.

25. The quotation is from Charles Lamb's 1811 essay "On the Genius and Character of Hogarth," in *Selected Prose,* ed. Adam Phillips (Harmondsworth: Penguin, 1985), 42.

See, in addition, Scott's discussion of Smollett's "inexhaustible richness of invention" and "wealthy profusion of varied character" (*Sir Walter Scott on Novelists and Fiction*, 66); "It is . . . chiefly in his profusion, which amounts almost to prodigality, that we recognize the superior richness of Smollett's fancy . . . there is so much of life, action, and bustle, in every group he has painted; so much force and individuality of character" (67, 69). See also R. H. Horne's remarks on the "profusion and prodigality of character" in the works of Hogarth and Dickens (*A New Spirit of the Age*, 1:21). The standard history of the idea of luxury is by John Sekora: *Luxury: The Concept in Western Thought, Eden to Smollett* (Baltimore: Johns Hopkins University Press, 1977).

26. George Orwell, "Charles Dickens," in *The Collected Essays, Journalism and Letters of George Orwell*, vol. 1, ed. Sonia Orwell and Ian Angus (London: Secker and Warburg, 1968), 443, 455; first published 1939. I also draw on W. J. Harvey's "Character and the Context of Things," chap. 2 of *Character in the Novel* (Ithaca: Cornell University Press, 1968), 36–37.

27. Terry Eagleton, *Criticism and Ideology*, quoted in Tony Bennett, "Marxism and Popular Fiction," in *Popular Fictions: Essays in Literature and History*, ed. Peter Humm et al. (London: Methuen, 1986), 261.

CHAPTER ONE

1. Laurence Sterne, *The Life and Opinions of Tristram Shandy*, ed. Graham Petrie (Harmondsworth: Penguin, 1967), 74. Subsequent citations are to this edition and appear in the text. Henry Fielding, *An Inquiry into the Causes of the Late Increase of Robbers*, in *The Complete Works* (New York: Barnes and Noble, 1967), 13:14; Hume, quoted in Jerome Christensen, *Practicing Enlightenment: Hume and the Formation of a Literary Career* (Madison: University of Wisconsin Press, 1987), 158.

2. See Terence Cave, *Recognitions: A Study in Poetics* (Oxford: Clarendon, 1988), especially chap. 4, "The Decline of Recognition: Eighteenth-Century Variants."

3. For this reason, in this chapter I necessarily anticipate developments that later chapters address explicitly. Even though in acknowledging such anticipations I run the risk of seeming to play fast and loose with history, I still prefer not to present the long-term redefinition of character either as a matter of a single decisive reaction against the past or as a process of steady development. Instead I would like to emphasize the coexistence of contrary tendencies within the debates on the added stroke of character.

4. In discussing the problems that inhere in any discussion of "the" novel as a genre, I rely on Tony Bennett's *Outside Literature* (London: Routledge, 1990) and follow his suggestion that "the concept of genre is more usefully interpreted when used as a means for analysing historically and culturally variable systems for the regulation of reading and writing practices than as a kind of writing amenable to a socio-genetic explanation" (81).

5. I am indebted here to Richard W. F. Kroll, *The Material Word: Literate Culture in the Restoration and Early Eighteenth Century* (Baltimore: Johns Hopkins University Press, 1991) and Douglas Lane Patey, *Probability and Literary Form: Philosophic Theory and Literary Practice in the Augustan Age* (Cambridge: Cambridge University Press, 1984). Patey's examples testify to the longevity of arguments founded on the notion that the phenomenal world was replete with identifying signatures—what Sterne's *Sentimental Journey* will call nature's "shorthand." John Ogilvie's *Philosophical and Critical Observations on the Nature, Characters, and*

Various Species of Composition (1774), for instance, sets out a method for discriminating various styles of composition, each marked " 'by those radical signatures, in their full strength, which nature stamps as indelibly on the mind as on the countenance' " (quoted on 227). Seventeenth-century philosophers such as Francis Bacon and John Ray had argued against a Paracelsian doctrine of signatures, one founded on notions of microcosmic-macrocosmic relations. They retained, however, the notion of a signifying nature: "The issue was not the reading of signs in nature," Patey remarks, "but only what kinds of signs nature actually contains" (46).

6. These examples are culled from Haywood's runaway hit of 1719, *Love in Excess, or, the Fatal Enquiry*, ed. David Oakleaf (Peterborough, Ontario: Broadview, 1994), 127, 138, 75. Subsequent references to this book (hereafter *Love*) are to this edition and appear in the text.

7. Daniel Defoe, *An Essay upon Literature; Or, An Enquiry into the Antiquity and Original of Letters* (London, 1726), 2. Subsequent references to this work appear in the text. Eighteenth-century definitions of character are helpfully elucidated by Paul J. Korshin, "Probability and Character in the Eighteenth Century," in *Probability, Time, and Space in Eighteenth-Century Literature* (New York: AMS, 1979), 63–77; Patrick Coleman, "Character in an Eighteenth-Century Context," *The Eighteenth Century: Theory and Interpretation* 24 (1983): 51–63; and David Oakleaf, "Marks, Stamps, and Representations: Character in Eighteenth-Century Fiction," *Studies in the Novel* 23 (1991): 295–311.

8. Kroll, *The Material Word*, 20.

9. Jane Barker, *The Lining of the Patch Work Screen*, in *The Galesia Trilogy and Selected Manuscript Poems*, ed. Carol Shiner Wilson (Oxford: Oxford University Press, 1997), 178–79. Subsequent references, keyed to this edition, will be to *Lining* and will appear in my text. I will likewise key my references to this book's predecessor, *A Patch-Work Screen for the Ladies* (hereafter *Patch-Work Screen*) to this edition and include them in the text.

10. [Abbé Pernetti], *Philosophical Letters upon Physiognomies. To which are added, Dissertations on the Inequality of Souls, Philanthropy, and Misfortunes*, 2d ed. (London: R. Griffiths et al., 1751), 132; John Donaldson, *The Elements of Beauty* (Edinburgh: Charles Elliot and T. Cadell, 1780), 47; Johann Georg Sulzer, *Allgemeine Theorie der Schönen Kunste* (1777), cited in Barbara Maria Stafford, *Body Criticism: Imaging the Unseen in Enlightenment Art and Medicine* (Cambridge: MIT Press, 1991), 84. In *The Order of Things: An Archaeology of the Human Sciences* (New York: Vintage, 1973), Michel Foucault attends to the central role this particular concept of character—as "the structure selected to be the locus of pertinent identities and differences"—plays in eighteenth-century natural history (140).

11. Anthony Ashley Cooper, third earl of Shaftesbury, *Second Characters, or, The Language of Forms*, ed. Benjamin Rand (Cambridge: Cambridge University Press, 1914), 99; John Evelyn, *Numismata: A Discourse on Medals, Antient and Modern* (London: Tooke, 1697), 335; John Ray, *The Wisdom of God Manifested in the Works of the Creation* (1692), cited in Marcia Pointon, *Hanging the Head: Portraiture and Social Formation in Eighteenth-Century England* (New Haven: Yale University Press, 1993), 81. Subsequent references to *Second Characters* are to the Cambridge edition and appear in the text.

12. Locke, *An Essay Concerning Human Understanding*, ed. Peter H. Nidditch (Oxford: Clarendon, 1975), 104. Subsequent citations are to page numbers in this edition and appear in the text. On Locke and collecting see his "New Method of a Common-Place Book," in *Works* (London: Thomas Tegg et al., 1823), 3:331–50.

13. On the role collections of medals and portraits are to play in the formation of gentry identity see Evelyn's *Numismata* and Jonathan Richardson's *An Essay on the Theory of Painting* (1715). For a context for both these texts, see Pointon's "James Granger and the Politics of Collecting Engraved Historic Portrait Heads" in *Hanging the Head*, 53–62. A grangerized book is one that is personalized by having engravings pasted into it: in 1769 James Granger published *Biographical History of England, from Egbert the Great to the Revolution: Consisting of Characters disposed in different Classes, and adapted to a Methodical Catalogue of Engraved British Heads.* Granger's book, by soliciting customizing practices of this sort, seems to have functioned for its readers in ways that anticipate the booklets designed for stamp collectors today.

14. It is notable that Evelyn's instructions to Restoration-era collectors in *Numismata* conclude with "A Digression Concerning Physiognomy." The coin-countenance analogy suggests how physiognomy of the first part of the eighteenth century conceptualizes the face as a field of inscription, the screen on which the characters of a universally consistent grammar or code—the language of "the passions," for instance—become visible. The analogy suggests how the meanings that the mid-eighteenth-century countenance embodies are not in our sense personal meanings (they are not confined to the singular individual); nor are they conceptualized as deep-seated or ineffable meanings. It is only by the end of the eighteenth century, and under the Romantic influence of Johann Caspar Lavater, that the effort will be made to understand the face as, by contrast, a language or, more precisely, an idiolect, which expresses, rather than inscribes, the unique personality (or character) of the individual.

Since it is the proposition of this study that "character" has no general form, that it is not the same sort of object at the start of the eighteenth century that it is at the start of the nineteenth, it seems important to note here that what people see when they look at faces is equally subject to change, not only because, for instance, technological changes make mirrors cheaper and more ubiquitous and allow people to build more windows into their walls and illuminate one another's features more thoroughly, but also because the metaphors that organize people's viewing of faces, and the relationships that they assume between what is visible and what is not, are not constant through time. Such changes are worth keeping in mind because they are implicated in turn in the recalibrations of the relationship between the discourses of character and of physiognomy.

15. Henry Fielding, *The History of the Adventures of Joseph Andrews,* ed. Douglas Brooks-Davies (Oxford: Oxford University Press, 1970), 79. Subsequent citations are to this edition and appear in the text.

16. Daniel Defoe, *Roxana,* ed. John Mullan (Oxford: Oxford University Press, 1996), 74, 161. Subsequent citations are to this edition and appear in the text.

17. Jean-Christophe Agnew, *Worlds Apart: The Market and the Theater in Anglo-American Thought, 1550–1750* (Cambridge: Cambridge University Press, 1986), 58.

18. Delarivier Manley, *The New Atalantis,* ed. Ros Ballaster (Harmondsworth: Penguin, 1992), 45, 34; we see the uses of pocketbooks in Haywood's *Love in Excess,* 111. On legible bodies and seducing texts in Manley and Haywood see Ballaster's *Seductive Forms: Women's Amatory Fiction from 1684 to 1740* (Oxford: Clarendon, 1992), 132–36, 170–75.

19. See Joel Weinsheimer, "Theory of Character: *Emma,*" *Poetics Today* 4 (1979), esp. 186–90.

20. Sarah Fielding [with Jane Collier], introduction to *The Cry: A New Dramatic Fable*

(London: Dodsley, 1754), 18; Henry Gally, *A Critical Essay on Characteristic-Writings* (London, 1725; reprint, Los Angeles: William Andrews Clark Memorial Library, 1952). Subsequent citations of Gally are to this edition and appear in the text.

Prefacing his sister's *The Adventures of David Simple* (1742), Henry Fielding takes pains to align Sarah's narrative with the kinds of character sketches that occupy Henry Gally: "As to the Characters here described[,] . . . *they are as wonderfully drawn by the Writer, as they were by* Nature *herself.* There are many strokes in *Orgueil, Spatter, Varnish, Le-vif,* the *Balancer* and some others, which would have shined in the Pages of *Theophrastus* . . . or *La Bruyere*" (*The Adventures of David Simple*, ed. Malcolm Kelsall [Oxford: Oxford University Press, 1969], 7) (emphasis in original).

21. I draw my examples of the "characters" available at print shops from *Sayer and Bennett's Catalogue of New and Valuable Prints* (London, 1775; reprint, London: Holland, 1970).

22. Samuel Butler, *Characters,* ed. Charles W. Daves (Cleveland: Case Western Reserve University Press, 1970), 185–86, 219. Compare Wye Saltonstall's Waterman to Butler's Busy Man and Hypocrite: "A Waterman is like a peece of Hebrew spel'd backeward, or the embleame of deceite, for he rowes one way & lookes another (*Picturae Loquentes, or, Pictures Drawne forth in Characters* [London, 1631; reprint, Oxford: Basil Blackwell, 1946], 40).

23. Christensen, *Practicing Enlightenment,* 31; see also Christensen's fifth chapter for discussion of the press and the copy theory of knowledge.

24. *Pantocrator* appears as an epithet for God in the General Scholium to book 3 of Newton's *Principia;* Constantine George Caffentzis asserts that Pantocrator was also Newton's name for his copying machine in *Clipped Coins, Abused Words, and Civil Government: John Locke's Philosophy of Money* (Brooklyn: Autonomedia, 1989), 239 n. 109.

25. John Brewer, *The Sinews of Power: War, Money, and the English State, 1688–1783* (New York: Knopf, 1989), 179.

26. Christensen, *Practicing Enlightenment,* 184, 187.

27. I quote the *OED* definitions of *correspondence* and Francis Jeffrey's review of *The Correspondence of Samuel Richardson* (edited by Anna Laetitia Barbauld), which appeared in the *Edinburgh Review* in 1804 and was reprinted in Jeffrey, *Contributions to the Edinburgh Review* (New York: Appleton, 1879), 128. John Mullan's comment on what is at stake in Richardsonian talk of the heart is helpful: "The heart is not a principle of characterization, so much as a principle of writing, of the coherence of narrative itself" (*Sentiment and Sociability: The Language of Feeling in the Eighteenth Century* [Oxford: Clarendon, 1988], 68). For Johnson's comparison of Richardson and Fielding, see James Boswell, *The Life of Johnson,* ed. R. W. Chapman (Oxford: Oxford University Press, 1980), 389.

28. Carol Kay, *Political Constructions: Defoe, Richardson, and Sterne, in Relation to Hobbes, Hume, and Burke* (Ithaca: Cornell University Press, 1988), 140.

29. Samuel Richardson, *Clarissa* (London: Dent, 1979), 2:435. Subsequent references to *Clarissa* are to this four-volume Everyman edition and appear in the text.

30. Jane Austen, *Pride and Prejudice,* ed. James Kinsley (Oxford: Oxford University Press, 1990), 327.

31. Kay, *Political Constructions,* 177.

32. [Georgiana Spencer Cavendish, the duchess of Devonshire], *The Sylph: A Novel, In*

Two Volumes (London: T. Lowndes, 1779), 1:245; Samuel Richardson, *The History of Sir Charles Grandison*, ed. Jocelyn Harris (Oxford: Oxford University Press, 1986), 220; Frances Sheridan, *Memoirs of Miss Sidney Biddulph*, ed. Patricia Köster and Jean Coates Cleary (Oxford: Oxford University Press, 1995), 225.

33. Mullan, *Sentiment and Sociability*, 84–85.

34. Samuel Person, *An Anatomical Lecture of Man, Or a Map of the Little World* (London, 1664), cited in J. W. Smeed, *The Theophrastan "Character": The History of a Literary Genre* (Oxford: Clarendon, 1985), 263 (emphasis in original); Ralph Johnson, *The Scholar's Guide* (London, 1665), quoted in Daves's introduction to Butler, *Characters*, 5.

35. Compare Christensen, *Practicing Enlightenment*, 136 n. 20.

36. I quote E. H. Gombrich's "The Experiment of Caricature," in *Art and Illusion: A Study in the Psychology of Pictorial Representation* (Princeton: Princeton University Press, 1960), 343.

37. Julie Stone Peters, *Congreve, the Drama, and the Printed Word* (Stanford: Stanford University Press, 1990), 136–38.

38. Refinement, Susan Stewart writes in her work on the detailed and minute description, "has to do with not only the articulation of detail but also the articulation of difference, an articulation which has increasingly served the interests of class." Stewart follows Baudrillard in underlining how refinement is a "class-related phenomenon" and in instancing the bourgeois interior—dependent on "the discretion of 'tints and nuances' "—so as to reveal refinement in operation (*On Longing: Narratives of the Miniature, the Gigantic, the Souvenir, the Collection* [Baltimore: Johns Hopkins University Press, 1984], 29). I have already suggested how Locke conceptualizes the mind as a printed page. I want to move now to considering Locke's empiricism—which operates as a program for discovering discreet "tints and nuances," disengaging the differences from within apparent samenesses—as a "class-related phenomenon of refinement." The pursuit of refinement can be seen as a response to an issue that became compelling in a period of commercialized print. The fact that the copy theory of knowledge that is elaborated in eighteenth-century moral philosophy depends on a metaphorics of printing also suggests the problem that arose at this moment—a moment when thinking about knowledge no longer meant thinking about minds as wax tablets, which varied, which could be thicker or thinner, more or less smooth. The problem is this: if the mind is not a wax tablet but, instead, an imprinted page, what is the difference—especially in an age in which correspondence, commerce, and print have rendered experience increasingly uniform and mass-mediated—between one person's page and another's?

39. Chandra Mukerji, *From Graven Images: Patterns of Modern Materialism* (New York: Columbia University Press, 1983), 21.

40. On the character books' overloading of the hitherto prevailing schemes for categorizing people see Agnew, *Worlds Apart*, 82–83.

In Renaissance thinking the humors begin to be disjoined from Galenic medicine. No longer serving to assemble individuals into groups (by slotting them into the category of the "phlegmatic," "the choleric," etc.), the humor became a device for talking about people's distinctive differences, as in William Temple's insistence that the idiosyncracies of the English, a nation of "humourists," marked their superiority over the French, who "look as if they were cast all by one Mould, or cut out all by one Pattern." "Humour," William Gally wrote, is "peculiar to our Nation"; Englishmen "afford a greater Variety of Subject Matter than any other People" (*Critical Essay on Characteristic-Writings*, 94). For an extended discussion of changes in the meaning of *humorist* see Stuart M. Tave, *The Amiable Humorist* (Chicago: University of Chicago Press, 1960); Tave cites William Temple on 94.

41. Richard Flecknoe, *Enigmaticall Characters*, cited in Smeed, *The Theophrastan "Character,"* 181.

42. Warton's comments appeared in the periodical *The Adventurer* no. 49, and are cited in Smeed, *The Theophrastan "Character,"* 65.

43. Here I draw on Peter Stallybrass and Allon White's discussion of the ambivalence that figures such as Swift and Pope evince as they try to "associate *everyone else* with the vulgarity of the fair whilst repudiating any connections which they themselves might have with such a world" (*The Politics and Poetics of Transgression* [Ithaca: Cornell University Press, 1986], 104). See also Lance Bertelsen, *The Nonsense Club: Literature and Popular Culture, 1749–1764* (Oxford: Clarendon, 1986).

44. The quotation is from Henry Fielding's "Essay on the Knowledge of the Characters of Men," *Miscellanies*, ed. Henry Knight Miller (Middletown, Conn.: Wesleyan University Press, 1972), 1:162.

45. In this decade and the following the Darlys solicited caricature sketches from aristocratic amateurs in these fulsome terms: " 'Ladies and gentlemen sending their designs may have them neatly etch'd and printed for their own private amusement, or for publication shall have every grateful return and acknowledgment for any comic design. Descriptive hints in writing (not political) shall have due Honor shewn them" (quoted in the introduction to *English Caricature 1620 to the Present* [London: Victoria and Albert Museum, 1984], 15). Mary Darly, a figure who deserves to be considered independently of her husband, published *A Book of Caricaturas* in 1762. On Pond see Louise Lippincott, *Selling Art in Georgian London: The Rise of Arthur Pond* (New Haven: Yale University Press, 1983).

46. Complaints about caricaturists tend, that is, to focus on the problems of excess and the detail: and this is despite the fact that comic abbreviation—reducing the person to a stick figure—is one of the chief weapons in the caricaturist's arsenal.

47. *The Artist's Repository* is quoted in Pointon, *Hanging the Head*, 86; the complaint against Townshend appeared in *Baratariana, a select collection of fugitive political pieces* (Dublin, 1773), quoted in Diana Donald, " 'Calumny and Caricatura': Eighteenth-Century Political Prints and the Case of George Townshend," *Art History* 6 (1983): 57.

48. Norman Bryson, *Looking at the Overlooked: Four Essays on Still Life Painting* (Cambridge: Harvard University Press, 1990), 53. Fuseli's lectures to the Royal Academy are cited in John Barrell, *The Political Theory of Painting from Reynolds to Hazlitt: "The Body of the Public"* (New Haven: Yale University Press, 1986), 286.

49. The phrase "pictorial abstemiousness" is Barbara Stafford's: *Body Criticism*, 152. "Droll subjects, comic figures, sundry characters, caricatures, &c." are the categories of printed matter found in *A Catalogue of Darly's Comic Exhibition at No. 39, in the Strand* (n.d.; quoted in Diana Donald, *The Age of Caricature: Satirical Prints in the Reign of George III* [New Haven: Yale University Press, 1996], 3). As the catalog's wording suggests, differentiating the caricature from other sorts of comic printed matter was not a priority, and in my usage of *caricature* I aim to reflect that attitude (which was also Hogarth's). The term should be understood as taking in the whole range of comic prints.

50. Joshua Reynolds, *Discourses on Art*, ed. Robert R. Wark (New Haven: Yale Univer-

sity Press, 1975), discourse 3, 44. Subsequent citations are to this edition and appear in the text, where I cite discourse and page numbers.

51. For a discussion of the place of character in Barry's lectures see Barrell, *Political Theory of Painting*, 173–82.

52. Johann Joachim Winckelmann in 1755 compared the classical Greek face with the modern European face, to the disadvantage of the latter: "Modern works are distinguished from those of the Greeks by numerous little hollows, by too many conspicuous dimples . . . in the physical beauty of the Greeks . . . there was a greater unity of construction, a nobler integration of the parts, and a higher degree of completeness" (*Thoughts on the Imitation of the Painting and Sculpture of the Greeks*, reprinted in *German Aesthetics and Literary Criticism*, ed. and trans. H. B. Nisbet [Cambridge: Cambridge University Press, 1984], 37). The Abbé Du Bos and Montesquieu both opined that the characteristically inferior bodily structure of the English (a product of English weather) would impede England's success in the arts of design.

53. Graphic art, throughout the century a prime English export to the Continent, seemed to many commentators conspicuous evidence of a particularly English ideology of "liberty," whether they considered the irreverence toward public figures evidenced in the political cartoons of the mid-to-late eighteenth century or the freedom of draftsmanship that distinguished the comic print in general—the "artless" regression to scribbling that fascinates many psychoanalytically minded commentators on the art of caricature. Something of the social function of the English face—a function that it performed when it was simultaneously decried for its ugliness and celebrated as a manifestation of English liberty—is suggested by the establishment in the eighteenth century of "ugly clubs" in which English men drank, sang, networked, and reveled in their physiognomic oddities. The cheeky (so to speak) defiance of the Royal Academy's ideals of beauty that these men engaged in is one element in the complex negotiations that formed a "middling culture": see Donald, *Age of Caricature*, 10–11.

54. Quoted in ibid., 20.

55. See Marcia Pointon, "Portrait-Painting as a Business Enterprise in London in the 1780s," *Art History* 7 (1984): 187–205.

56. My sources here are Bertelsen, *Nonsense Club;* Sean Shesgreen, ed., *Engravings by Hogarth: 101 Prints* (New York: Dover, 1971); Ronald Paulson, *Hogarth*, vol. 2, *High Art and Low* (New Brunswick, N.J.: Rutgers University Press, 1992); and William Hogarth, *Analysis of Beauty*, ed. Joseph Burke (Oxford: Clarendon, 1953). Subsequent citations of the *Analysis* and also of Hogarth's "Autobiographical Notes" (included in Burke's edition) appear in the text.

57. Letter signed "George Bout-de-Ville," *Public Advertiser*, 5 June 1765; quoted in Donald, *Age of Caricature*, 50.

58. Paulson, *Hogarth: High Art and Low*, 123.

59. Ibid., 195.

Hogarth has a starring role whenever nineteenth-century Britons describe themselves as heirs to a culture well stocked with characters. See, e.g., Charles Lamb's 1811 "On the Genius and Character of Hogarth" (*Selected Prose*, ed. Adam Phillips [Harmondsworth: Penguin, 1985], 27–44), Lecture 7 of William Hazlitt's *Lectures on the English Comic Writers* (London: Taylor and Hessey, 1819), and R. H. Horne's *A New Spirit of the Age* (London: Smith, Elder, and Co., 1844). Texts such as these portray Hogarth as being in his "true element," as Horne says (21), whenever he deals with "characters full of . . . life," and as belonging to a tradition that includes Shakespeare, Sterne, and Dickens rather than other graphic artists. Given this portrayal of Hogarth, we have all the more reason to recognize his mixed feelings about the project of character drawing and to acknowledge that for him the identity of the character was not self-evident.

60. B. Walwyn, *Essay on Comedy* (London, 1782), cited in Devin Burnell, "The Good, the True, and the Comical: Problems Occasioned by Hogarth's *The Bench*," *Art Quarterly* n.s. 1 (1978): 29.

61. Barrell remarks of Reynolds' system of species and classes, "The difficulty of this position . . . is that there is no limit to the number of classes we can invent . . . and the more we do invent, the more we seem to shatter the uniformity of human nature which a public art exists to represent" (*Political Theory of Painting*, 105). Note too the problems Reynolds has in coping with the painter's need to depict the expressions of the passions: "If you mean to preserve the most perfect beauty *in its most perfect state,* you cannot express the passions, all of which produce distortion and deformity" (*Discourses on Art*, 5:78; emphasis in original).

62. *The Monthly Review* (20 Sept. 1758), cited in Burnell, "The Good, the True, and the Comical," 18.

63. Francis Grose, *Rules for Drawing Caricaturas, with An Essay on Comic Painting* (London: Samuel Bagster, 1788), 5, 4.

64. Smart is quoted in Paulson, *Hogarth: High Art and Low*, 248. The entertainment provided on the mid-eighteenth-century stage was also closely allied with that provided by the print shop window. Theatergoers were on the lookout for players' mimicry of the physical tics that distinguished the members of rival acting troupes. Theater was a kind of animated caricature.

65. James Beattie, *Essays on Poetry and Music* (London, 1776), cited in Patey, *Probability and Literary Form*, 86.

66. Warton's praise of Garrick's "little touches of nature" is cited in George Winchester Stone, Jr. and George M. Kahrl, *David Garrick: A Critical Biography* (Carbondale: Southern Illinois University Press, 1979), 39.

67. For the conversation with Burney, see Boswell, *Life of Johnson*, 663. Johnson's remarks to Thrale are cited in Cecil Price, *Theatre in the Age of Garrick* (Totowa, N.J.: Rowan and Littlefield, 1973), 18.

68. Aaron Hill, *An Essay on the Art of Acting* (London, 1746), as cited in George Taylor, " 'The Just Delineation of the Passions': Theories of Acting in the Age of Garrick," in *The Eighteenth-Century English Stage*, ed. Kenneth Richards and Peter Thomson (London: Methuen, 1982), 65.

69. Samuel Foote, *A Treatise on the Passions, so far as they regard the Stage* (London, 1747; reprint, New York: Benjamin Blom, 1971), 1. Subsequent citations (to *Treatise*) appear in the text.

70. Denis Diderot, "Le paradoxe sur le comédien," as cited in Alan T. McKenzie, " 'The Countenance You Show Me': Reading the Passions in the Eighteenth Century," *Georgia Review* 32 (1978): 766. I have drawn on the sophisticated account of Garrick's "naturalism" that Leigh Woods offers in *Garrick Claims the Stage: Acting as Social Emblem in Eighteenth-Century England* (Westport, Conn.: Greenwood, 1984).

71. *Theophilus Cibber to David Garrick, Esq.* (London, 1759), cited in Woods, *Garrick Claims*

the Stage, 18; see the same page for Charles Macklin's normative sense of how " 'the restless abundance of [Garrick's] action and his gestures . . . exceeded the fair business of character.' "

72. Abbé Le Blanc, *Letters on the English and French Nations* (London, 1747), cited in Price, *Theatre in the Age of Garrick,* 15.

73. I cite Charles Le Brun, *A Method to Learn to Design the Passions,* trans. John Williams (London, 1734; reprint, Los Angeles: William Andrews Clark Memorial Library, 1980), 31. On Hamlet's wig see Woods, *Garrick Claims the Stage,* 121.

74. The *London Chronicle*'s review of *Harlequin Skeleton* is cited in Price, *Theatre in the Age of Garrick,* 74; Horace Walpole is cited in Woods, *Garrick Claims the Stage,* 18. Stone and Kahrl trace Garrick's involvement with the pantomimic tradition throughout their biography of the actor: see chaps. 2 and 7.

75. E. J. Clery, *The Rise of Supernatural Fiction, 1762–1800* (Cambridge: Cambridge University Press, 1995), 41. Clery's description of the experience of early-eighteenth-century playgoing could, as a whole genre of popular prints indicates, just as easily describe what it was like to join the crowd in front of a print shop window. This suggests in turn how readers who were invited to think of themselves as connoisseurs of character, rather than of caricature, were also being invited to think of themselves as habitués of the domestic interior rather than buyers off the street.

76. For the argument that the preface to *Joseph Andrews* concerns itself with the shift from crowd entertainment to literary representation, see Judith Frank, "The Comic Novel and the Poor: Fielding's Preface to *Joseph Andrews,*" *Eighteenth-Century Studies* 27, 2 (winter 1993–94): 217–34. Walpole's *Book of Materials* is quoted in *Reynolds,* ed. Nicholas Penny (New York: Harry Abrams, 1986), catalog entry 42, 205.

77. Thus, aesthetic treatises of the late eighteenth century such as Isaac d'Israeli's *A Dissertation on Anecdotes* [1793] tend to find the single stroke of character to be more meaningful "than an elaborate delineation, as a glance of lightning will sometimes discover what has escaped us in full light" (cited in Patey, *Probability and Literary Form,* 124). For another example of dissatisfaction with the notion of character as an aggregate of discrete signs, see *The Spirit of the Age,* where William Hazlitt implies that "personal character" is *not* "a machine or a collection of topics" (London, 1825; reprint, Menston, Yorkshire: Scolar, 1971), 320–21.

78. Tobias Smollett, *The Adventures of Roderick Random,* ed. Paul-Gabriel Boucé (Oxford: Oxford University Press, 1981), 395; *The Adventures of Peregrine Pickle,* ed. James L. Clifford, rev. Paul-Gabriel Boucé (Oxford: Oxford University Press, 1983), 273–74, 335.

79. Laurence Sterne, *A Sentimental Journey through France and Italy,* ed. Ian Jack (Oxford: Oxford University Press, 1968), 50, 51. In these remarks on the novel and meticulousness, I draw on Susan Stewart's discussion of description in *On Longing,* 27–29.

80. Chatterton, [Letter 6 from "A Hunter of Oddities," 15 June 1770] in *The Complete Works of Thomas Chatterton,* ed. Donald S. Taylor (Oxford: Clarendon, 1971), 1:593–94. The Pinchbecks are featured in the Fillinham collection of print ephemera, vol. 5, British Library, London.

81. See the entries "queer card," "rum fellow," and "quiz" in E. Cobham Brewer, *The Dictionary of Phrase and Fable* (1894; reprint, New York: Avenel, 1978). The *OED* calls this anecdote about the invention of the term *quiz*—supposed to have occurred in 1791— apocryphal and ascribes the first use of the term to Frances Burney in 1782.

CHAPTER TWO

1. George M. Kahrl, "Smollett as a Caricaturist," in *Tobias Smollett: Bicentenary Essays Presented to Lewis M. Knapp*, ed. G. S. Rousseau and P.-G. Boucé (New York: Oxford University Press, 1971), 188; Tobias Smollett, *The Adventures of Roderick Random*, ed. Paul-Gabriel Boucé (Oxford: Oxford University Press, 1979), 70, 283. Subsequent references to *Roderick Random* are to this edition and appear in the text.

2. Henry Fielding, *Tom Jones*, ed. Sheridan Baker (New York: Norton, 1973), 526; subsequent references to *Tom Jones* are to this edition and appear in the text; Sarah Fielding, *The Adventures of David Simple*, ed. Malcolm Kelsall (Oxford: Oxford University Press, 1969), 27, 28; [Joseph Addison], *The Spectator* no. 69 (19 May 1711), in *Selections from the Tatler and the Spectator*, ed. Angus Ross (Harmondsworth: Penguin, 1982), 437.

3. Joshua Reynolds, *Discourses on Art*, ed. Robert R. Wark (New Haven: Yale University Press, 1975), 44–45.

4. John Barrell, *English Literature in History, 1730–1780: An Equal, Wide Survey* (New York: St. Martin's, 1983), 35. Barrell's introduction considers eighteenth-century debates about who could claim this sort of disinterested viewpoint; his third chapter offers an extended reading of Smollett's and Henry Fielding's discussions of the gentleman.

5. Tobias Smollett, *The Adventures of Peregrine Pickle in which are included Memoirs of a Lady of Quality*, ed. James L. Clifford, rev. Paul-Gabriel Boucé (Oxford: Oxford University Press, 1983), 108, 18. Subsequent references to *Peregrine Pickle* are to this edition and appear in the text.

6. This arrangement also predicts the habit that illustrators of Dickens's novels would have of equipping his insipid ingenus and ingenues with blank, unlined faces and accentuating the peculiarities adorning everyone else's. Franco Moretti remarks on something like this division of labor when he characterizes (in overly general terms, I believe) "the" tradition of the English novel: "As if to make the slightly colorless universalism of the 'common' hero stand out, and to balance it with an entirely different value system, the English novel surrounds the protagonist with a dense array of peculiar, maniacal and unmistakable characters incarnating the opposite principle" (*The Way of the World: The Bildungsroman in European Culture*, trans. Albert Sbragia [London: Verso, 1987], 192).

7. Cited in Leigh Woods, *Garrick Claims the Stage: Acting as Social Emblem in Eighteenth-Century England* (Westport, Conn.: Greenwood, 1984), 139.

8. Those anxieties perhaps inform an odd assertion Samuel Johnson made to Boswell: Johnson first confirmed that "Garrick's great distinction is his universality" and then continued, illogically enough, "He can represent all modes of life, but that of an easy fine-bred gentleman" (James Boswell, *The Journal of a Tour to the Hebrides with Samuel Johnson, LL.D.*, ed. Peter Levi [Harmondsworth: Penguin, 1984], 227).

9. I quote *The Life and Adventures of Bampfylde-Moore Carew, The Noted Devonshire Stroler and Dog-Stealer* (n.p: Joseph Drew, 1745) in *Bampfylde-Moore Carew: The King of the Beggars*, ed. C. H. Wilkinson (Oxford: Clarendon, 1931), 22; see, as well, *An Apology for the Life of Bampfylde-Moore Carew* (London: W. Owen, 1748 [?]), included in the same volume. The author of the second biography refrains from recounting a scene of farewells between Carew and his family because, he says of himself, he lacks "the fertile Imaginations" of the authors of *Roderick Random* and *Tom Jones* (150); in his conclusion he maintains that Carew has a better claim to "Immortality" than the fictitious heroes of his age (272–73).

On the Smollett-loving spy, see Andrew Lang, *Pickle the Spy, or the Incognito of Prince Charles* (London: Longman, 1897).

10. Taking refuge in patriotism while he refuses to apologize for his practice of putting the narrative cart before the horse, one narrator from 1770 declares, "I do not claim an hereditary right to it as an Englishman; but Englishmen I hope have a right to take some small liberties that way now and then." Thomas Bridges, *The Adventures of a Bank-Note*, 4 vols. (London: T. Davies, 1770–71), 1:205. I draw here on two helpful discussions of the picaresque: Susan Stewart, *Nonsense: Aspects of Intertextuality in Folklore and Literature* (Baltimore: Johns Hopkins University Press, 1979), 141; and Barbara A. Babcock, " 'Liberty's a Whore': Inversions, Marginalia, and Picaresque Narrative," in *The Reversible World: Symbolic Inversion in Art and Society*, ed. Barbara A. Babcock (Ithaca: Cornell University Press, 1978), 106.

11. I am interested in the tensions between these emphases, but in what follows I won't be valorizing these tensions as, say, a symptom that brings to light the ideological contradictions of the period. John Barrell and Harriet Guest have advised scholars of eighteenth-century literature to think hard about how literary works are not always embarrassed by their contradictions. Like the poetry Barrell and Guest discuss, mid-century characteristic writing may have been "performing the function of *enabling* contradictions to be uttered" ("On the Use of Contradiction: Economics and Morality in the Eighteenth-Century Long Poem," in *The New 18th Century*, ed. Felicity Nussbaum and Laura Brown [New York: Methuen, 1986], 123). It might well have been the flexibility with which these narratives bridged public and personal meanings that made them useful for people adapting to what J. G. A. Pocock calls an "increasingly transactional universe . . . in which relationships and interactions with other social beings and with their products became increasingly complex" ("Virtue, Rights, and Manners," in *Virtue, Commerce, and History: Essays on Political Thought and History, Chiefly in the Eighteenth Century* [Cambridge: Cambridge University Press, 1985], 48).

12. Tobias Smollett, *The Adventures of Ferdinand Count Fathom*, ed. Paul-Gabriel Boucé (Harmondsworth: Penguin, 1990), 43. Subsequent references to *Count Fathom* are to this edition and appear in the text.

13. Henry Home, Lord Kames declares "that natural objects readily form themselves into groups": *Elements of Criticism*, 2d ed. (London, 1763; reprint, New York: Huntington and Savage, 1845), 164; see also Johnson's discussion of Shakespeare's characterization in his preface to *The Plays of William Shakespeare* and in particular the reference to how Shakespeare manages to "vary [many casts . . . of dispositions] with great multiplicity; to mark them by nice distinctions; and to *show them in full view by proper combinations*" (*The Oxford Authors: Samuel Johnson*, ed. Donald Greene [New York: Oxford University Press, 1984], 439; emphasis mine).

14. Delarivier Manley, *Memoirs of Europe, Towards the Close of the Eighth Century* (London, 1710), in *The Novels of Mary Delariviere Manley*, ed. Patricia Köster (Gainesville: Scholars' Facsimiles and Reprints, 1971), 2:297; Alain René Le Sage, *Le Diable boiteux*, ed. Roger Laufer (Paris: Gallimard, 1984); Claude Lévi-Strauss, *The Savage Mind* (Chicago: University of Chicago Press, 1966), 24. See the remarks on Le Sage in Ronald Paulson, *Satire and the Novel in Eighteenth-Century England* (New Haven: Yale University Press, 1967), 175.

15. Laurence Sterne, *A Sentimental Journey through France and Italy*, ed. Ian Jack (Oxford:

Oxford University Press, 1984), 30, 86. Subsequent references to *A Sentimental Journey* are to this edition and appear in the text.

16. For an extensive discussion of the circulation of bodily fluids in *Tom Jones* see Ronald Paulson, "The Iatrohydraulic System," in *Popular and Polite Art in the Age of Hogarth and Fielding* (Notre Dame: University of Notre Dame Press, 1979), 172–89. The scene near the close of the novel in which Tom and Sophia are reunited at Lady Bellaston's London house is also of interest if we want to consider Fielding's characters as one another's mirrors: it is when she looks in the drawing-room mirror to contemplate "her own lovely Face" that Sophia first sees Tom's. " 'Oh Heavens! Indeed, I am surprised. I almost doubt whether you are the person you seem' " (559). Building on Sophia's doubt, one might well ask, in what sense are these two distinct characters at all?

In an extended discussion of *Tom Jones* and *Joseph Andrews,* Jill Campbell traces how at moments like these Fielding seems to mobilize a myth of a primal androgyny and challenge the polarization of masculinity and femininity that characterized his culture (*Natural Masques: Gender and Identity in Fielding's Plays and Novels* [Stanford: Stanford University Press, 1995]). My point is that the suggestions of a continuity between selves that these episodes offer might also be valued, not in mimetic terms, and not for what they suggest about Fielding's views of real people, but rather for what they tell us character is and is not. Other scenes with mirrors in *Tom Jones* also illustrate the indeterminacy of the hero's and heroine's identities but do so in ways that suggest how his reliance on distinctions of class, as well as his ambivalence over the emerging distinctions of gender, condition what Fielding can do with character. In a conversation Sophia has with her maid Honour, which occurs as the one assists the other at her toilette, it is Honour who launches into encomiums in which Tom figures as a "pretty . . . Creature" and enumerates "many Particulars, . . . ending with the Whiteness of his Skin" (155). This scene shows us Fielding exploiting the convention whereby the chatty maidservant features as the mouthpiece of her mistress, for the sentiments to which Honour gives voice in the scene are Sophia's own. Fielding's assumptions about characters and the means of communication make the relation between the characters Sophia and Honour a relation of job-sharing. It is also notable that Honour's enumeration of Tom's beauties makes Sophia blush, but Honour doesn't notice Sophia's face—because, we are told, her eyes are locked on a "Looking-glass, . . . most commodiously placed opposite to her, [which] gave her an Opportunity of surveying those Features, in which of all others, she took most Delight." Honour's, Tom's, *and* Sophia's features end up strangely intermingled in this episode, confirming one's sense that Fielding is as interested in unraveling identities as establishing them.

17. [George Hickes,] *Some Queries Propos'd to Civil, Canon, and Common Lawyers . . . In order to prove the Legitimacy of the Pretender* (London: S. Popping, 1712), 19; *The Great Bastard, Protector of the Little One. Done out of the French* ([London], 1701), 3.

18. See Paul Monod, *Jacobitism and the English People* (Cambridge: Cambridge University Press, 1989), chap. 3, " 'Look, Love, and Follow': Images of the Last Stuarts in Jacobite Art."

19. [M. Michell, ascrib.], *Young Juba: or, The History of The Young Chevalier from His Birth to his Escape from Scotland, after the Battle of Culloden* (London, 1748), 277–78; *Ascanius; or, the Young Adventurer: Containing an impartial history of the Rebellion in Scotland in the years 1745–6* (Belfast, 1841), 123; 116. It is worth noting that this nineteenth-century edition of *Ascanius*

(original edition 1747) is published in a series that also includes novels—*Gulliver's Travels, The Vicar of Wakefield,* and so on.

20. Catherine Gallagher, *Nobody's Story: The Vanishing Acts of Women Writers in the Marketplace, 1670–1820* (Berkeley and Los Angeles: University of California Press, 1994).

21. See Homer Obed Brown's discussion of Tom Jones's nobodiness in just these terms: "*Tom Jones:* The 'Bastard' of History," *boundary 2* 7 (1979): 201–33. The phrase "children of the nation" appears in *Some Queries Propos'd to Civil, Canon, and Common Lawyers;* arguing that questions about illegitimacy that are usually confined to private families have been inappropriately transferred to the Stuarts' case, George Hickes states that children who have rights to a crown are "children of the Nation"—"this is the Reason why they are called by the Name of the Nation, and not by that of their Family" (13).

22. This is in fact the motto of *The Connoisseur,* the periodical essay series that, reviving the *Spectator,* Bonnell Thornton began to publish in 1754. In his first number, "Survey of the Town" (31 January), Mr. Connoisseur declares, "I am a Scotchman at Forrest's [Coffeehouse], a Frenchman at Slaughter's, and at the Cocoa-Tree, I am—an Englishman. . . . Wherever the WORLD is I am."

23. Gallagher, *Nobody's Story,* 174.

24. David Hume, *A Treatise of Human Nature,* ed. Ernest C. Mossner (Harmondsworth: Penguin, 1969), 414. I quote above from Joshua Reynolds's third Discourse, 47.

25. Hume, *Treatise of Human Nature,* 408; Adam Smith, *An Inquiry into the Nature and Causes of the Wealth of Nations,* ed. Kathryn Sutherland (Oxford: Oxford University Press, 1993), 177.

26. Bridges, *Adventures of a Bank-Note,* 1:7. Subsequent references to this narrative appear in the text.

27. James Thompson, "Patterns of Property and Possession in Fielding's Fiction," *Eighteenth-Century Fiction* 3, no. 1 (1990): 21–42, esp. 23–24.

28. The standard history of English currency is A. E. Feaveryear, *The Pound Sterling: A History of English Money* (Oxford: Clarendon, 1931). See Feaveryear, 169, on the liquidity crisis the British state faced at the start of its war with revolutionary France, when fears of an invasion induced people to hoard their metallic money. The Restriction Bill was intended to compensate for this shortage of specie.

29. Aileen Douglas, "Britannia's Rule and the It-Narrator," *Eighteenth-Century Fiction* 6, no. 1 (1993): 71.

30. On physiognomy and the misrepresentations endemic in the early modern marketplace, see Jean-Christophe Agnew, *Worlds Apart: The Market and the Theater in Anglo-American Thought, 1550–1750* (Cambridge: Cambridge University Press, 1986), 58–60; Roy Porter, "Making Faces: Physiognomy and Fashion in Eighteenth-Century England," *Etudes Anglaises* 18 (1985): 385–96.

31. [Helenus Scott], *The Adventures of a Rupee, Wherein are interspersed various anecdotes Asiatic and European* (London: J. Murray, 1782), 7, 145.

32. Douglas, "Britannia's Rule and the It-Narrator," 73–74; Douglas quotes *The Adventures of a Corkscrew* (London, 1775).

33. As in *Tom Jones,* the narrator of *Miss Betsy Thoughtless* cultivates a certain facetiousness and garrulousness, teasing the reader with chapter titles that manage both to be explicit and to disclose nothing crucial in the way of plot twists. To define the reading process,

both Fielding's and Haywood's narrators use the metaphor of the long stagecoach journey and speak of their readers as travelers who stop at inns.

34. Eliza Haywood, *The History of Miss Betsy Thoughtless* (London: Pandora, 1986), 34, 31, 373, 107. Time works differently for a circulating woman—whose beauty, she is constantly reminded, will fade—than it does for a circulating man. She will also have a different relationship to space. No space is off-limits to either a Tom Jones or a banknote, and in a sense all spaces are commensurable. Betsy, by contrast, risks losing her character by going into the wrong places, as Haywood suggests in the episodes that see Betsy wander off the path while visiting some gardens at Oxford and that see her pulled over the threshold of a rascally viscount's townhouse. Betsy's story unfolds, that is, not within the neutral, homogenized space of a modern commercial society, but in a landscape of romance— full of areas of darkness and ill-doing and (to cite the phrase from amatory fiction that Betsy reuses) "perplexing labyrinth[s]" (184).

35. Bruce Robbins, *The Servant's Hand: English Fiction from Below* (New York: Columbia University Press, 1986), 35.

36. On *copia* and copying, see Jonathan Goldberg, *Writing Matter: From the Hands of the English Renaissance* (Stanford: Stanford University Press, 1990), 158–59. Natalie Zemon Davis's essays "Printing and the People" and "Proverbial Wisdom and Popular Errors" demonstrate that proverbial wisdom was one of the most characteristic products of early print technology (*Society and Culture in Early Modern France* [Stanford: Stanford University Press, 1975]).

37. In *Tom Jones*, Partridge, the would-be manservant to the eponymous hero, if not to the Young Pretender himself, cites this same Latin adage, echoing Strap's echo of Juvenal's well-worn tag (658).

38. Here I follow Susan Stewart's discussion of the aphorism: see *On Longing: Narratives of the Miniature, the Gigantic, the Souvenir, the Collection* (Baltimore: Johns Hopkins University Press, 1984), 53.

39. Barrell, *English Literature in History*, 190. In addition to learning from Barrell's reading of *Roderick Random*, I have drawn on the following discussions: James H. Bunn, "Signs of Randomness in *Roderick Random*," *Eighteenth-Century Studies* 14 (1981): 452–69; Aileen Douglas, " 'Surrounded with Bodies': Social Experience in *Roderick Random*," chap. 3 of her *Uneasy Sensations: Smollett and the Body* (Chicago: University of Chicago Press, 1995); and Richard W. F. Kroll, "The Politics of Plot in Smollett's *Roderick Random*" (paper delivered for the American Society for Eighteenth-Century Studies, Pittsburgh, April 1991).

40. This marks a difference between what Fielding and Smollett are doing with character. For Fielding, as the story of the banknotes' recognition demonstrates, nothing is ever lost. For Smollett, no one is every really found. In this sense, Smollett's use of character caters to more modern convictions about the unknowability of identity.

41. On Narcissa, see Douglas, *Uneasy Sensations*, 68. On the estate as personality-sustaining property, see J. G. A. Pocock, *The Machiavellan Moment: Florentine Political Thought and the Atlantic Republican Tradition* (Princeton: Princeton University Press, 1975). Ann Louise Kibbie has extended Pocock's work with provocative speculations on how this ideal of the estate was gendered: "Sentimental Properties: *Pamela* and *Memoirs of a Woman of Pleasure*," *ELH* 58 (1991): 561–77.

42. The most famous of these stories centered—aptly, for my purposes—on one Rod-

erick Mackenzie, who "died under English bullets crying, 'You have slain your Prince' "
(Lang, *Pickle the Spy*, 15).

43. *The Life and Adventures of Bampfylde-Moore Carew* (1745), in Wilkinson, *Bampfylde-Moore Carew*, 98.

44. Sarah Fielding [and Jane Collier], *The Cry: A New Dramatic Fable* (London: Dodsley, 1754), 18.

45. Gallagher, *Nobody's Story*, 180–81.

46. Paulson, *Satire and the Novel in Eighteenth-Century England*, chap. 5. I also draw here on Stuart M. Tave, *The Amiable Humorist* (Chicago: University of Chicago Press, 1960).

47. "Mr Joseph Andrews . . . was of the highest Degree of middle Stature. . . . His Forehead was high, his Eyes dark, and as full of Sweetness as of Fire. His Nose a little inclined to the Roman. His Teeth white and even. His Lips full, red, and soft . . ." (34).

48. I am grateful to Richard Kroll for reminding me of the Scottish associations of red hair. John Barrell's remarks on the sign of Scottish origin that Roderick does lose— his accent—are helpful: he notes that Roderick's accent "identifies him as a Scot on a number of occasions in the early part of the novel. . . . It seems to be only by about the time that he believes himself (however erroneously) to be a 'gentleman in reality' that he ceases to be identifiable by his accent" (*English Literature in History*, 198).

49. "The money-owning individual is confronted with an infinite number of objects the enjoyment of which is equally guaranteed by public order": George Simmel, *The Philosophy of Money*, trans. Tom Bottomore and David Frisby (London: Routledge and Kegan Paul, 1978), 309.

. 50. That Joseph wears the gold on a ribbon around his neck would to mid-eighteenth-century British readers have recalled how parents who left their infants at the Foundling Hospital would leave with them one-half of a broken coin—pledge of a blood relation that might resume when the two halves were reassembled. Campbell's *Natural Masques*, which emphasizes the prominent role such losses and reunions play in Fielding's fiction, authorizes my decision to treat *Joseph Andrews* as a novel of sentimental masculinity.

51. Henry Mackenzie, *The Man of Feeling* (1771; reprint, New York: Norton, 1958), 31–32. Subsequent references are to this edition and appear in the text.

52. On Sterne's snuffbox and the miniature of Eliza Draper, see Arthur Cash's biography: *Laurence Sterne: The Later Years* (New York: Methuen, 1986).

53. R. F. Brissenden, *Virtue in Distress: Studies in the Novel of Sentiment from Richardson to de Sade* (London: Macmillan, 1974), 119; John Mullan, *Sentiment and Sociability: The Language of Feeling in the Eighteenth Century* (Oxford: Clarendon, 1988), 119.

54. Mullan, *Sentiment and Sociability*, 61; Kibbie, "Sentimental Properties," 568.

55. Barbara M. Benedict, "Reading Faces: Physiognomy and Epistemology in Late Eighteenth-Century Sentimental Novels," *Studies in Philology* 92, 3 (1995), 327, 321.

56. Hippolyte Taine, *The History of English Literature*, trans. H. Van Laun, 4 vols. (new ed., London: Chatto and Windus, 1877), 3:268.

57. This is Richard Sennett's point in *The Fall of Public Man: On the Social Psychology of Capitalism* (New York: Vintage, 1978), 64–88.

58. *Capital*, quoted in Gillian Brown, *Domestic Individualism: Imagining Self in Nineteenth-Century America* (Berkeley and Los Angeles: University of California Press, 1990), 52. To understand how the personal effect and the impersonal medium of money seem to trade

places in these two odd vignettes, see also Simmel's *Philosophy of Money:* "In so far as money is the symbol as well as the cause of making everything indifferent and of the externalization of everything that lends itself to such a process, it also becomes the gatekeeper of the most intimate sphere, which can then develop within its own limits" (470).

59. In eighteenth- and nineteenth-century British society, inheritance of real property (land) tended to be reserved for male beneficiaries; gentlewomen, more associated with the volatile realm of circulation, got their wealth in the form of personal property—troublingly liquid assets, such as shares of stocks, or troublingly portable and transferable things. Women have, accordingly, had more compelling reasons than men to strive to bind proprietorship and self-expression. Concluding her examination of the records of one Lancashire gentry family, Amanda Vickery notes that "women's records consistently reveal a more self-conscious, emotional investment in household goods, apparel and personal effects" ("Women and the World of Goods: A Lancashire Consumer and Her Possessions, 1751–81," in *Consumption and the World of Goods,* ed. John Brewer and Roy Porter [London: Routledge, 1993], 294).

In the chapters that follow, 4 and 5 especially, I shall, accordingly, concentrate on women readers and female characters. This does not mean that I am turning toward a "separate" or "minor" tradition of character reading and writing. As my previous remarks on the mid-eighteenth-century gendering of impersonality might suggest, adopting a woman-centered focus means examining exactly those areas of culture in which new questions about character, questions that hinged on *personality,* were going to be asked with the greatest degree of insistence and eloquence.

60. Gallagher, *Nobody's Story,* 174; William Wordsworth, *Home at Grasmere,* ed. Beth Darlington (Ithaca: Cornell University Press, 1977), Ms. D., at 449, ll. 686–87.

CHAPTER THREE

1. Ian Watt, *The Rise of the Novel: Studies in Defoe, Richardson, and Fielding* (1957; reprint, Harmondsworth: Pelican, 1972), 33. See the discussions of Watt in Ian Hunter, "After Representation: Recent Discussions of the Relation Between Language and Literature," *Economy and Society* 13 (1984): 397–430, and Clifford Siskin, *The Historicity of Romantic Discourse* (New York: Oxford University Press, 1988).

2. Robert Langbaum, *The Poetry of Experience,* cited in Alexander Welsh, *Strong Representations: Narrative and Circumstantial Evidence in England* (Baltimore: Johns Hopkins University Press, 1992), 103. In *Character and the Novel* (Ithaca: Cornell University Press, 1965), W. J. Harvey is quite insistent—in ways characteristic of an era in which "socialist realism" was something of an American bugbear—that no authentically novelistic novel can be written in an illiberal society. Because novelists must accept their characters "as asserting their human individuality and uniqueness in the face of all ideology," there can be no Marxist novel (25). Replaying Taine's discussion of the "character novel," Harvey ascribes to character the glamor of the soon-to-be-doomed: "liberalism is a luxury rarely allowed by history" (26).

3. E. M. Forster, *Aspects of the Novel,* ed. Oliver Stallybrass (Harmondsworth: Pelican, 1962), 80.

4. [J. Wilson Croker], review of *Waverley, Quarterly Review* 11, no. 22 (1814): 354–55; Ioan Williams, ed., *Sir Walter Scott on Novelists and Fiction* (London: Routledge and Kegan

Paul, 1968), 99 (on Reeve) and 227 (on Austen). On the Burney school of novelists, see, for example, the review of *Henry and Isabella, Critical Review* 65 (June 1788): 485, and the *Analytical Review*'s 1788 review of Charlotte Smith's *Emmeline. Emmeline* was also heralded— once again by the *Critical Review*—as announcing "a new aera in novel-writing" (quoted in Mary A. Favret, "Telling Tales about Genre: Poetry in the Romantic Novel," *Studies in the Novel* 26 [1994]: 285).

5. As Franco Moretti suggests in his discussion of the bildungsroman, ordinary walks of life are where "relationships, intimate as well as public, are only worthwhile in their contribution to the development and consolidation of personality": *The Way of the World: The Bildungsroman in European Culture* (London: Verso, 1987), 39–41.

6. According to Michael Crump, the 1770s witnessed a 20 percent increase in the number of such new "novels" issued in England, the 1780s, another 20 percent increase, and the 1790s—the crucial decade for the consolidation of the novel—a 64 percent increase: "Stranger Than Fiction: The Eighteenth-Century True Story," in *Searching the Eighteenth Century: Papers Presented at the Symposium on the Eighteenth Century Short Title Catalogue in 1982*, ed. Michael Crump and M. Harris (London: British Library, 1983), 61–62, cited in Catherine Gallagher, *Nobody's Story: The Vanishing Acts of Women Writers in the Marketplace, 1670–1820* (Berkeley and Los Angeles: University of California Press, 1994), 219.

7. Roland Barthes, *S/Z,* trans. Richard Miller (New York: Hill and Wang, 1974), 191.

8. *Capital,* cited in John Guillory, "Canonical and Non-Canonical: A Critique of the Current Debate," *ELH* 54 (1987): 492.

9. On Lane's circulating libraries, see E. J. Clery, *The Rise of Supernatural Fiction, 1762– 1800* (Cambridge: Cambridge University Press, 1995), 135–36; my quotations from Lane's advertising are taken from Dorothy Blakey, *The Minerva Press, 1790–1820* (Oxford: Oxford University Press, 1939), 120–21.

10. *The Case of the Appellants and Respondents in the Cause of Literary Property, Before the House of Lords,* quoted in Trevor Ross, "Copyright and the Invention of Tradition," *Eighteenth-Century Studies* 26, no. 1 (fall 1992): 3.

11. Ann Radcliffe, *The Romance of the Forest,* ed. Chloe Chard (Oxford: Oxford University Press, 1986), 82.

12. See Jane Austen, *Pride and Prejudice,* ed. James Kinsley (Oxford: Oxford University Press, 1970), 166, 189; Michel Foucault, "What Is an Author?" in *Language, Counter-Memory, Practice: Selected Essays and Interviews,* ed. Donald F. Bouchard (Ithaca: Cornell University Press, 1977), 120, 116.

13. Austen, *Pride and Prejudice,* 220.

14. Moretti, *Way of the World,* 69.

15. Austen, *Pride and Prejudice,* 246.

16. Brian Doyle, *English and Englishness* (London: Routledge, 1989), 14.

17. On "literature" as an invention of the late eighteenth century, see, inter alia, Siskin, *Historicity of Romantic Discourse,* 67–93; Michel Foucault, *The Order of Things: An Archaeology of the Human Sciences* (New York: Vintage, 1973), 303–7; Alan Richardson, *Literature, Education, and Romanticism: Reading as Social Practice, 1780–1832* (Cambridge: Cambridge University Press, 1994), chap. 6; Ross, "Copyright and the Invention of Tradition." The idealist credos that emphasize the autonomy of works of literature were perhaps boosted as the novel wrote off the tropes of political economy that had pervaded the older writing of character. It is tempting to push this point further and propose that such protocols emerged

because the novel dropped the episodic plots of the mid-eighteenth century, when character writers had presented the peregrinations of their heroes as if they were monitoring commodities' movements through the circuits of exchange. The round character at the center of the period's new style of novels, the figure who cannot be slotted into any one of the *Quarterly Review*'s "classes of men," does not speak nearly as explicitly as its forerunners did about the social and material supports of meaning. This character does not direct our attention to systems of type faces and coin faces and circuits of reproduction, distribution, and exchange—to the material apparatus that, as characteristic writings would suggest, underwrites its significance and worth. From being a means to meaning, the character comes to organize the axiomatics of romantic reading as a source of meaning in its own right.

18. Philippe Lacoue-Labarthe and Jean-Luc Nancy, *The Literary Absolute: The Theory of Literature in German Romanticism* (Albany: SUNY Press, 1988), passim. I also draw on Pierre Bourdieu, *Distinction: A Social Critique of the Judgement of Taste*, trans. Richard Nice (Cambridge: Harvard University Press, 1984), whose term "aristocracy of culture" I have borrowed.

19. Foucault, "Nietzsche, Genealogy, History," in *Language, Counter-Memory, Practice*, 142. The same might be said of the novel: for an essay that argues the point, see Homer Obed Brown, "Of the Title to Things Real," *ELH* 55 (1988): 917–55.

20. Maurice Morgann, *Essay on the Dramatic Character of Sir John Falstaff* (London: P. T. Davies, 1777), 58. Subsequent references to Morgann will appear in the text. Morgann's essay was reprinted in 1820 and 1825.

21. Mackenzie's essays on Hamlet and on Falstaff appeared in, respectively, *The Mirror*, nos. 99–100 (17 April, 22 April 1780), and *The Lounger*, nos. 68–69 (20 May, 27 May 1786). William Richardson's works include *Essays on Shakespeare's Dramatic Characters of Richard the Third, King Lear, and Timon of Athens, With Additional Observations on Shakespeare's Dramatic Character of Hamlet* (1783) and *Essays on Shakespeare's Dramatic Character of Sir John Falstaff* (1788). Thomas Robertson published "An Essay on the Character of Hamlet" in *Transactions of the Royal Society of Edinburgh* 2 (1788): 251–67. Many of these essays are excerpted in Brian Vickers, ed., *Shakespeare: The Critical Heritage* (London: Routledge and Kegan Paul, 1981), vol. 6.

22. In his provocative essay on Morgann's *Essay* and A. C. Bradley's *Shakespearean Tragedy*, Alexander Welsh also thinks about what connects Falstaff and Hamlet (*Strong Representations*, 101–36) but doesn't mention their shared weight problem. If we bear in mind that in the nineteenth century Shakespearean heroines replace Falstaff and Hamlet as favorite subjects for the reveries of the character appreciation, it is interesting to note that Falstaff and Hamlet also have in common a persisting association with femininity. Falstaff is in women's clothing for part of *The Merry Wives of Windsor* (in the guise of the "fat woman of Brainford"), and Hamlet has been a prize role for cross-dressed actresses ever since Sarah Siddons played him at the turn of the nineteenth century. Fittingly, in his 1881 *The Mystery of Hamlet*, Edward P. Vining queried whether Shakespeare may not in fact have been "compelled . . . to gradually modify his original hero into a man with more and more of the feminine element, may not at last have had the thought dawn upon him that this womanly man might be in very deed a woman" (cited in Marjorie Garber, *Vested Interests: Cross-Dressing and Cultural Anxiety* [New York: Routledge, 1992], 38). In "Literary Fat Ladies and the Generation of the Text," Patricia Parker also discusses the effeminacy

of Hamlet, but does so, unlike Vining, without resorting to the postulate that really round characters escape their makers' intentions, and without resorting to transhistorical stereotypes about female psychology in the effort to motivate Hamlet's indecisiveness, garrulity, and ineffectuality. Parker associates the Prince of Denmark, as well as Falstaff, with the rhetorical tradition that linked the figure of *dilation*—the figure for lengthening and fattening texts—to women's linguistic unruliness and bodily excessiveness. Her essay is highly suggestive, not least in inviting us to speculate that the history of psychological meaning, a history in which femininity and psychological complexity are persistently intertwined, may be construed as a process of working over and working through Renaissance rhetoric's tacit link between wordiness, female corporeality, and discourse "pregnant" with meaning (chapter 1 of *Literary Fat Ladies: Rhetoric, Gender, Property* [New York: Routledge, 1987], 8–35).

23. *The Lounger*, no. 69 (27 May 1786), in *Eighteenth-Century Critical Essays*, ed. Scott Elledge (Ithaca: Cornell University Press, 1961), 2:978–79.

24. Samuel Taylor Coleridge, "Hamlet," *Lectures* (1818), in *Poems and Prose*, ed. Kathleen Raine (Harmondsworth: Penguin, 1957), 273; Mackenzie, *The Mirror*, nos. 99–100 [17 April, 22 April 1780], in Vickers, *Shakespeare: The Critical Heritage*, 6:279.

25. The shift in critical aims is described by Brian Vickers in the introduction to *Shakespeare: The Critical Heritage*, 6:16–25. Vickers cites Thomas Whately's *Remarks on Some of the Characters of Shakespeare* (1785), which opens with a forthright attempt to shift the target of Shakespearean commentary and replace "fable" with "character" (6:408).

26. Henry Fielding, *Tom Jones*, ed. Sheridan Baker (New York: Norton, 1973), 373–74.

27. In other words, as in Doug Allen's "Steven," these inferior characters are—suspiciously—never glimpsed from the side.

28. Thomas Robertson, "An Essay on the Character of Hamlet," in Vickers, *Shakespeare: The Critical Heritage*, 6:482.

29. The neoclassical critic's concern with the "preservation of character" found its authorization in the *Ars Poetica*: "[I]f you boldly fashion a fresh character, have it kept to the end even as it came forth at the first, and have it self-consistent" (quoted in Vickers's introduction to *Shakespeare: The Critical Heritage*, 6:17). Compare Fielding, *Tom Jones*, 307.

30. Margreta de Grazia, *Shakespeare Verbatim: The Reproduction of Authenticity and the 1790 Apparatus* (Oxford: Clarendon, 1991), 223–24; William Richardson, "Additional Observations on Shakespeare's Dramatic Character of Hamlet," in Vickers, *Shakespeare: The Critical Heritage*, 6:367–68; my emphasis.

31. "To understand the character of *Hamlet* we had best take it at two different times, before the death of his father and after that period": Robertson, "An Essay on the Character of Hamlet," in Vickers, *Shakespeare: The Critical Heritage*, 6:481.

32. G. M. Woodward, *Eccentric excursions: Literary and pictorial sketches of character and countenance* (London: Allen, 1797), chap. 16, pl. 66. Compare the similar Victorian paintings memorializing the relation between immortal characters and their perishable creators, for example, Robert W. Buss's *Dickens's Dream* and Luke Fildes's *The Empty Chair*.

33. *Critical Review* 57 (1784) and Richard Stack, "An Examination of an Essay on the Dramatic Character of Sir John Falstaff," *Transactions of the Royal Irish Academy* 2 (1788), both cited in Vickers, introduction to *Shakespeare: The Critical Heritage*, 6:18, 23.

34. Ian Hunter, "Reading Character," *Southern Review* 16 (1983): 230. Stubbes' *Some*

Remarks on the Tragedy of Hamlet is excerpted in Vickers, *Shakespeare: The Critical Heritage*, vol. 3; see particularly 57.

35. Anne Thackeray Ritchie, *A Book of Sibyls—Mrs. Barbauld, Miss Edgeworth, Mrs. Opie, Miss Austen* (London: Smith, Elder, 1883), 211, 206 (revision of an essay series first published in *Cornhill Magazine* 24 [Aug. 1871]); Kathryn Sutherland, "Fictional Economies: Adam Smith, Walter Scott and the Nineteenth-Century Novel," *ELH* 54 (1987): 118. See also Francis Jeffrey's 1804 review of Anna Laetitia Barbauld's edition of Samuel Richardson's *Correspondence*, particularly Jeffrey's remarks on Richardson's (by 1804 retroactively rounded) characters: "[W]e get so intimately acquainted with [them], and so impressed with a persuasion of their reality, that when any thing really disastrous or important occurs to them, we feel as for old friends and companions" (*Contributions to the Edinburgh Review* [New York: Appleton, 1879], 128).

36. Samuel Richardson, *Clarissa, or, The History of a Young Lady* (London: Dent, 1932), 2:408.

37. Friedrich Schiller, *On the Aesthetic Education of Man*, cited in Ian Hunter, "Aesthetics and Cultural Studies," in *Cultural Studies*, ed. Lawrence Grossberg et al. (New York: Routledge, 1992), 350.

38. As early as 1825, the reviewer for the Tory *Blackwood's Edinburgh Magazine* combats the utilitarian plans for working-class education proposed by "the Fox and Bentham schools"—instruction in political economy and science—with a plan to put *novels* into the hands of the lower orders: "Brougham on the Education of the People," *Blackwood's* 17 (May 1825): 550.

39. William Wordsworth, preface to *Lyrical Ballads* (1802), in *The Oxford Authors: William Wordsworth*, ed. Stephen Gill (New York: Oxford University Press, 1984), 606.

40. Henry Smith, "The Education of the Citizen," cited in James Donald, *Sentimental Education: Schooling, Popular Culture, and the Regulation of Liberty* (London: Verso, 1992), 72 (emphasis mine). More generally, see Ian Hunter, *Culture and Government: The Emergence of Literary Education* (Basingstoke: Macmillan, 1988), esp. 119–49, and Michel Foucault, "The Subject and Power," afterword to Hubert Dreyfus and Paul Rabinow, *Michel Foucault: Beyond Structuralism and Hermeneutics* (Chicago: University of Chicago Press, 1982). In my use of "government" and "governmentality" I follow Foucault: " 'Government' . . . designated the way in which the conduct of individuals or of groups might be directed: the government of children, of souls, of communities, of families, of the sick. It did not only cover the legitimately constituted forms of political or economic subjection, but also *modes of action, more or less considered and calculated, which were destined to act upon the possibilities of action of other people. To govern, in this sense, is to structure the possible field of action of others* ("Subject and Power," 221; emphasis mine). It's worth stressing that to propose with Foucault that subjectivity is an effect of the machinery of government is not equivalent to claiming that subjectivity is the *realization* of that machinery.

On the "infinitization of literature," see Lacoue-Labarthe and Nancy, *The Literary Absolute*.

41. William Gilpin, *Dialogues on Various Subjects* (London: T. Cadell and W. Davies, 1807), 152 (emphasis in original). See Kim Ian Michasiw, "Nine Revisionist Theses on the Picturesque," *Representations* 38 (1992): 76–100, for a careful exposition of the politics of the picturesque.

42. I quote Jonathan Crary, *Techniques of the Observer: On Vision and Modernity in the Nineteenth Century* (Cambridge: MIT Press, 1990), 98.

43. Sarah Stickney Ellis, *The Women of England, their Social Duties and Domestic Habits* (1836; reprint, New York: Appleton, 1843), 22–23; Austen, *Pride and Prejudice*, 32. On the social status that accrued to owners of large collections of books and on the addition of libraries to country houses, see Gary Kelly, *English Fiction of the Romantic Period, 1789–1830* (New York: Longman, 1989), chap. 1; for the evolution in Jane Austen's lifetime of a new interest in "interior decoration" (a term coined in the period) see Philippa Tristram, *Living Space in Fact and Fiction* (New York: Routledge, 1989).

44. I owe this point to Crary, *Techniques of the Observer*, 9; cf. M. H. Abrams, *The Mirror and the Lamp: Romantic Theory and the Critical Tradition* (1953).

45. Colin Campbell, *The Romantic Ethic and the Spirit of Modern Consumerism* (Oxford: Blackwell, 1987). Campbell's point of departure is Neil McKendrick, "Home Demand and Economic Growth: A New View of the Role of Women and Children in the Industrial Revolution," in *Historical Perspectives: Studies in English Thought and Society in Honour of J. H. Plumb*, ed. Neil McKendrick (London: Europa, 1974). As McKendrick suggests, in the course of the eighteenth century, women of the propertied classes found increasing opportunities for individual agency in their guise as arbiters of the "tasteful" and as custodians of the domestic sphere and so of the main site at which people developed relations with the new consumer goods. But in thinking about how some women were empowered through the consumer revolution we need not reproduce the celebratory tone that characterizes this work. We should not overlook how since the eighteenth century the marketplace has been a site where the injuries of class have been reproduced—the processes described by Bourdieu in *Distinction*. That shopping is an occasion for discontent and snobbery more often than it is an occasion for pleasure is an important feature of the psychology of consumerism—as I will emphasize when I turn in the next chapter to agoraphobia in the novels of Frances Burney.

46. Campbell, *Romantic Ethic*, 89, 92.

47. G. J. Barker-Benfield evocatively describes the historical significance of the various accessories and knickknacks that constituted the prime matter of the eighteenth-century world of goods. "An increasing range of personal and domestic items were invested with a particular combination of the culture's feelings, that is, with taste. . . . Commercially produced and advertised items included the famous smelling bottles, hartshorn drops, and handkerchiefs—in the phrase used by Wollstonecraft, Radcliffe, and Hays, 'every inanimate object'—with which women were concerned": *The Culture of Sensibility: Sex and Society in Eighteenth Century Britain* (Chicago: University of Chicago Press, 1992), 211.

48. Campbell, *Romantic Ethic*, 92.

49. Alison Light, *Forever England: Femininity, Literature, and Conservatism between the Wars* (London: Routledge, 1991), 13. In the nineteenth century physiognomy too was harnessed to projects of self-culture. Mary Cowling (*The Artist as Anthropologist: The Representation of Type and Character in Victorian Art* [Cambridge: Cambridge University Press, 1989]) has established how physiognomy, inflected by new anthropological notions of race, supplied the Victorians with a way of making the crowd into a readable object; a text from 1815, Mary Anne Schimmelpenninck's *Theory on the Classification of Beauty and Deformity* (London: John and Arthur Arch), suggests what else physiognomical reading could do by the nineteenth century. Schimmelpenninck argued with the previous generation of neoclassical aestheti-

cians by proposing that there were many standards of beauty rather than one, and she reconceptualized physiognomy as a set of guiding principles that would aid individual women in discovering the distinct types of beauty ("sentimental," "sprightly," and so forth) to which they might appropriately aspire. In her introduction, Schimmelpenninck explains that she first took an interest in physiognomy in her childhood, when she would draw the profiles of visitors and amuse herself by matching them to "every variety of costume": "It could not fail to strike the most inattentive eye, that whilst some of [the costumes] only travestied the individual . . . ; [others] imparted a new and bold relief to the expression; and, as with the touch of Ithuriel's spear, bid the original character start up to light, in all its native magnitude" (vi). When the Abbé Pernetti set out his physiognomical system in 1751 he emphasized its capacity to undo the disguising and the deceiving that fashion, by eroding distinctions of rank, fostered. In *Theory on the Classification of Beauty and Deformity* we see physiognomy setting the particular terms on which the individual will participate in the fashion system, promoting her efforts to elaborate her individual style. Physiognomical principles guide the individual in choosing between muslin and brocade, Grecian or Highlander's costume. See also Ann Bermingham, "The Picturesque and Ready-to-Wear Femininity," in *The Politics of the Picturesque: Literature, Landscape, and Aesthetics since 1770,* ed. Stephen Copley and Peter Garside (Cambridge: Cambridge University Press, 1994).

50. Jon P. Klancher, *The Making of English Reading Audiences, 1790–1832* (Madison: University of Wisconsin Press, 1987). To align those processes of class formation with the transformation that saw the proper knowledge of character become a deep and private knowledge allows us to broaden the history that Klancher assembles, one restrictively focused on the periodicals of the romantic period and on Wordsworth, Coleridge, and Percy Shelley. If we think about the novel of manners as a site at which new audience relations and new controls over interpretation were established, we are in a better position than Klancher is to acknowledge women writers' participation in the project of audience-making: we can learn how the processes of class formation unfolded on the home front.

51. Austen, *Pride and Prejudice,* 138; compare Michasiw ("Nine Revisionist Theses," 95), who remarks on how Austen is "very precise on the class locations of her various students of the picturesque."

52. Klancher, *Making of English Reading Audiences,* 11.

53. William Richardson, "Additional Observations on Shakespeare's Dramatic Character of Hamlet," in Vickers, *Shakespeare: The Critical Heritage,* 6:368; anonymous review of *Pride and Prejudice, Critical Review,* 4th ser. (1813), in B. C. Southam, *Jane Austen: The Critical Heritage* (London: Routledge and Kegan Paul, 1968), 47.

54. Klancher, *Making of English Reading Audiences,* 12.

55. Wordsworth, preface to *Lyrical Ballads,* 599; Samuel Taylor Coleridge, *Biographia Literaria,* ed. George Watson (London: Dent, 1975), 21.

56. Review of *Tales of Fashionable Life* by Maria Edgeworth, *Edinburgh Review* 4 (1804): 329.

57. See Ina Ferris, *The Achievement of Literary Authority: Gender, History, and the Waverley Novels* (Ithaca: Cornell University Press, 1991), 41–42; Ferris quotes the *Gentleman's Magazine* 75 (1805) and the *New Monthly Magazine* 14 (1820).

58. For an argument linking the work of academic critics to Wordsworth's gaze, see Siskin, *Historicity of Romantic Discourse,* 85.

59. Ferris, *Achievement of Literary Authority*, 34; cf. Clery, *Rise of Supernatural Fiction*, chap. 6.

60. See Margaret Anne Doody, "George Eliot and the Eighteenth-Century Novel," *Nineteenth-Century Fiction* 35, no. 3 (1980): 260–91; John Bender, *Imagining the Penitentiary: Fiction and the Architecture of the Mind in Eighteenth-Century England* (Chicago: University of Chicago Press, 1987), 212.

61. Austen, *Pride and Prejudice*, 320–23.

62. Coleridge, *Lectures*, in *Poems and Prose*, 235.

63. Thank you to Adela Pinch for supplying me with this formulation. The *New Monthly Magazine*'s 1826 assessment of Ann Radcliffe's fiction is helpful here: "[I]t may be true that her persons are cold and formal; but her readers are the virtual heroes and heroines of her story as they read" (quoted in Maggie Kilgour, *The Rise of the Gothic Novel* [London: Routledge, 1995], 6–7).

64. Jane Austen, *Northanger Abbey*, ed. John Davie (Oxford: Oxford University Press, 1980), 36.

65. Ann Radcliffe, *The Italian, or the Confessional of the Black Penitents,* ed. Frederick Garber (Oxford: Oxford University Press, 1971), 91, 197, 211. See also Eve Kosofsky Sedgwick, "The Character in the Veil," chap. 4 of her *The Coherence of Gothic Conventions* (New York: Methuen, 1986); and Andrea Henderson, " 'An Embarrassing Subject': Use Value and Exchange Value in Early Gothic Characterization," in *At the Limits of Romanticism: Essays in Cultural, Feminist, and Materialist Criticism,* ed. Mary A. Favret and Nicola J. Watson (Bloomington: Indiana University Press, 1994).

66. For example: "The monk, whose face was still shrouded, he thought advanced, . . . and, lifting the awful cowl that had hitherto concealed him, disclosed—not the countenance of Schedoni, but one which Vivaldi did not recollect ever having seen before!" (*The Italian*, 318). Comparable scenes of unveiling can be found in vol. 1, chap. 11 and vol. 3, chap. 6.

67. Frances Burney, *The Wanderer, or, Female Difficulties,* ed. Margaret Doody, Robert L. Mack, and Peter Sabor (Oxford: Oxford University Press, 1991), 44–45.

68. Mary Brunton, *Self-Control* (1811; reprint, New York: Pandora, 1986), 1; Regina Maria Roche, *The Children of the Abbey* (1796; reprint, Philadelphia: J. B. Lippincott, 1864), 7.

69. Jane Austen, *Persuasion,* ed. John Davie (Oxford: Oxford University Press, 1990), 71; Susan Ferrier, *The Inheritance* (Mill Green, Oxfordshire: Three Rivers Books, 1984), 884.

70. Roche, *Children of the Abbey*, 343–44. In *Bleak House,* the classic Victorian example of a narrative motivated by the veiling and disfiguring of women's faces, Dickens replays the romantic writers' insistence on separating the meanings of selfhood from meanings that appear when he places the recognition scene that reunites Esther Summerson with her mother immediately after the heroine's recovery from the bout of smallpox that divested her of her "old face" and left her unrecognizable.

71. Susan Ferrier, *Marriage* (London: Virago, 1986), 4; Roche, *Children of the Abbey*, 177.

72. Jane Austen, *Catherine and Other Writings,* ed. Margaret Doody and Douglas Murray (Oxford: Oxford University Press, 1993), 5.

73. Lady Morgan [Sydney Owenson], *Woman; or, Ida of Athens* (London: Longman, Hurst, Rees, and Orme, 1809), 2:158, 1:ix.

74. As Morgan's allusion to the custom of purdah attests, the dichotomies ordering

this system of value could also be redeployed for Orientalist ends: characters whose significance was exhausted in the work of bodily exhibition could kindle the race-thinking of the second British empire.

75. Thank you to Roy Roussel for help with this formulation.

76. On oppositions between the essential and the ornamental, see Bourdieu, *Distinction*, 486 and Naomi Schor, *Reading in Detail: Aesthetics and the Feminine* (New York: Methuen, 1987). I quote the anonymous review of Elizabeth Norman's *The Child of Woe: A Novel*, *The Analytical Review* 3 (1789), anthologized in Ioan Williams, ed., *Novel and Romance, 1700–1800: A Documentary Record* (New York: Barnes and Noble, 1970), 368. This review has been ascribed to Mary Wollstonecraft. For examples of how the personal questions tendered by the heroine's foil can turn the heroine into a fashion plate, see Evelina's interaction with the Branghtons (Frances Burney, *Evelina, or, the History of a Young Lady's Entrance into the World*, ed. Edward A. Bloom [Oxford: Oxford University Press, 1982], 69), or see Roche, *Children of the Abbey*, 153.

77. Preface to vol. 6 of *Ballantyne's Novelist's Library*, anthologized in Williams, *Sir Walter Scott on Novelists and Fiction*, 44.

78. Fielding, *Tom Jones*, 435; Hannah More, *Strictures on the Modern System of Female Education*, in *Works of Hannah More* (New York: Harper, 1840), 1:343.

79. Ferrier, *Marriage*, 6. For Lady Juliana's misadventures with circulating-library novels, see 237–38. Miss Bingley, in *Pride and Prejudice*, is arraigned for similar readerly misconduct; see 48.

80. William Hazlitt, "Standard Novels and Romances" (review of Burney, *The Wanderer*), *Complete Works of William Hazlitt*, ed. P. P. Howe (London: Dent, 1934), 16:19; "On Fashion," *Works*, 17:54–55.

81. Brummel is cited in Elizabeth Wilson, *Adorned in Dreams: Fashion and Modernity* (Berkeley and Los Angeles: University of California Press, 1987), 180. See also Philippe Perrot, *Les Dessus et les dessous de la bourgeoisie: Une histoire du vêtement au XIXᵉ siècle* (Paris: Fayard, 1981); Richard Sennett, *The Fall of Public Man* (New York: Knopf, 1977).

82. Kaja Silverman, "Fragments of a Fashionable Discourse," in *Studies in Entertainment: Critical Approaches to Mass Culture*, ed. Tania Modleski (Bloomington: Indiana University Press, 1986), 141.

83. In his account of the Great Masculine Renunciation, Flugel in fact was concerned not only with gentlemen's habit of dressing down but also with the compensatory displacement elsewhere of fashion, first and foremost onto women of the propertied classes— the gentlemen's wives and daughters. In "On Fashion," Hazlitt applauds an apparent democratization in women's as well as in men's clothing: "a white muslin gown is now the common costume of the mistress and the maid" (55). However, those muslin gowns that are in vogue at the turn of the nineteenth century (as heroine description of the era testifies) quickly gave way to a phantasmagoria of hoop skirts, extravagantly shaped muttonchop sleeves, flowers, ribbons, and feathers—a fluid body image that ceaselessly restated rather than reformed the ancien régime language of woman's apparel. As Silverman writes, following Flugel, "[t]he endless transformations within female clothing construct female sexuality and subjectivity in ways that are at least potentially disruptive, both of gender and of the symbolic order, which is predicated upon continuity and coherence. . . . [T]he uniform of orthodox male dress . . . [has been] a rock against which the waves of female fashion crash in vain" ("Fragments of a Fashionable Discourse," 148). My next

chapter explores how Burney addresses some consequences of this sexual division of the labor of fashion.

84. Cited in Perrot, *Les Dessus et les dessous,* 206; my translation.

85. I owe thanks to Aileen Ribeiro for telling me about the unseemly underside of eighteenth-century vestimentary exhibitionism: the sloppy basting stitches, the unfinished or absent facings, and so on.

86. I quote the remarks on sleeve buttons in Sennett, *Fall of Public Man,* 166; on cravats, see Perrot, *Les Dessus et les dessous,* 208–9; see also Perrot's remarks on dandyism, 250.

87. Ritchie, *A Book of Sibyls,* 151–52.

CHAPTER FOUR

1. Frances Burney, *Evelina, or, the History of a Young Lady's Entrance into the World,* ed. Edward A. Bloom (Oxford: World's Classics, 1968), 77. All subsequent references to *Evelina* are to this edition and appear in the text, as do references to the following works by Burney: *Cecilia, or, Memoirs of an Heiress,* ed. Peter Sabor and Margaret Anne Doody (Oxford: Oxford University Press, 1988); *Camilla, or, A Picture of Youth,* ed. Edward A. Bloom and Lillian D. Bloom (Oxford: Oxford University Press, 1983); *The Wanderer, or, Female Difficulties,* ed. Margaret Anne Doody, Robert L. Mack, and Peter Sabor (Oxford: Oxford University Press, 1991).

2. Quoted in Mark Seltzer, *Bodies and Machines* (New York: Routledge, 1992), 143. Julia Epstein proposes that the dance—"its oppressive nonchoice of partners for women and the complacent 'disposal' of women by unself-consciously possessive men—serves as a metaphor for the female condition throughout *Evelina*": *The Iron Pen: Frances Burney and the Politics of Women's Writing* (Madison: University of Wisconsin Press, 1989), 110.

3. See, for example, Burney, *Cecilia,* 34: "The moment Cecilia appeared, she became the object of [Sir Robert Floyer's] attention, though [not] . . . with the look of admiration due to her beauty, . . . but with the scrutinizing observation of a man on the point of making a bargain, who views with fault-seeking eyes the property he means to cheapen."

4. Margaret Anne Doody, *Frances Burney: The Life in the Works* (New Brunswick, N.J.: Rutgers University Press, 1988), 256. Perhaps because her career coincided with the book market boom that began following the resolution of *Donaldson v. Becket* in 1774, and because she was the first well-known novelist to exploit the possibilities of "popular" authorship, Burney's corpus was often read as a mere transcription of marketplace messages—a reading like that elicited by the bodies of the fashion victims who are portrayed in the pessimistic accounts of consumer culture.

5. Igor Kopytoff, "The Cultural Biography of Things: Commoditization as Process," in *The Social Life of Things,* ed. Arjun Appadurai (Cambridge: Cambridge University Press, 1986), 64.

6. Charlotte Brontë, *Jane Eyre,* ed. Margaret Smith (Oxford: Oxford University Press, 1975), 277, 272; Sandra M. Gilbert and Susan Gubar, *The Madwoman in the Attic: The Woman Writer and the Nineteenth-Century Literary Imagination* (New Haven: Yale University Press, 1979), 44; *The Journals and Letters of Fanny Burney (Madame d'Arblay),* vol. 3, ed. Joyce Hemlow (Oxford: Clarendon, 1973), 117 (18 June 1795; emphasis in original).

7. I draw here on Karen Newman's critique of the concept of agency that organizes feminist thinking about markets: see "Directing Traffic: Subjects, Objects, and the Politics of Exchange," *Differences* 2 (1990): 50.

8. Claude Lévi-Strauss, *The Savage Mind* (Chicago: University of Chicago Press, 1966).

9. See Claudia L. Johnson, *Equivocal Beings: Politics, Gender, and Sentimentality in the 1790s: Wollstonecraft, Radcliffe, Burney, Austen* (Chicago: University of Chicago Press, 1995), and Doody, *Frances Burney* for excellent discussions of Camilla's double bind.

10. See, for example, Miranda J. Burgess's discussion of Burney's late novels in "Courting Ruin: The Economic Romances of Frances Burney" (*Novel* 28, no. 2 [1995], 131–53), which insightfully illuminates the complicity between eighteenth-century defenses of credit in the commercial economy and the promotion of sensibility in conduct writers' guides to courtship but says very little about the historicity of the notions of intrinsic worth and fixed propriety that Burney summons to counter this alliance. The phrase "desire-based relativism" is Burgess's: see 135.

11. Hannah More, *Works* (New York: Harper, 1840), 1:389.

12. The seesaw in itself is a traditional emblem of mutability, and one that is often exploited in jokes about the physical and moral fragility of female pleasure-seekers. So much is suggested by the air of abandon and the disheveled state of the falling woman who is pictured in *The Play of See-Saw*, one in the series of paintings that Francis Hayman executed in 1740–41 for the supperboxes at Vauxhall Gardens and a painting that Burney most certainly knew.

13. Doody, *Frances Burney*, 236.

14. See, for example, Rachel Bowlby, *Just Looking: Consumer Culture in Dreiser, Gissing, and Zola* (New York: Methuen, 1985), 32.

15. Rosalind Williams is quoted in Roy Porter, "Premodernism and the Art of Shopping," *Critical Quarterly* 34, no. 4 (1992), 6. By the 1790s customers were also free to give themselves up to this visual allure, because the shop interior no longer represented a place where they had to be ready to haggle: by this decade fixed-price retailing had become the norm. On this change in retail practice, see Neil McKendrick, "The Commercialization of Fashion," in McKendrick et al., *The Birth of a Consumer Society: The Commercialization of Eighteenth-Century England* (Bloomington: Indiana University Press, 1985), 86, and Hoh-Cheung and Lorna H. Mui, *Shops and Shopkeeping in Eighteenth-Century England* (Kingston and Montreal: McGill-Queen's University Press, 1989), chap. 12.

16. Anne Friedberg, *Window Shopping: Cinema and the Postmodern* (Berkeley and Los Angeles: University of California Press, 1993), 35–36.

17. For a terrific discussion of Mrs. Mittin, see Elizabeth Kowaleski-Wallace, *Consuming Subjects: British Women and Consumer Culture in the Eighteenth Century* (New York: Columbia University Press, 1996), 92–98.

18. Friedberg, *Window Shopping*, 15–38. The panorama was a 360-degree, cylindrical painting of a broad vista (usually a cityscape) that was lit from above and viewed from within a darkened room—one reached, at least in the case of Leicester Square panorama (1791), by means of a mechanism that was the forerunner of the elevator. The diorama supplemented the panoramic scene with moving lights that recreated the effects that the passage of time—sunrise to sunset, for instance—had on a scene. For more on "building-machines . . . designed to transport—rather than to confine—the spectator-subject" (*Window Shopping*, 20), see Richard D. Altick, *The Shows of London* (Cambridge: Harvard University Press, 1978), chaps. 9–16, and William H. Galperin, *The Return of the Visible in British Romanticism* (Baltimore: Johns Hopkins University Press, 1993).

19. The locket's physical characteristics underscore this oddity, since it has a blank

space "left for a braid of hair, or a cypher" (92), a space that indicates that it *could* be personalized but as yet has not been.

20. M. M. Bakhtin, "The Bildungsroman and Its Significance in the History of Realism," in *Speech Genres and Other Late Essays,* ed. Caryl Emerson and Michael Holquist (Austin: University of Texas Press, 1986); Kristina Straub, *Divided Fictions: Fanny Burney and Feminine Strategy* (Lexington: University Press of Kentucky, 1987), 194.

21. I am indebted for this formulation to Gillian Brown's "Anorexia, Humanism, and Feminism," *Yale Journal of Criticism* 5 (1991), 189–215.

22. But even the *Lady's Magazine* does not assume that its readers are content when they contemplate the "fluctuations in fashions." The *Lady's Magazine* promotes style—and promotes its illustrations, as well as the "elegant patterns for the Tambour [and] Embroidery" that it supplies—not by urging readers to embrace "innovation[s] in the female dress" but, as the "Address to the Fair Sex" that opens the magazine's inaugural number suggests, by portraying those innovations as facts of social experience that must be tolerated. The lady will make the best of them: "[W]e shall endeavour to render [the news of fashion] the more worthy of female attention, by an assiduity which shall admit of no abatement, and by an eagerness of intelligence which shall preclude anticipation" (advertisement to vol. 1 [1770]).

23. Friedberg, *Window Shopping,* 57.

24. Straub, *Divided Fictions,* 191, 82–83.

25. I am assisted here by Gillian Brown's discussion of individualism and female bodies in "Anorexia, Humanism, Feminism."

26. Seltzer, *Bodies and Machines,* 143.

27. Nancy Armstrong, *Desire and Domestic Fiction: A Political History of the Novel* (New York: Oxford University Press, 1987), 76. Thomas Broadhurst's reflections on "the large class of superficial women" appear in *Advice to Young Ladies on the Improvement of A Mind and Conduct of Life* (1810) and are quoted on this same page of *Desire and Domestic Fiction.*

28. Englishwomen's willingness to self-identify as potential wearers of clothes and users of cosmetics contributed to the boom in the English fashion trades that began in the 1790s. On this boom, also spurred by the wartime embargo on products from the Continent, see, inter alia, Adburgham, *Shops and Shopping, 1800–1914* (London: Allen and Unwin, 1964); for the growth in the perfumers' trade in the eighteenth century, see *Faces* (booklet published to accompany a special exhibition at the Museum of London, 1986).

29. Tom Furniss, *Edmund Burke's Aesthetic Ideology: Language, Gender, and Political Economy* (Cambridge: Cambridge University Press, 1993), 25, 34.

30. Clifford Siskin, "Wordsworth's Prescriptions: Romanticism and Professional Power," in *The Romantics and Us: Essays on Literature and Culture,* ed. Gene Ruoff (New Brunswick, N.J.: Rutgers University Press, 1990), 310; Burney, *Journals and Letters* (18 June 1795), 117 (emphasis in original).

31. Dorinda Outram, *The Body and the French Revolution: Sex, Class and Political Culture* (New Haven: Yale University Press, 1989), 52.

32. On the ways in which the Industrial Revolution involved not only the transformation of ways of working but also a reconstituted understanding of women, see Deborah Valenze, *The First Industrial Woman* (New York: Oxford University Press, 1995).

33. On the Burneys, shows of mechanical wonders, and Charles's player piano, see Altick, *Shows of London,* 69. Commentary on the drawing of the mechanical woman, which

has been ascribed to various members of the Burney circle, has construed it as evidence for Burney's biography, as, specifically, an image of the author's condition following her mastectomy in 1812. Rejecting this biographical focus, I choose instead to read the drawing as an image of a female *machine* as well as of a female body, and to highlight rather than obscure its relation to the material conditions in which women worked in the age of manufactures.

34. For Adam Smith's representations of the human hand, severed from the human body, see *An Inquiry into the Nature and Causes of the Wealth of Nations*, ed. Kathryn Sutherland (Oxford: Oxford University Press, 1993), 16; for his discussion of the mental mutilation of the worker, "whose whole life is spent in performing a few simple operations, of which the effects too are, perhaps, always the same," see 429 and 435. For useful discussions of automatons' relation to the steam engines and to nascent processes of industrialization, see Jean-Claude Beaune, "The Classic Age of Automata: An Impressionistic Survey from the Sixteenth to the Nineteenth Century," in *Fragments for a History of the Human Body*, pt. 1, ed. Michel Feher (Cambridge: MIT Press, 1989), 430–80, and Seltzer, *Bodies and Machines*.

35. The *OED* quotes Mill's *On Liberty* (1859). I draw in this paragraph on two especially interesting discussions of the spectacle of the other's determination: Rey Chow's "Postmodern Automatons," in *Feminists Theorize the Political*, ed. Judith Butler and Joan W. Scott (New York: Routledge, 1992), 101–20, and Amanda Anderson's "Prostitution's Artful Guise," *diacritics* 21, nos. 2–3 (1991): 102–22.

36. Burney's interest may well derive from her knowledge of the controversy over "animal magnetism" that occurred in the 1780s. In that decade, Mesmer's séances graphically demonstrated how thoroughly individuals could, in William Godwin's words, be "subjected" to "their senses" and how thoroughly they could give themselves up to "mechanical imitation." For a history of this controversy, and for the suggestion that the mesmerist's victims would have been linked by the public to the automatons of popular entertainments, see Simon Schaffer, "Self Evidence," in *Questions of Evidence: Proofs, Practice, and Persuasion Across the Disciplines*, ed. James Chandler et al. (Chicago: University of Chicago Press, 1994), 80; Schaffer quotes William Godwin's translation of Franklin and Lavoisier's joint investigation into animal magnetism (1785). On female automatons specifically see "The Wooden Daughter of Descartes," a story in *Lady's Magazine* 26 (1795), 7.

37. Johnson, *Equivocal Beings*, 152.

38. I borrow here from Anne McClintock's description of how two founding texts of feminist literary criticism, Gilbert and Gubar's *The Madwoman in the Attic* and Nina Auerbach's *Woman and the Demon*, emplot the emancipatory task of the woman writer: *Imperial Leather: Race, Gender, and Sexuality in the Colonial Conquest* (New York: Routledge, 1995), 96.

39. Gilbert and Gubar, *The Madwoman in the Attic*, 350–53; cf. Joseph Litvak's insightful remarks on this passage in *Caught in the Act: Theatricality in the Nineteenth-Century English Novel* (Berkeley and Los Angeles: University of California Press, 1992), 35–36.

40. I draw on Amanda Anderson's analysis of how the figure of the painted lady—the fallen woman who has "lost her character"—highlights the tensions between plot and character that are constitutive of the novel: "Prostitution's Artful Guise," esp. 104.

41. The market, it is worth recollecting, invites women to convert the social anxieties of looking as one ought, the anxieties of being in a body, into achievements of identity. But the agoraphobic in Burney also casts the market as a site of menace, so that while finding her self through shopper's methods, a heroine may also "lose her character."

42. Here I draw on Brown's "Anorexia, Humanism, and Feminism," esp. 214 n. 46.

43. When Burney chronicles the story of the bills that Camilla racks up with the milliners and drapers of Southampton, fashion epitomizes the social contingencies that override individual desires or powers. Just when she's trying to practice economy, Camilla finds that "all she wore, by the quick changes of fashion, seemed already out of date" (689). Burney's next novel also portrays fashion in these terms, but the Wanderer, by contrast to Camilla, inhabits the kind of world that Deborah Valenze depicts when she describes the effects the winds of fashion had on women engaged in the cottage industry of straw plaiting: " 'The size of the bonnet was important,' a historian of the craft pointed out, 'for an increase of only two inches in the size of the ridiculously small bonnets worn in the middle of the [eighteenth] century would have required twice as much plait.' Straw plaiters simply fell victim to all of these variables, and available work and wage rates fluctuated mercilessly, ranging anywhere from 6s. or 10s. to only 2s. 6d. a week" (Valenze, *First Industrial Woman*, 119–20, citing Dony, *History of the Straw Hat Industry*).

44. I owe this insight to Gillian Brown's discussion of authorship in *Domestic Individualism: Imagining Self in Nineteenth-Century America* (Berkeley and Los Angeles: University of California Press, 1990), 146.

45. It is no accident that the Wanderer finds herself "advertised" in a newspaper. Transported across the Channel and into the novel by a smuggler, she is from the start of her narrative associated with commodities such as French lace and face powder, contraband goods that female shoppers in particular might hanker after (e.g., 406, 720).

46. Christine Cullens, "Female Difficulties: English and German Women Writers, 1740–1810" (Ph.D. diss., Stanford University, 1988), 485.

47. In the seventh chapter of the novel, the protagonist tries to collect letters that the post office has been holding for L.S. This is the closest she gets in the first third of the narrative to owning a name, adopting one that is applied more properly to the pounds and shillings of English currency and that allies her with the money-centered narratives I discussed in chapter 2. Doody's introduction to *The Wanderer* offers a number of provocative suggestions about the resonances of this name.

48. Here I take issue with Miranda Burgess, who in "Courting Ruin" seems to argue that Burney is unremittingly antagonistic toward figures such as Hume and Burke. But see, for instance, the passage (319) in which the narrator accounts for why the Wanderer's merit as a musician is undervalued by her audience: "The public at large is generally just, because too enormous to be individually canvassed; but private circles are almost universally biassed by partial or prejudiced influence." I don't think that this vindication of the heroine's worth and this critique of the world's faulty powers of discrimination underwrite a critique of the Whigs' belief in a self-regulating, impersonal market: instead, the point of the passage is that the economy in which the Wanderer must operate is imperfect because it's insufficiently impersonal.

49. To understand the effects here of Burney's adoption of a pointedly impersonal perspective, we might draw on a distinction that Catherine Gallagher lays out in her discussion of *Evelina* and note that the crucial fact about the Wanderer at this point is not, as it was previously, her namelessness. Instead, it's the fact that she's *nobody*—for this figure in the landscape could be anybody or everybody. Namelessness draws attention to the self that's operating incognito: asserting the existence of a secret, it grants to the self the substance and distinctness of a "somebody." By contrast, to consider the Wanderer's condition

in this scene is to move from "the altogether private to the altogether public." See Gallagher, *Nobody's Story: The Vanishing Acts of Women Writers in the Marketplace, 1670–1820* (Berkeley and Los Angeles: University of California Press, 1994), 214.

50. Johnson's remarks on the "extensive views" of the practitioner of political economy are quoted in Kathryn Sutherland's introduction to Smith, *Wealth of Nations*, x. The description of the individual's moment of sublime vision as a "summons to self-consciousness" is that of Geoffrey Hartman, whose discussion of Wordsworth's locodescriptive poetry is cited in Frances Ferguson, *Solitude and the Sublime: Romanticism and the Aesthetics of Individualism* (New York: Routledge, 1992), 125. Ferguson discusses how the fascination with sublime vision was a fascination with technologies of individuality: "Against the . . . fear of a diminution of consciousness produced by the very act of communication, the sublime establishes nature as the instrument for the production of individuality itself" (130). The natural scenes in question are, customarily, ones whose magnitude brings the viewer face to face with "the limitations of individual perception" and at the same time recuperates that limitation by providing an occasion where human reason proves itself able "to think past those very perceptions" (138). It is because intellectual phantasms like "commerce" also force the mind to confront what is supersensible that Burney can so easily move between the extensive views of political economy and the expansive prospects of aesthetic theory.

51. Adam Ferguson is quoted in John Barrell's introduction to *English Literature in History, 1730–80: An Equal, Wide Survey* (New York: St. Martin's, 1983), 46, 30.

52. John Barrell, "Visualising the Division of Labour: William Pyne's *Microcosm*," chap. 5 of *The Birth of Pandora and the Division of Knowledge* (Philadelphia: University of Pennsylvania Press, 1992), 90; Smith, *Wealth of Nations*, cited in Michael Ignatieff, *The Needs of Strangers* (New York: Viking, 1985), 105.

53. Chow, "Postmodern Automatons," 110: this phrase comes from Chow's characterization of an essay ("Fiction and Its Phantoms") in which Hélène Cixous talks back to Freud and talks for E. T. A. Hoffmann's clockwork woman.

54. Chow, "Postmodern Automatons," 109.

55. For a discussion in similar terms of new feminist uses for autobiography, see Elspeth Probyn, *Sexing the Self: Gendered Positions in Cultural Studies* (New York: Routledge, 1993).

Chapter Five

1. Sophie von LaRoche, *Sophie in London, 1786, being the Diary of Sophie v. La Roche*, trans. Clare Williams (London: Jonathan Cape, 1933), 192 (Sept. 9); Edmund Burke, *Reflections on the Revolution in France*, ed. Conor Cruise O'Brien (Harmondsworth: Penguin, 1968), 271; Adam Smith, *An Inquiry into the Causes and Nature of the Wealth of Nations*, ed. Kathryn Sutherland (Oxford: Oxford University Press, 1993), 175.

2. LaRoche, *Sophie in London*, 123 (Sept. 11); Susan Stewart, *On Longing: Narratives of the Miniature, the Gigantic, the Souvenir, the Collection* (Baltimore: Johns Hopkins University Press, 1984), xii.

3. In this paragraph, I draw on Neil McKendrick, "The Commercialization of the Potteries," in McKendrick et al., *The Birth of a Consumer Society: The Commercialization of Eighteenth-Century England* (Bloomington: Indiana University Press, 1985), 99–145. McKendrick quotes from manuscripts in the Wedgwood museum, Stoke-on-Trent.

4. Jane Austen, *Persuasion*, ed. John Davie (Oxford: Oxford University Press, 1971), 42–43. Subsequent references to *Persuasion* are to this edition and appear in the text.

Throughout this chapter, references to Austen's other novels are handled in the same way: I have used the Oxford editions of *Sense and Sensibility* (ed. James Kinsley [Oxford: Oxford University Press, 1970]), *Pride and Prejudice* (ed. James Kinsley and Frank W. Bradbrook [Oxford: Oxford University Press, 1970]), *Mansfield Park* (ed. James Kinsley [Oxford: Oxford University Press, 1970]), *Emma* (ed. James Kinsley [Oxford: Oxford University Press, 1971]), and *Northanger Abbey, Lady Susan, The Watsons, and Sanditon* (ed. John Davie [Oxford: Oxford University Press, 1971]).

5. The only other discussion of noise and Austen with which I'm acquainted occurs in Adela Pinch's account of the lyricism of *Persuasion*: "Lost in a Book," chap. 5 of *Strange Fits of Passion: Epistemologies of Emotion, Hume to Austen* (Stanford: Stanford University Press, 1996). I am greatly indebted to Pinch's discussion throughout this chapter.

6. For example, for Marilyn Butler (*Jane Austen and the War of Ideas* [Oxford: Clarendon, 1975], 274), Austen "masters the subjective insights that help to make the nineteenth-century novel what it is, and denies them validity."

7. Ian Watt, *The Rise of the Novel: Studies in Defoe, Richardson, and Fielding* (1957; reprint, Harmondsworth: Pelican, 1972), 338.

8. See David Kaufmann's pithy comments on novels' disciplinary distinction (*The Business of Common Life: Novels and Classical Economics Between Revolution and Reform* [Baltimore: Johns Hopkins University Press, 1995], 63): "[Political economics and the novel] show the relation of the part to the whole, the individual to the alien totality that appears to stand over and against that individual. Nevertheless they are not redundant. Economics began by looking at the general and inferred the individual; the novel began with the individual and allegorized the general."

9. See Barbara M. Benedict, "Jane Austen's *Sense and Sensibility:* The Politics of Point of View," *Philological Quarterly* 69 (1990): 453.

10. See Mary A. Favret, *Romantic Correspondence: Women, Politics, and the Fiction of Letters* (New York: Cambridge University Press, 1993), 145.

11. On *Persuasion* as a "second novel," see Tony Tanner, *Jane Austen* (Cambridge: Harvard University Press, 1986), 211. For the argument that almost all Austen's love stories are framed as repetitions of a prior narrative, see Daniel Cottom (*The Civilized Imagination: A Study of Ann Radcliffe, Jane Austen, and Sir Walter Scott* [New York: Cambridge University Press, 1985], 90): "There is no such thing as an original love in Austen's novels," Cottom writes. Another way to say this is to say that Austen's hero and heroine, who never fall in love at first sight, also never really see each other as strangers. The couple in Austen is the product of an erotic alchemy that affects, in Susan Morgan's words, "people who are already familiar to each other": Darcy may look perfect for the part of the glamorous stranger, "but the first movement of his feelings is a failure and he must return to propose again" (*In the Meantime: Character and Perception in Jane Austen's Fiction* [Chicago: University of Chicago Press, 1988], 187). The look of love is always a second glance at someone who is already known and remembered. When Elizabeth Bennet visits the picture gallery at Pemberley, she finds that there are "many family portraits, but they could have little to fix the attention of a stranger. Elizabeth walked on in quest of the only face whose features would be known to her. At last it arrested her—and she beheld a striking resemblance of Mr. Darcy, with such a smile over the face, as she remembered to have sometimes seen, when he looked at her" (220).

12. Pinch, "Lost in a Book," 160 (emphasis in original).

13. Discussing how in *Persuasion,* more than in other novels by Austen, the heroine's consciousness seems to monopolize the narrative voice, Elizabeth Deeds Ermarth characterizes the novel as the record of the conversation that Anne sustains with herself (*Realism and Consensus in the English Novel* [Princeton: Princeton University Press, 1983], 166).

14. To cap this equation, Austen presents Louisa's change of heart—her turn from Captain Wentworth to Captain Benwick—as a change in reading matter: Byron's *Giaour* replaces the navy list. What Austen wants us to notice is how the book-man analogy is retained.

15. Austen would have known that Samuel Johnson in his *Dictionary* used Pope's poem to illustrate the definition of *character* as "personal qualities; particular constitution of the mind."

16. See, among the many readings of the novel, James Thompson's discussion of *Pride and Prejudice* in "Character and Interpretation," chap. 3 of his *Between Self and World: The Novels of Jane Austen* (University Park: Pennsylvania State University Press, 1988). *Northanger Abbey,* a novel more frequently associated than *Pride and Prejudice* and *Persuasion* are with lessons in literacy, defines the enterprise of reading character similarly: Catherine's misreadings of Northanger Abbey happen because she proceeds as if General Tilney's covert nastiness might be recognized in, and pinned down to, a single flamboyant deed (preferably one that would produce a corpse or depend on a dungeon). Instead the general's villainy can be established only from the dispersed and multiple strands of meaning that compose his "character."

17. These conversations are Austen's versions of the nostalgic tours that her contemporaries include in the final chapters of their novels, and in which the heroine and her new husband revisit the scenes of their story: in Frances Burney's *The Wanderer,* "every cottage in which the Wanderer had been harboured" (ed. Margaret Doody, Robert L. Mack, and Peter Sabor [Oxford: Oxford University Press, 1991], 872), and, in Ann Radcliffe's *Romance of the Forest,* "the Swiss mountains, the sight of which revived a thousand interesting recollections in the mind of Adeline" (ed. Chloe Chard [Oxford: Oxford University Press, 1986], 359). These carriage journeys down memory lane operate in the same way as the conversations that engage Austen's couples—as a means of interiorizing plot as reminiscence.

18. August Schlegel, cited in Philippe Lacoue-Labarthe and Jean-Luc Nancy, *The Literary Absolute: The Theory of Literature in German Romanticism,* trans. Philip Barnard and Cheryl Lester (Albany: SUNY Press, 1988), 112.

19. Freud, "Dynamics of Transference," in *Standard Edition of the Complete Psychological Works of Sigmund Freud,* trans. and ed. James Strachey (London: Horgarth, 1958), 12:168. Both stereotypes and clichés were used to provide duplicates of printing formes, which meant, according to Michael Twyman, that "the original could be preserved from damage in printing and that more than one forme could be printed at a time when large editions were needed quickly" (*Printing 1770–1970: An Illustrated History of Its Development and Uses in England* [London: Eyre and Spottiswoode, 1970], 22).

20. Stuart Cosgrove, "The Circulation of Genres in Gibbon's *Decline and Fall of the Roman Empire," ELH* 63 (1996): 109.

21. Samuel Taylor Coleridge, *Biographia Literaria,* ed. George Watson (London: Dent, 1975), 21. The keys of a barrel-organ, according to the *OED,* "are mechanically acted on by a revolving barrel or cylinder studded with metal pins." See also the *OED*'s quotation

from the 1796 *Monthly Review:* "A barrel-organ . . . would do the business much more to his satisfaction than the fingers of a man of genius."

22. Review of J. Wedderburne Webster, Esq., *Waterloo, and Other Poems, Quarterly Review* 30 (July 1816): 345.

23. [Sydney Smith], review of *Delphine,* by Madame de Staël-Holstein, *Edinburgh Review* 2 (1803): 176, 177.

24. Thomas Carlyle, "Goethe," *Works of Thomas Carlyle* (London: Chapman and Hall 1905), 26:229; "The Projector," no. 49, *Gentleman's Magazine* 75 (1805), quoted in Ina Ferris, *The Achievement of Literary Authority: Gender, History, and the Waverley Novels* (Ithaca: Cornell University Press, 1991), 43.

25. Ferris, *Achievement of Literary Authority,* 43. In addition to Ferris's incisive remarks on the critical tropes that put novels in their place, see Sonia Hofkosh's discussion of romanticism and a "circulating library sensibility" ("The Writer's Ravishment: Women and the Romantic Author—The Example of Byron," in *Romanticism and Feminism,* ed. Anne K. Mellor [Bloomington: Indiana University Press, 1988], 93–114).

26. That Bath is a site where one must immerse oneself in conventionality is made clear in the chapter in which Catherine first meets Henry Tilney. Henry shows us that conversation there follows a script that every one, Catherine aside, knows in advance. He remarks on how he has " 'hitherto been very remiss . . . in the proper attentions of a partner here' ": " 'I have not yet asked you how long you have been in Bath; whether you were ever here before; whether you have been at the Upper Rooms, the theatre, and the concert; and how you like the place altogether' " (11–12). Having set the conversational ball rolling in this fashion, Henry then proceeds to make those very enquiries.

27. Studying the novel's use of free indirect discourse, Narelle Shaw argues that Austen returned to the manuscript of *Northanger Abbey* shortly before beginning work on *Sanditon* ("Free Indirect Discourse and Jane Austen's 1816 Revision of *Northanger Abbey,*" *Studies in English Literature* 30 [1990]: 591–601).

28. On Minerva fiction and publishers' chicanery see E. J. Clery, *The Rise of Supernatural Fiction, 1762–1800* (Cambridge: Cambridge University Press, 1995), 140. I quote the description of such fashionable retail practices offered by "The Projector," no. 88, *Gentleman's Magazine* 78 (1808): 884.

29. On this topic see Tanner's chapter on *Sanditon* in *Jane Austen;* D. A. Miller, "The Late Jane Austen," *Raritan* 10 (1988): 55–79; John Wiltshire, *Jane Austen and the Body: The "Picture of Health"* (Cambridge: Cambridge University Press, 1992).

30. Tanner, *Jane Austen,* 259.

31. Barbara Johnson, *The Critical Difference: Essays in the Contemporary Rhetoric of Reading* (Baltimore: Johns Hopkins University Press, 1980), 3.

32. In referring to how Austen recycles novel slang I quote from the letter in which she guides Anna Austen in the latter's first attempts at a novel. "I wish you would not let him plunge into a 'vortex of dissipation.' I do not object to the Thing, but I cannot bear the expression;—it is such thorough novel slang—and so old, that I dare say Adam met with it in the first novel he opened" (*Jane Austen's Letters,* ed. Deirdre Le Faye [Oxford: Oxford University Press, 1995], 277; 28 September 1814). Austen is being somewhat disingenuous here. She herself feels free to put novel slang into the mouth of a Sanditonian like Sir Edward Denham; what Anna has not learned from her aunt's fictions, perhaps,

is that in that context novel slang is always in virtual quotation marks. It is never used, and never to be read, "straight."

33. Patricia Meyer Spacks, *Gossip* (New York: Knopf, 1985), 49.

34. Favret, *Romantic Correspondence*, 152–53. For guidance in thinking about Austen's capacity to be comfortable and to comfort readers, I am indebted to Clifford Siskin's discussion of Austen's canonization and what it can tell us about the history of the category of literature. Siskin focuses on the ways her novels respond to worries about the proliferation of writing. "The discomforting question is whether we become what we read. Austen's answer—an answer that I would argue signals a change in writing's status from a worrisome new technology to a more trusted tool—is 'Yes and no, but don't worry.' Catherine Morland does, at times, behave somewhat like the gothic heroines she reads about but she is neither 'born' . . . to be such a heroine or doomed to become one. The linkage is too complex to be predictable" ("Jane Austen and the Engendering of Disciplinarity," in *Jane Austen and the Discourses of Feminism,* ed. Devoney J. Looser [New York: St. Martin's, 1995], 60–61).

35. Literally, a hackneyed language is a language hired out by others—as the *OED*'s definition has it, "worn out like a hired horse by indiscriminate or vulgar use." In eighteenth-century usage, the word *hackney* is also freighted with suggestions of prostitution. Marianne's complaint about the hackneyed language of books thus points to the connections that commentators who were worried about female reading and writing often made as they linked automatic, indiscriminate reading to automatic, indiscriminate sexuality.

36. *Monthly Review* 1:419; *Critical Review* 32:144; *Edinburgh Review* 4:208: all quoted in Richard G. Swartz, "Dorothy Wordsworth, Local Tourism, and the Anxiety (or Semiotics) of Description," *Prose Studies,* forthcoming.

37. Claudia L. Johnson, "A 'Sweet Face as White as Death': Jane Austen and the Politics of Female Sensibility," *Novel: A Forum on Fiction* 22 (1989): 159–74; cf. Deborah Kaplan, "Achieving Authority: Jane Austen's First Published Novel," in *Jane Austen: Modern Critical Views,* ed. Harold Bloom (New York: Chelsea, 1986), 203–18.

According to Colonel Brandon, Marianne resembles his first love, Eliza Williams, in body and mind; she likewise resembles Eliza's namesake and illegitimate daughter in being the second victim of Willoughby's charms. Johnson aligns the Elizas in their turn with a long list of heroines that extends from Clarissa to Charlotte Temple; Nicola J. Watson, concentrating on anti-Jacobin tales of seduction that flourished in the 1790s, also locates them within a crowd of fictional predecessors (*Revolution and the Form of the British Novel, 1790–1825: Intercepted Letters, Interrupted Seductions* [Oxford: Clarendon, 1994], 89 n. 28).

38. Benedict, "Politics of Point of View," 458.

39. For one of the most adept examples of such a reading see Casey Finch and Peter Bowen, " 'The Tittle-Tattle of Highbury': Gossip and the Free Indirect Style in *Emma,*" *Representations* 31 (1990): 1–18.

40. Cottom, *Civilized Imagination,* 91.

41. Emma is the exception, perhaps, since she is, as Miss Bates inadvertently discloses, a topic for Highbury's gossip. She looks like a heroine to them. But Emma's conviction that the incentives women usually have for marrying do not apply to her make her much readier to identify other people's desires than she is to identify her own: she does, however deludedly, consider herself Harriet Smith's foil.

42. I draw here on the discussion of narrative omniscience in Ermarth, *Realism and Consensus.*

43. Eve Sedgwick, "Jane Austen and the Masturbating Girl," *Critical Inquiry* 17 (1991): 830. A germinal account of the technical innovations in *Sense and Sensibility* is Butler, *Jane Austen and the War of Ideas.*

44. Benedict, "Politics of Point of View," 464.

45. In a strange way, the story that Willoughby recounts to Elinor to explain his conduct toward Marianne becomes Elinor's property—a personal effect. Austen emphasizes the "heightened" degree of "influence" Willoughby exercises "over [Elinor's] mind" (292). She also has Elinor first withhold the story and then retell it with "address," first to Marianne, and then to Mrs. Dashwood, doling it out selectively and to a slight degree begrudgingly: "it was neither in Elinor's power, *nor in her wish*, to raise such feelings in another . . . as had at first been called forth in herself" (305, 307; emphasis mine).

46. See Favret, *Romantic Correspondence*, 146–52.

47. Here I receive assistance from Nancy Bentley's suggestive discussion of Henry James and manners: *The Ethnography of Manners: Hawthorne, James, Wharton* (New York: Cambridge University Press, 1995), 1–18.

48. For a good discussion of Austen's endings, see Cottom, *Civilized Imagination.*

49. Gilles Deleuze and Félix Guattari, "November 20, 1923: Postulates of Linguistics," in *A Thousand Plateaus: Capitalism and Schizophrenia*, trans. Brian Massumi (Minneapolis: University of Minnesota Press, 1987), 76.

50. Margreta de Grazia, "Sanctioning Voice: Quotation Marks, the Abolition of Torture, and the 5th Amendment," in *The Construction of Authorship: Textual Appropriation in Law and Literature*, ed. Martha Woodmansee and Peter Jaszi (Durham, N.C.: Duke University Press, 1994), 288–89.

51. See Jane Barker, *The Lining of the Patch Work Screen* in *The Galesia Trilogy*, ed. Carol Shiner Wilson (Oxford: Oxford University Press, 1997), 271–72.

52. Cottom, *Civilized Imagination*, 91–92.

53. Lionel Trilling, "Manners, Morals, and the Novel," in *The Liberal Imagination: Essays in Literature and Society* (New York: Harcourt Brace Jovanovich, 1979), 194.

54. Pinch, "Lost in a Book," passim. On overhearing and eavesdropping, see the discussions of *Persuasion* offered by Keith Thomas ("Jane Austen and the Romantic Lyric: *Persuasion* and Coleridge's Conversation Poems," *ELH* 54 [1987]: 893–924) and Cottom (*Civilized Imagination*, 119–20).

55. Quoted in Carol Shiner Wilson, "Lost Needles, Tangled Threads: Stitchery, Domesticity, and the Artistic Enterprise in Barbauld, Edgeworth, Taylor, and Lamb," in *Revisioning Romanticism: British Women Writers, 1776–1837*, ed. Carol Shiner Wilson and Joel Haefner (Philadelphia: University of Pennsylvania Press, 1994), 182.

56. See Pinch, "Lost in a Book," 139 ff.

57. Ibid., 155.

58. For an extended discussion of the barriers to communication in *Persuasion*, see Tanner, *Jane Austen*, 236.

59. The allusion to the eleventh number of the *Spectator* is noted by Cottom (*Civilized Imagination*, 122).

60. Pinch, "Lost in a Book," 162.

61. Watson, *Revolution and the Form of the British Novel*, 79. By reauthenticating the episto-

lary mode, *Persuasion* reopens questions about the language of individual feeling that Austen seemed to have settled when *Sense and Sensibility* gave preference to an unspoken language of selfhood—to the free indirect discourse that puts Elinor's inner life in the safekeeping of an impersonal narrator—over Marianne's epistolary self-representations. Unlike the practitioners of characteristic writing, Austen does not comfortably make her characters into men and women of letters. The letters that Marianne writes to Willoughby are intended as words from the heart. Her commitment to a private, unmediated expression aside, however, Marianne's clandestine correspondence is exceedingly public. As Mary A. Favret and Nicola Watson each point out in discussions of the romantic-period decline of the novel-in-letters, Elinor and Colonel Brandon both see the letters to Willoughby that Marianne sends to the post, and Willoughby's fiancée reads them. Marianne's dependence in volume 2 of the novel on the institution of the two-penny post is, ironically enough, another result of her conviction that self-respect entails rejection of social forms. That dependence is problematic in a culture increasingly perturbed by commercial growth and by the growth of a state committed to the surveillance of the post: it points up the overlap between the interchange of sentiments and the traffic in circulating goods and intelligence. It muddles the distinctions between the realm of personal relationships and the realm of the market and the state.

62. Favret, *Romantic Correspondence*, 171.

63. Morgan, *In the Meantime*, 176–82.

64. The first paragraph of *Northanger Abbey* is reported (by the editor of the most recent Oxford edition) to contain one such in-joke: Catherine Morland's father, the narrator informs us, was "a very respectable man, though his name was Richard" (1). The general public has yet to come up with an explanation of this grudge against the name "Richard," and the Oxford editor surmises that the name must have some private associations for the Austen family; the editor surmises, that is, that public bafflement was Austen's point.

65. J. E. Austen-Leigh, *A Memoir of Jane Austen* in *Persuasion*, ed. D. W. Harding (Harmondsworth: Penguin, 1965), 339. Austen-Leigh's memoir of his aunt was first published in 1870. The parallel between the scene in the *Memoir* and the scene in *Persuasion* is also noted by Adela Pinch in the course of her excellent discussion of "domestic white noise" ("Lost in a Book," 159).

66. Deborah Kaplan, *Jane Austen among Women* (Baltimore: Johns Hopkins University Press, 1992), esp. chap. 4.

67. In an 1870 essay (*North British Review* 12), Richard Simpson described Jane Austen as the "ironical censurer" of her contemporaries; for illuminating remarks on these ways of separating Austen from the women's writing of her time, see Clifford Siskin, "Jane Austen and the Engendering of Disciplinarity."

68. Virginia Woolf, review of *Jane Austen: Her Life and Letters. A Family Record* by William Austen-Leigh, in *Essays (1912–1918)*, vol. 2, ed. Andrew McNeillie (London: Hogarth, 1986), 10. On Austen's reception history in the first part of this century see my "At Home with Jane Austen," in *Cultural Institutions of the Novel*, ed. Deidre Lynch and William B. Warner (Durham, N.C.: Duke University Press, 1996).

CONCLUSION

1. For a critical account of how Eliot focuses fiction on the question of the individual's relation to society—and of what it means to accept that there is indeed a discontinuity

between these two categories—see Daniel Cottom, *Social Figures: George Eliot, Social History, and Literary Representation* (Minneapolis: University of Minnesota Press, 1987).

2. Ian Duncan, *Modern Romance and Transformations of the Novel: The Gothic, Scott, Dickens* (Cambridge: Cambridge University Press, 1992), 51.

3. See Kathryn Chittick, *Dickens and the 1830s* (Cambridge: Cambridge University Press, 1990), chap. 4. On early-nineteenth-century collections and histories of "the" novel, see Chittick's chapter 3 and Ina Ferris, *The Achievement of Literary Authority: Gender, History, and the Waverley Novels* (Ithaca: Cornell University Press, 1991).

4. Allan Cunningham, "British Novels and Romances," *The Athenaeum* (1833), reprinted in *A Victorian Art of Fiction: Essays on the Novel in British Periodicals, 1830–1850*, ed. John Charles Olmsted (New York: Garland, 1979), 1:149; John Dunlop, *The History of Fiction* (London: Longman, 1814), 2:231; Julia Kavanagh, *English Women of Letters: Biographical Sketches* (London: Hurst and Blackett, 1863), 1:61–62; [R. H. Hutton], "Novels by the Authoress of 'John Halifax,' " *North British Review* 29 (1858): 472–73.

5. Eaton Stannard Barrett, *The Heroine, or, Adventures of a Fair Romance Reader* (London: Henry Colburn, 1813), 1:v, 2:201. See Catherine Gallagher's excellent discussion of how it is "an affective pulsation between identification with fictional characters and withdrawal from them" that makes fiction go (*Nobody's Story: The Vanishing Acts of Women Writers in the Marketplace, 1670–1820* [Berkeley and Los Angeles: University of California Press, 1994], xvii–xviii).

6. Colin Campbell, *The Romantic Ethic and the Spirit of Modern Consumerism* (Oxford: Basil Blackwell, 1987), 8; Barrett, *The Heroine*, 1:viii.

7. Frances Burney, *The Wanderer, or, Female Difficulties*, ed. Margaret Doody, Robert L. Mack, and Peter Sabor (Oxford: Oxford University Press, 1991), 630.

8. Brontë to W. S. Williams, 12 April 1850, *The Brontës: Their Lives, Friendships, and Correspondences in Four Volumes*, ed. Thomas James Wise and John Alexander Symington (Oxford: Basil Blackwell, 1932), 3:99; Brontë to George Henry Lewes, 12 January 1848, *The Brontës*, 2:179.

9. T. H. Lister, review of Mrs. Gore's *Women as they Are*, *Edinburgh Review* 51 (July 1830), reprinted in *Victorian Art of Fiction*, 1:58; "Literary Women: No. II. Jane Austen," *The Athenaeum* (1831), reprinted in *Victorian Art of Fiction*, 1:74; Allan Cunningham, "British Novels and Romances," reprinted in *Victorian Art of Fiction*, 1:149.

10. Thomas Babington Macaulay, "Madame d'Arblay," in *Critical and Historical Essays* (London: Dent, 1907), 2:604–5.

11. For this epithet, see Burney's dedication to *The Wanderer*, 5.

12. "Of the twelve different classes of Engraved Portraits arranged by the late ingenious Mr. Granger, there is not one so difficult to perfect, with original prints, as that which relates to persons of the lowest description; the reason of which, it is evident, arises from the little estimation they were held in when first published; as it is sufficiently known, that prints of this class, that could not have sold originally for more than 12 pence, would at this time . . . produce near as many guineas" (Advertisement to James Caulfield, *Portraits, Memoirs, and Characters of Remarkable Persons* [London: J. Caulfield and Isaac Herbert, 1794]).

13. James Caulfield, *Blackguardiana* (London: J. Caulfield, 1795), ii; G. M. Woodward, *Eccentric excursions* (London: Allen, 1797), chap. 1. Woodward's enterprise is explicitly modeled after William Gilpin's project of delineating the picturesque features of the British landscape: "[W]hy should not the variegated forms of Nature, in the *physiognomy* of the

human race in respect to *countenance* and *character*, afford subjects equally worthy the exertion of the *pen* and *pencil?*" Woodward's second model for his "characteristic traveller" is Yorick: in chapter 2, we visit Sterne's grave.

14. Here I draw on Jon P. Klancher's remarks on the utopian desire that might motivate the encyclopedic aspirations of romantic-period mass journals such as *The Mirror* or *The Hive:* see *The Making of English Reading Audiences, 1790–1832* (Madison: University of Wisconsin Press, 1987), 81.

15. Norman Bryson, *Looking at the Overlooked: Four Essays on Still Life Painting* (Cambridge: Harvard University Press, 1990), 61.

16. R. H. Horne, *A New Spirit of the Age* (1844; reprint, New York: Garland, 1986), 1: 21.

17. Daniel Cottom, "The Enchantment of Interpretation," *Critical Inquiry* 11 (1985): 575.

❧ I N D E X ❧

acting: in *Camilla*, 176; and Garrick, 70–75; in
   The Wanderer, 201–2
Adventures of a Bank-Note, The. *See* Bridges,
   Thomas
Adventures of a Rupee, The. *See* Scott, Helenus
aesthetics, 218, 278n. 77, 291n. 49, 299n. 50;
   of Burke, 187–89; and the Royal Academy,
   60–61, 66–67, 276n. 53; of Shaftesbury, 39
Agnew, Jean-Christophe, 3, 267n. 3, 274n. 40
agoraphobia, 6; in Burney, 165–206, 257,
   297n. 41
Allen, Doug, 2, 16, 288n. 27
amatory fiction, 31, 37, 283n. 34
Analysis of Beauty, The (Hogarth), 61, 69, 70
Anderson, Amanda, 198, 297nn. 35, 40
animation. *See* automatons
antiprint rhetoric, 49, 221–23
Armstrong, Nancy, 186–87
Arnold, Matthew, 141
Ascanius; or the Young Adventurer, 92
audience. *See* readers; crowd
Austen, Jane, 8, 13, 45, 124–27, 130–32, 154–
   56, 162, 207–51, 301n. 17; Brontë on, 256;
   and the rise of the novel, 256; Scott's review of
   Emma, 9, 125. *See also specific works by title*
Austen-Leigh, J. E., 247, 305n. 65
automatons, 192–99, 204–5, 296–97n. 33. *See
   also* machines

Babcock, Barbara A., 86, 280n. 10
Bacon, Francis, 271n. 5
Bakhtin, M. M., 183
Barbauld, Anna Laetitia, 241
Barker, Jane, 29, 44, 47; *The Lining of the Patch
   Work Screen*, 32, 238; *A Patch-Work Screen for
   the Ladies*, 32, 34, 38, 42, 72, 133
Barker-Benfield, G. J., 290n. 47
Barrell, John, 104, 205, 277n. 61, 279n. 4,
   280n. 11, 284n. 48, 299n. 52
Barrett, Eaton Stannard, 254–55
Barry, James, 59, 66
Barthes, Roland, 14, 16, 128
Beattie, James, 71, 277n. 65
beauty. *See* aesthetics

Belsey, Catherine, 15, 269n. 19
Bench, The (Hogarth), 61–62, 67–69
Benedict, Barbara M., 116, 230, 232, 234,
   284n. 55
Bennett, Tony: on genre, 270n. 4; on "reading
   formations," 9
Blackstone, William, 93
body, 24–27; and the body politic, 25; reorga-
   nization of soul and, 187–90; of Roderick
   Random, 106; and signification, 30; of
   women, 166, 174, 183. *See also* face
book market: Austen and, 242, 247–48; Bur-
   ney and, 294n. 4; expansion of, 127, 129–
   31, 137, 153, 210; novels and, 221, 254. *See
   also* copyright law; literacy; print market;
   reading
Book of Nature, 30–33, 108
Boswell, James, 279n. 8
Bourdieu, Pierre, 19, 287n. 18, 290n. 45
Brewer, John, 41, 273n. 25
Bridges, Thomas, 7, 80, 95, 96, 280n. 10
Brissenden, R. F., 115, 284n. 53
Brontë, Charlotte, 168, 256; *Jane Eyre*, 149,
   170, 196, 257
Brown, Gillian, 183, 186, 198, 200, 296nn. 21,
   25, 298nn. 42, 44
Brunton, Mary, 154
Bryson, Norman, 58, 261, 307n. 15
Burgess, Miranda J., 295n. 10, 298n. 48
Burke, Edmund, 188–89, 223, 257, 298n. 48;
   Reflections on the Revolution in France, 208
Burney, Frances, 8, 13, 18, 127, 153–54, 164–
   207, 213, 224, 250–51, 255–61, 264–65,
   278n. 81, 290n. 45, 298n. 49, 299n. 50,
   301n. 17; reworking of the sublime by, 189,
   202–6, 299n. 50. *See also specific works by title*
Burney school of novelists, 7, 117, 125, 152,
   205, 213, 232, 285–86n. 4
Butler, Marilyn, 300n. 6
Butler, Samuel, 40, 42, 54

Caffentzis, Constantine George, 273n. 24
Camilla, or, A Picture of Youth (Burney), 167–201,
   204, 231, 257, 298n. 42

309

Sennett, Richard, 162, 294n. 86
Sense and Sensibility (Austen), 210–20, 228–40,
303n. 37, 304n. 45, 305n. 61
sensibility, 295n. 10. *See also* feeling; readers,
and sensibility
sentiment. *See* feeling
sentimental fiction, 43–44, 112–18
Sentimental Journey Through France and Italy, A
(Sterne), 89, 112–18, 270n. 5
servants, 103–5
Shaftesbury, Anthony Ashley Cooper, earl of,
41, 89; *Second Characters,* 33, 38–39, 49, 73
Shakespeare, 60, 89, 277n. 59; eighteenth-
century editing of, 14; Garrick in the plays
of, 71, 73, 74, 83; Johnson on, 23, 24, 280n.
13; writings on the characters of, 133–39,
147, 152. *See also* heroines
Sheridan, Frances, 46, 116
shopping. *See* consumer culture, and shopping
Silverman, Kaja, 160, 293nn. 82, 83
Simmel, George, 112, 284n. 49, 284–85n. 58
Simpson, Richard, 305n. 67
Sir Charles Grandison (Richardson), 14, 45–46,
72
Siskin, Clifford, 190, 303n. 34
Smith, Adam, 204, 208; *The Theory of Moral Sentiments,* 95; *The Wealth of Nations,* 96, 192, 205
Smith, Charlotte, 8, 153, 286n. 4
Smollett, Tobias, 7, 11, 18, 54–55, 76–77, 81,
82, 84, 99, 101–12, 283n. 40; and pretend-
ers, 86–94; Scott on, 270n. 25. *See also spe-
cific works by title*
society: the conceptualizing of, 13, 41, 77, 82,
88–89, 98, 104, 141, 201, 204–5, 250–51,
261, 264; the self and, 117, 152, 198–99,
203–4, 212, 231, 240
Sohn-Rethel, Alfred, 165
Spacks, Patricia Meyer, 228, 303n. 33
Spectator, 81, 243, 282n. 22
Stack, Richard, 139, 148
Stafford, Barbara, 59, 275n. 49
Stallybrass, Peter, 275n. 43
Steele, Richard, 243
stereotypes, 221–22, 227–28, 301n. 19. *See also*
types
Sterne, Laurence, 7, 18, 23–26, 77, 85, 113,
117, 270n. 5, 277n. 59. *See also specific works
by title*
Stewart, Susan, 86, 274n. 38, 280n. 10
Straub, Kristina, 183, 185
structuralism, and the realism debate, 14–16

Stuart, Charles (Bonnie Prince Charlie), 84,
90–93, 108
Stubbes, George, 139–40
Sutherland, Kathryn, 140, 289n. 35
sympathy, 86, 89, 92–94, 116; and Austen heroines, 233–35; and impersonality, 95; in
readers, 118, 152, 212

Taine, Hippolyte, 117, 285n. 2
Tanner, Tony, 226, 302n. 30
taste, 119, 127, 131, 189, 216, 219, 228, 248–
49, 290nn. 45, 47. *See also* Bourdieu, Pierre;
self-culture
Tel Quel, 14
Temple, William, 274n. 40
theater, 11, 277n. 64; and Garrick, 70–75
Theophrastan characters, 7, 27, 29, 39–40, 47,
54–55, 58, 86
third-person narration: in Austen, 230, 233; in
Burney, 201–2
Thompson, James, 97
Thornton, Bonnell, 282n. 22
Tom Jones (Henry Fielding), 35, 75, 81, 84, 87,
90, 91, 96–101, 135, 157, 279n. 9, 281n.
16, 282–83n. 33, 283n. 37
tourism, 126, 142–43, 180
Townshend, Marquess of, 58, 61–62
Trilling, Lionel, 239
Tristram Shandy (Sterne), 23–26, 48
Turner, James Grantham, 268–69n. 14
types: character, in Austen, 211, 227, 230;
characteristic writing and character, 47, 54–
55, 103; Royal Academy and ideal, 62, 66–
67
typographical culture, 24, 31–42, 46–47, 274n.
38; and acting, 70–71; and copying, 47–49,
221–28; defined, 5–6; novels situated within,
28; and *Sense and Sensibility,* 228, 240

Valenze, Deborah, 298n. 43
Vickery, Amanda, 285n. 59
von LaRoche, Sophie, 207–9, 218

Walpole, Horace, 74–75
Wanderer, or, Female Difficulties, The (Burney),
154, 161, 184–85, 198–206, 210, 255,
298nn. 42, 45, 48, 298–99n. 49, 301n. 17
Wanderer; or, Surprizing Escape, The, 92
Warton, Joseph, 55–56, 71
Watson, Nicola J., 244, 305n. 61
Watsons, The (Austen), 213

Printed in Great Britain
by Amazon

58246132R00199